11/09

CUNARD

Library

Out of respect for your fellow guests, please return all books as soon as possible. We would also request that books are not taken off the ship as they can easily be damaged by the sun, sea and sand.

Please ensure that books are returned the day before you disembark, failure to do so will incur a charge to your on board account, the same will happen to any damaged books.

1812:

RUSSIA'S
PATRIOTIC
WAR

At this point, Miloradowitch's adjutant, Bibikov, rode up and asked me to ride at once to his commander. I asked him which way; he raised an arm to point it out and a cannon ball ripped it off. He pointed again with his remaining arm and said 'There! Hurry!'
(General Wurttemberg at Borodino)

1812:

RUSSIA'S
PATRIOTIC
WAR

LAURENCE SPRING

First published 2009

Spellmount, an imprint of The History Press
The Mill, Brimscombe Port
Stroud, Gloucestershire, GL5 2QG
www.thehistorypress.co.uk

British Library Cataloguing in Publication Data.
A catalogue record for this book is available from the British Library.

ISBN 978-0-7524-4994-4

Printed in Great Britain

AUTHOR'S NOTE

There has been many books written on the 1812 campaign, but very few in English have looked at it from the Russian perspective. I hope this book will give the reader a more balanced view of the campaign from the 'other side', although I have not only used Russian, but also French, German, British, Irish and American eye-witness accounts.

Like most accounts, these vary in detail as well as accuracy. Some were written immediately after the event, while others were written years after, when the memory had faded. However, what is clear is that the Russians suffered the same terrible roads and weather conditions that the soldiers of the Grande Armée complained about.

Until the Russian Revolution in 1917, the Russian calendar was twelve days behind Western Europe, so the Battle of Borodino took place on 26 August, or 7 September by the Western or Gregorian one. All dates in this book are based on the Western calendar. I have also changed the Russian measurements, of a verst (0.66 of a mile or 1.06km) and a sazhen (7ft or 2.13m), into metric measurement.

Finally, I would like to thank the staff of the British Library and The National Archives for all their help, the Borodino Museum, the Hermitage and also the team on the website, www.museum.ru/1812/index.html, who have reproduced many articles and books on the Russian Army and the 1812 campaign.

CONTENTS

INTRODUCTION

'1812, what a magic word! What great memories! 24 years had passed since that unforgettable time. And the gigantic events are still occuring in our imagination,' recorded Rafail Zotov in his memoirs.[1] There has been a fascination with the campaign which the Russians have called the Patriotic War ever since. Those who took part in this and the subsequent campaigns saw it as a momentous event in history. Even before Napoleon's defeat in 1814, published accounts had begun to appear and tourists visited the battlefields. People in Britain and America could read about it in their newspapers, and funds were set up to help Russia in its hour of need. The Battle of Borodino has been celebrated in Russia annually ever since and on the 100th anniversary the last alleged surviving veterans were invited. One even claimed to have seen Napoleon himself, although he remembered him as a tall man with a beard.[2]

The campaign had not just a military impact on history, but also a social one. Many young officers came to respect the Russian serfs who made up the rank and file of the army. General Michael Vorontsov, who commanded a division at Borodino, set up a school in 1815 to teach his soldiers to read and write. One Russian officer wrote: 'Every day I meet peasant soldiers who are just as good and rational as any nobleman. These simple men have not yet been corrupted by the absurd conventions of our society and they have their own moral ideas which are just as good.'[3] These young nobility wanted serfdom abolished and the introduction of a liberal constitution so that they could enjoy the freedom they had seen in other European countries. Yet this idea was nothing new, Alexander himself had written before coming to the throne: 'nothing could be more degrading and inhuman than the sale of people, and a decree is needed that will forbid this forever. To the shame of Russia, slavery still exists.'

However, it is easy to exaggerate the effects that the 'children of 1812' – as the young nobility who had served in the army were known – had on society. During his stay in Paris the Tsar went so far as to have French soldiers guard him, instead of Russian ones, so that they would not see the 'freedoms' that other nations' soldiers enjoyed. While some of the nobility were freeing the serfs on their estates, Alexander's

favourite, Count Arakcheev, was setting up his 'military settlements'. At their height about a million serfs lived on these settlements, which taught the soldiers and their families farming techniques, but it was under strict military discipline.

Frustrated in their aims for the introduction of an enlightened society, some of the more radical nobles attempted a coup in December 1825. However the 'Decembrist Uprising' was badly organised and harshly put down, with five of the ringleaders being hanged and others sent to Siberia. By these actions the new Tsar, Nicholas I, introduced a stricter constitution and established a police force to impose it.

The 1812 campaign is also seen as a turning point in Russian culture, as Orlando Figes states: 'The nineteenth century quest for Russian nationhood began in the ranks of 1812.'[4] Since the time of Peter the Great, Russia had been a great power, but it had always looked to Western Europe for its culture, in arts, architecture and fashion. Even during the Napoleonic Wars parents hired French teachers to educate their children. French was the court language; some nobility could not even speak their native tongue. Now with the overthrow of Napoleon, in which Russia played a major part, it was filled with self-confidence, and the Russian language was taught once more to the children of the nobility. The nobility looked to the old Russian culture, which still existed among the serf population. At court women began to wear the national costume of a *sarafan* tunic and the *kokoshnik*, a crescent shaped headband. At balls in St Petersburg, Russian dances became just as popular as French ones.

Yet in 1812 many hoped for Napoleon to be successful. The countries of Lithuania, Poland and Moldavia had only been part of Russia since the 1790s and longed to be independent again, albeit under the protection of France. The popular view that the Russian serfs patriotically burned their homes and crops in an attempt to stop a foreign invader is false. In reality many had their houses burnt by the Cossacks and they had no say in the matter. Some Russian serfs hoped that Napoleon would set them free and so welcomed members of the Grande Armée; but it would not be until 1861 that they were finally emancipated.

1

PRELUDE TO WAR

On 24 June 1812 Napoleon crossed the Nieman at the head of an estimated army of 500.000 men. The world had turned since those distant days in 1807 when Emperor Napoleon and Tsar Alexander I had embraced each other at Tilsit and sworn eternal friendship. Though even then many believed that this was just a respite and that, as an English Colonel serving with the Russian Army recalled, the peace did not 'promise to be of long duration'.[1]

Alexander had been dazzled by their meeting; once it had finished he could not wait to write to his sister:

> God has saved us: instead of having to make sacrifices, we have emerged almost gloriously from the struggle. But what do you think of all these events? Just imagine me spending my days with Bonaparte, talking for hours quite alone with him! I ask you, does not all this seem like a dream? It is past midnight and he has only just left me. How I wish you could be an invisible witness of all that was going on!²

On 9 July, Alexander and Napoleon signed the Treaty of Tilsit, which officially brought an end to the War of the Fourth Coalition. By signing the Treaty, Russia agreed to recognise various states established by Napoleon, including the Duchy of Warsaw, and the Emperor was free to pursue his conquest of Western Europe. In return Russia had to join the Continental System, which banned trading with Great Britain. Russia was allowed to expand in the East against the Turkish Empire and pursue its claims against Finland. The Duke of Oldenburg, whose son was soon to marry Alexander I's sister, Catherine, was also to be reinstated in his Duchy, albeit with a French presence.

Russia's ally in the war, Prussia, did not get off so lightly. The King, Frederick William III, was practically ignored by Napoleon. Prussia had to give up her part of Poland, which she had annexed on 24 October 1795, to form the Duchy of Warsaw. Overnight the country had gone from a superpower to a second tier nation.

Despite these favourable terms to Russia, upon hearing the news of the Treaty of Tilsit, Admiral Shishkov wrote in his diary: 'The Tilsit peace lowered the head of mighty Russia by the acceptance of the most humiliating conditions.' While Admiral Mordvinov wrote: 'The sons of Russia would rather have given the last drop of their blood than have bowed in disgrace under [this] yoke.' These two admirals were by no means alone in their sentiments. Even Alexander's sister, Catherine was displeased with her brother:

> While I live I shall not get used to the idea of knowing that you pass your days with Bonaparte. When people say so, it seems like a bad joke and impossible. All the coaxing he has tried on this nation is only so much deceit, for the man is a blend of cunning, ambition and pretence.

In Russia itself, Martha Wilmot, an Irishwoman staying in Moscow recorded:

> On Saturday the 16th [July] arrived the news of Peace between the Russians and France. This Peace is very unpopular. However M de Tutolmin has given orders it should be celebrated magnificently and Sunday there was an illumination, ringing of all the bells till my ears ached, firing of cannon, a Te Deum and Buonaparte named Emperor and King instead of Buonaparte in all the Churches.[3]

Just over a year later, on 27 September 1808, Alexander and Napoleon met again at Erfurt to reaffirm their friendship. This time however, it was the Tsar who held the advantage, because the Grande Armée had suffered a series of setbacks in Spain and Napoleon needed Alexander's help to keep Prussia and Austria from rearming, while he stabilised the situation in Spain. Alexander promised France military aid if it was attacked by Austria, 'to the best of her abilities'. In return the Tsar wanted the French troops evacuated from Prussia and the Duchy of Warsaw, which could be used to threaten Russia, and that Napoleon recognise Russia's territorial claims to Finland, Moldavia and Wallachia. Napoleon argued that the French troops were needed in Prussia in case Austria attacked him, but agreed to evacuate the Duchy of Warsaw and although he did recognise Russia's claim to Finland, Napoleon gave only a vague assent about Moldavia and Wallachia.

At the Congress of Erfurt, Alexander had an unexpected ally in Charles Maurice de Talleyrand – Napoleon's former foreign minister – who suggested to Alexander

> You are predestined to save Europe and you will be able to do it only if you do not give in to Napoleon. The French nation is civilised, but its sovereign is not; the Russian sovereign is civilised, whilst his people are not. Therefore the Russian Emperor should be an ally of the French people and not to the French Emperor.[4]

On 12 October 1808, an agreement was signed and two days later Alexander and Napoleon departed. It would be the last time they would meet. In the event Russia failed to stop Austria rearming and the War of the Fifth Coalition broke out in 1809.

Napoleon failed to withdraw his troops from the Duchy of Warsaw, so Franco-Russian relations began to deteriorate.

One of the main causes was that Russia had a desperate need for free trade, so the Continental System was bringing hardship upon the country. The rouble fell in value by 25 per cent and Russian ships were often seized by the Royal Navy, which increased the price of imports even more. The price of coffee more than doubled and sugar trebled in price. Faced with mounting financial problems, Russian merchants began to break the sanctions against Great Britain.

It was also discovered that Napoleon had been issuing licences to French merchants to import goods from Great Britain, thus breaking the Continental System himself. Nonetheless, Napoleon was furious with Russia, which he saw as betraying him. In his attempt to enforce the blockade of Great Britain, Napoleon annexed Holland in June 1810 and then in December of the same year, the Hanseatic cities, including the Duchy of Oldenburg, the independence of which had been guaranteed by the Treaty of Tilsit.

Alexander sent a letter of protest to the French foreign minister, Jean Baptiste de Nompere de Champagny, but this protest was treated with contempt, without the Foreign Minister even reading it. On 31 December 1810 Alexander issued an Imperial Decree opening Russia's ports to American ships that imported British goods, and imposed a tax on French imports. Napoleon sent more troops to central Europe to 'help' the coastal towns and countries enforce the Continental System but Russia saw these troops as a threat to her sovereignty.

There was a further cause for the decline in Franco-Russian relations. For years Napoleon had believed he was infertile. However, during the War of 1807 he had met a young Polish countess, Marie Walewska, who became his mistress and on 4 May 1810 gave birth to their son, Alexander Florian Joseph. Napoleon realised that there was still a chance for a legitimate heir to carry on his dynasty, and so he divorced Empress Josephine and began looking for a new wife.

At first Napoleon set his eyes on Catherine, Alexander's favourite sister, who was quickly married off to the Duke of Oldenburg; then they settled on Grand Duchess Anna. Although she was only 14 years old at the time and Napoleon was 40, in 1809 he instructed the imperial ambassador to St Petersburg, Armand Caulaincourt (1773–1827) to ask Alexander for her hand in marriage. Upon hearing of this proposal Maria Feodorovna, Alexander's mother, wrote to her other daughter Catherine:

> What a miserable existence the child [Grand Duchess Anna] would have united to a scoundrel to whom nothing is sacred and who knows no restraint because he does not even believe in God! ... What would she see, what would she hear in that school of wickedness and vice?[5]

Maria Feodorovna also had to look out for her son, the Tsar, and what 'troubles and misfortunes [would be brought] down upon him', if she refused. Finally, in February 1810 after much delay, Caulaincourt was informed that there would be no wedding between Napoleon and Anna, the official line being that she was too young.

By this time, the War of the Fifth Coalition had broken out between Britain and Austria on the one side and France and her allies on the other. Once again Napoleon was victorious. This war ended on 14 October 1809 with the Treaty of Schonbrunn and by the time Alexander had sent his answer on the Russian marriage, negotiations had already begun with the Austrian Emperor, Francis I, for his daughter's hand in marriage. On 11 March 1810, Napoleon married Marie Louise at Vienna and again on 1 April in Paris. It was obvious that Napoleon had been in negotiations with the Austrian Court even before Alexander had given his answer to Napoleon and this was seen as an insult to Russia.

The Treaty of Schonbrunn extended the Duchy of Warsaw by annexing Western Galicia, and the following year Napoleon refused to confirm that the Duchy would not be expanded further. Russia feared that it would be at its expense, since it was now the sole controller of part of Poland, granted to her by the 3rd Partition of Poland in October 1795. Alexander toyed with the idea of pre-empting Napoleon and defining his own Poland. The Polish nobleman, Adam Czartoryski, recalled his conversation with the Tsar and the suggestion of the formation of

> ... a Kingdom of Poland out of the Duchy of Galicia, and to allow the inhabit-
> ants of the Polish provinces of Russia to serve the new kingdom, as if it were their
> own country. This idea surprised me; but the Tsar explained that the Poles, being
> thus satisfied, would have no reason to oppose Russia, that there then would be no
> longer any cause of dissension between Russia and France, and that the evil would
> thus be got rid of by amputation instead of cure.[6]

Having mulled over the suggestion, Czartoryski wrote to the Tsar on 30 January 1811 about the subject of Poland, suggesting that

> The reunion of Poland into a national body under a constitutional regime, would be
> received with gratitude and eagerness from everyone that could offer it ... However
> just the grievances of the Poles against Napoleon may be, he has persuaded them
> that it was not want of power which prevented him from carrying the wish of their
> regeneration any further ... and that at the first rupture with Russia, Poland would
> be restored. To this feeling is added gratitude for what Napoleon has already done
> and repugnance at the idea of turning against him, just at the moment when he
> most reckoned upon co-operation from the new Polish state which he has created.
> To all these considerations must be added the fact that the French and the Poles are
> brothers in arms and the idea that while the French are the friends of Poland the
> Russians are her bitter enemies – an idea which has been considerably strengthened
> by the events of the late war ... Moreover in the expectation of a war with Russia,
> many Poles have sent their children to be educated in Paris, as being at present the
> safest place in Europe; and these would be so many hostages in Napoleon's hands.
> Finally Napoleon has hitherto been so uniformly successful even in the most dan-
> gerous undertakings, that people think he will always conquer in the end, however
> much appearance may be against him.[7]

Czartoryski suggested that to overcome these problems Alexander should restore the constitution of 3 May 1791 and reunite the whole of Poland under one ruler and re-establish trade, the lack of which was ruining the country. However, Alexander also needed a reasonable prospect of success in a war against Napoleon. In the event, neither monarch was able to bring themselves to restore Poland, but it would take several years of tension to realise it.

Napoleon felt that the decline of Franco-Russian relations had begun in 1809 when he had asked the Tsar to supply troops to invade Galicia, which was part of the Austrian Empire, but Russia had acted slowly and supplied only a small army. However, at the time Russia was already fighting two wars, one with Turkey (1806–1812) and the other with Sweden (1808–1809), so had limited resources. Furthermore, Russia had demanded part of the Grand Duchy of Warsaw as payment for her services, which Napoleon was not willing to grant. Napoleon saw that before he could turn on Spain and drive the British out of the Iberian Peninsula he had to deal with Russia, or else she might invade the Duchy and unite Austria and Prussia against him.

As early as April 1810 Alexander also expected a war with Napoleon; he told Czartoryski:

' … it [the war] will now be nine months hence.' While saying these words, and indeed throughout the conversation, the Emperor had a severe and fixed look, which reminded me of his haggard gaze after Austerlitz.[8]

Alexander was not the only one to think this way; in 1810, the Minister of War, General Barclay de Tolly, wrote to Alexander:

A power has now drawn near the frontiers of Russia; it is France, and she will certainly not be satisfied to stay where she is. If one can judge the future by the past or by the manifest intentions of the French Emperor with his unlimited ambition to use any means to dominate Europe.[9]

On 4 January 1811, General Barclay de Tolly ordered that Russia's western frontier was to be better guarded, with the construction of fortifications, hospitals and magazines. The frontier was to be divided into sections each of about 160km with each section further divided into fifteen parts. Each was to be policed by a Cossack regiment and a troop or *sotnia* divided into three to guard a single part, so 30 Cossacks were responsible for 10 to 11 km. A regular officer was to be in command of each sector. Behind these Cossacks were three armies designated the 1st, 2nd and 3rd Western Army under the command of Barclay de Tolly, Prince Peter Bagration and Tormasov.

On 2 April 1811 a letter to the British Foreign Office reported that cannon were being sent to the frontier and that garrison troops were being incorporated into regular regiments.

Many generals commanding divisions of the army assembled in those provinces have successively arrived at [St] Petersburg under the pretext of settling their private

affairs, but in reality for the purpose of conferring on orders with the Minister of
War [and] on the state of their respective corps …

The manufacture of military weapons has increased. The number of muskets
already finished has been increased from 50,000 to 500,000 and there are 2000
pieces of cannon ready to be mounted upon the new fortifications erected on the
banks of the Dwina.[10]

Military expenditure rose from 134,405,000 roubles in 1808 to 274,037,000 in 1811.
The army was to be modernised, no longer was the army to be organised on Prussian
military lines, instead the French corps system was to be adopted and new regiments
raised. Orders for more men to be conscripted were issued, three 'souls' or male peasants in every 500 were to be raised in 1810, and four in 500 in 1811, to bring the
regiments up to strength.

Having been at war almost continually since 1805, the Russian Army was not the
same as that which had fought at Austerlitz (1805) or Eylau (1807). In 1810 Barclay de
Tolly complained:

> In place of strong and brave troops, our regiments consist in large measure of green
> soldiers, unaccustomed to the rigours of war. The present prolonged war [the
> Russian–Turkish War] has smothered their traditional heroic virtues. Their patriot-
> ism, as well as their physical strength have begun to weaken with the beginning of
> this intense and useless war.[11]

Napoleon agreed with this, later opining that 'the Russian Army which fought at
Austerlitz would not have lost the Battle of Borodino.'[12]

Many Russian generals wanted an offensive war before Napoleon's European
Army was ready and bombarded Alexander with their plans for occupying the Duchy
of Warsaw, so that, according to Bagration, 'the theatre of war will leave the limits of
our empire.'

Alexander contemplated an attack on the Duchy of Warsaw. As early as 25 February
1811, Alexander proposed the occupation of the Duchy, but these preparations were
halted after Marshal Joseph Poniatowski, whom Adam Czartoriski was trying to persuade to change sides, informed Napoleon of Alexander's intentions. Czartoryski
suggested to the Tsar that 'such a plan was obviously chimerical; its difficulties were
palpable, and it involved a war against Napoleon with uncertain chances of success'.[13]

In May 1811, Napoleon replaced Caulaincourt, whom he considered as too pro-
Russian, with Jacques Alexandre Bernard Law, Marquis de Lauriston, as the French
ambassador to Russia. Before Caulaincourt's departure from St Petersburg, Alexander
had an audience with him, when according to the ambassador he warned:

> If the Emperor Napoleon makes war on me … it is possible, even probable that
> we shall be defeated, assuming that we fight. But that will not mean that he can
> dictate a peace. The Spaniards have often been defeated; and they are not beaten,
> nor have they submitted. But they are not so far away from Paris as we are, and they

have neither our climate nor our resources to help them. We shall take no risks. We have plenty of room; and our standing army is well organised, which means, as the Emperor Napoleon has admitted, that we need never accept a dictated peace, whatever reverses we may suffer. What is more, in such circumstances the victor is forced to accept the terms of the vanquished. The Emperor Napoleon made a remark [concerning this] to Chernishev [Alexander's ADC] in Vienna after the Battle of Wagram [1809]. He would not have made peace then if Austria had not kept an army intact. Results have to keep pace with his thoughts, because being often absent from France, he is always anxious to return there. This is the teaching of a Master. I shall not be the first to draw my sword, but I shall be the last to sheathe it. The Spaniards have proved that lack of perseverance has been the undoing of all the States on which your master has made war. The Emperor Napoleon's remark to Chernychev, in the latest war with Austria, shows clearly enough that the Austrians could have obtained better terms if they had been more persevering. People don't know how to suffer. If the fighting went against me, I should retire to Kamchatka [in eastern Siberia] rather than cede provinces and sign, in my capital, treaties that were really only truces. You Frenchmen are brave; but long privations and a bad climate [will] wear him down and discourage him. Our climate, our winter, will fight on our side. With you, marvels only take place where the Emperor is in personal attendance; and he cannot be everywhere, he cannot be absent from Paris year after year.[14]

Some historians have claimed that Caulaincourt wrote this with hindsight, but it fits with the temperament of the time.

On 18 June 1811 a letter to the British Foreign Office recorded:

The Court of St Petersburg was said to be divided into two parties, both of them look upon a war as inevitable, but the one thinks that Russia should commence hostilities without delay. Whilst the other (whose opinion is sanctioned by that of the Emperor) thinks that the Russian Army, fortifying and concentrating itself upon the frontier, should not act offensively until attacked by the French.

With the growing tension between Russia and France, Austria tried to mediate, however this was believed to have been

… suggested by France in order to lull Russia until France be ready to attack her with advantage. France it is added would already have done this had it not been for the war in the peninsula, which absorbs the greatest part of her army.[15]

On 15 August 1811, at Tuileries all the senior officers and dignitaries came to pay their respects to Napoleon on his 42nd birthday. When it came to the Russian ambassador, Prince Kurakin, Napoleon inquired about the Russian victory over the Turks at Ruschuk, and why the Russian troops had subsequently withdrawn from the Turkish War. When Kurakin said it was because of financial constraints, Napoleon exploded saying that the Tsar had withdrawn troops from the Turkish front to reinforce the

Russian armies massing on the border of the Duchy of Warsaw, and that the outrage shown by Russia over the occupation of Oldenburg was just an excuse to declare war on him. Kurakin tried to answer, but Napoleon would not let him. Finally Napoleon asked him whether he had power to negotiate a treaty, to which Kurakin replied that he had not and so Napoleon walked away.

Napoleon was correct, the Russian troops fighting the Turks were badly needed for the forthcoming war. In fact General Kutuzov, who had taken over the command of the Russian Army, had withdrawn troops from Russia's western border to reinforce his army, so the war had to be brought to a quick conclusion. French diplomacy was trying to prolong the war, so that these troops would be tied down. On the other hand Sweden and Great Britain sent diplomatic missions to mediate between Turkey and Russia for a quick peace.

Meanwhile Kutuzov had surrounded the Turkish Army, which prompted the Sultan to ask for an armistice. The Congress of Bucharest was set up to discuss a final peace, but made slow headway, and dissatisfied with progress, the Tsar sent Admiral Paul Chichagov to replace Kutuzov as the commander of the Army of Moldavia. In the draft that followed, Turkey even suggested it might be willing to supply troops to help Russia, but these never materialised. On 28 May 1812, the Peace of Bucharest was signed. It was ratified by Alexander on 23 June 1812, the day before Napoleon crossed the frontier.

In the meantime Alexander sent Count de Nesselrode to Paris to mediate. Whether this was a publicity feint or if Alexander actually wanted peace is unknown, but by now neither side could back down and save their honour and so war between the two nations was inevitable. To add to this, the armies on both sides of the Russian border were increasing. Among those watching the Russian soldiers marching to the frontier was 13-year-old Alexander Pushkin, who attended school about twelve miles from St Petersburg:

> To begin with we saluted all the regiments of the Guard which marched through Tsarskoe-Selo. We were always there as soon as they came in sight, and we even went out to meet them during lessons. We accompanied them with a fervent prayer, we kissed our relations and friends, and grenadiers wearing heavy moustaches blessed us with a sign of the cross without leaving the ranks. How many tears we shed![16]

However, the waiting was having a detrimental effect on the Russian Army, as General Ivan Paskevitch, who commanded the Orel Infantry Regiment, recalled:

> In February 1812 the 2nd Army moved closer to the border. This campaign undertaken in the impassable roads and terrible mud from early spring had created in the army a scorbutic illness. Of the 1,200 men in the regiment about 400 were sick. In April and May 150 men died. Only about 700 to 800 men remain in the ranks of the regiment.[17]

Baron Uxkull, a cornet in the Horse Guards, recorded his thoughts in his diary for 13 May 1812:

I dislike our inactivity very much, we'll soon have been in this part of the country for four weeks. It is said that the French Army is getting closer to our borders. Why don't we go to meet them? Why? Because there are men, our chiefs in Russia, who have more brains than I have, and who have less vanity than I, but [there] are also men who don't love their country as I do, and who are sacrificing the public interest for their private interests. This is true, but since it can't be remedied it's better to have patience. Which the Good Lord will give us.'[18]

General Ermolov: 'Accurate intelligence soon confirmed a colossal force being concentrated near our borders.'[19] The Russians believed that Napoleon had about 300,000 men in central Europe, whereas in reality he had about 500,000, drawn from all over western Europe, including Austria and Prussia, with whom Alexander had hoped to form an alliance. In April 1812 Napoleon was even prepared to negotiate with Great Britain for peace, so that he could use the troops in Spain to reinforce his Grande Armée. The British Government refused his overtures and Napoleon had to send much needed supplies and replacements to Spain rather than Germany. Great Britain had technically been at war with Russia since 1807, but signed a peace treaty on 18 July 1812, although it had been supplying Russia with arms and money long before this date.

With all hopes of a grand alliance, as had been alive in 1805, dashed, Alexander saw that Russia had no option but to fight a defensive war when it came. The border fortifications would have to be abandoned and General Phull, the Tsar's military adviser, suggested a fortified camp at Drissa, to where the armies could retreat.

Although on paper Russia's army was estimated at anything between 550,000 and 900,000 men, of these Barclay's 1st Western Army was reported to have 120,210 men and 580 guns, Bagration's 2nd Western Army had 49,423 men and 180 guns and Tormasov's 3rd Western Army had 44,180 men and 168 guns. The remainder had to be used to guard Finland, and the Russo-Turkish border, and for internal security.

The Grande Armée was widely dispersed, so that the Russians would be kept guessing where Napoleon would strike in force. This prompted Russia to disperse its army along its border. The gap between the 1st and 2nd Western Armies was 100km, and between the 2nd and 3rd Armies 200km, with the Pripet marshes between them. Barclay, as Minister of War issued the following strategy to Tormasov and Bagration for the forthcoming campaign:

After the commencement of military operation, you are to execute the following [orders] a) to constantly harass the enemy. b) to attack the enemy rear and flanks, to capture enemy transports and destroy everything that facilitates his actions, especially the hospitals. c) to eliminate any provisions and transports that can be utilised by the enemy, to demolish bridges, ships, depots and stores … The local population should be allowed to keep only minimal supplies.

Unfortunately for Russia, Napoleon had a secret network of spies, which included Polish inhabitants living in Russia; and the various newspapers reported the Russian

Army's movements! Both helped give Napoleon a fairly accurate picture of the Russian deployment along the border.

On the other hand Russia also had its spies in all the Royal Courts of Europe, including France. In coded letters they sent information back to St Petersburg, Alexander was known as Louise and Napoleon was referred to as Terence Petrovich or Sophie Smith, and the marriage as 'La Karpovka'.[20] Among those who ran the network of spies in France was Alexander Ivanovich Chernishev, the Russian colonel who had been at Napoleon's side at the Battle of Wagram and enjoyed his confidence. Chernishev's network of spies included many influential Frenchmen, including Michel who was on the General Staff of the French Army. He borrowed various reports on the French Army to be copied and then returned them to the French Minister of War. Talleyrand was also said to supply Alexander with information on occasion. In this way Russia was able to gather intelligence on the movements of troops and in 1811 knew where every French regiment in Europe was stationed.

However, Chernishev and Michel soon aroused the suspicion of Napoleon's counter intelligence organisation and when Chernishev heard that his lodgings were about to be searched he decided to return to Russia. He burnt all his papers that might reveal his network of spies, except one document that had found its way under his carpet incriminating Michel. Michel was promptly arrested and was executed on 2 May 1812, along with three others.

At beginning of 1812, Kurakin thought he saw signs that the war might be averted. However, he did not know that on 27 January Napoleon had issued a proclamation declaring his complaints against Russia and calling for his allies to muster their troops by 15 February.[21] On 23 April Kurakin wrote: 'Everything points to the conclusion that war was decided upon long ago in the mind of the French Emperor.'

On 26 April Alexander arrived at Vilna, the headquarters of the 1st Western Army. The following day, in a final effort to prevent war, Prince Kurakin asked Napoleon to evacuate French troops from Prussia, which Napoleon refused. The next day, Kurakin held talks with the French Minister of Foreign Affairs, in which he said that Russia was willing to drop all its demands over the Duchy of Oldenburg, beneficial duty would be placed on all French imports to Russia, in exchange for the evacuation of Prussia. These concessions were rejected.

On 9 May Napoleon considered the Grande Armée was ready for the invasion of Russia and he set out to join it. He does not seem to have worried that the Russians might attack first and decided to meet the various heads of states of his Empire, so that they could pay their respects. Two days later Kurakin asked for his passport to leave France.

While Napoleon was travelling to join the Grande Armée, the Tsar was hard at work preparing for the imminent invasion. 'The council of war at the Emperor's headquarters,' records Captain P. Cumming of the Royal Navy, 'sits daily from 11 o'clock in the morning till 3 o'clock in the afternoon.' Those who were present had 'the privilege of giving their opinion in writing or verbally in matters relating to the army or to the war', but with so many generals being allowed to speak this council of war made little headway.[22]

Russian propaganda would have it that the plan to retreat, or rather in the words of the propagandists, the 'advance' into Russia, had been devised as early as May 1811. This could not be further from the truth and up to the actual invasion the Russians still had not finalised their strategy. On 20 June 1812 Bagration was still suggesting an offensive war to the Tsar. 'Any retreat encourages the enemy and will give him great amounts of this territory, and take away our spirit … What are we afraid of and why do we have to exhaust the army?' General Ermolov, the 1st Army's Chief of Staff, wrote in June 1812: 'At the present moment, everything is arranged for the offensive: armies are deployed close to the frontiers, huge warehouses are established … on the frontiers of our territory.' Instructions were issued and then superseded, Barclay de Tolly promised Bagration that he would not give up Vilna without a fight – but was already making plans to abandon it.

The Russian politicians and generals knew that a war was coming in 1811. In the night sky a comet appeared, which to a superstitious people was always a sign that a great catastrophe would soon occur. Among those who saw the comet was Sister Antonia of the convent, who recalled, 'Every night this comet blazed in the sky, and we all asked one another "What misfortunes will it bring upon us?"'[23] Soon the Russian people would know.

Notes

1 *An Englishman in the Russian Army,* 1807 ed. Laurence Spring p.20
2 Quoted in L.I. Strakhovsky *Alexander I of Russia* p.42
3 *The Russian Journals of Catherine and Martha Wilmot,* p.299 Tutolmin was Governor General of Moscow
4 Quoted in Leonid Strakhovski's *Alexander I of Russia* p.96
5 Quoted in Henri Troyat's *Alexander of Russia* pp.123–124
6 *Memoirs of Prince Adam Czartoryski* vol 2 p.203–204
7 Ibid, pp221–222
8 Ibid, vol. 2 p 204
9 Quoted in Michael and Diana Josselson *The Commander, a life of Barclay de Tolly* p.73
10 TNA FO 65/77 ff1-7
11 Quoted in Laurence Spring *Russian Grenadiers and Infantry* p.42
12 Ibid, p.42
13 *Memoirs of Prince Adam Czartoryski* vol 2 p.203-204
14 Caulaincourt *With Napoleon in Russia* pp.5–6
15 TNA FO 65/77 f15
16 Quoted in Antony Brett-James *1812* p.77
17 Quoted in *1812 v vospominanye sovremennila* p.76–77
18 Baron Uxkull *Arms and the Woman* pp.39–40
19 Ermolov *Zapiski 1812* p108
20 *Memoirs of Nesselrode* vol.3 pp.225–227.
21 Edward Foord *Napoleon's Russian Campaign of 1812* p.9
22 BL Add ms 41,366 f.31
23 Quoted in Brett James *1812* p.10

2

VILNA

War was imminent, but for the civilians life went on as usual. In June 1812 Countess de Choiseul-Gouffier who lived in Vilna, wrote in her memoirs:

> A storm was ready to break over our heads, and yet in full security, no one thought of anything but pleasure and of the happiness of having the Emperor [Alexander] there. Not only were we far from foreseeing his departure and from suspecting that the troops of Napoleon were near the Nieman, but we were even ignorant of the fact that the French had crossed Germany.[1]

June 23 was a special day for Alexander, that day he had ratified the Peace of Bucharest so ending the Russo-Turkish War, before attending a ball held in his honour at General Levin Bennigsen's house at Zakrat, a few miles from Vilna. Bennigsen had commanded the last Russian Army to confront Napoleon in 1807, and many tipped him to be the commander in chief of the army this time.

The Countess de Choiseul-Gouffier was present at Bennigsen's ball and recorded her impressions:

> The evening was beautiful, the whole place was ornamented with orange trees in full bloom which perfumed the air … The musicians of the Imperial Guard played choice bits of music in different parts of the grounds … the sight of this brilliant assembly of beautifully dressed women and the military in splendid uniforms with their diamond decorations; this company scattered over the green lawns. The old trees forming masses of verdure; the villa that reflected … the blue heaven and the colours of the setting sun. The hills, whose tops disappeared in the soft clouds, all offered a sense of enchantment. But when the Emperor appeared, no one saw anything but him.[2]

As the guests danced and the band played the forthcoming war seemed a thousand miles away; but then General Balashov, Alexander's minister of Police arrived, in an agitated state. He whispered in the Tsar's ear that Napoleon's forces had begun to cross the River Nieman at about 9pm.[3] To avoid causing panic Alexander stayed for a while longer and then left to organise his forces.

Reports of Napoleon's movements were being received at Russian head-quarters, and by a British agent, Captain P. Cumming, who wrote to London on 27 June 1812:

> The French crossed the Russian borders on 24 June in four different places, viz at Georgenburg, Rawna, Olita and Miritsch … but only a few of their piquets were resisted and partly taken by the Cossacks. It was expected that a battle would be fought on 27th … The Russian Army, it would really appear, is in the most complete and effective order, and the officers (even those who were dispirited on a former occasion in the highest spirits and in the conviction that as long as they act on the defensive, Bonaparte cannot possible make any impression on them. I was told today and from a source which I conceive perfectly authentic that the Russian Army only consists in all of about 200,000 men, including the reserve. This I confess surprised me much after hearing on my arrival yesterday people estimating it at 300 to 400,000 men including all the reserves.[4]

The Duke of Wellington would later criticise Napoleon for beginning a campaign in June when many crops were still not ripe, since the majority of his army had to forage. However Napoleon's plan was simple; in a lightning campaign he planned to confront the 1st Western Army, before turning on the 2nd Army, which would force Alexander to surrender. Such a campaign would perhaps take about twenty days, or so Napoleon believed. Now his army was crossing the Nieman at Kovno on pontoon bridges, with the words of Napoleon's proclamation ringing in their ears:

> Soldiers, the second Polish War has begun. The first was ended at Friedland and Tilsit … The Second Polish War will be glorious for French arms, like the first: but the peace we shall conclude will carry with it its guarantee, and put an end to that proud influence Russia has exercised for fifty years over the affairs of Europe.[5]

No doubt the veterans of the First Polish War in 1807 still remembered the hardships of that campaign, the Russian soldiers' fierceness in battle, the cold and then the heat of Poland. Even now the Grande Armée was marching through torrential rain and soon it would turn very hot. Furthermore, Napoleon irritated many of the Germans in his army – which made up the greater part of it – when he referred to the war as being 'glorious for French arms'. Worst still, a rabbit had frightened Napoleon's horse, which threw its rider. While the Emperor was getting to his feet, some senior generals commented that this was a bad omen.

The main thrust of the invasion force was made up of Napoleon's Imperial Guard, Marshal Davoust's I Corps, Oudinot's II Corps (French and Swiss troops), Marshal Ney's III Corps, composed of French troops, and Generals Nansouty's I Cavalry Corps and Montbrun's II Cavalry Corps.

A few days after Napoleon's invasion force crossed the Nieman, Prince Eugene's Army of Italy, containing Eugene's IV Corps, with mainly Italian soldiers but also French and Croatians, Marshal St Cyr's Bavarian VI Corps, and General Grouchy's III Cavalry Corps crossed the Nieman at Pilony, south of Kovno. Grodno was chosen as the second supporting army's crossing point. This was commanded by Jerome Bonaparte, Napoleon's brother and King of Westphalia, composed of Prince Poniatovski's Polish V Corps, General Regnier's Saxon VII Corps and Jerome's Westphalian VIII Corps, plus General Latour-Maubourg's IV Cavalry Corps. An Austrian Army under Prince Schwarzenburg, which was to operate in the south of Russia, crossed the Nieman at Drotgitschin. Marshal Macdonald's X Corps of Polish and Prussian troops that would operate against Riga crossed at Tilsit.

Both sides believed that the Russian Army would defend Vilna, but orders were issued for the Russian Army to begin its retreat. On 25 June, thinking not only of the army but also of Russia, the Tsar, who was described at this time as 'his usual calm self and in his normal mood', wrote to Count Soltikov, the commander in chief of St Petersburg, informing him of the invasion:

> I have full confidence in the zeal of my people, and in the bravery of my troops; being menaced in their homes they will defend them with the firmness and intrepidity which characterise them.
>
> Providence will bless our just cause; the defence of the nation, the preservation of independence and of the national honour, has forced us to draw the sword. *I will not sheathe it again whilst a single enemy remains in arms on the territory of my empire.*[6]

At the same time, Alexander issued a proclamation to his army, which after recounting his efforts to end the situation diplomatically, went on:

> The French Emperor, by an attack upon our troops at Kovno, has already commenced war, and consequently nothing farther remains for us, but (while we invoke the aid of the Sovereign of the Universe, the Author and defender of Truth) to place our force in opposition to the force of the enemy. It is unnecessary to remind our Generals, our officers and soldiers, of their duty and valour. In their veins flows the blood of the Scavonians, so highly renowned of old for their victories. Soldiers! You are the defenders of your country and independence. I am with you. God is on our side.[7]

Despite the stirring rhetoric, Alexander wanted to give diplomacy one more chance, so he summoned General Balashov and according to the General told him

> You will undoubtedly be surprised when you hear why I sent for you. I intend to send you to Emperor Napoleon. I have just received a report from St Petersburg that our Minister of Foreign Affairs has received a note from the French Embassy explaining that our ambassador, Prince Kurakin, has asked for his passports twice in a single day and that France regards this action as a rupture. In consequence, Count

Lauriston has been commanded to ask for his passport and leave Russia. Though this is a very flimsy reason, it is, as far as I know Napoleon's first pretext for making war on us. What makes it all the more paltry is that Kurakin acted on his own account and not on my orders.

Between you and me I do not expect your errand will stop the war. But at least Europe will know and this will prove once more, that we did not begin it.

Alexander gave Balashov a letter for Napoleon early next morning and added:

If he wants to enter into negotiations, they can begin at once, on one unalterable condition: his armies must retire beyond the frontier. Otherwise, the Tsar gives his word of honour that so long as a single armed French soldier remains on Russian soil, he will neither utter nor listen to a single word of peace.[8]

Balashov then set out for the French lines, but it would be five days before Napoleon would see him.

On 26 June Mikhail Oginski, a Russian diplomat of Polish origins, wrote in his memoirs:

When I awoke the next morning I learnt that the Tsar had left Vilna three hours after midnight, and one was made aware of this fact by the general bustle throughout the town … Every arrangement for the evacuation of Vilna by the military was carried out in the best possible order, but what a picture! Here one saw lines of vehicles overtaking one another in their efforts to get out of the town; there one noticed carts blocking the way and, once they had got clear of the gates, bustling along to give warning of the enemy's approach. At every square and crossroads groups of people stood discussing what they should do.[9]

Major Baron Woldemar von Lowenstern, who had served in the French Army in 1805 and now was a member of the Russian staff, also described the evacuation of Vilna:

The tumult, the noise, and the anxiety were extreme. All horses were commandeered in the streets. Disorder was at its height. The inhabitants took refuge inside their houses and barricaded themselves in. At the gates of Vilna preparations were made to offer a stout resistance. The Commander in Chief [Barclay de Tolly] sent the troops at his disposal into a camp near the town. He made frequent reconnaissances and he alone did not belie his character. He remained calm throughout, but uncommunicative.

All the news we had from our advance guard left us in no doubt that the enemy were concentrating with a view to forcing the Vilna position. At two o'clock in the morning all the aide de camps were summoned to the Commander in Chief [de Tolly] and we were sent off in all directions, time after time.

The question had not seemed to have been decided yet as to whether we were to oppose the enemy or retreat. Eventually General Barclay de Tolly called me into his office and instructed me to write to His Majesty the Tsar and lay before him the reasons why he was going to abandon Vilna without firing a shot.[10]

The Russians were rushing about preparing to leave, burning any stores that they could not take with them so they would not fall into enemy hands. Bridges were also burnt to slow down the enemy. Countess de Choiseul-Gouffier, one of the Tsarina's maids of honour, also records the events at Vilna:

> Not only did the Russian troops evacuate Vilna, but the Russian individuals who had lived there for a great many years hastened to leave with their wives and children and everything they possessed. All the horses in the town and those privately owned were requisitioned in these circumstances of dire necessity – all, that is except for those belonging to my father, who had not even taken the precaution of hiding them, as some people had done, placing their horses in the loft where the police never thought of looking for them … On the night of the 27-28 June the Russian troops filed past in good order, and in a most impressive silence. No, this was certainly not a flight as has been stated.[11]

Napoleon remained at Kovno until the morning of 27 June, overseeing the crossing of his army, then moved to Yeve, just 30 miles from Vilna. On 28 June, at 1.00pm, with the forward elements of the Grande Armée already in the town, the Russian Headquarters left Vilna. Countess de Choiseul-Gouffier, who had recently entertained the Tsar, now witnessed the arrival of the first elements of the Grande Armée and remembered her Polish ancestry:

> I can find no words to describe my emotions when I saw some Polish troops! Poles who were galloping at full speed, sabres drawn and laughing, waving their lance pennants, which were in the national colours. I was wearing these for the first time! I stood at an open window, and they saluted me as they passed. The sight of these real compatriots set my heart racing. I felt that I was Polish by birth, that I was going to become Polish again. Tears of joy and enthusiasm streamed down my face. This was a delicious moment, but it was not to last long.[12]

It was not just the Polish civilians who were excited by the prospects of becoming 'Polish again', some Polish soldiers within the Russian Army deserted in the hope that they would be able to join the new Polish Army once Napoleon had created a new Poland. However their hopes were to be dashed. Napoleon could not bring himself to sign the Edict while he was at war with Russia, whose army – once he had brought the Tsar to heel – he needed for a possible invasion of India, then part of the British Empire.

Napoleon had other things to worry about. The Grande Armée had one fatal flaw: unlike the French troops who had their own organised commissariat system, his German allies had to rely on living off the countryside. His army had plundered its way across Europe, robbing the inhabitants, demanding money to buy food and pay the troops and pulling the thatch from the roofs of the houses to feed their horses. Now on Russian soil the plundering continued with renewed vigour, with the French troops now joining in with the justification that they were in enemy territory. Countess de Choiseul-Gouffier continues:

The French Army who entered Vilna had not had bread for three days … The country through which the Grande Armée had passed had been ravaged and pillaged and its corn had been cut green for cavalry; it could not, therefore, supply the needs of the capital, and the people dared not even expose their convoys on the roads which were infested by marauders.

Besides, the disorderly behaviour of the army was a consequence of the sentiment of the chief, for after having crossed the Nieman Napoleon in an order of the day declared to the troops that they were about to set foot on Russian territory. It was like this that the liberator of Poland, so much desired, announced himself to the Lithuanians. In consequence of this Proclamation Lithuania was considered and treated as a hostile country, while its inhabitants, animated by patriotic enthusiasm flew to welcome the French. They were soon to be desported and outraged by those who they regarded as the instuments of the deliverance of their country and compelled to abandon their homes and their property to pillage. Many took refuge in the depths of the forest, carrying with them that which they hold the most dear – the honour of their wives and children.

Each day brought the recital of new excesses committed by the French soldier in the country. Vilna seemed to have become a seat of war, soldiers bivouacked in the streets, which resounded with the clash of arms, the blare of trumpets, the neighing of horses and the confusion of many languages.[13]

On 30 June, General Balashov was shown into the same room where the Tsar had interviewed him five days before. This time it was Napoleon who was in the room and he was in no mood for diplomacy. After saying that Alexander had insulted him by his actions, he went on:

I know that a war between France and Russia is no trifling matter for either Russia or France. I have made extensive preparations, and my forces are three times as large as yours. I know as well as you do, perhaps better than you, the size of your army. You have 120,000 infantry and 60 or 70 thousand cavalry. In a word under 200,000 men, all told. I have three times as many.

Napoleon then criticised the generals that Alexander had gathered around his person, even referring to Bennigsen's involvement in the assassination of Tsar Paul I in 1801. However, it is when Napoleon came to Barclay de Tolly that he is most revealing;

I do not know Barclay de Tolly, but judging from his first moves in the campaign, he is rather lacking in military talent. Never have you begun a war in such confusion … You have burnt many stores. Why? Either you should not have assembled them, or you should have used them according to their purpose. Did you imagine that I would merely have a look at the Nieman and would refrain from crossing it? Aren't you ashamed? From the time of Peter I, from the time when Russia became a European power, no enemy has penetrated your borders, and now I am in Vilna. I have conquered an entire province without firing a shot. If only out of respect for your Emperor, who for two months had been in Vilna with his headquarters, you should have defended it![14]

So the diatribe went on, with Balashov trying to get a word in. It was only interrupted when a window blew open for a second time, so Napoleon ripped it off its hinges. Napoleon's insults about the Tsar and Russia went on all day, until Balashov was finally able to take his leave of Napoleon and return to the Russian Army.

Countess de Choiseul-Gouffier, who met Napoleon several times during his stay at Vilna, also commented on Napoleon's behaviour at this time.

> [He] entered Vilna anxious and discontented. The easiness of this victory dismayed him, he had too much judgement not to see that the retreat of the Russians was not inspired by the fear of his name, but covered deep designs. 'I had believed that the taking of Vilna would cost me twenty thousand men at least,' he said … The scarcity of food, the disorder of the army, the mistake by Prince Jerome, the continued losses among the cavalry, all combined to make him look the sad result of this campaign in the face as a thing inevitable. But the fatal *genius* of Napoleon pushed him forward and it was thus that from illusion to illusion he rushed to his ruin, rejecting the truth as an apparition whose presence he could not endure.[15]

Napoleon had wanted a quick campaign, he had believed that the Russians would throw themselves on his much larger army before he had reach Vilna. Now without provisions for his army and a decisive battle, he was at a loss, he now knew that the war would be a long one.

He stayed in Vilna until 16 July. For almost three weeks he attended to various military and civil matters, built fortifications and ordered the establishment of magazines where provisions could be stored. Caulaincourt, the former French ambassador to Russia, who was with the Emperor, states Napoleon worked hard during this time, scanning every report from his corps commanders on the Russians' movements. However, his place was with the army, which was even now spreading out across Russia in search of the foe. The French general Jomini, one of the leading tacticians of his day, thought that staying in Vilna so long was Napoleon's biggest mistake.

Notes

1   *Memoirs of Alexander I and the court of Russia* by Countess de Choiseul-Gouffier p.90
2   *Memoirs* Countess de Choiseul-Gouffier p.92
3   This was General Morand's Division of Davoust's Corps
4   BL Add ms 41366 ff 15–17
5   Quoted in Robert Kerr Porter, *Narrative of the campaign in Russia* pp.16–17
6   Sir Robert Wilson, *The French Invasion of Russia*, pp.24–25

7 The *Windsor and Eton Times*
8 Eugene Tarle, *Napoleon's Invasion of Russia 1812* p.46
9 Memoirs de Michel Oginski sur la Pologne et les Polonais pp.150-151
10 Lowenstern *Memoires du general major Russe* p.189-190
11 *Memoirs* Countess de Choiseul-Gouffier pp.92-95
12 Quoted in Brett-James *1812* pp. 42-43
13 *Memoirs* Countess de Choiseul-Gouffier pp.98-99
14 Quoted in Tarle, *Napoleon's Invasion of Russia* p.49
15 *Memoirs* Countess de Choiseul-Gouffier p.100

THE 1ST WESTERN ARMY

Although the various Russian corps were quickly informed of the Grande Armée crossing the River Nieman, it was not until 26–27 June that the corps commanders were given the order to retreat. By this time General Dokhturov's 6th Corps, which was stationed between Lida and Grodno, found itself cut off from the army. However, by forced marches in heavy rain and along almost impassable roads Dokhturov's Corps managed to cut its way through the encircling French cavalry at Olshani and Bolshie Solecniki and was able to join Bagration's 2nd Western Army.

The Russians did not understand why they were retreating, they wanted to confront Napoleon's army and defeat him. On 4 July Baron Boris Uxkull wrote in his diary:

> The bearing of my men is admirable; the infantry, especially, is magnificent. Very soon, perhaps, a battle will decide our destinies and the destinies of the two most powerful empires, and the lives of several thousand men will be at stake. May Almighty God grant us the victory, for the right is on our side! ... If fate has decided that I am to meet my death in one of the fields covering the Russian land, and if this Diary comes into the hands of my parents one day, I beg them to grant me the following requests: Take care of my two servants ... Keep my grey horse until it dies and pay my debts ... But this sounds like a Will, and I have no desire to make one, since I'd much rather go on living.[1]

However there was no battle and the next day Baron Uxkull wrote:

> It is inconceivable! Why are we always being made to fall back without giving battle? Yet our army is so big. We've marched 53 km; our quarters are in one of the villages that belong to Count Manuzzi; it is a very pretty location, [however] it will all soon be the prey of the flames, for according to all one hears, the French mark their advance by the most atrocious cruelties – pillaging, ravaging and burning everything they come across. It's so sad to see the peasants and their families leaving the

places where they came into the world. But what shocks me most is that the fields, full of wheat and the fruits of nature, are trampled by the hooves of the cavalry. There's no longer any order among us concerning supplies and fodder; everyone grabs what he finds. This ruination of the peasants and the gentry afflicts me a great deal, even though the latter deserve it, because their tyranny is well known.[2]

Little did the Russian Army know that this scorched earth policy was their best strategy of defence. In the meantime, through heavy rain and impassable roads, they had to try and out-march the Grande Armée. A. I. Antonovski, an officer in the 26th Jager Regiment of the 14th Division belonging to Wittgenstein's I Corps:

We were not allowed to sleep or even sit down. In addition, the road turned out to be a country track with many marshes, which exhausted everyone. At first a few men dropped out of their regiments; some said openly that they lacked any more strength, others claimed a sudden onset of illness and therefore they could not go on, though it was clear to see what kind of ailment was causing their legs to fail. Stern measures to force them could not be used, but after seeing the greater number of stragglers, it had to be accepted that the fast pace had to slacken. We went slower, but this did not improve our situation at all. The number of officers on duty in the regimental columns was doubled, and they were ordered to see that no one fell out. However, these measures were also not entirely effective. We had to leave to their own uncertain fate those who could not go on at all. Whatever overtook them is unknown, but many did not return to their units … To crown our misery it rained and the weather turned gloomy; mud, slush – these brought everyone to their limit.

It was not until 1 July that the 26th Jagers were finally allowed to rest. They had not slept for four days and nights, but the following day 'set off again, happy and cheerful'.[3]

Nor were the Russian Imperial Guard spared the rigours of the campaign, Captain Pushkin of the Semenovski Regiment recorded in his journal the long marches and the sufferings of his regiment:

30 June. A march from Sventsian to the Camp at Davgelishek. Setting out at 4 o'clock in the morning, it rained … The way is difficult, we are going continually for 11 hours. In the regiment 40 men are hurt and one dead.

1 July … Luckily during the day the rain having an interval, we used it to dry our clothes a little. Our commander, Colonel Kridner, today is positively excited, we captured many enemy, seized several officers for a mere trifle. Brought into our camp [Captain] Count Segur. This is the first French captive.

2 July. In camp between the rivers Desnoi and Vitzeu. Our Corps leaves at 4.30 in the morning … My Sergeant Major reported to me that three soldiers, Poles, deserted …

3 July. We heard some cannon volleys in the rearguard …

4 July. Camp at Vidzei, the Corps of Tuckhov and Uvarov arrived at 6 o'clock in
the morning … We received orders to set out and followed after them. We went to
Vidzu, where the sovereign set out to inspect us. Passing the town we turned on to
the right-hand road and stopped about 2 km from the town. The march being in all
16 km, but the very hot weather wearies us.

5 July. Camp at Zamoski. Our corps arrived at 2 o'clock at night making 42 km in
the course of 15 hours. The weather is still very hot … but in spite of three rests, the
men are exhausted.

6 July. Camp at Ikasni. Our Corps arrived at 7 o'clock in the evening, being absolutely dark, when we pitched a bivouac, not having either a fire nor firewood for
cooking food.[4]

The long retreat was also exhausting for the cavalry. On 7 July, at Polotsk, Baron
Uxkull had a chance to write in his diary:

We marched all night … I was overcome by a desire to sleep so suddenly that I
slumped over beneath a tree, holding my horse by the reins. I slept three hours; then
I followed after the rearguard until I caught up with the regiment.[5]

On 9 July the advanced guard of the 1st Western Army, including Alexander, arrived
at the fortified camp at Drissa, followed by Barclay de Tolly and the main body two
days later. The Fifth Russian Army Bulletin reported:

All the corps belonging to the First Army have joined, and will tomorrow
march into the entrenched camp on the borders of the Dwina, near to Drissa.
Our troops have sustained the difficulties of the march with their accustomed
hardihood.

All the endeavours of the enemy to cut off some of the separate corps of the
First Army and to turn our right flank have been fruitless. At present his main force
is directed against our left wing in order to take a station between the First and
Second Armies. Prince Bagration has received orders to attack these corps of the
enemy which are in the front, and the necessary dispositions for the purpose are
already made in the First Army.

Since the small actions which took place at the passage of the Dwina, our rearguard has not sustained any attack of consequence from the enemy.[6]

No doubt Alexander had heard of the Lines of Torres Vedras in Portugal, where
Wellington had beaten off the invading French army under Marshal Massena and
he imagined he would do the same at Drissa. One crucial difference was that the
Lines of Torres Vedras were protecting the port of Lisbon, so Wellington could have

evacuated his army if necessary. The camp at Drissa did not have this advantage; nevertheless Alexander was determined to fight and issued a proclamation:

Russian Warriors

You have at last obtained the result which you proposed when the enemy dared to invade the boundaries of our empire. You were on the frontiers to observe him.

Until the reunion of the army, it was necessary by a momentary and indispensable retreat to restrain your ardour for the combat, that you might check the rash march of the enemy. All the corps of the first army are now united on the position pre-selected.

A new occasion offers to manifest your tried valour, and to enable you to gather the recompense for the labours you have endured.

May this day, distinguished by the victory of Poltava, serve for your example; may the remembrance of your glorious ancestors animate you to equally glorious exploits. In following their steps you will overthrow the projects of the enemy directed against your honour, your country, and your families.

God, who sees the justice of your cause, will give you His blessing.[7]

He also issued a proclamation to the Russian people:

Every day tends to unfold the plan which was adopted by the Russian government as far back as May 1811, when it became evident that Bonaparte's pretension and encroachments could only be counteracted by force … different foundries in a short time produced 200 pieces of cannon, a quantity of which was secretly sent to the frontiers, but the far greater part of which has been mounted in the new fortifications which have been erected on the banks of the Dwina, particularly in the neighbourhood of Dunaburg and Drissa. This is the line in which the Russians have concentrated themselves and there will be the scene of the first great conflict, which there is every reason to expect will be obstinate and bloody.[8]

It has been assumed that the 1st Army was to occupy the camp at Drissa, while Bagration would attack the Grande Armée, but according to General Lowenstern the camp of Drissa was to have been garrisoned by 80 battalions of reserve troops. This would leave the 1st and 2nd Armies free to operate against Napoleon. These 80 battalions, however, were nowhere to be seen.[9] Even if the plan had worked, the camp would still have pinned the armies of Bagration and Barclay de Tolly down, so that Napoleon could have defeated the two Russian armies, and then if necessary laid siege to the camp.

Fortunately for the Russians, on seeing the camp even the Tsar realised that his military adviser Colonel Phull's plan was idiotic. An embarrassed Alexander who had issued a proclamation stating that the army was about to fight, now had to issue another stating why it had not:

Beloved Subjects! In pursuance of the policy advised by our Military Council, the armies will, for the present, quit their positions, and retire farther into the interior, in order the more readily to unite. The enemy may possibly avail himself of this opportunity to advance; he has announced this intention. Doubtless, in spite of his boasts, he begins to feel all the difficulties of his menaced attempt to subjugate us and is anxious therefore to engage; he is desperate and would therefore put every thing upon the issue of a battle. [For] the honour of our Crown ... it is necessary that he should be made sensible of the madness of this attempt.

He encouraged (and ordered) the Russian people:

If, urged by the desire of obtaining provisions and forage, or goaded by an insatiable cupidity for plunder, he should be blind to the danger of further committing himself at such an immense distance from his territories, it would become the duty of every loyal Russian – every true friend to his country – to co-operate cheerfully with us in impeding equally his progress or his retreat, by destroying his supplies, his means of conveyance; in short, everything which can be serviceable to him. We, therefore, order that such of our subjects in the provinces of Vitebsk and Pskov, as may have articles of subsistence, either man or beast, beyond their immediate want, to deliver them to officers authorised to receive them and for which they shall be paid the full value out of the Imperial Treasury. The owners of growing crops within the distance of the line of the enemy's march, are commanded to destroy them, and of magazines, either of provisions or clothing, are required to deliver them to the commissaries for the use of the army, and they will be liberally remunerated. In general, the spirit of this Order is to be carried into execution in regard to all articles, whether of subsistence, of clothing, or of conveyance, which may be considered useful to the invaders; and the Magistrates are made responsible for the due fulfilment of these.[10]

Even before this proclamation was published, cattle and goods were being seized, as Mr Levy, a British civilian with the 2nd Western Army, witnessed:

All the horses and oxen that were within the districts through which the army marched were seized, either by order or connivance of the Russian government. This probably was an act of necessity to prevent their falling into the hands of the Austrians and the French, who certainly by these means would have greatly facilitated their respective marches in the rear and flank of the Prince's [Bagration] Army.[11]

The commissariat issued vouchers for any provisions or cattle brought into the army, but if these vouchers were ever redeemed then it was far below the market value of the goods. How widespread this destruction of property was is not known. As an example that suggests this was not a vigorously executed scorched earth policy, when the French occupied Minsk they found the magazines still intact.

Embarrassed by the failure of General Phull's plan, Alexander now shunned the General. Cold-shouldered by the Imperial court and the other generals, Phull remained with the army for several days before quietly returning to St Petersburg.

On 17 July, after burning the magazines stored there, the Russians marched out of the camp and proceeded to Vitebsk. Before they left Barclay de Tolly had another proclamation printed, this time for the invading army:

French soldiers! – You are forced to march to a new war; you are told that it is because the Russians do not do justice to your valour, no comrades, they appreciate it, you shall see this on the day of battle. Reflect that one army, if necessary, will succeed another, and that you are 400 leagues from your reinforcements. Suffer not yourselves to be deceived by our first movements; you know the Russians too well to believe that they flee before you; they will accept the combat, and your retreat will be difficult. They address you as comrades, return home in a mass, believe not these perfidious words, that you are fighting for peace; no, you are fighting for the insatiable ambition of a Sovereign who wishes not for peace. Otherwise he would have had it long ago, and who makes sport of the blood of his brave troops. Return to your country, or accept, in the meantime, an asylum in Russia, you will there forget the words – conscription, levy, ban and arriere ban – in short, all that military tyranny of which you are every moment condemned to feel the yoke.[12]

The Russian staff and ministers knew that they had to get rid of one impediment, Alexander himself, but how to tell him? Certainly his heart was with his men, but he was apt to interfere. However, no one had the courage to ask the Tsar to leave. 'Knowing that he deemed his presence with the troops absolutely necessary, and that he considered it ignominious not to be with them, could I hope that my words and arguments might overcome in him his own prejudice and pride?' wrote Secretary of State Shishkov. Finally Shishkov, Arakcheev and Balashov plucked up enough courage to write to Alexander:

The example of sovereigns who have led their armies cannot serve as a model for the reigning Tsar and Emperor, because they had special motives. Peter the Great, Frederick the Second and our present enemy Napoleon have had to do it: the first, because he had raised regular troops; the second because his entire kingdom was, so to speak, transformed into a military force: the third, because he has come to the throne, not by birth, but by chance and good fortune. None of these reasons exists for Alexander the First.[13]

Alexander's sister, Catherine, also wrote to the Tsar suggesting that it would be a mistake to remain with the army:

Of course I consider you as capable as your generals, but you must act not only the part of an army leader, but also that of a sovereign. If one of them [the generals] should do his work badly, censure and punishment await him. But if you should commit an error, everything would fall upon your head. This would destroy faith in the sole arbiter of the destinies of the Empire, who should be our support.[14]

On 18 July at Polotsk the Tsar decided to leave the army. According to Lowenstern, he embraced Barclay de Tolly, and 'just when His Majesty was stepping into his carriage, he shook his hand warmly and said "Goodbye, General. Again Goodbye and au revoir. I recommend my Army to you. Do not forget that it is the only one I have. Always bear this in mind."' Alexander proceeded to Moscow, to make arrangements for new supplies and recruits. From there he returned to St Petersburg.

Although the Russian high command may have been pleased to see the back of Alexander, the rank and file were disappointed. According to Ermolov,

> The Tsar's departure had an unpleasant effect on the troops. [Wtih his] appearing every day with a serene and calm look, no one thought about danger and everyone was encouraged by his presence.[15]

The Russian Army's problems were of course far from over. Their pre-war plans to retire to the camp at Drissa were now known to be an unacceptable strategy, but what could they do now? Certainly they must unite with Bagration and above all not give battle to Napoleon's vastly stronger army.

Even at the beginning of the war the retreat had been unpopular; now with the Tsar gone, people would blame Barclay de Tolly for his strategy, which they considered as treason:

> People resented General Barclay. Secret meetings were held and plots hatched …
> The operations of the Commander in Chief were criticised openly; people wanted
> to make him disgusted with his command by a thousand vexations, which were set
> in train at leisure. General Bennigsen, Duke Alexander von Wurttemberg and the
> Grand Duke of Oldenburg discussed freely, and with anyone who was prepared to
> listen, the errors that had been made and what they regarded as the incompetence
> of the man who had given the orders. They corrupted a group of officers who, as a
> crowning misfortune, had the support of the Grand Duke Constantine; and he – I
> do not know by what fatality – had been influenced by General Ermolov, who deep
> down hated Barclay while pretending to be extremely attached to him.[16]

Meanwhile the retreat continued; the delay at Drissa had given the Grande Armée the chance to catch up with the 1st Western Army. By now the heavy rains had given way to stifling heat; the summer would prove one of the hottest in living memory.

It was now essential for the 1st Army to unite with Bagration's forces, so Barclay decided to wait for the 2nd Western Army at Vitebsk. However Barclay needed to gain time for Bagration to rendezvous, so on 24 July, Barclay ordered Count Ostermann-Tolstoy, who had recently been appointed as commander of the 4th Corps, to delay the French at Ostrovno.

When Murat arrived near Ostrovno he saw some Russian artillery deployed near a dense wood. Without waiting for orders he ordered his cavalry to charge the batteries, but he failed to notice the Russian infantry that were concealed in the woods until it was too late. His cavalry were repulsed with loss; without waiting for infantry support he launched his depleted cavalry into another charge, with the same results.

By now Delzon's Division of Eugene's 4th (Italian) Corps had arrived and began deploying on the battlefield. It also attacked the Russians and this time the Russians were driven into the woods. Ermolov:

> The enemy attacked vigorously; our troops, having grumbled about continual retreat, seized the opportunity of engaging the French and the distance from reinforcements seem to double their courage. The forested and rolling terrain prevented the enemy from utilising his advantage; cavalry acted in isolation which helped our weaker cavalry. Facing fresh enemy forces Count Osterman had to yield ground for some distance and darkness ended the battle.[17]

The main Russian Army was near Vitebsk, a few miles away, waiting for orders to support Ostermann's Corps. Baron Uxkull wrote: 'I'm lying in my tent. You can hear sustained cannon fire from the distance. The French are already showing themselves on the other side of the Dwina. Are we finally going to come to the point of measuring arms with them?' That evening he wrote:

> We're bivouacking 6 km on the other side of Vitebsk. The sight of the wounded, who are being moved into Vitebsk is so sad! Some of them, without arms or legs, were swimming in their own blood; others, slashed to pieces by sabre strokes, were hiding their pains and agonies while trying to look brave. The Hussars of the Guard are said to have acquitted themselves well. Nineteen kilometres from Vitebsk we called a halt in order to take up battle formation. The number of wounded and captured kept growing. Thus the night fell.[18]

During the night, Ostermann pulled back a short distance to a stronger position. His front was covered by a ravine and his flanks were protected by the river Duna and a dense wood. The battlefield itself was intersected by woods, which were occupied by skirmishers. The rest of the army slept in their accoutrements ready at a moment's notice to form up and support their brothers in arms, but no word came.

The battle recommenced the following day, this time the whole of Prince Eugene's 4th (Italian) Corps had arrived. It advanced on the Russian position, covered by Murat's cavalry, although bombarded by Russian artillery all the way. To draw the fire of the Russian artillery, Eugene deployed the artillery of the Italian Imperial Guard. By now the Franco-Italian force had come close to the Russian position, when all of a sudden Russian cavalry burst through the woods, routing Murat's cavalry and Huard's infantry brigade. As the rest of his infantry began to waver, Eugene tried to rally them, but with Russian infantry bearing down upon them it was no use. However, the Russian infantry were charged by a Polish lancer division, which killed and wounded many of them, and so the crisis in the Italians' ranks passed.

General Konovnitsyn's 3rd Division and later Tuchkov's 1st Grenadier Division were sent to reinforce Ostermann's corps, but the sheer weight of numbers began

to tell on the outnumbered Russians who were being driven back towards Vitebsk.
Baron Uxkull continues:

> Soon the battle broke out at all points. We were placed on a height in order to attack
> the enemy columns that were constantly pressing forward. The defensive fire from
> the woods was very lively. The cannon were being fired successfully; the whistling
> of the shells, the shouts of fighting and the commands of the officers produced
> a general effect that was very marked and impressive. This whole spectacle took
> place at our feet. The broad expanse of the field was speckled with troops. It began
> to grow dark, so that every cannon shot, scattering death, was all the more visible.
> The engagement ended to our disadvantage, at ten o'clock. The French set up their
> camp fires opposite us, with sangfroid and an air of security that astounded us. Even
> from a distance you could make out their voices and hear what they were saying.
> We were quite still, for our hearts were as heavy as the shadows that surrounded us.
> The complaints of the wounded, who were being trampled by our horses, added to
> our despondency. A number of them wanted to drag along after us in order not to
> fall into the hands of our pursuers, but being too feeble, they fell time after time. So
> that's the glory of the soldier! ... But thank God this is a just and true war![19]

At about 3.00 pm Napoleon arrived on the field, but he decided to wait for the rest
of his army and attack the following day. Bagration was still nowhere to be seen and
with 'the bridge and the warehouses being already on fire', Barclay de Tolly decided
to abandon Vitebsk.

That night, leaving their campfires burning to mask their withdrawal, the Russian
Army continued its retreat; 2,500 Russians had been either killed or wounded compared to 3,000 of the Allies. Since the Russians abandoned the battlefield, Napoleon
was able to claim another victory.[20] This boast belied the fact that he had not destroyed
the Russian Army and that he would have to march deeper into Russia and so extend
his lines of communications farther.

In 1813 Barclay admitted that he had no choice but to retreat from Vitebsk, but
at the time he blamed Bagration's slowness for forcing him to abandon the town.
According to Sir Robert Wilson:

> Napoleon on the 28th entered Vitebsk with his Guards, a deputation having come
> out of the city with the keys; but notwithstanding this submission, and the presence
> of Napoleon, to whom in person the keys were delivered, and who had some time
> previously prohibited pillage 'under pain of death' the greater part of the city was
> sacked as if it had been a storm prize.
>
> The confederate army [as Wilson called the Grande Armée] ... from the
> moment of its entrance into the Russian territory, notwithstanding order on order,
> and some exemplary punishments, had been incorrigibly guilty of every excess.
> It had not only seized with violence all that its wants demanded, but destroyed
> in mere wantoness what did not tempt its cupidity. No Vandal ferocity was ever
> more destructive.[21]

Many Russian peasants had welcomed members of the Grande Armée, hoping that they would be liberated from serfdom, but they had seen their huts burnt and possessions stolen. It would be a lesson that they would not forget, and when the time came they would make the invader pay for his unruliness.

The 1st Army continued its retreat, this time towards Smolensk. At one point intelligence was received that Napoleon had outflanked the Russian Army and was already nearing Smolensk, but this intelligence was later proved to be incorrect. In fact Napoleon remained at Vitebsk until 13 August, building four bridges over the river Duna and two over the Berezina to ease his passage and so Barclay de Tolly was able to march to Smolensk unmolested.

On 1 August Barclay de Tolly's army entered Smolensk, despite the many clashes of the rearguard, it had remained intact and although exhausted from its long marches, it had been well fed, as General Carl Clausewitz, a Prussian officer serving with the Army, remembers:

It [the 1st Western Army] halted where most convenient, established itself as well as possible and neither man nor horse experienced any want of subsistence; the former, indeed, went generally without bread, and had to content himself with bad biscuit, which was, however, not unwholesome, and scarcely less nourishing than bread; grits, meat and brandy were in abundance; the horses seldom had corn, but Russian horses are accustomed to live upon hay, and the Author for the first time here observed that this food is more nourishing than is usually imagined. Hay was plentiful and good; the Russians give their horses from 15 to 20 lbs a day, and they rejected the sheaves of ripe oats, which lay on the field, thinking them less wholesome.

The cavalry of the rear-guard alone (and this, indeed, was the great number) was worse off, because it could seldom unsaddle. The Author scarcely remembers to have seen through the whole retreat a light cavalry regiment unsaddled; almost all the horses were galled. We may gather from this that in physical respects the Russian Army was well off in its ten weeks of retreat. It only suffered diminution from casualties in action, and lost few by sick or stragglers.

On 30 July Glinka confirmed Clausewitz's view:

Our army is not numerous, but the troops never were in such organisation, and the regiments never had such fine men. The troops receive the best foodstuffs: the noblemen donate all. From all sides [people] convey baked bread, drive cattle and deliver all the necessary goods to our soldiers, who burn with desire to fight at the walls of Smolensk.[22]

The same could not be said of Bagration's Army.

Notes

1   Uxkull *Arms and the Woman*, p.62
2   Ibid, pp.62–63

3 'Notes of A.I. Antonevski' translated by Mark Conrad in *The Kiwer* issue 8 pp.14–17
4 Dnevnika, *Pavla Pushkin* pp.26–27
5 Uxkull *Arms and the Woman*, p.66
6 Fifth Russian Army Bulletin dated 21 July 1812, Quoted in the *Edinburgh Evening Courant* 15 August 1812
7 Wilson *The French Invasion of Russia* p.42
8 The *Edinburgh Evening Courant* 6 August 1812
9 Memoirs of General Lowenstern pp.205–206
10 Quoted in *Jackson's Oxford Journal* 29 August 1812
11 BL Add ms 30,132 *The Journal of Mr Levy*
12 The *Edinburgh Evening Courant* 15 August 1812
13 Quoted in Tarle *Napoleon's Invasion of Russia 1812* p.61
14 Ibid, p.61
15 Ermolov Zapiski, *1812* p.116
16 Quoted in Brett James, *1812* p.61
17 Ermolov Zapiski, *1812* p.121
18 Uxkull, *Arms and the Woman*, p.68
19 Ibid, pp.68–69
20 Napoleon's Tenth Bulletin, published 31 July 1812 at Vitebsk.
21 Sir Robert Wilson *The French Invasion of Russia* pp.56–57
22 Glinka's *Pisma* pp.146–147

3

THE 2ND WESTERN ARMY

To pursue the 2nd Western Army, Napoleon allocated Prince Poniatowski's V (Polish) Corps, General Reynier's VII Corps and the VIII Corps under Jerome Bonaparte, the King of Westphalia. As King of Westphalia, Jerome was given the honour of commanding this force, however he had none of the military talents of his older brother and this appointment would cost Napoleon dear in the forthcoming campaign.

On 28 June Bagration's Army began its retreat. His army was supported by General Platov's Cossacks, which would have the first blood of the campaign that day against Jerome's force near Grodno. The following day, Napoleon ordered Marshal Davoust with a flying column made up of General Valence's Cuirassier and Pajol's light cavalry divisions, with an infantry division from his own I Corps, and probably the Corps' cavalry, to march to Minsk and cut Bagration's Army off from Barclay de Tolly. Generals Grouchy and Nansouty's cavalry divisions were also ordered to support Davoust. However, Murat ordered Nansouty to join him instead and Grouchy lost contact with Davoust, so the Marshal was left without much of his cavalry support.

Bagration planned to be in Minsk by 5 July, knowing that the enemy would try and cut him off there, but on 30 June he received orders from the Tsar not to march on Minsk, but to proceed along the River Shara and link up with the 1st Western Army near Novogrudok or Belitsy. However, after marching along this route Bagration discovered the countryside was too marshy for his troops and that French troops were blocking his path, so he decided to ignore the order and continued his march towards Minsk. Covering an average of 40 km a day, the 2nd Western Army managed to outmarch the Grande Armée, although Bagration's rearguard was often threatened.

Nikolai Ivanovich Andreev, an officer in the 50th Jager Regiment recalled this forced march:

> … quite often making 75 km in twenty four hours, not having time to cook
> kashitsi [a thin gruel] for the soldiers, after hanging the kettles over a lighted fire
> and in an instant this cooking is wasted, poured out onto the ground and the

retreat continued. Being the beginning of June [sic], the heat is intolerable ... we were exhausted.[1]

To speed up his march Bagration destroyed all the army's unnecessary baggage and sent the remainder to Minsk. The officers were only allowed one carriage, the division commanders two.

With his now more mobile army Bagration was able to cross the River Nieman on 4–5 July at Nikolaev, which was swollen because of heavy rain. With the river between him and the enemy, Bagration allowed his army to rest for a short time before setting out again towards Mir. He ordered the ferries at Nikolaev and Koledzany to be destroyed once Platov's Cossacks had crossed. Fortunately for Bagration it was not until 6 July that Jerome left Grodno. Had he been more aggressive, Jerome's three Corps could have easily defeated Bagration's smaller army, but he complained of bad roads, the exhaustion of his troops and the weather.

Bagration still had to reach Minsk before Davoust's force, a distance of 250 miles, while the latter only had to cover 160 miles. The difficulty was compounded by the fact that Davoust was probably the best of Napoleon's marshals and was easily capable of accomplishing the task set him. Alexander Benkendorf, ADC to the Tsar, was sent to the town to destroy the stores there, but the local population convinced him that the enemy were not far off. Fearing the imminent arrival of the French he distributed some of the provisions to the inhabitants, and abandoned the town without destroying the remainder, so most of the stores fell into the hands of the French.[2]

Bagration received the news that Davoust had beaten him to Minsk and so he knew that his army would either have to fight its way through or find another route. Bagration decided on the latter strategy, although he knew he would incur the Tsar's displeasure. At least he would have saved his army from destruction. However, according to Mr Levy, the Englishman who was marching with the Russian Army, on 7 July

[Bagration] left Mir and marched to Swierzen 30 km from this place. It was intended to march to Minsk in order to join the First Army, but on our arrival at Swierzen we learnt that the French were near Minsk in full force, we therefore struck in again onto the Niesewies Road. It seems however from later information that it was only a strong detachment of the enemy's vanguard that was near Minsk, if we had pushed boldly forward we might have got the start of them, before the main [body] of their army could come up.[3]

The same day, to encourage his men Bagration issued a proclamation:

I am confident in the courage of my army ... Division commanders must assure private soldiers that [the enemy] are scoundrels from all over the world, while we are Orthodox Christians; that they cannot fight vigorously; and are particularly afraid of our bayonets. [We must] attack them! The bullet can miss but the bayonet will not ... At Hollabrun [1805] the chivalrous regiments – Kiev Grenadiers, 6th Jager and the Chernigov Dragoons witnessed how we were opposed by 100,000 men [a huge exaggeration] being only 4,000 men strong … Knowing your love for the Fatherland, I expect everything from the courageous troops. You always distinguish yourselves under my command and now you must excel.[4]

It was not until the following day that the French entered Minsk. Bagration had lost four days trying to pursue Alexander's strategy. Fortunately for Bagration, since Jerome made only a half-hearted advance, the Russians were able to escape, otherwise they could have been caught in a pincer movement.

Bagration did not understand why the Russian armies were retreating and believed that they should attack Napoleon at once. On 7 July he found time to write to General Ermolov.

The retreat is intolerable and dangerous … The army was in an excellent condition; but now it is exhausted … [for] ten days it has marched on sandy terrain, in hot weather … surrounded by the enemy. Nevertheless, we defeated the adversary every time we opposed him! I do not understand your [the 1st Army's] witty manoeuvres. My manoeuvre is to seek and attack![5]

The following day Bagration wrote to Arakcheev complaining:

I am not to blame for anything. First they stretched me out like a gut, while the enemy broke into our lines without a shot. We began to retreat, no one knows why. You will get no one in the army, or in Russia, to believe that we have not been betrayed. I cannot defend all Russia alone … I am completely encircled and cannot say yet where I shall break through. I implore you to advance against the enemy … It does not befit Russians to run. We are behaving worse than the Prussians … One feels ashamed … You will continue retiring, and I am asked to break through. If my person cannot be borne here, better have me released from the yoke which is on my neck and send someone else to command. But why torment the soldiers without purpose and satisfaction?[6]

On 9 July, a brigade of Polish lancers from the French 4th Cavalry Corps under General Turno appeared in front of the town of Mir. The Cossack outposts retreated into the town, hotly pursued by the lancers. In the town they came face to face with Platov's Cossacks. In their attempt to escape, the Poles were surrounded and annihilated. Another brigade of cavalry coming to their aid also met a similar fate.

The following day the French approached more cautiously, but after a fierce fight lasting all day, Platov received reinforcements, which enabled his Cossacks to drive the enemy off.

The enemy had upwards of 800 men killed and 200 prisoners were taken, among the number were 12 officers, two lieutenant colonels were brought to the headquarters … When Hetman Platov had despatched his men in pursuit of the enemy, he very quietly went to bed saying that his children (the Cossacks) would do the business without him.[7]

This action not only gave Bagration an opportunity to rest his men, but also raised the morale of his troops. By now the torrential rain had given way to stifling heat, so Bagration decided to begin his march at dawn and dusk, and give his troops a rest during the hottest part of the day. Bagration knew that to survive he must impose strict discipline on his troops. On 9 July he issued the following order:

> I am informed of the excesses committed by the regular troops and Cossacks …
> The duty of each soldier is to protect the subjects of His Majesty and any offender
> against these rules will be executed. I admire soldiers, respect their courage, but
> I equally demand their discipline. Therefore, I declare anybody found guilty of a
> violent act against the local population will be executed on the spot, and the com-
> manders of the division, squadron or brigade will be reduced to the ranks.[8]

Even before Davoust had reached Minsk, Napoleon had appointed him commander of Jerome's force, without telling his brother. It was not until 14 July that Jerome finally found out about this change in command. Sulking, he halted his force and returned to Westphalia. The pursuit resumed the following day, but another day had been lost by the French.

Bagration had crossed the Berezina at Bobruisk, so that he could march via Mogilev and Orsha to Vitebsk. On 14 July Platov's Cossacks again defeated a French force at Romanov. The same day, Davoust left Minsk; he was still ahead of Bagration and managed once again to out-march the Russians and seized Mogilev, with its important ferry across the Dnieper.

Bagration had no choice but to order Raevski's 7th Infantry Corps to launch a diversionary attack against Davoust. While part of his army pinned the enemy down at Mogilev, Bagration would try and find another crossing between Mogilev and Stari Bikhov. On 23 July Bagration wrote to Raevski: 'If Our Lord gives us an oppor-tunity to find a ferry between you and Stary Bikhov, then we shall immediately cross the river.' Paskevitch, who was with Raevski, described the deployment,

> … having been informed by Prince Bagration that in Mogilev there were about
> 7 to 10,000 of the enemy. Therefore the prince ordered me to attack them and
> after it to occupy the town. General Raevski had taken with him from the 12th
> Division the 6th and 42nd Jager Regiments, and from my division two battalions.
> I had chosen one battalion of the Orlov and the other from the Nishki Novgorod
> Regiment, and in order to go quicker ordered them to leave [their] knapsacks. Early
> in the morning of 11th we began to advance. Between us and the enemy was a
> distance of 5 km. In one and quarter kilometres we encountered his infantry of the
> advanced guard and ousted them from the wood …
>   Marshal Davoust himself expecting an attack, had beforehand prepared for the
> defence. The bridge at Saltanovska had been demolished and the walls of the tavern
> were cut through with gun loopholes, situated on the left side of the ravine covering
> all the line of the French. The bridge at the Fatovoy Mill had been demolished and
> in the neighbouring houses loopholes were also made. Three battalions had been

placed near Saltanovska; one battalion at Fatovoy, having for themselves in reserve another five battalions, four battalions were between Fatovoy and the village of Seltsen and near the ravine and in front of the last village had been placed two more battalions. All the cavalry consisting of the cuirassiers of General Shastelya's Division and the horse Jager regiment of General Bordesult's Brigade were situated in reserve behind the right wing of the village of Seltsen on the road leading from it to the place of Starı-Buınıch. Five battalions had been placed still more to the right, near the town of Zactenke, and finally, the last five battalions, were in front of Mogilev.

The infantry of Marshal Davoust consisted of two regiments of Compans' Division, in which were 25 battalions, the cavalry had consisted of 48 squadrons, moreover the enemy expected to be reinforced by a detachment of General Pazholya's and the Polish Legion of the Vistula, but these troops joined him only after the battle. Prince Bagration, not having exact intelligence about the strength of the enemy and believing that there was no more than 6000 against us, had sent his adjutant with an order to General Raevski that he, having collected all the troops of his Corps, should boldly attack the positions of the French and capture Mogilev. General Raevski had sent for other troops. As the knapsacks of the two battalions of the 26th Division had been left, the other two battalions should bring them. They only arrived toward the end of the fighting, therefore the 26th Division had only eight battalions and the 12th ten battalions. All the Corps consisted of five regiments of the 26th Division and three regiments of the 12th Division, twenty squadrons of cavalry, three Cossack regiments and 72 guns.[9]

Raevski ordered Paskevitch's Division with three regiments of Cossacks and the Ahtirski Hussar regiment to outflank the French right wing through some woods and attack them from the rear, while the 12th Division would attack their centre:

In the middle of the wood I met our engaged skirmishers, withdrawing from the French skirmishers. The enemy on this road outflanked our left. The firing of my first battalion had stopped and had overrun the enemy. I ordered [the battalion] to drive them to the edge of the woods and followed with the rest of the troops. The head of my column consisted of a battalion of the Orlov and one of Nizhegorod, behind them twelve guns, then the Poltav Regiment, six more guns and the Ladozh Regiment with the other Nizhegorod battalion, two guns and finally the cavalry, leaving the woods ... skirmished with the enemy, lying behind a small rising, in front of the town of Fatovoy. Behind them I caught sight of the glittering bayonets of two French columns. The distance between them was no more than 130 metres. The dense wood did not allow me to turn the troops in column, I was forced to move to the right by sections, to leave the wood and form them in front of the edge. The firing continued. In order to form platoons I had to go out in front 60 metres from the enemy ...

Only two battalions had been extended in line and I ordered Colonel Ladizhenski to attack with a shout of 'Ura!' on the enemy as far as the stream, to overthrow [those] on the bridge, and having occupied the first houses on that side, to wait for my orders. The enemy was immediately overthrown and ran ... as far as the bridge. Seeing that the battalion passed the bridge I brought forward 12 guns onto the height and ordered the Poltava Regiment, under the cover of the battery, to go also on that side ... The enemy infantry stood in two lines from the main road as far as the wood. In a 3rd line there was the cavalry. Having moved up to the battery six more guns and having placed the Ladoga Regiment on the left flank, I set off to the right flank. To my astonishment I found that the enemy skirmishers were ensconced there in the ravine ... Our artillery, losing men and horses, drew off from the position. I stopped them. Meanwhile, I saw the Poltava Regiment was withdrawing, the colonel having been wounded. Having ordered the Regiment to halt, riding farther and expecting to meet the Orlov and Nishki Novgorod battalions and seeing two battalions departing from the wood in the rear of my position, I galloped towards them, but to my surprise I saw at 30 paces French grenadiers. Colonel Ashar ordered about. The French charged our battalion ... 'Lads, forward!' I shouted to the Poltava Regiment. They hesitated, 'Ura! Charge!' ... From the men I heard a voice, 'Even the artillery is with us.' 'Well', I said 'hold here.' Riding down towards the artillery arranged behind my position was a battery of four guns returning towards the Poltava Regiment ... The enemy having seen their retreat, began with shouts of 'Forward!' The regiment made way and caseshot struck into the French battalions, They stopped, confused, I drew up to the Poltava Regiment, ordered 'Forward!' They charged and drove the enemy up to the bridge. Here my horse was wounded by two bullets.

The Poltava Regiment was carried away, I could hardly stop it ... [reforming] they were drawn up in line and appeared there a sufficiently strong column. Doubling the skirmishers, I ordered all 18 guns to open fire on the enemy's column. The action was violent, that I saw myself, how they continuously moved and changed places, removed [themselves] out of range of the caseshot. Their losses were great. Finally they retreated, redoubling the artillery meant the battle became equal ...

The Nishki Novgorod and Orlov battalions at first overthrew the enemy and crossed the bridge, occupied an inn and the little village of several peasant huts on that side of the ravine. Barely had they been deployed, when from this small village four French battalions appeared; lying in the rye, they rose up at a distance of 60 metres, volleyed and charged with the bayonet. The fighting was entered into hand-to-hand. The French rushed on the white ensign of the Orlov Regiment and captured it by killing the ensign. [One of] our NCOs snatched it away from the Frenchman, but he was killed. The ensign was again lost. Once again it was seized up, and in the fight the staff was broken. At this time the adjutant of the Orlov Regiment rushed into the middle, took away the ensign and bore it from the fight. Colonel Ladyzhenski was wounded in the jaw ... Half of our two battalions were killed or wounded. They were forced to retreat and thrown back on to the wood. They were pursued by two battalions. Setting the battery, we fired for more than one and a half hours.[10]

Meanwhile, at the head of the Smolensk Infantry Regiment, Raevski, accompanied by his sons Alexander and Nickolai, aged 16 and 11 respectively, launched his attack against the French centre at Saltanovka, supported by the 6th and 42nd Jager Regiments. Paskevitch continues:

> At the time I heard on the right side a severe fire fight. This was General Raevski attacking the front of the enemy's position. The woods, surrounding the village of Saltanovka, did not allow any other approach. On the main road was an enemy battery. At the end of the road … was a bridge. The Smolensk Regiment of the 12th Division moved forward with astonishing firmness, but could not seize the bridge. Generals Raevski and Vasilchikov dismounted to walk in front of the columns, but the advantage of the [enemy] situation destroyed all the exertions of courage of our soldiers. They could not burst into the village and on the road endured all the fire of the enemy's battery.[11]

After heavy resistance the Russians forced the French to withdraw, but from the prisoners taken, Raevski learned that Davoust was concentrating his main force upon the 7th Infantry Corps, instead of pursuing Bagration.

> …exchanging fire with the enemy I sent a report to General Raevski that I had encountered on the left flank, not 6,000 but maybe 20,000. Therefore if it was necessary to dislodge them, [he must] dispatch to me reinforcements of several battalions. General Raevski answered that the attacks on him were beaten off, but that he had lost many men and consequently could not send any more than one battalion.
>
> It was about 4pm, my troops were already tired, only the cavalry not being in the fighting and that only because the woodland position did not allow the use of them. I obtained the despatch of a battalion of the 41st Jager Regiment and went into the woods in a wide enveloping movement on the right flank of the enemy. The elderly Colonel Savoini was ordered to appear from the woods and descend on the enemy, in order that he … [could] cross the bridge at Fatovoi and attack the French at bayonet point. On the left flank I found Colonel Ladizhenski with the Nizhegorod battalion, who directed a vigorous skirmish across the ravine … General Raevski's adjutant arrived with orders to retreat.

Paskevitch's Division was severely pressed by the French, and he did not have the luxury of waiting until darkness before he could retreat. Moreover, he learnt that the 12th Division was already retreating and neither Bagration nor Raevski could be found. Paskevitch was able to persuade General Vasilchikov of the 12th Division to cover the retreat of the 26th Division:

> Vasilchikov stopped the troops and commanded 'forward!' and here was displayed all the strength of mind and discipline of the Russian soldier. The troops rushed on the enemy, overthrew them and again occupied the wood. I galloped to them in order to organise the retreat, the withdrawal being 220 metres from the enemy. With all the advantages of the position in their favour it was a difficult business.

Paskevitch also had the two battalions, which had stayed with the knapsacks and the 41st Jager Regiment, still not committed. He instructed them to form in squares by echelons. These, supported by artillery and the Ladozh and Poltava Infantry Regiments, took up position at the edge of the wood.

> To provide time for the troops to organise, I ordered the artillery to move off, [only] two guns from the flank being left at the entrance of the wood ... The others passed through the wood at a trot. The skirmishers were told that when the last two guns were removed, they could rush back [and reform] on the flanks of the artillery. This was all carried out precisely. The enemy, seeing this apparent retreat, rushed head-long on us, but here, being met by caseshot from the two guns and the battalion fire of the two regiments, they stopped and we passed the wood so successfully that I did not lose any guns.
>
> Behind the wood there was a glade and 1000 metres on a village. On the glade I put the regiments in line, placed a battery ... The enemy began to appear, [we] opened fire from all the guns of the battery. Here I found the 12th Division, holding the position and being in line with mine. We continued to retreat, covering the horse on the flanks and occupied the heights behind us ... The cannonade did not stop.[12]

In his account of the battle Raevski reported to Bagration:

> The combined bravery and diligence of Russian troops spared me destruction by a superior enemy and in such a disadvantageous place; I bear witness that many officers and soldiers, wounded twice, having bound up these wounds, returned to battle as if to a feast. I must praise the bravery and the art of the gunners: on this day everyone was a hero.

Raevski reported a total of 2,548 officers and men either killed, wounded or missing, including one unknown Russian officer of the Poltava Infantry Regiment, who, having lost an arm by a cannonball, 'calmly picked it [the arm] up and left the battlefield. As he was passing Bagration, he saluted him with the remaining hand'.[13]

Meanwhile the remainder of Bagration's Army continued its retreat, and had built a bridge over the Dnieper at Novi Bikhov. His army began to cross on 25 July, but was hampered by the many refugees who had left their homes before the French arrived. Among them were the inhabitants of Chaus:

> News of [the invasion] reached this small town of Chaus (Mogilev province). The unexpected appearance of the French army within the borders generated in the simple people a ridiculous idea that Napoleon is the Anti-Christ, the precursor of the end of the world ... Fearing the consequences of a war, the inhabitants of Chaus ... began to gather for daily meetings in houses, in the streets and even beyond the gate on the road going to Mogilev, in order to learn something from passers by ... of what is happening and what is undertaken in the provincial towns. Every messenger, every courier sent to the First Army in Krasnoe (Smolensk Province), was stopped and

hounded with enquiries about the movement of our armies and about battles. But when the inhabitants learned that the enemy's army were already near Mogilev, that after giving battle our armies retreated, many started to think and confer about escaping to the neighbouring Chernigov Province. I was then 11 years old, but I vividly remember how once in the evening at sunset, beyond the gates, we heard a kind of distant rumble, and put an ear to the ground to make sure that the uninterrupted roll was cannon shots. Indeed there was a battle at the village of Saltanovka, near Mogilev.

Soon after that in Chaus our troops came through, Cossacks, Kalmucks, Bashkirs and artillery, on the faces of whom was seen despondency; they entered and passed through the town without songs, without music, without drumbeat, that brought still more fear and despair to the peaceful inhabitants. Our forces, with a small gap, passed by day and night throughout the week, if not longer. That was the corps of Bagration and Platov … the last group of Cossacks … set fire to the provisions depot with the bread, so that it was not procured by the enemy … With the removal of the last detachment of Cossacks our town was left to the mercy of fate; complete anarchy then reigned: the town authorities having run away, they were replaced by a kind of Polish municipality. The priest and gentlemen rejoiced and sang in honour of Napoleon, patriotic Hymns in the church were already replaced by a chorus of French ones.[14]

Many of the inhabitants decided to leave Chaus and set out towards the town of Chernigov.

Our long string of carts [carried] trunks, suitcases, feather beds and various chests, with favourite cats, dogs and even canaries. This string of carts, stretched almost a kilometre, consisting of different kinds of Antedeluvian carriages, britshas, tilt carts, carriages and simple hand carts. Passing 40 km, the string of carts stopped at a lodging for the night at the estate of Princess Muruzi, where the manager was a friend of my father. Here we were horrified at the news that all the bridges and ferries over the rivers, through which we should cross, had been burnt by the Cossacks on their retreat. What should we do? Continuing the journey was impossible; by turning back, we could be captured by the enemy and lose the last of our property. Not until midnight did we nomads sleep, thinking, changing our minds, then the general general opinion was that it was better to return home and anticipate one's fate … With the break of day, when all was ready to depart our string of wagons … started the return journey, on the way the young people, except for the children, went on foot.[15]

The following day they arrived home and awaited the arrival of the French:

[We] did not dare appear in the streets. In the evening of the same day we heard a heavy knock and a sound of weapons at the gate of our house. Resistance was impossible … removing the latch from the gate, five French cavalrymen entered the house, with a rattling of spurs and sabres … My brother and sister were frightened by the sound of the weapons and ran and hid where they could, except me as a grown up [at 11 years old] … Our uninvited visitors, whom we met with fear, treated my father, as with the clergy, politely. The senior among the French, with the appearance of an officer, examined all the rooms and not finding anything attractive or to his liking demanded the delivery to him of the domestic cattle, cows and horses. But my father explained to him that all the cattle had been seized and driven away by the last detachment of Cossacks. The officer restricted the order to preparing a dinner for him tomorrow, and sent to the Jewish tavern where the Frenchman lodged. The enemy detachment's stay with us was not prolonged; they were replaced frequently by officers: there were French, Saxons, Westphalians and Polish. They did not occupy the rooms in the houses but bivouaced on the area in the meadow close to the river, where now and again they exercised drill and manoeuvres, quite often in a comical fashion; for example, they moved off from the halt by a signal from a bugle.[16]

And so the summer passed for the inhabitants of Chaus, and many other villages under the occupation of the French and their allies, with the odd Cossack raid into the village.

During the retreat, Bagration seems to have heard very little from Barclay. Finally giving up writing to him and not receiving a reply, Bagration wrote to General Ermolov, the 1st Western Army's chief of staff:

I have written to you twice, but there is no answer. I asked the Minister [Barclay] where is he leading the army? I wrote to him, but there is no answer. I do not understand, what does it mean?! Why do you run so and to where do you hasten? What is happening with you, why do you neglect me? It is no time for jokes. If I write, it is necessary for you to answer.

At last on 25 July, Count von Wolzogen arrived at Bagration's headquarters and informed him of the situation. However Bagration was still not satisfied, and two days later again complained about Barclay's conduct of the campaign:

One feels ashamed to wear the uniform. I feel sick … What a fool … The minister himself is running away, yet he orders me to defend all of Russia. We were brought to the frontier, then scattered about everywhere like pawns and there we stood, our mouths agape, befouling the entire frontier and then running away … I must confess, I am so disgusted with the whole business that I am nearly out of my wits … As for me, I am going to swap my uniform for a peasant's robe.[17]

On 29 July, Bagration received a letter from Barclay accusing him of marching too slowly and of disloyalty.[18] The following day Bagration wrote to Barclay defending himself against these accusations:

I am deeply hurt to see your doubts as to my devotion to the Fatherland. My deeds clearly showed the opposite: despite of all impediments, I accomplished the mission; twenty five days of continuous, forced marches, four resolute battles and Marshal Davoust's inaction could easily justify my actions.[19]

On 30 July, Bagration informed Barclay de Tolly that the 2nd Army would arrive at Smolensk on 3 August. Despite their forced marches, when the 2nd Western Army finally arrived at Smolensk it was in good spirits, as Ermolov recalled:

> The 1st Army was exhausted by the continuous withdrawal and soldiers began to mutiny; there were cases of insubordination and agitation … At the same time, the 2nd Western Army arrived [at Smolensk] in entirely a different state of mind. The music, joyful songs animated the soldiers. These troops showed only pride in their escape from the danger and readiness to face and overcome new jeopardy. It seemed as if the 2nd Western Army did not retreat from the Nieman to the Dnieper, but covered this distance in triumph.[20]

General Neverovski recalled, 'We covered over 850 km in 22 days at an average march of 44–53 km [per day] … In addition, the enemy had a direct route to Minsk, Borisov and Orsha, while we made a circuit.' Another eyewitness noticed

> The difference in spirits of both armies was that the 1st Army relied on itself and the Russian God, while the 2nd Army also trusted Prince Bagration … Bagration's presence, his eagle-like appearance, cheerful expression, keen humour inspired the soldiers.[21]

Notes

1 Russkii Arkhiv 1879 vol 3 pp.174–202
2 BL Add ms 30,132 The Journal of Mr Levy
3 BL Add ms 30,132
4 General Bagration, Sbornik, dokumentov I materialov pp.179–180
5 Ibid, p.50
6 Ibid, pp. 215–16
7 BL Add ms 30,132 The Journal of Mr Levy
8 Bagration, Sbornik, dokumentov I materialovo p.183
9 Quoted in 1812 v vospominanye sovremennila, pp.84–89
10 1812 v vospominaniyah sovovremennikov pp.84–86
11 1812 v vospominanye sovremennila, pp84–89
12 1812 in vospominaniyah sovovremennikov pp.87–88
12 Quoted in Russkii Invalid 1912
14 'The French in Chaus' in *Russkii Starina* 1877 pp.688–696
15 Ibid, pp.688–696
16 Ibid, pp.688–696
17 Quoted in Tarle, *Napoleon's Invasion of Russia*, p. 91
18 Bagration, Sbornik, dokumentov I materialov, p.214
19 Ibid, p213.
20 Ermolov, *Zapiski* 1812 p.155
21 Gribanov *Bagration v Peterburge* p.185, Zapiski *General Neverovskago*, p.77

4

RUSSIAN OFFENSIVE

Napoleon had failed in his aim to destroy the two Russian armies separately and now they were united. However, when Bagration arrived at Smolensk on 3 August he was in no mood to be civil to Barclay. Barclay de Tolly had criticised Bagration for his slow retreat, not realising what he had had to face, whereas Barclay de Tolly was seen as a traitor for allowing the Grande Armée to occupy such a large part of Russia without a battle. Both generals had also written to the Tsar – and whoever else would listen – on each other's faults. According to Lowenstern

> When Prince Bagration, accompanied by all his staff ... came for the first time to see the Commander in Chief [Barclay], I persuaded the latter to go out to the ante-room to meet the prince, sword and hat in hand, and to say that he was on his way to pay him a visit. This step, which had not been anticipated by Bagration, had a tremendous effect on him and on all his suite, who had jealously noted that Bagration, though senior to General Barclay, had been placed under his orders by command of the Tsar. Barclay's modesty and his usual lack of pretensions, above all this considerate step, had captivated them all in his favour ...
>
> The interview lasted only a quarter of an hour. Thereafter Barclay took over command of the two united armies, and although Prince Bagration was hurt to find himself placed under the orders of a junior, he mastered his keen disappointment and went openly to work.[1]

Both commanders realised that if they fell out with each other now Russia might be lost, so Bagration praised Barclay's withdrawal from Vitebsk, who in turn complimented Bagration on his march to Smolensk. Bagration even went so far as to write to Alexander recommending that he appointed Barclay commander of both armies, 'since a single overall command is necessary to save the motherland'. However, Bagration did not know of a secret letter that Barclay wrote to the Tsar:

I was … obliged, in order to get a course of action common to the two armies and to make them aim at the same objective, to use every endeavour to restore the essential harmony between Prince Bagration and myself, because our earlier correspondence about the slowness of his movements had created considerable ill feeling between us. I was obliged to flatter his vanity and to give in to him in several matters against my better judgement, solely with a view to gain agreement to the carrying out of more important enterprises. In short, I had to behave in a manner I find most repugnant, and one totally contrary to my character and feelings. However, I hoped thereby to gain my object, but the results convinced me of the reverse, because intrigues and party spirit soon reared their heads. Scarcely had the two armies linked up than offensive opinions and malevolent rumours began to circulate and were deliberately spread in St Petersburg.[2]

This ill feeling was not confined to Barclay and Bagration. There had been tension since the beginning of the campaign over the strategy used and the nationality of the officers who had proposed it. With their arrival at Smolensk the ill feeling boiled over. Two factions had formed, a 'Russian Party' headed by Bagration, and a 'German Party', composed of German officers who had joined the Russian Army since Prussia's defeat in 1807 and were seen as having the ear of the Tsar. This faction was mainly found on Barclay's staff.

In a letter to Arakcheev, Bagration complained that Barclay's headquarters 'is so full of Germans that a Russian can not breathe' (see page 56). It was this 'German party' that was blamed for the strategy of retreat. Whereas the 'Russian party' had wanted to take the offensive. According to Denis Davidov:

> Inspired with ardent love to our Motherland, Prince [Bagration], with the unrestrained ardour characteristic of all Asians, felt anger against Barclay; this feeling, based only on antipathy to the German party, considerably increased due to constant retreat of our troops.

The senior Russian officers called Barclay de Tolly '*Boltai da i tolko*' – 'All talk and nothing more' in front of their men and so undermined Barclay's authority. Muravyev recalled 'all our generals and officers … unanimously detested Barclay'; which is ironic since Barclay was Russian, albeit with Scottish ancestry, and Bagration was in fact Georgian. Militarily speaking Bagration was senior to Barclay de Tolly, but politically – as the minister of war – Barclay was senior to Bagration.

The officers in the 'Russian party' wanted Bagration to be the commander in chief. General Vasyl'chykov recalled:

> Ermolov [urged] Bagration to oppose him [Barclay], not to be subordinate to a junior in rank, to this *German*, and to take the overall command. It is obvious what disastrous results these intrigues could bring at a time when the fate of Russia was at stake and everything depended on good relations between the commanders.[3]

There is no doubt that Bagration would have liked to have been appointed commander in chief, but in a letter to Ermolov he wrote, 'I would not write to the Tsar asking for the command, because this would be attributed to my ambition and vanity, not my merit and abilities.'

If the Russian party had succeeded in their aims, then the history of the campaign and the Napoleonic Wars would perforce have been very different. To add to Barclay's problems Grand Duke Constantine rejoined the army at this time and promptly started his own scheming. The *Russian Army bulletin* of 5 August ignored these divisions in the high command:

> The corps of General Barclay de Tolly and Prince Bagration joined each other [at]
> … Smolensk. Throughout Russia glows a patriotism which has but a few examples
> in history, every citizen offering himself to become in some way useful to the state.
> The youth vie with each other for the glory of becoming the defenders of their
> nation. Husbands fly to arms and leave their wives and children, in the joyful hope
> of releasing them from the power of their tyrants and all appear united in the same
> sentiments, that when their native country is in danger, all private interests should
> be sacrificed to it.[4]

Now that the two armies had united, all looked forwarded to taking the offensive, Captain Pushkin of the Semenovski Regiment wrote in his journal:

> The Second Western Army of Prince Bagration joined us, we are [now] able to
> take decisive action. All of us are burning with impatience to fight, everyone of
> us is ready to shed his blood until the last drop and we are well led, we will cause
> the enemy a lot of harm. New military laws in our army are very severe. Two were
> shot for pillaging today, one man from every company was ordered to be present
> at the execution.[5]

Glinka recalls the soldiers' feelings:

> Our soldiers wished … to fight. Approaching towards Smolensk they shouted 'We
> see the beards of our fathers! Time to fight!' Finding out about the fortunate joining
> together of all our corps, they spoke in their own way, extending the hand and the
> palm with parted fingers, 'Before we were so! (that is the corps in the army, and the
> fingers on the hand were parted) now we are so,' they said with clenched fingers
> making a fist. 'So it is time (raising a hefty fist) to give the French one like that!'

As early as 30 July Barclay de Tolly had written to Bagration, stating that once the two armies were united

> I intend to anticipate the enemy and prevent him from penetrating deeper into our
> country. I am firm in my decision not to retreat under any circumstances and will
> fight a battle despite the united forces of Napoleon and Davoust.[6]

On 6 August, Barclay de Tolly held a council of war where many of the senior generals urged him to take the offensive now the two armies were united. Eventually Barclay was forced to accept the plan for the offensive. Intelligence reports suggested that Napoleon's troops were scattered over a wide area, the 5th and 8th Corps around Moghilev, the 6th Corps to the south at Dnieper, the Imperial Guard and the 4th Corps around Vitebsk – where Napoleon's headquarters was – and to the north the 1st, 3rd and Murat's cavalry were between Orsha and Rudnya. Colonel Toll suggested attacking the French at Rudnya, which would divide the Grande Armée and then the Russians could defeat each section of the army in turn.

On 7 August the Russian Army launched their offensive in three columns along a 20-mile front, the right wing commanded by General Tuchkov and the centre by General Dokhturov, and the 2nd Western Army formed the left column. Platov's Cossacks proceeded ahead as a cavalry screen, while a division remained behind at Smolensk. The soldiers now sang, 'since it was the first time in the campaign that they marched west, not east'.[7] Barclay was not convinced by this plan, his aide de camp Lowenstern recalled:

> On the one hand, he [Barclay] was aware of the possible gains from the manoeuvre, while on the other, he saw the dangers of attacking a far superior force … and of engaging, so to speak, in a manoeuvring match with that past master Napoleon.

By the evening, Barclay had reached Prikaz Vydra and Bagration halted at Katan. However, the following day intelligence was received that Prince Eugene's Corps was marching towards Porechye. Worried that Napoleon was concentrating his forces, instead of pressing home the attack, as the council of war had agreed, Barclay halted his column for three days fearing that Napoleon might encircle his northern flank and attack Smolensk. The Russian counter-attack ground to a halt. To counteract the threat of encirclement, Barclay ordered Tuchkov's column to protect the Porechye-Smolensk Road, while Dokhturov was ordered to move to Prikaz-Vydra and Count Pahlen's cavalry, which also formed the centre, was ordered to march to Rudnya to support Platov. Bagration was ordered to march north and protect Prikaz-Vydra. Bagration objected to this order and wrote to Barclay:

> We do know that the enemy troops are assembled at Porechye, Vitebsk, Rudnya, Lubovichi, Babinovichi, Orsha, Dubrovka and Moghilev, but we still do not know exactly where his main forces are located. Therefore, if we deploy the 1st Army on the Porechye route, and the 2nd Army on the Rudnya route, the enemy would attack our left flank and destroy our troops at Krasnoe … Any inactivity would give the enemy enough time to concentrate his forces in advantageous positions. Therefore, we should immediately continue to advance and find out his intentions and if possible prevent them.[8]

Barclay ignored Bagration's suggestion and moved his army towards Porechye. On 8 August, Platov clashed with General Horace Sebastiani's division near Inkovo, east of Rudnya. In his account of the skirmish Platov wrote: 'The enemy did not ask for mercy and the raging Cossacks slaughtered them.'[9]

On 10 August, Bagration wrote to Barclay to remind him that his army could not remain at Prikaz–Vydra.

> The state of my army requires us to leave these positions, since there is neither water nor provisions here; sickness is rife and the number of sick soldiers has considerably increased, further weakening the army … the enemy could leave Orsha on the route to Smolensk and assail my left flank … Thus, if we continue to waste time here, he [Napoleon] could march to Smolensk, forestall me there and cut route to Moscow.

The same day Bagration also wrote to Arakcheev:

> I am being treated without frankness and with an unpleasantness beyond the power of words … I cannot get along with the Minister. For God's sake, send me anywhere, if only to command a regiment in Moldavia or in the Caucasus. But I do not want to be here. The whole headquarters is so full of Germans that a Russian cannot breathe and the whole thing does not make any sense. I swear to God, they drive me mad with their changes every few minutes … My 40,000 men are called an army, and I am ordered to stretch them out like a thread and pull them in all directions.[10]

Sick of Barclay's inactivity, Bagration had had enough; in the 10 August letter to Barclay he continued:

> Since Your Excellency does not intend to advance against the enemy and attack him in accordance with the approved plan, I do not see any necessity of protecting the Rudnya road … Therefore I kindly appeal to you for permission to withdraw my troops to Smolensk.[11]

Without waiting for orders, Bagration began marching back to Smolensk, informing Neverovski, whose 27th Division had been ordered to occupy Krasnoe, just in case Napoleon sought to outflank him by the Orsha to Smolensk Road, to guard his flank as long as possible.

Barclay seems to have been confused at this time; the Russian historian Eugene Tarle wrote that Barclay's army 'moved aimlessly, now towards Rudnya, now away from Rudnya'. Certainly this is a view taken by Captain Pushkin of the Semenovski Regiment:

> 9 August. Camp on the road at Porechye. We were to move off from our position at 5am, but owing to a new order remained at the place until 8pm. Formed in columns, we again set out on the Smolensk Road and made 5–6 km in this direction, made a stop. In three hours we moved and covered 2 km, turned towards the

left. Not knowing what's happening is awful. My horse (recently we are allowed to have two horses) got stuck constantly, pain and a shortage of sleep [made me] very tired. Thus we passed the night from Saturday to Sunday. We spent Sunday in front of a wood. Darkness and the rain increased and made the conditions in our encampment intolerable. [Setting out] along the Smolensk to Poreschye Road, we again made a halt until dawn, then we advanced 10 km towards Porechu and made a bivouac in battalions. Platov remained on our position having fought with the enemy and captured 1,000 prisoners.

10 August. We caught up with a large part of our army.

11 August. The first order to set out at 8 o'clock was countermanded … I acquired a very small tent, which I was always able to set up very quickly, whereas the setting up of a cabin required time.

12 August. On this day (9 August) the carriage of General Sebastini was captured … in his pocket was a notebook, in which [he] records the date and place, day-by-day movements of our corps and its numerical strength [was] passed to … the chief of staff [with] all the suspicious persons in the volume, dates and ADCs.

13 August. Our experience in military affairs showed at every step, orders to go to Shelomets, the village which we passed in the night of 8th to 9th; being given simultaneously to 3rd and 4th Corps and also the 2nd and 3rd Cavalry Divisions. Our 5th Corps probably set out last of all.[12]

However this seems to have been through a lack of firm intelligence of Napoleon's whereabouts, rather than any desire to deliberately end the offensive.

Clausewitz believed the plan was doomed from the start, because if all had gone well the Russians might have surprised, and perhaps overwhelmed an enemy corps, but this would have given Napoleon time to unite his forces. Either way, the Russians would have to continue their retreat or fight a battle against superior numbers.

By now the soldiers were exhausted because of the heavy rain and counter marching. On 14 August the 5th (Guards) Corps again set out at 4.00am, marched all day, and arrived at Prikaz-Vidri after dark. Pushkin records that their column was approached by a woman that day, who questioned some of the officers; a gust of wind blew off 'her' hat revealing that 'she' was in fact a man. He was arrested as a spy and taken away.

The Russian's delayed advance allowed Napoleon to regroup his army at Babinovichi, before trying to cut off the Russian armies from Smolensk. Instead of marching north as Barclay had feared, Napoleon took the Orsha to Smolensk Road – the southerly road – and would threaten the Russian's left flank as Bagration had predicted. When they reached Krasnoe, they found Neverovski's 27th Infantry Division, in all ten battalions of infantry, supported by four squadrons of cavalry, three Cossack regiments and twelve guns. The Vilenski Infantry Regiment, which belonged to this Division, had remained at Smolensk as part of its garrison.

At about 10am on 14 August a party of Cossacks came galloping into Krasnoe and reported that a large body of French were close behind them. Neverovski called his division to arms. He would later report:

> I was attacked by 40 regiments of cavalry and seven of infantry, under the leadership of the two kings, I had little cavalry, who were quickly slaughtered by the enemy, so the fight was completely up to my infantry.[13]

The 1st Battalion of the 49th Jagers deployed in front of Krasnoe in a skirmish line, while the 3rd Battalion of the 50th occupied the town, supported by several pieces of artillery.

The 1st Battalion of the 50th Jagers was in reserve. The commander of this battalion sent Nikolai Ivanovich Andreev, a junior officer in the 50th Jager Regiment, with a small detachment, to build a bridge over the Lostvinu stream in case the Russians had to retreat. After demolishing some huts and old buildings to use the wood for the bridge, Andreev

> ... with another officer, went to the church tower, where we saw the enemy, with a great number of cavalry, emerging from the wood about a kilometre along the main road from the small town of Lyadov ... Emerging from the woods, they began to deploy in the field to the right and left; others went along the road towards the town. Here galloping past us were all the Cossacks and dragoons, the Jagers of the 49th Regiment, after making several shots ... they retired and ran past us at the double. Scarcely had the enemy begun to enter the town than they were greeted by caseshot from the guns and the battalion fire of our Jagers. I was on the main road and saw how several enemy columns were overturned.[14]

The 41st Jagers were also involved in the skirmishes in front of the town.

> Close to the two roads from Lyadov and Romanov (to Krasnoe) they engaged the enemy skirmishers and flankers with excellent fortitude and then withdrew across the river at a ford ... During the retreat, [they] repulsed a cavalry attack.

However, not all the Russian cavalry fled. Lieutenant Colonel Baron Saken, 'with two squadrons [of the Kharkov Dragoons] repulsed the first efforts of the enemy skirmishers by the road in the suburbs of Krasnoe ... [and] covered the withdrawal of four guns of the [Don] battery'. He then directed the battery to fire upon the French who were attacking the 50th Jagers.[15]

Despite this initial success, weight of numbers slowly drove the Russians back into the town, where they made another stand. Through the streets of Krasnoe the soldiers fought hand to hand. Major Slonimski of the 41st Jagers, 'with intrepidity and courage engaged in the town [Krasnoe] the enemy's skirmishers and when at the appearance in the market place of the enemy's column, deployed and advanced on the battalion on the left flank. He [led a] bayonet charge and overthrew them.'[16] Meanwhile a detachment of 41st Jagers, 'courageously attacked the skirmishers and then when the column drew near, [they] put down a heavy fire that repulsed them and did not allow the battalion to be outflanked'.[17] Another officer to be recognised for his bravery that day was Stab Captain Tinovski:

> … on the appearance of the enemy's columns on the right flank of the battalion, the commander being with the grenadier company, repulsed them … I allowed the enemy to come up with my flank, gave a volley and charged with the bayonet and in this way overthrew [them].[18]

Despite this fierce fighting the Russians were forced to retire behind the town. Andreev:

> Here ran from the town the Jagers, our battalion and the 49th Regiment deployed in the field, began to run towards the infantry column and those also incorporated into one mass. I was on horseback and seeing the dragoons deployed in order galloping in the field with the Cossacks, I took it into my head to escape also with them, but I saw the enemy cavalry pursuing them and sabring without mercy. I turned my horse towards the mass of our infantry, (it was impossible to call this mass a detachment) … nobody thought to arrange the order, column or square. I returned to the throng, riding into the middle of the men and seeking safety from Polish and French horsemen … The Poles made most of the attacks upon us, but the attacks were not persistent … Our crowd was similar to a herd of sheep, which always compressed in a mass under attack … The field where we deployed was wide and flat. One of our troubles was that the enemy did not allow us to retire on the road, which from the reign of Catherine the Great was bordered by two rows of densely packed birches that prevented more cavalry riding nearer to us. They shot at us several cannon balls and caseshot from the guns they captured from us, but later, as the harnesses had been cut, the crews could not drag the guns away … Their firing lost us about 40 men … a musketeer near me had his hand cut off, but his other, in the heat of the moment, still carried his musket.

General Paskevitch, whose division was sent to assist Neverovski's, recalled:

> [Neverovski] formed up [his] division, posting the battery guns on the left flank, covering them the Kharkov Dragoon Regiment with the Don Cossack Regiments stationed on the right flank … The enemy had 15,000 cavalry. It turned the left flank, the Kharkov Dragoon Regiment, seeing the attack, rushed forward, but was overthrown and pursued 12 km. The the battery remained without cover. The enemy rushed on it, overthrew and captured five guns, the other seven were left on the Smolensk Road. The Cossacks also did not hold firm. So Neverovski from the very beginning of the battle was without artillery, without cavalry, with only infantry. The enemy surrounded him on all sides with his cavalry. [Neverovski said to Paskevitch] the infantry attacked 'from the front, we sustained and repulsed the

attack and began to withdraw. The enemy, seeing the retreat, redoubled the cavalry attacks.' Neverovski closed the ranks of the infantry into columns covered by
the trees, which were planted at the edge of the road. The French cavalry repeatedly attacked the flanks and the rear of General Neverovski, finally offering him a
chance to surrender. He refused. The men of the Poltava Regiment with him this
day, shouted that they would die but not surrender. The enemy was so close that
they could exchange words with our soldiers. After the fifth kilometre of our retreat
came the biggest French onslaught, but the trees and the broken road prevented
them forcing their way into our columns.

Neverovski knew his force would be annihilated if he remained near Krasnoe and
so sent a detachment to find a ford across which they could make their escape.
Meanwhile the remainder of his division began to make a fighting withdrawal.

D. V. Dushenkyevitch, a junior officer in the Simbirski Regiment of the 27th
Division, records that after crossing the River Dnieper

> The many survivors, joined and reformed in the field ... in a general square. As the
> enemy had already prepared for us on two sides of the division for a formal attack
> ... Neverovski rode around the square with a drawn sword ... saying to those under
> his command, 'Children! Remember what you learnt in Moscow ... and no cavalry
> can defeat you, do not hurry firing, fire well, aim in front of the enemy. The third
> rank – hand over the musket as it should be, and nobody must begin without my
> command ...
>
> [The square] stood silently in good order like a wall ... at the command 'alarm!'
> the drummers picked this up, the battalion aimed, started quickly shooting and in an
> instant an arrogant enemy with their horses around the square covered the earth by
> the line of our bayonets.

Another account of the Simbirsk Infantry Regiment records

> The enemy artillery and infantry continually caused caseshot and musket fire [to
> be poured] into the square which shot it to pieces. Then the numerous cavalry for a
> distance of 13 km relentlessly attacked it [the square], attacks courageously repulsed
> every time. The regiments were newly formed from recruits and soldiers inexperi-
> enced in war. Although suffering great losses, their courage and orders alone obliged
> them bravely to endure all the enemy's attacks, which every time were beaten off.[19]

Andreev continues:

> The attack continued but we returned fire ... we were on the run and in the battle
> from 10am until 8pm, covering 27 km and every step was fought over. At 8pm on
> the road we saw coming into sight in the distance a wood and before it a high
> and long hill extending before us ... The reserve of one battalion of our regiment
> formed up in one rank of Jagers and stopped them [the enemy]. ... The Don's two

guns from the height rained several shots down on the enemy. The French, believing that [they were] a great reserve of infantry and artillery … stopped, and we, running past them, began to form up in regiments, arriving in order and we got to the woods towards Smolensk, which was only 16 km away.[20]

General Paskevitch:

The resistance of our infantry destroyed the energy of their impact. The enemy incessantly entered new regiments into the fighting, and all of them were beaten off. Ours, without distinguishing the regiments, mixed up in one column and withdrew, firing back and repulsing the attacks of the enemy cavalry. Thus Neverovski withdrew 7 more kilometres. In one place, a village, he was nearly thrown into confusion in his retreat when the birches and broken road ran out. In order not to be completely destroyed Neverovski was forced to leave some of the troops which had been cut off. The others withdrew, fighting. The enemy seized upon the rear of the column …. Fortunately they did not have any artillery and consequently they could not destroy this handful of infantry. When Neverovski began to approach the river, those two guns he had sent him before opened fire. The enemy thought that here were the expected Russian reinforcements and cleared the rear and we successfully crossed the river. Here they held out until evening. During the night [Neverovski covered] 20 km, as far as the ravine situated 7 km from Smolensk; where I found them, reduced to a third of the number.[21]

Neverovski's division finally managed to withdraw to Smolensk.

According to Neverovski, his division lost '1,200 privates killed and wounded, 20 field and commissioned officers and my adjutant, Yevsukov, who beside me was mortally wounded and died there and then'. Denis Davidov wrote: 'I remember how we looked at this division that approached us in the midst of smoke and dust. Each bayonet shined with an immortal glory.' Bagration wrote to Alexander praising the soldiers of Neverovski's division, 'one could not find another example of such courage.' Even the French praised the 27th Division, according to Count Segur they 'retreated like lions'.

At the beginning of the battle, Neverovski had despatched a courier to Barclay and Bagration warning them of the impending danger, who ordered their armies to retire on Smolensk, fearing that Napoleon would get there before them. Fortunately, General Raevski's Corps had been delayed at Smolensk, because it had been ordered to leave the city after 2nd Grenadier Division. But according to General Ermolov: 'the division was commanded by Lieutenant General Karl von Mecklenburg. Having spent the previous night with friends, he was drunk and awoke very late the next day; only then was he able to order his troops to march.'

The 2nd Grenadier Division had left three hours late, so by the time Raevski received orders to return to Smolensk, he was only ten miles from the city. Arriving early on 16 August, his corps was more or less the only troops available to defend Smolensk. Later that day the French arrived. With a message in his hand from

Bagration: 'I shall not march to rejoin you, I shall run. I only wish I had wings. Courage! God will help you.'

Raevski knew that he had to hold out as long as possible.

Notes

1   Quoted in Brett-James *1812* p.79
2   Ibid, pp.79–80
3   Pogodin, A.P. Ermolov: Materiali dlia ego biografii, sobrannie Pogodinim pp.445–46
4   Quoted in the *Edinburgh Evening Counrant*, 3 September 1812
5   Dnevnik, *Pavla Pushkin* p.38
6   Bagration, Sbornik, dokumentov I materialov p.214
7   Kochetkov, *Barclay de Tolly* p.36
8   Bagration, Sbornik, dokumentov I materialov, p.220
9   Donskoe kazachestvo v Otechestvennoi voine 1812 goda pp.16–17.
10 Bagration, Sbornik, dokumentov I materialov, p.226
11 Ibid, pp.225–227
12 Dnevnik, *Pavla Pushkin* pp.39–41
13 *Zapiski General Neverovski* p.79
14 *Andeev Russkii Arkhiv* 1879 p.184
15 *Russkii Invalid* 1912
16 Ibid
17 Ibid
18 Ibid
19 Ibid
20 *Andeev Russkii Arkhiv* 1879 p185–186
21 Quoted in *1812 v vosponinaye* pp.91–92

6

THE BATTLE OF SMOLENSK

Sir Robert Wilson, who joined the Russian Army at this time, was impressed by the city of Smolensk and describes it as follows:

[The walls], about thirty feet high and eighteen feet thick at the base … form a semi-circle of about three miles and a half. Thirty towers, irregularly placed and built, some being round, some square, with roofs made of wood, butt out from the walls … In front of the walls … [is] a deep dry ditch and a covered way and glacis, but the covered way had no regular communications with the city until they were made by the Russians at the moment of attack. There were three gates: one by the side of the river led over a bridge covered by an old *tête du pont* to the St Petersburg suburb, which was called from its size 'La basse Ville'. This suburb was populous and wealthy, but the houses were made of wood.

Two other gates, Malakhov and Nikols opened on the country; a half-moon work of earth covered the Malahkovski or Krasnoe Gate, which was flanked on the left by an old bastion, also of earth, and on the right by an earthwork polygon of five bastions, not palisaded, easily scaleable and open in the rear.

The towers could not receive artillery, and the Russians had no heavy guns to plant in any part of the works.[1]

The suburbs of the city were formed in a semi-circle. From west to east were Stasnia and Krasnoe, which were both on the river Dnieper, and the Mitslavl, Roslavl and Nikolski suburbs to the south of the city. The Ratchevka and Rayzenka suburbs were on the east of the city on the bank of the Dnieper. To the north of the city was the St Petersburg suburb.

The Russians were spread very thinly in the defence of the city, having just Raevski's Corps and Neverovski's weak division. In the Krasnoe suburb were the Ladozh, Nizhegorod and Orlov Infantry Regiments of Paskevitch's 26th Division and by the Royal bastion were the remainder of the 26th Division, the Poltava

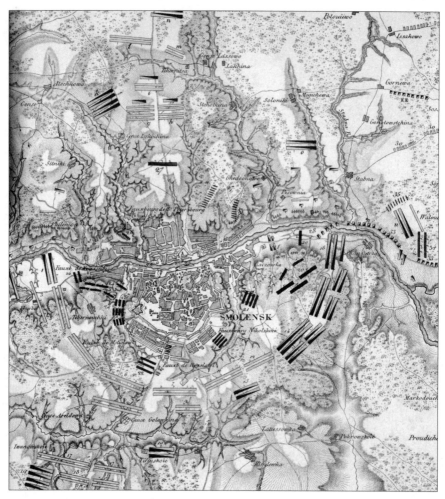

Plan of the battle of Smolensk.

Infantry and the 5th and 42nd Jagers, plus eighteen guns. Within Smolensk itself was the Vilenski Infantry Regiment of 27th Division and a composite battalion of several hundred men who had been released from hospital too late to join in the Russian offensive. The Mstislavski suburb was occupied by the Narva, Smolensk, Alexopol and Novo Ingermanland Infantry Regiments of Major General Vasil'chikov's 12th Division, with 24 guns. The Odessa and Tiraspol Infantry Regiments of 1st Brigade, 27th Division, commanded by General Stavitski, occupied the Roslavl suburb, which was in front of a cemetery, with 24 guns. The 6th Jager Regiment of 12th Division was in the Nikolski suburb with four guns. The bridge over the Dnieper was protected by the Simbirsk Infantry Regiment and the 41st Jagers. In reserve was the 49th and 50th Jagers of the 27th Division. The New Russia Dragoons and the Lithuanian Horse of the 4th Reserve Cavalry Corps and four regiments of Cossacks arrived during the night of the 16th and were placed on the Moscow Road on the left flank of the Russians.

Napoleon, who had arrived on the outskirts of Smolensk early in the morning of 16 August, knew he had to capture the city before the arrival of the entire Russian Army, so he ordered an immediate attack. He had only three corps with him at this time. In a crescent shape he posted Murat's cavalry to the east, Ney's corps to the west and Davoust's to the south. The attack began at about 6.00am when the French guns opened fire. About 9.00am, according to Paskevitch

We saw three large columns of French infantry … One of them coming straight at the bastion, another towards the cemetery, the third along the Dnieper, on our right flank. I rushed towards the six battalions lying in reserve, leading them from behind the covered way. All 70 of our guns were already in action. But the enemy disregarded the shot and the grapeshot and came nearer to the ravine, making for the moat of the Smolensk fortress. I only just managed to form up one battalion, as the French were already on the glacis. The Orlov Regiment opened fire and stopped the enemy. They sometimes attempted to leave the ravine, sometimes rushing on our infantry, but every time were met by our violent fire and were compelled to return to the ravine. Their bodies covered the glacis. Noticing that the enemy attacks grew weaker I ordered the 1st Battalion of the Orlov Regiment to rush on them with the bayonet.

The battalion coming out from the covered way, but seeing that the 2nd Battalion behind it did not come, stopped. I sent my adjutant Borodino. He stood on the glacis a few paces from the enemy, cried 'Ura!' and both battalions with shouts rushed on the French. During this time the Ladozh and Nizhegorod Regiments attacked with the bayonet, and the enemy was beaten out of the ravine. Their corpses covered all the ground from the glacis to the opposite side of the ravine. My regiment rushed to pursue the enemy. I beat the retreat, they returned and the battalions reformed on the other side of the covered way. Shortly after the enemy received reinforcements, and approached us again, but this time they stopped on the other side of the ravine. [We] fired at each other and [they were] not courageous enough to make a new attempt upon us.

On the left flank the enemy commenced firing and the columns approached towards our batteries, advancing their own artillery. They were met with grapeshot. General Raevski, being afraid of losing the guns, ordered them to withdraw, but the commander of the company, Lieutenant Colonel Zhurakovski, decided to stand firm and continued to fire caseshot. Shortly after there was a general charge and the enemy were [driven off] from this side with great losses. On the left in the suburbs occupied by the 12th Division, there was no attack …

At this time the whole French Army began to gather at Smolensk, taking up position and surrounding the city. I saw about 200,000 men standing in dark masses. The enemy, seeing that their attacks had failed, organised a battery and began to fire at the walls of the city … Entire regiments approached in battalion columns and extended in a skirmish line. We at the covered way lost a few men … My battalions had bad muskets, so I ordered them to pick up the muskets of the French and distribute them throughout the regiment.[2]

Although the 50th Jagers of Neverovski's Division had been placed in reserve, the regiment was soon called upon to hold the line, as an officer in the regiment recalls:

> Our 1st battalion, formerly at the Krasnoe [suburb] … was placed in the kitchen gardens, in skirmish order. But as the enemy's skirmishers were much stronger than our unfortunate battalion of a thousand men, and no more than a quarter of an hour, hardly 300 men remained, the rest were wounded, so that it was only possible to assemble one company. It remained somewhere in the city during both days of the battle … From the beginning of the battle our battalion deployed on the right flank of the city or beyond the city towards the cemetery. We were all day in skirmish order in the cover of a little brushwood. I was sent to General Raevski to ask for assistance, for from four until ten o'clock in the morning … we had lost a considerable [number of] men.[3]

By the river Dnieper the Polish Horse and Cossacks waited. Nadezhda Durova, who was with the Polish Horse, recalls in her memoirs:

> For two hours we waited for orders by the wall of the Smolensk fortress; at last we were commanded to march on the enemy. As the inhabitants of the city watched us go by in disciplined ranks, with heroic bearing and confidence in our own strength, they saw us off with joyful exhortations. A few, especially the old men, continually repeated 'God help you! God help you!' in an uncommonly solemn tone, which made me shudder and deeply moved me.
>
> Our regiment is positioned on both sides of the road. Farther to the left are brick sheds. The spot assigned to us is so awkward for cavalry manoeuvres that we will not be able to withstand the enemy's first onslaught. The entire field is so pitted, strewn with scraggly bushes, and cut by ruts that in any rapid movement, the squadron would have to jump either a ditch or a bush or a pit at every step. Since this was where they dug clay for the bricks, there are countless pits and, moreover, all of them are full of rainwater.

As the Polish Horse surveyed the battlefield they did not notice a brigade of light cavalry from Poniatowski's corps approaching them. Suddenly the regiment's priest came galloping up to them, pointing towards the body of enemy cavalry;

> We glanced to where he was pointing and saw the enemy cavalry galloping up on our flank. Instantly Podzhampolski ordered 'second half squadron left wheel', and, once it was facing the enemy, ordered me to take command and immediately attack the onrushing horsemen. It was a trilling moment for me! … But suddenly my order 'from your places, charge, charge!' merged with the thunderous voice of our commander resounding behind the lines 'Back! Back!' My half squadron turned around instantly and galloped at breakneck speed down the highway, leaving me behind. The squadron was galloping in disarray in a dense throng across bushes, hummocks and ruts …

When we reached a smooth spot, we repaid the enemy for our chaotic flight: the squadron, obeying the voice of their officers, took only a minute to form ranks and rush like a menacing storm cloud to meet the enemy. The earth groaned under the hooves of our ardent steeds, the wind whistled in the pennons on our lances, and it seemed as if death with all its horrors was racing ahead of our brave uhlans' formation. The enemy could not withstand the sight and, trying to get away, was caught, beaten, scattered, and driven off with a much greater loss than we had sustained when we were forced to retreat so impetuously across the hummocks and ruts.[4]

As the day wore on, more Russian regiments began to arrive. The 2nd Cuirassier Division arrived at the beginning of the battle and was placed in reserve on the right bank of the Dnieper. At about midday the 2nd Grenadier Division also arrived. The Siberian Grenadier Regiment was sent to reinforce Paskevitch's hard-pressed division and the Kiev Grenadiers to the 50th Jagers. However, weight of numbers began to tell and after several hours of fighting the 50th Jagers and their supporting regiments were driven into Smolensk. Andeev recalled: 'The battalion was reduced by more than a half. Two company commanders were killed on the spot, one of them, Lieutenant Kuntsevitch, killed near his house; two are severely wounded and another officer with me was hit in the face. Out of 21 eight remain.'

Meanwhile the inhabitants of Smolensk had not been idle. D.V. Dushenkyevitch, a junior officer in the Simbirski Infantry Regiment of Neverovski's Division saw 'the citizens of both sexes rushing in front of the walls towards the field of battle, taking hold of the arms of the wounded. Tearing up their clothes to wrap around their wounds … they carried [them] away from the place of danger to the city.'[5]

Towards evening the 1st Army began to arrive. Captain Edward Lowenstern who was the ADC to Count Peter Pahlen, who had commanded the Russian rearguard before being wounded:

At Smolensk we found General Raevski, who was holding the storming French out of the city. As I now had no official duties I rode out to a battery in order to watch the battle. Here I found General Schevich of the Imperial Guard's Hussars who was inspiring the gunners by his presence. Also standing there was a Russian priest from the city; he was personally laying several guns. The artillery officer, a young man of about my own age [22] distinguished himself, showed a bold front, allowed the French to come close as possible and then, as soon as they came within case shot range [about 200 yards] shattered great heaps of them to the ground. In the many battles and actions in 1806 and 1807, and also in this campaign, I had often seen soldiers fall, but never in my experience had I seen so many felled by a single salvo, weltering in their own blood and without arms or legs. A second earlier these poor victims of battle had advanced with fixed bayonets and pale faces. Now most of them lay dead or mutilated. Another column soon advanced and, with a hail of bullets, avenged the death of their comrades. Many of our artillerymen were shot.

I ducked behind a breastwork and the bullets whistled overhead. Being a mere spectator I had no job to do here, and did not wish to get myself killed to no purpose, so I made off and rode into Smolensk. The city seemed dead. A few wounded or drunken men staggered around the deserted streets. The suburbs were on fire, the magazines and a few houses had been plundered, while outside the battle thundered. The bloodbath I had just witnessed had upset me dreadfully. I felt completely forsaken, and I was suddenly overcome by such fear that I would willingly have hidden in a mouse hole. Every loud bang made me tremble.[6]

That evening Raevski's battered corps was replaced by that of Dokhturov's, reinforced by the 3rd Infantry Division of General Konovnitsin, and the 27th Infantry Division of General Neverovski was replaced by the 6th Jagers Regiment from 12th Infantry Division. In the Krasnoe suburb and Royal bastion was General Lihachev's 24th Infantry Division and in the Mstistlavski and Roslavski suburbs was the 7th Infantry Division of General Kaptevich. On the left flank the Irkutski, Siberia and Orenburg Dragoons and Cossacks were drawn up. Two pontoon bridges were built for better communication with the right bank of the Dnieper. Above and below Smolensk, two strong batteries of artillery were placed under the command of General A.I. Kuitaisov.

By 17 August the majority of the Grande Armée had arrived. They drew up in a large crescent, so that they surrounded Smolensk on three sides; only the river Dnieper prevented Napoleon from completely encircling the city. The 10th, 11th and 25th Infantry Divisions and a light cavalry division of Ney's Corps were deployed opposite the Krasnoe suburb, while in the centre stood the divisions of Davoust's Corps and on the right was Poniatowski's Corps. The cavalry divisions of Murat still occupied the eastern approaches to the city and part of the 3rd Cavalry Corps stood in reserve with the Imperial Guard.

Napoleon hoped that the Russians would draw out in front of Smolensk and so the decisive battle of the campaign would be at hand. 'At last I have them!' he is reported to have said. However, on the morning of 17 August, Barclay and Bagration held a council of war, where it was decided that Napoleon's attack on Smolensk might be a feint, while he sent a force to outflank them. To prevent this, Bagration was to march to Dorogobouzh, while the 1st Army would defend Smolensk. It would not be until 4pm that the 2nd Army took up position on the Moscow Road behind the Kolodria stream about 8 km from Smolensk. This was a wise move because Napoleon had sent Junot's Corps to the right to try and outflank the Russians.

At dawn on 17 August a musket and artillery dual commenced, then at 10am records D.V. Dushenkyevitch, 'Marshal Davoust's Corps moving to the right towards the wood, marching past in sight of us… Napoleon being there [cries of] "Vive l'Empereur!" wafted to us and confirmed the advance of the French line.'

Paskevitch described the fighting on the Nicolski suburb:

Our courageous resistance notwithstanding, Smolensk was at no time endangered, [even when] when Napoleon sent the Polish Corps with the right flank to the rear of the city, where the wall in one place had collapsed. On this side we had few troops and few guns. The Poles could easily have broken in, but they lacked the courage. They were only at a distance of 100 paces from the break, but withdrew. [I was] surprised that General Barclay de Tolly placed on the flank only 24 guns, he could have put 100 there. In that case there would be less risk and less loss of men.[7]

Neverovski's Division, which had been relieved by Dokhturov's Corps, refused to leave the battlefield, and retired into Smolensk to support the Vilenski Infantry Regiment manning the walls of the city. The soldiers of the 12th Division had orders to set fire to the suburbs if necessary. Sir Robert Wilson (referring to himself somewhat bizarrely in the third person):

Ney directed his corps against the bastion called the citadel, and the suburb of Krasnoe. Davoust directed Gudin to carry the Mistilaul and Morand the Roslaul and Nikolskoi suburbs. Friant connected Morand with Poniatowski, who was charged with the assault on the Raczenka suburb and the eastern quarter of the city. Murat at the same time charged and drove into the Russian cavalry stationed in that flank; their retreat enabled Poniatowski to establish sixty pieces of cannon on the height above Raczensk, whence he enfiladed the Russian bridges till a Russian battery was established on the opposite side of the river, and on equal heights, by the English General Sir Robert Wilson, which raked his line of battery, and compelled its removal from the position; by this withdrawal the bridges were preserved. The battle now raged with mutual fury and carnage through the whole semi-circle, and continued for two hours before the Russians withdrew from the suburbs; but even then they left troops in the covered ways. Once, indeed, the suburb of Nikolskoi was reoccupied by a sally of the division of Konovnitsin, but again relinquished.

As soon as the suburbs were in the possession of the enemy, a hundred and fifty pieces of cannon, many of them twelve, and some eighteen pounders, played incessantly upon the walls of the city to batter a breach; and about five o'clock a daring assault was made on the Malakofskia gate, which for a moment was gained; but Konovnitsin and the gallant Prince Eugene of Wurttemberg, always most conspicuous in every danger and who had just been sent by Barclay to reinforce the garrison, charged forward and recovered possession.

The enemy's grape [shot] and shells continued to pour into and sweep the covered ways, compelling their abandonment, and setting fire to the roofs of the towers and many of the houses in the city; but neither projectiles nor flames could dislodge the Russians from the ramparts.[8]

All this time Barclay had 'the air of not being occupied by the imminent danger which surrounded him and gave orders with the greatest calm'.[9] On one occasion Barclay was surrounded by enemy cavalry and had to be rescued by his escort and ADCs. Some regiments were eager to advance upon the French, as one anonymous eyewitness recalled:

I found the commander of the regiment, Major-General Tsibulsky [commander of 1st brigade, 24th Division of Dokhturov's 6th Corps], in full uniform, mounted on horseback among his skirmishers. He replied that he was unable to restrain his men, who after exchanging a few shots with the French ... repeatedly tried to dislodge them by bayonet assaults, without awaiting orders. Even as he spoke, there was a shout of 'Hurrah' from the line of men. He [Tsibulsky] began to shout, even drove the skirmishers back with his sword. At his presence, his command was obeyed, but only a few paces from him the cry of 'Hurrah!' resounded again and again, and the men flung themselves on the enemy. Many other regiments acted likewise ... Light wounds were ignored until the wounded fell from exhaustion and loss of blood.[10]

Prince Eugene of Wurttemberg:

The enemy attack commenced at this time at all points ... the enemy columns advanced on our left in the suburbs of Ratschanka threatening the bridges. I found myself at that time close to General Barclay. He was placing a strong battery against the suburbs of Ratschenka, but the news about General Dokhturov made the general in chief very anxious, he engaged me in consequence to return with General Dokhturov and see with my own eyes the state of affairs and then give him an account ... an Aide de Camp of the general in chief joined me and told me that the 4th Division was to follow me and wait for my orders in the middle of the city ... The brigade of General Rossi received notice to move at once to the left after crossing the bridge and to take possession at all costs of the suburb of Ratschenka.

This order was followed with zeal. The Polish brigade of General Grabowski was overthrown and the general died by a bayonet thrust of a grenadier of the Tobolski Regiment. The Volhynia Regiment had its Colonel, Kurnossov, grievously wounded. Majors Wolf and Reibnitz of the Tobolsk Regiment distinguished themselves in the most brilliant manner. The suburbs were retaken, but the regiments received orders to evacuate [and place] themselves ... on the covered way defending the eastern part of the city in concert with the 6th Jagers and the Jagers of the Imperial Guard Regiment.[11]

D.V. Dushenkyevitch recorded that little mercy was shown to the Polish troops: 'Our soldiers succeeded in capturing some of the French but all of the Poles were victims of [our] revenge.'

Wurttemberg and Dokhturov's troops tried to make their way through the city, but were blocked by the large numbers of wounded returning from the battle. Wurttemberg continues

I rejoined the General this side of the Malachov bridge at the moment when his troops entered into the city, pressed close by the enemy and in a disorganised state, which was the natural outcome of the furious battle enjoined in the suburbs and of the difficulties of the retreat ... It seemed to me nevertheless, considering the thickness and the height of the walls and the narrow passages by which the troops withdrew that ... [there was little chance] of disputing the bridge until the arrival of the 4th Division, and I ran in front to hasten their march; they finally drew near, but they lost a great number of men from the bullets during that advance in the streets. General Dokhturov wanted me first to make a sortie to dislodge the enemy from the houses that they occupied opposite the gate. This enterprise seemed to me very difficult and perilous … [but] after several attempts the men finally succeeded in reaching General Konovnitsin and we got to the bridge before the tower that covered the gateway … The throng filled the gateway … General Konovnitsin took charge of clearing it … and I placed myself at the head of the 4th Jager Regiment to fulfil my orders from the General. Arriving at the gateway, we suffered in the meantime such a rate of fire that the regiment hesitated, but Major Heideggen, at the head of some gallant soldiers began to run forward and … he occupied the covered way … All cried almost in one voice 'to the covered way!' and soon all the regiment was there, sustaining a very lively exchange of fire with the enemy troops who were in the houses opposite. The 4th Regiment had the honour of saving the city at that moment …

General Konovnitsin had in the meantime prepared General Pichnitzki's Brigade [which was] despatched to the right side of the citadel where it fought a very fierce skirmish … Towards evening Potemkin's brigade of the 17th Division also passed the bridge and drove back the enemy from the Krasnoe suburb.

At the moment when I arrived at the bridge I found the 6th Jager Battalion [sic] there and that the affair was already decided. The enemy announced his presence to us by a very heavy cannonade which again caused casualties to the 1st Brigade of the 4th Division. The retreat was executed during the first hour after nightfall; all General Dokhturov's Corps and the 3rd Division were placed at the end of the St Petersburg suburb and the Jagers of the 3rd Division occupied the same suburb. The 30th Jagers of the 17th Division were charged with burning the bridge.[12]

Meanwhile, in the Roslavlski suburb according to Sir Robert Wilson:

Napoleon, finding that the Russian Army continued to fight within the walls, commenced a violent assault, about midday, on the southern suburbs of the city: the attack was executed and maintained with such vigour that the enemy, after encountering for two hours as resolute a resistance, obtained possession of the three central suburbs; but he was repulsed in numerous attempts to make a more forward lodgement. Finding that every effort, notwithstanding high encourage-ment to those efforts, was unavailing, towards the afternoon he wheeled his right flank forward to the eastern face of the city, and opened on that side a very heavy fire from above sixty pieces of cannon under the direction of Prince Poniatowski. But a Russian battery which was established immediately on the right bank of the Dnieper, and on a corresponding elevation, although very inferior in number of guns and weight of metal, obliged the enemy's guns, which it enfiladed, to withdraw from the position whence they commanded the pontoon bridges and the original wooden bridge of the city, dismounted several of them, and occasioned six different explosions of powder wagons.

But the enemy's bombardment with above a hundred and fifty pieces of cannon, although failing to make any impression on the walls and works, succeeded in firing the city in several different places, and in enveloping the northern suburb in a volume of flames that extended above half a mile; a spectacle that no person present can ever forget, and a calamity (for it was a holy city) which every Russian resolved to avenge.

Despite this heavy fighting a large part of the 1st Army was drawn up to the north of the city and remained uncommitted to the battle, to the disgust of those engaged.

Bagration's army was still protecting the crossing of the Dnieper at Dorogobusch and was also not engaged in the battle. But where was Junot's VIII Corps which had been sent to outflank the Russians? Upon receiving his orders, Junot had set off, but not knowing the country he had a peasant brought before him to act as a guide. Unfortunately, none of Junot's staff could speak Russian and the peasant could not speak French, so the VIII Corps was marched in circles around the Russian countryside for two days. When the marshal discovered this, he ordered the peasant to be shot. Unfortunately, history does not record the name of this peasant, but he must be considered among the heroes of the 1812 campaign, because Junot's corps would have been decisive if it had taken part in the battle of Smolensk.

By now the day began to look black for the Russians, as Baron Uxkull, who had been seconded to Barclay's staff wrote in his diary:

> The outer parts of the city were burning. Fighting continued in the city itself until nine in the evening; it was then that a sight as fearsome as it was beautiful presented itself to my eyes. I was standing on the mountain; the carnage was taking place at my very feet. Shadows heightened the brilliant sheen from the fire and the shooting. The bombs, which displayed their luminous traces, destroyed everything in their paths. The cries of the wounded, the Hurrahs! of the men still fighting, the dull confused sound of the rocks that were falling and breaking up – it all made my hair stand on end. I shall never forget this night! For who could imagine all the horrors I've just seen without having been present! The poor city has become a heap of stones; its a considerable loss! This encounter is going to have important consequences for us.[13]

The inhabitants, who had believed that the Army would be victorious, now looked to flee this scene of horror. D.V. Dushenkyevitch:

> What an awful confusion I witnessed within the walls; the inhabitants, believing that the enemy would be repulsed, had remained in the city, but that day's strong and violent attacks had convinced them that it would not be in our hands tomorrow. Crying out in despair; they rushed to the sanctuary of the Mother of God, where they prayed on their knees. Then they hurried home, gathered up their weeping families and left their houses, crossing the bridge in the utmost confusion. How many tears! How much wailing and misery and in the end how many victims?

N. N. Sukhanin, an artillery officer, also witness the inhabitants leaving:

> The inhabitants fled in horror, dragging their valuables. Here I saw a good son, bearing on his shoulders an infirm father, there a mother making her way along a safe path towards our positions clutching her little ones in her arms, having sacrificed everything else to the enemy and to the fire.[14]

Meanwhile, Dushenkyevitch's regiment decided to get a better position:

> We with difficulty climbed onto the collapsing walls … and occupied all the loopholes and surveyed such a majestically threatening scene! As it began to grow dark the heat of battle around had not calmed down, transforming the suburbs into ashes, the lake of flames separating us from the French horde.

Ivan Maslov recorded the scene that evening:

> The burning suburbs, the dense multicoloured smoke, the red glow, the crash of exploding bombs, the thunder of cannon, the seething musket fire, the beating of drums, the moans and groans of old men, women and children, the whole people falling on their knees with arms outstretched to the skies – such was the picture that greeted our eyes and tore at our hearts. Crowds of inhabitants ran from the flames, not knowing whither … The Russian regiments ran into the flames, some to save lives, others to sacrifice their own. A long line of carts rolled on slowly, bearing the wounded. In the deep twilight the Icon of the Smolensk Mother of God was carried out of the city; the dismal tolling of bells merged with the crash of falling houses and the din of battle.[15]

The fighting continued into the evening, the fires from the burning suburbs lighting the combatants. For two days the Russian Army had fought Napoleon's forces, which were still bombarding Smolensk. Despite this many believed that they could renew the battle the following day. Bagration had met Barclay in the afternoon to persuade him to hold out. Despite giving Bagration assurances that he would stand and fight, during the night of 17–18 August Barclay gave the order to abandon the city. Many officers requested that their regiment should stay and garrison the city, but Barclay rejected their appeals.

That night the Russian Army began its evacuation of Smolensk. Dushenkyevitch's regiment

> … were ordered to leave the walls, with caution in order that the enemy would not notice, and afterwards led us through the ruins of the city towards the bridge over the Dnieper, covered with straw, while others prepared to burn it. Before dawn the bridge flared up, the French at that minute launched, with music, an attack, but nobody [was there] except the retreating rearguard.

However, a battalion of the 50th Jager Regiment had been forgotten. Had it not been for Andeev, who could not sleep that night, his men would have been captured:

I could not sleep and took it into my head to ride along the river to the bridge …
Approaching towards the bridge I saw that troops were crossing. I approached a
field officer of the retinue of His Majesty, he asked me whether there were any
troops from whence I came? I said that I did not know of any others, but there
was my battalion in line on the right flank. He asked me to gallop and order the
battalion to quickly come here for the army was leaving the city and that this was
the appointed hour to set fire to the bridge … I galloped to announce this to our
Major Antonov, who for a long time did not dare to leave his post without orders
from his superiors, but sawayed by my conviction he ordered us to move. In a
quarter of an hour an adjutant of ours came galloping towards us with orders to
run, because the bridge is to be set on fire. Barely had we run across it, than it was
blown up.

The 30th Jagers of 17th Division of Baggovut's corps were given the task of destroying the bridge, as Wurttemberg described:

The 30th Jagers delayed executing their orders and the French voltigeurs arrived on
the other bank before the bridge had been entirely destroyed. The 30th had arrived
and the enemy seized the suburbs. The [musket] balls reached the 4th Division, but
they did not have the time to proceed forward. General Konovnitsin was found still
close to the Jagers of his brigade, commanded by Prince Schachovskoi, who made
[a charge] with him upon the enemy and threw them back beyond the bridge.

The Jagers of the 3rd and 17th Divisions then extended the length of the left bank
of the Dnieper and maintained almost during the whole day a fire fight with the
enemy. The Jagers of the 4th Division remained in reserve on the heights behind the
St Petersburg suburb and the rest of the 4th Division came to rejoin the 17th on the
extreme right of the army.

The losses of the 4th Division during the battle of the proceeding day had sur-
passed 1,300 of all ranks. Major Mamanov commanded the Volhynie Regiment
instead of Colonel Kurnossov. The loss esof Potemkin's brigade are unknown to me.

The troops had barely rested when I was informed of the passage at a ford of two
detachments of enemy cavalry opposite my Division. The banks of the Dnieper
were concealed from this side by thick brushwood.

I had sent out at first a battalion of the Tobolsk Regiment commanded by Major
Wolf to resist this cavalry. It appeared that their intention was to be foraging …
Major Wolf fell upon the enemy … and drove [them] back to the other side, but
he was forced to retire in his turn having endured the fire of a battery placed on
the right bank. I [saw] … the enemy's position opposite us, Marshal Ney's Corps
and a great number of cavalry bivouacked en masse within musket shot of the river
without having taken the least precautions.

We were uncertain of retirement the next day and there could be no better cover
than causing an alarm on the left of the enemy's army during the night. It was
part of my idea suggested to General Baggovut. I was the first person to report
to Headquarters. In effect all the artillery of the 2nd Corps was to assemble that

evening under my orders and be placed on the heights opposite the enemy Corps in an attempt to create terror in the middle of the night. A few regiments of Cossacks positioned behind the second Corps were appointed to ford the Dnieper and alarm the great park of artillery that we could see on the extreme left of the French; and the 4th Division was to protect our battery ... All measures possible were taken to make the enemy repent his temerity.[16]

Orders were received at 11.00pm to follow the 4th Corps through the St Petersburg suburb and along the Poriestsch Road; but this did not end the battle. On 18 August Baron Uxkull wrote:

The engagement has resumed. Our batteries are having great success and our sharpshooters are performing miracles. The French, dead drunk, scrambled up the walls and, falling back became ladders for the men following. The ditches are filled with corpses.[17]

Wilson also gives an account of the fighting on the 18th:

Towards eight o'clock a Spanish and Portuguese brigade crossed the river about mid-deep under the walls of the city, and entered the suburb on the right bank, but they were attacked and many of them killed, wounded or made prisoners.

When General Barclay heard from some of the prisoners that the city was full of artillery and powder wagons, he ordered some shells to be thrown into it; but the artillerymen executed the order with great reluctance, as, notwithstanding the removal of their Saint, they did not feel sure that the bombardment would not be considered a religious offence.

Upon hearing that Barclay had abandoned Smolensk, and had again lied to him Bagration complained to Rostopchin.

I owe a great deal to General Rayevsky. He commanded a corps and fought with dash ... Neverovski's new division fought with incredible bravery. But that wretch, scoundrel and vermin, Barclay, gave up a splendid position for nothing. I wrote to him very seriously, I implored him in person not to withdraw, yet no sooner had I set out for Dorogobouzh than he began to follow me ... I swear to you that Napoleon would have been defeated, but Barclay never listens to me and does everything that is useful to the enemy ... I can tell you that we would have covered Napoleon with shame if only the minister had held firm ... All the French prisoners tell me that he [Napoleon] was saying that once he vanquished Bagration, he could take on Barclay with his bare hands ... I do not rely on Barclay anymore and ... can assure you that he will bring the enemy to you. I must admit that I am thinking of leaving Barclay and joining you, I would rather fight with the Moscow militia.[18]

He later added:

It is painful and sad, and the entire army is in despair, because they gave up the most important position, and all for nothing. Our troops fought and are fighting as never before. With 15,000 men, I held them back victoriously for over 35 hours, but he refused to make a stand for 14 hours. This is shameful, a stain on our army. As for him, it seems to me he should not go on living. If he reports that our losses are great, he is lying. We lost perhaps four thousand, no more than that, surely less. But suppose it were ten thousand, what of that? This is war, after all.

General Ermolov probably echoed the sentiments of all the Russians when he wrote

The destruction of Smolensk introduced me to a completely new feeling which a war outside your native land cannot inspire. I had never witnessed the destruction of my homeland or seen my cities burning. For the first time in my life, my ears heard the lament of my compatriots and my eyes were opened to the horror of their terrible condition. I do consider mercy a gift from God, but now I could never allow it into my heart before revenge was satisfied.[19]

One of the reasons why Barclay wanted to make a stand at Vitebsk but not at Smolensk might have been that at Vitebsk he had underestimated the Grande Armée's strength, whereas he overestimated it at Smolensk. Akhsharumov, who wrote an account of the campaign in 1813, stated that the Russians had exactly 110,000 men to Napoleon's 205,000 – but the Russians did not realise how effective their strategy had been. The French 3rd Corps, which had began the campaign 39,342 strong could now muster 22,282 men and the 1st Cavalry Corps, which mustered 8,577 ,was now 5,413 men. Even the Imperial Guard had began the campaign with 40,373 men and was now 24,600 strong.[20] The Russians' scorched earth policy had caused the soldiers of the Grande Armée to go hungry and desertion was rife. Moreover, in his advance across Russia, Napoleon was forced to leave troops to garrison large towns and protect his lines of communications, thus depleting his army further.

Clausewitz writes that from

... successive retreats from Drissa to Vitebsk, and thence on Smolensk, no one entertained the idea that the French force would so soon dissolve away, the idea of clinging to the Moscow line was quite natural, in order to preserve that important place as long as possible.

At Smolensk, the relative proportions were 180,000 to 120,000, and as calculations might be erroneous, it might be considered possible that the French there had 200,000. The Russian generals then were not to be blamed, if, under these circumstances, they would not yet commit themselves.[21]

According to Caulaincourt, Napoleon now decided to remain at Smolensk. 'I will rest the troops and dominate the country from this pivotal position and we'll see how Alexander likes that.' But Smolensk was in no state to quarter an army. Before the battle it had about 2,250 buildings, but now only about 350 remained. Most of the city's 15,000 inhabitants had fled, leaving only 1,000. During the engagement the Russians lost about 12,000 men, while the French casualties amounted to some 10,000 killed and wounded. The number of soldiers and civilians who perished in the flames is not known.

While the Grande Armée plundered what remained of Smolensk, the Russian Army was not out of danger yet.

Notes

1 Sir Robert Wilson, *The French Invasion of Russia* pp.85–86
2 Quoted in 1812 *in vospominaniyah sovovremennikov* pp.92–95
3 Andreev, *Russkii Arkhiv* 1879 p.187
4 Durova, *The Cavalry Maiden* pp.135–137
5 Zapiski, *D V Dushenkyevitch* 1st book p.111
6 Quoted in Brett-James *1812* pp.85–86
7 1812 *in vospominaniyah sovovremennikov* p.96
8 Wilson, *The French Invasion of Russia* pp.87–88
9 Lowenstern, *Memoires du general major russe* p.220
10 Quoted in Tarle *Napoleon's Invasion of Russia* p.106
11 *Journal of Prince Eugene of Wurttemberg* p.5
12 Ibid, p.5
13 Uxkull, *Arms and the Woman* pp.73–74
14 N.N. Sukkhanin, 'Iz zhurnala uchadtnika voiny 1812 goda' *Russkaia Starina,* 1912
15 Tarle, *Napoleon's Invasion of Russia* p.104
16 *Journal of Prince Eugene of Wurttemberg* p.7–8
17 Uxkull, *Arms and the Woman* p.73-74
18 Dubrovin, *Patriotic War in Letters of Contemporaries,* p.96
19 Ermolov Zapiski *1812* p.57
20 Count Ostermann Sacken Feldzug von 1812 pp.317–318. However ,Tchuyhevitch in his *Reflections of the War of 1812* (1813) puts Ney's Corps in June 1812 at 42,569 and the Guards at 43,606
21 Clausewitz, *Campaign of 1812* p.145

7

THE BATTLE OF LUBINO

By the evening of 18 August, after both armies had faced each other most of the day, the Russians drew off. Barclay divided his army in to two columns. The first column commanded by Dokhturov left at 7.00pm and with orders to march to Prouditchi. The second column, under Tuchkov III, began to withdraw two hours later and was to march to Bredikhino, via Lubino. The Russians' aim was to march all night and put enough ground between them and Grande Armée as possible. Since the Russians had destroyed the bridges over the river Dnieper, the French did not pursue Barclay's army. The 2nd Army was also able to withdraw unmolested along the Moscow Road.

General Korf's rearguard, which was the last to leave the suburbs of Smolensk at about 2.00am, lost its way and marched in a large semicircle and so as 19 August dawned it once again found itself close to Smolensk. By now the French had finished rebuilding the bridges over the Dnieper and had begun crossing the river. For Korf's rearguard the situation was serious:

> In this critical situation, nothing was left but to endeavour to maintain his (Korf's) present position; not doubting but that the Commander in Chief, [Barclay] on finding the rearguard had been attacked, would lose no time in sending troops to its support. According to this resolution, Korf ordered the right column to form on the ground where it then stood; and the left to station itself on a command-ing point to the town of Valutina. Prompt as the troops were in obeying these directions, they were not completely executed before another body of the enemy appeared on the Smolensk side. These new corps waited not an instant but attacked with a sudden and tremendous shock. This was the signal for a general assault … Ney's troops began the business, by charging the rear of the right column of the Russians before it had time to finish its formation. He made the onset with the bayonet, it being his design, by the surprise and impetuosity of his movement, to drive them from their ground.

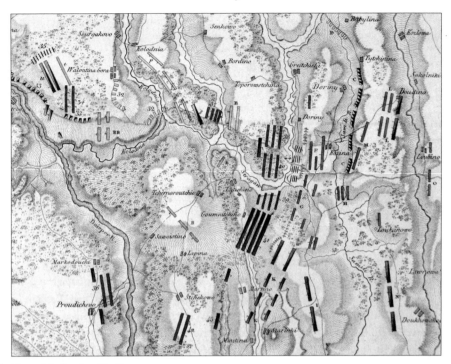

Plan of the battle of Lubino.

General Korf perceiving the difficulties of his situation increase, judged it pru-
dent to release himself, if possible, from these unequal and desperate encounters,
by making a junction with his left column, which was forming very rapidly, and
had already opened a heavy fire upon the advancing bodies of the enemy. To this
effect, he ordered two battalions, supported by several guns, to remain on his present
ground, to cover his movement while retiring upon the other column.

The brave men selected for this duty performed it with unshaken firmness, notwithstanding the most violent efforts to dislodge them: nor did they recede one
step, until their General had gained his object; although to secure it, nearly one half
of their undaunted comrades sacrificed their lives.[1]

Meanwhile, Barclay ordered Prince Eugene von Wurttemberg to support the hard
pressed rearguard. He appears only to have had three regiments at his disposal, the
Tobolsk Infantry Regiment from the 1st Brigade of his 4th Division, from which
Wurttemberg placed a battalion to hold the village of Gedeonovo, with four pieces of
cannon. The other battalion of the regiment, under Major Wolf, was sent to occupy
the woods in front of Gedeonovo. The other regiments were the Wilmanstandt
Infantry Regiment and the Belozersk Infantry Regiment, from General Zakhar
Olsufiev's 17th Division. A battalion of the Wilmanstand Regiment was placed in the
brushwood by a dried up stream between Gedeonovo and the Moscow Road. The
other battalion, with two pieces of artillery, was to hold a bridge over the stream and
to destroy it once the rearguard had passed.

As a French column moved out of the St Petersburg suburb, Eugene von Wurttemberg takes up the story:

> Several battalions of this column (among others the Portuguese of Razout's Division) went to my left against the town of Gedeonovo and towards the height where Major Wolf was found. All the Tobolsk Regiment and a battalion of the Belozerki was little by little engaged at these points in a very lively fire fight. The battalion of Major Wolf profited by an ancient redoubt on the height for cover against the repeated attacks of the enemy who were reinforced by tmen from the head of the columns leaving the woods.
>
> The admirable resistance of this battalion allowed my detachment to remain in its precarious position during more than two hours. The forces of the enemy were increasing nevertheless from one moment to the next. I was forced to send to Major Wolf the order to retreat; but before he could the French surrounded [him] and at the same time, redoubled their efforts against the town of Gedeonovo. They were therefore on the point of seizing the two pieces placed in front of them, but a battalion of the Belozerski was brought from the reserves by my ADC Captain Wachten to attack in front very resolutely and Major Wolf benefited from the advantage to make a gap through the enemy in order to regain Gedeonovo. At this time a formidable mass of cavalry crossed the dried-up river in front of the Wilmanstandt Regiment and attacked its skirmishers in the brushwood. The moment seemed to me as critical and decisive.

Wurrtemburg had only a squadron of the Isum Hussars at hand to counterattack, but

> Very fortunately at this moment General Dokturov, on the left with Tuchkov's cavalry detachment, that is to say with the rest of the Isum Hussars and the Elizabethgrad Hussars, charged the French cavalry and hurled them back on the infantry. The skirmishers of the Wilmanstandt [Regiment] ran to support the action of the hussars and we enjoyed a similar kind of success as we had against the enormous masses that the enemy presented to us near the suburbs. A French battery on the left bank of the Dnieper caused us several losses, however.[2]

It may have been this cavalry melee that Barclay – who had galloped back towards his rearguard with his staff to see what was happening – was caught up in.

> In one of the cavalry charges which took place during the morning when we were fighting along with Baggovut's corps to allow General Korf's disengagement. I had the good luck to save the General in Chief from a grave situation.
>
> He was mounted on a very dashing horse, which had been given to him by the brave General Dokhturov. This horse was very tired and was accordingly frisky and would hardly go forward. Some Polish lancers, having thrown back and driven into our skirmishers, threw themselves upon the group made up of the General in Chief and his staff. He spurred his horse to avoid the danger to his person, but at this the

horse turned and turned, not advancing, bucked and was unwilling to be put to the gallop. I had already given the horse several blows with the flat of my sword to force it to move, but seeing that nothing worked on this cursed beast and that the danger was becoming ever more pressing, I dismounted my horse and compelled the General in Chief to take my own. General Barclay, with great coolness and without saying a word, dismounted from his and briskly mounted mine, continuing on his way, looking to the right and left to see any squadron to facilitate our retreat. While waiting, I jumped up onto his horse and, being more youthful and vigorous than he, I put this wearisome horse of his in hand such that it was only with some difficulty that it was possible to stop him.

Captain Leon Narischkine, commander of a squadron of the Isum Hussars, at this moment made an excellent charge, throwing back the enemy and giving us time to complete our reconnaissance.[3]

Wurttemberg's actions on the heights behind Gedeonovo had given General Korf's rearguard the chance to reform. The order now came for Korf and Wurttemberg's forces to withdraw towards the crossroads at Lubino. They were followed by Ney's advance guard.

Meanwhile, the main body of the 1st Army was marching on another road, which ran parallel to the north of the Moscow Road until it took a sharp curve at the village of Kochaeva and intersected the Moscow Road near the village of Lubino. Bagration had given General Gorchakov orders to hold the crossroads until the 1st Army appeared then proceed along the Moscow Road to Dorogbouzh. However, when a detachment of Baggovut's men came into view, Gorchakov mistook them for the main body of Barclay's army and abandoned the crossroads, leaving just 300 Cossacks to hold it.

The 1st Army was still some way off from the crossroads and was ignorant of the impending danger.

Dawn was breaking when the troops, having marched for some 10 km, had to halt because Uvarov had ordered the 1st Cavalry Corps to gather forage and lay hay for their horses. I [Ermolov] sent him a very respectful note and, with due regard to my rank, invited him to proceed, without infantry, to the crossroads. Soon, we heard the sound of artillery fire and I ordered the infantry to march as fast as possible. Yet, we could not find Tuchkov, the commander of the entire column, as he was calmly resting in a nearby village.

Fortunately, Konovnitsyn was at hand to order the column to march quickly to the crossroads. Upon hearing that the crossroads was guarded only by an outpost of Cossacks, Barclay ordered General Paul Tuchkov (III) with 3,000 men to secure it. The terrain by the side of the roads was marshy and surrounded by woods, unsuitable for cavalry, guns and wagons, so the crossroads was to be defended at all costs until the Russians had passed. If this crossroads was lost then much of Barclay's army would be cut off.

The French were marching by a more direct route towards the crossroads and could have easily got there first if it had not been for Korf and Wurttemberg's courageous resistance, which gave Tuchkov's men time to reach the crossroads first. Tuchkov deployed his men on the heights west of Lubino, overlooking the crossroads. The Russians were still not safe, to their rear was the river Jarownia with only one bridge across it, a bottleneck if things went wrong.

It was afternoon, some accounts say 2.00pm, others 3.00pm, when the second stage of the day's fighting began. Ney's forces fell on Tuchkov's men in a desperate fight to capture the crossroads before the main body of the Russians could get there. Sir Robert Wilson:

> The enemy's attack on General Tuckhov commenced about three o'clock in the afternoon, with great vigour, and before General Barclay's column had gained the main road, mutual charges were given and repelled; but the superiority of the enemy's numbers increasing every moment, they must have prevailed if some of the infantry first debouching from the cross road had not opportunely arrived to check their advance.[4]

After heavy fighting Tuckhov was forced to withdraw from the heights to behind the river Stragan, which ran behind his position. The situation was critical and at one point Tuchkov seems to have ridden back to Barclay to ask for reinforcements. Upon seeing that Tuchkov had abandoned his post, Barclay was furious and said: 'Go back to your post and get yourself killed. If you come back again, I will shoot you!'

It was obvious to Barclay, however, that Tuchkov needed reinforcements and so he ordered Uvarov with the 1st Cavalry Brigade, along with Lieutenant General Nikolai Tuckhov's 3rd Corps and Major General Passek's artillery, to the crossroads. Lieutenant General Ostermann-Tolstoy's 4th Corps was also close behind these reinforcements. General Ermolov's report recorded:

> The battle soon began in earnest. The enemy directed its attacks down the main road, but advantageous terrain and the fact that the enemy artillery had not arrived yet allowed us to retain our position. The enemy increased its tirailleurs against Major General Tuchkov's left. On Tuchkov's orders, the 20th Jagers under Major General Prince Shakhovsky contained the enemy and gained time for the Chernigov, Murmsk and Seleginsk regiments of the 3rd Division [of Tuchkov's 4th Corps] to arrive and take up position.
>
> The enemy's artillery soon arrived and artillery fire on both sides greatly increased, just then Your Excellency arrived. The enemy cavalry also appeared and halted on their right flank like a dark cloud. We needed to shift our cavalry, except for the 1st Corps, to our left. The enemy had superior forces and the advantage of better terrain. Our cavalry and artillery had a marshy stream behind them, which was difficult to cross. However, Major General Prince Gurieli's brigade quickly drove the enemy infantry from the forest and inhibited their progress. In addition, the Pernov Regiment under Major General Choglokov, supported our cavalry by falling on the

enemy. 24 Guns then made our cavalry invincible. Even so, it seemed as though a single cavalry attack would annihilate our left wing, but because of the gallantry of our troops, each French attack was driven back with heavy casualties, much to the shame of the French. I ordered Adjutant General Count Orlov Denisov to take over the command of the cavalry and Cossacks. Both sides attacked over a prolonged period of time.[5]

Wilson's also witnessed the day's fighting:

It was about sunset when the enemy on the main road upon the left bank, flattering themselves that their right was gaining ground made a desperate effort to force the hill, on which several Russian guns were placed, and which commanded the whole position and also in reverse the outlet of the cross road, beyond which a boggy rivulet ran intersecting the route; over this only one bridge with loose planks afforded passage for the artillery and infantry until night, when two others were thrown across by Duke Alexander of Wurttemberg. For an instant the Russian guns and troops supporting, overwhelmed with shells, shot and musketry, flew back to seek shelter behind the crest of the hill; but General Barclay, who had been superintending the action with his rear guard, admonished by the cannonade at Lubino and Valutina Gora of the new danger to his advanced guard, opportunely arrived at this moment, and seeing the extent of the danger to his column, galloped forward, sword in hand, at the head of his staff (including myself, with two Russian officers attached to me as aides de camp), orderlies, and rallying fugitives, and crying out 'Victory or death! we must preserve this post or perish!' by his energy and example reanimating all, recovered possession of the height, and thus under God's favour, the army was preserved![6]

According to Lowenstern, the Duke Alexander von Wurttemberg ordered him to build another bridge over the River Jarownia for the army to cross. The existing bridge was to be used by the Russian baggage train.

I dismounted a squadron of Hussars of the Guard, and had demolished a number of peasant hovels, which were to be found in the area. I put to work a detachment of pioneers under the orders of Baron Salza and, by the activities of this young officer, the Duke had the satisfaction of seeing the bridge quickly constructed, roads laid out and our columns start to march on with some facility.[7]

Once this bridge was completed the Russian Army began to cross the river, and resumed its march along the Moscow Road. Ermolov continues:

Meanwhile, the 17th Division of Lieutenant General Olsufiev and the exhausted regiments of Adjutant General Baron Korf's rearguard went to reinforce our right, which was some distance from the enemy's attacks. The enemy batteries were increased in the centre, but the Chernigov, Murmsk and Selenginsk regiments of the 3rd Division fearlessly held their ground and repulsed the enemy who fled in disorder to the main road and disorganised the French troops deployed there. At this moment, Flugel Adjutant Colonel Kikin serving as duty general, my adjutant Lieutenant Grabbe of the Life Guard Horse Artillery and General Miloradovitch's adjutant, Staff Rotmeister Dejunker, who was attached to me, rallied our troops, led a bayonet attack and quickly cleared the road, restoring communications between our various units. Failing in its designs, the enemy directed its last attack against our right. Our battery of four guns was destroyed and, not trusting the exhausted regiments of the 17th Division to restore order, I personally led the Leib Grenadiers against an enemy battery, as Your Excellency witnessed yourself. Acting with competence and courage, Colonel Zheltukhin overthrew everything in his path. I had already reached the battery when devastating canister fire routed my gallant regiment. However, the enemy attacks ceased. My regiment returned to its position and a fierce exchange of musket fire began. The Ekaterinoslav Grenadiers arrived to reinforce my troops and the regiments of the 17th Division were now mostly deployed as tirailleurs. Major General Tuchkov overwhelmed a strong enemy column but, carried away by this success, he was captured. Despite intense enemy fire, Lieutenant General Konovnitsyn drove the enemy back on the right and retained the field. He then established his outposts, withdrew the artillery and troops in complete order and we retreated to Dorogobouxh, joining the 2nd Army.[8]

While Ney was occupying the Russians, Murat's cavalry was trying to outflank them. Fortunately for the Russians the woods and marshes which had impeded them earlier now prevented Murat's cavalry from outflanking them.

According to Lowenstern, who wrongly credits Junot's corps for this action,

At this juncture, the enemy cavalry of Junot's Corps, started to appear in force upon our left wing. General Uvarov placed some regiments of Hussars at that point. It was not sufficient ... The General in Chief, completely occupied in the centre, did not order this movement soon enough. I therefore pressed General Uvarov to send all his light cavalry to this point, remarking to him [on] the danger that all the army was running if the French were allowed to seize the heights to our left. He would have none of it, assuring me that the terrain was unfavourable.

There was not a moment to lose. We were in imminent danger. I galloped back to the Commander in Chief, to make him see the urgency with which our light cavalry should be set in motion to carry our left.

Indignant that General Uvarov had not appreciated it himself, he sent me back to him with the order for a general advance, and with the utmost speed, with all our light cavalry. That was done and, as the body moved up through a swamp many horses becoming enmired whereupon it was vigorously charged, but because they had sufficient force, they were able to stand and make a charge against the enemy in their turn, throwing them back and giving our right and centre the time to withdraw in good order ... Our grenadiers worked marvels. Colonel Jeltoukhine with the grenadiers du corps (combined grenadiers) made several charges with the bayonet.[9]

After marching around the Russian countryside for three days, Junot's corps finally put in an appearance on the battlefield, but did nothing. According to contemporary and modern historians of the battle, if Junot had moved faster with his VIII Corps, then the Russians would have been trapped.

When Murat came across Junot's corps he found that his infantry had piled arms and were resting; on hearing of Junot's actions that day, Napoleon declared: 'Junot has let the Russians escape, he is losing the campaign for me.' However, it is the Russian General Paskevitch who comes to Junot's defence: 'They attributed failure of their attempts this day to a mistake of General Junot who was not able to turn our left flank, but I think that this turning movement was not even possible behind the marshes.' Paskevitch added 'In our retreat from Valutino, the Poles found the chance to show us their hatred. In sight of us they killed the Russian wounded prisoners.'[10]

The fighting continued long into the night. The French lost approximately 7,000 men, while the Russian casualties amounted to 6,000 men, but the Russian Army once again was able to slip away. In one of the charges, General Paul Tuchkov (III) had been wounded and captured while fighting General Gudin's 4th Division at the head of Ekaterinoslav Grenadier Regiment, and the French general was killed.

With Smolensk abandoned the truce between Bagration and Barclay ended. On 20 August, Bagration wrote to Arakcheev about his disagreements with Barclay, the letter partly quoted on page 76.

I imagine that the Minister has already made his report on the abandoning of Smolensk. It is distressing, heart breaking, and the whole army is in despair. To think that we abandoned the most important position unnecessarily... The enemy has lost masses. Napoleon was right up against it and compelled to make promises and give large sums of money to the commanders to capture the positions, yet they were repulsed everywhere.

Our artillery and my cavalry did marvels. The enemy was hard pressed. What would it have cost us to hold on for two days longer? They would have left of their own accord, because there was no water for the horses or men. He gave me his word he would not retreat. That is no way to fight. We shall lead the enemy right up to the walls of Moscow...

Barclay has no grounds for complaint against me; I am not only perfectly polite, but docile too, even though I am senior to him. It is sad, but I love my Sovereign and benefactor, and I obey. The misfortune is to see the Tsar trust a magnificent army to such people! Bear in mind that our retreat has cost us more than 15,000 men from exhaustion or sickness, and a battle would not have cost us as much. And what with Mother Russia say about our cowardice? And why has so good and dear a country been delivered to Vandals? Why does she inspire in her children only disgust and contempt? Why on earth are we afraid, and of whom? It is not my fault if the Minister is a feeble, cowardly, muddle-headed dawdler – everything that is worst. The whole army weeps over it, and condemns him out of hand.[11]

In another letter, Bagration wrote that he was 'not to blame that the Minister [Barclay] is irresolute, cowardly, senseless and slow, that he has every bad quality. The entire army weeps, and curses him to death.'

He knew it would be shown to the Tsar.

Notes

1 Sir Robert Kerr Porter, *Campaign of 1812* pp.109–110
2 *Journal of Prince Eugene de Wurttemberg* pp.9–10
3 *Lowenstein Memoires du general major russe* p.229
4 Sir Robert Wilson, *The French Invasion of Russia* p.107
5 Ermolov, *Zapiski 1812* pp.59–65
6 Wilson, *The French Invasion of Russia* pp.107–109
7 Lowenstein, *Memoires du general major russe* pp.226–228
8 Ermolov, *Zapiski 1812* pp.143–145
9 Lowenstein, *Memoires du general major russe* p.227
10 Quoted in *1812 v vosponinanye* pp.98–99
11 Quoted in Brett-James *1812* pp.96–97

8

KUTUZOV!

While the army was retreating, the country was mobilising for its defence; regiments of militia or Opolchenye were being raised. The militia had been raised in 1807, but the war was over before they could see action. Now serfs flocked to the colours. Smolensk offered Alexander 20,000 militiamen to reinforce his army, while the province of Moscow raised 34,867 men, Kaluga raised another 15,370.[1] During his stay in Moscow Alexander wrote on 26 July:

> The dispositions in Moscow are excellent, the Government of Moscow has offered me 80,000 men. The difficulty lies in arming them, because, to my great astonishment, we have no muskets left, whereas in Vilna you seemed to think that we had an abundant supply of them. For the time being, I shall form large detachments of cavalry, armed with pikes. I shall see to it that the infantry also are supplied with them, until we can obtain muskets.[2]

Rostopchin, the Governor of Moscow wrote: 'in 24 days the militia was ready, divided into companies and provided with attire; but as there were not enough muskets, we armed them with pikes, which were useless and harmless.' The arsenal at the Kremlin, which was full of muskets, does not appear to have been touched.

At the end of July, the nobles of St Petersburg asked Kutuzov to raise and command their province's Opolchenye. With the invasion of Russia, Kutuzov surely hoped that he would be offered a role with the army, which would suit his experience. So at first he refused, but then after further persuasion from the nobility, and with no better offers, he reluctantly agreed.

With the retreat from Smolensk, the dispute between Barclay and Bagration had escalated and it became increasingly obvious that a new commander had to be found. But who could the Tsar appoint?

Bagration outranked Barclay as senior general, but Barclay outranked Bagration as Minister of War. Furthermore, the Tsar hated Bagration because he had a

1812: Russia's Patriotic War

relationship with his sister against Alexander's wishes, while Barclay was seen as a traitor to the Motherland and the army because of his strategy during the campaign.

On 12 August, General Count Shuvalov wrote to the Tsar exaggerating the unrest in the army:

> If Your Majesty would not give both armies a single commander, then I must attest on my honour and conscience that everything may be irrevocably lost ... The army is so dissatisfied that even the rank and file openly complain. The army has not the least confidence in the present commander ... The supply system is badly organised, the soldiers are often without food, the horses have been without oats for days. The commander-in-chief is entirely responsible for this state of affairs; he plans the marches so badly that *l'intendant general* cannot do a thing. General Barclay and Prince Bagration do not get along; the latter is justly dissatisfied ... A new commander is necessary, one over both armies and Your Majesty should appoint him immediately; otherwise, Russia is lost.[3]

On 17 August, the day Alexander received Shuvalov's letter, it was clear to the Tsar that the Russian high command was in disarray and that a supreme commander was needed. He appointed a committee to examine the question of who was to command the combined armies. Generals Bagration, Bennigsen, Tormasov, Dokhturov and Pahlen, were all considered and rejected.

Finally they decided upon Kutuzov, who although 67 years old, was the obvious candidate. The committee reported their findings to Alexander that evening, but it was not until 20 August that the Tsar finally signed his commission. The Tsar wrote to Kutuzov:

> Mikhail Illarionovich, your well known military talents, your patriotism and the repeated examples of splendid heroism which you have shown us, fully entitle you to the confidence I hereby place in you. Choosing you for this important task, I pray to Almighty God to bless your deeds and the glory of Russian arms, and to justify the hopes our country places in you. Assuring you of my favour, Alexander.[4]

On the same day, the Tsar wrote to Barclay and Bagration informing them of his decision. Barclay received the news on 27 August and was deeply hurt by it. On 29 August he wrote to Alexander

> Had I been guided by blind, senseless ambition Your Imperial Majesty would have received reports of battles and even so, the enemy would be at the gates of Moscow, because we did not have sufficient forces to resist him.[5]

Before Kutuzov left St Petersburg, according to the *Moscow Gazette*

> The Commander in Chief of the Russian armies, Prince Kutuzov, conformable to the duties of a Christian, went the evening preceding his departure for the armies to

the metropolitan church of Kazan to implore the aid of the Almighty. After the Te
Deum, the priest gave to this great captain of the Russian warriors a holy cross and
some blessed water. After this he performed homage to a fine image of our Lady of
Kazan, enriched with ornaments of gold. The celebrated man, penetrated with faith,
having received this holy offering, suspended it from his neck, fervently imploring
the benediction of the Almighty, whilst the temple filled with an immense con-
course of people, shedding tears of joy and affection, blessing the hero ready to set
out. All lifted up their wishes and benedictions with veneration towards Heaven
for the sacred monarch who had purposefully entrusted the conduct of the brave
Russian warriors to that great man, so experienced in the art of war, and the true
son of his country. All hearts were filled with a firm confidence in the Russian
armies.

Kutuzov, despite his age – and girth, according to Bennigsen he had great difficulty in staying on horseback – was now seen as the saviour of Russia. Sergei
Glinka described his passage to the armies:

The removal of Kutuzov from St Petersburg to the field army was a kind of tri-
umphant procession … The inhabitants of the towns left their work and trades to
look out on the main road, [for his coach] … The honoured citizens brought bread
and salt. The clergy addressed the leader of the army with prayers. In the vicinity
of the monasteries the monks were sent to him with icons and blessings from the
saints; and the people, not finding any other means to mark their simple heartfelt
excitement, resorted to the old hospitality custom of unharnessing the horses and
conveying the carriage on themselves. The inhabitants of villages, leaving the field
work (for this was harvest time), lay in wait in the same way near the road, in order
to look, admire and with great zeal to kiss passionately the tracks left by the wheels
of the traveller … While the old bowed their grey heads to the ground. Mothers
from afar ran … knelt and with an involuntary cry lifted their babies upwards.[6]

Meanwhile, the armies continued their retreat. On 19 August, Captain Pushkin of
the Semenovski Regiment remembered that it was with some relief that the soldiers were finally allowed to undress and the cavalry unsaddled the horses. However,
this respite was short-lived because the following day they set out at 1.00am. After a
march of 47 km, they 'were very pleased to stop at the river and bathed luxuriously'.
   On 20 August, Baron Uxkull wrote:

We are on the highway to Moscow and Dorgabush; the French, who hold Smolensk,
are pursuing us with as much speed as success. We don't have even the time to rest.
We often have to abandon our dinner in order to flee. What a situation![7]

A possible battlefield was selected and then rejected; all the time they were retreating
Moscow was getting nearer and nearer. Baron Uxkull recorded on 21 August while
at Dorgabush:

We are running away like hares. Panic has seized everyone. Our courage is crushed; our march looks like a funeral procession. My heart is heavy. We are abandoning all our rich and fruitful land to the fury of an enemy who spares nothing [in] his cruelty.[8]

All the time, rumours of the French Army's atrocities continued to reach the Russians, as Baron Uxkull recorded on 22 August:

It is impossible to imagine the horrors the French are said to be committing. One hears that they're burning and desecrating churches, that the weaker sex or rather any individuals who fall into their frantic hands are sacrificed to their brutality and the satisfaction of their infernal lusts. Children, greybeards – its all the same to them – all perish beneath their blows. These rumours are producing a sensation among the peasants, who with the greatest sangfroid in the world set their juts on fire so as not to abandon them to the enemy. I see nothing but consternation, sadness and misery. This evening we went to sleep by the light of a number of such fires.[9]

The best news the Russian Imperial Guard was to hear was that 'Grand Duke Constantine has been sent back to St Petersburg by Barclay. It is a relief for us; he won't torture us any more with his exercises and orders.'[10] At every opportunity Grand Duke Constantine had held inspections and parades, forcing the exhausted guardsmen who should have been resting to clean their equipment and uniforms and to stand for hours on end.

On 21 August, at the suggestion of Colonel Toll, the army's quartermaster general, Bagration and Barclay looked at the fields near Usv'atye as a possible place to stand, but much to Colonel Toll's annoyance both generals rejected the position. This caused Colonel Toll to insult Barclay. What he said is not known, but he appears to have suggested that Barclay was incompetent. This show of disrespect was too much for Bagration, who rounded on him:

If you cannot choose a position, that is not to say that others cannot also! How dare you, you unlicked cub, address the commander-in-chief so? He owes his position to his great qualities, and deserves every consideration. I am his senior, but I set the example by serving under him. But you think that you honour him by serving under him. Yet it is the other way. It is disgraceful that a young big head like you should use such language towards the man on whom depends the fate of the army and the empire. Thank his generosity that worse does not befall you, for if I had my way I would change that blue ribbon [of the Order of Knight of St. Andrew] for a common soldier's belts![11]

The generals might have called Barclay incompetent and his actions treasonous, the soldiers might also have complained about the retreat, but the 'mutiny of the generals', as it has been called, was for high ranking officers only, not a mere colonel. After Bagration's outburst there was an embarrassed silence among the generals' staff.

Bagration suggested a possible position near Dorogobouzh, but when the generals saw the position, it was also rejected and so the retreat continued. On leaving Dorogobouzh, according to I. Radozhitski, a member of the artillery, 'the soldiers were disappointed, looking downcast … Everybody was concerned for the future of the army.'[12]

The Grande Armée was also suffering, Napoleon needed peace, and quickly. On 25 August, Paul Tuchkov, who had been captured at Lubino, was summoned to see Napoleon. Napoleon asked Tuchkov to deliver a letter to Alexander proposing that peace talks should begin. Tuchkov refused to take it, which would result in two years of captivity for the general and the continuation of the war.

Kutuzov arrived at army headquarters on 29 August and the army's morale soared, Nadezhda Durova rejoiced: 'Kutuzov has arrived! Soldiers, officers, generals – all are ecstatic. Misgivings have given way to calm and confidence. Our entire camp is ebullient and imbued with courage.'[13] Glinka saw the same: 'The pleasure of the troops is indescribable … the military conversation around the fires is more joyful. The smoky fields of the bivouacs start to be filled with songs.'[14]

The following day, Glinka wrote in a letter that Kutuzov:

Went around the regiments for the first time. The soldiers began to fuss, started to clean themselves up, to move one after the other to form up. 'It is not necessary! It does not matter' said the Prince [Kutuzov]. 'I have only come to see whether you are healthy my children! A soldier on campaign does not need to think about the parade. It is necessary to have a rest after work and to prepare for victory' … When His Highness examined a regiment, an eagle soared above him … all the troops cried 'Ura!' On this day the commander in chief ordered all the regiments to celebrate with prayers to the Divine Mother and that the icons of her held by the army be used to make a new proper ark.[15]

Some of the senior officers were not so happy to see Kutuzov's return. They remembered their humiliating defeat at the Battle of Austerlitz (2 December 1805). Although the Tsar had been blamed for the defeat, they believed that Kutuzov had not done enough to protest against the battle plan, which had been proposed by the Austrians, and that he had sulked during the battle.

Kutuzov confirmed Barclay and Bagration in their positions as commanders of the First and Second Armies. Clausewitz observed 'No one doubted that the battle would take place soon and would halt the French offensive.'[16] However, the retreat continued, but now – as it was Kutuzov who was retreating – it had to be for strategic reasons, rather than treasonous ones. A Russian officer by the name of Liprandi who was attached to the staff of the 6th Corps, seems to have had a sharp eye turned on this confused picture of events:

I venture to conclude that neither before nor until Moscow itself did we have any defined plan of action. Everything happened according to circumstances. When the fore was distant, our leaders showed determination to fight a general battle, and according to all calculations they thought they would win. Once the foe approached, everything changed. The retreat resumed, and this too was justified by accurate calculations. The whole immense correspondence of Barclay and Kutuzov himself clearly proves that they themselves did not know what they would or should do.[17]

On 30 August, 2,000 reinforcements arrived under the command of General Miloradovich and a few days later the army arrived near a little village called Borodino.

Notes

1   Other provinces were Ryazan, Vladimir, Vologda, Olonets, Nizhniy Novgorod, Penza, Simbirsk and Kazan, Poltava, Chernigov.
2   Quoted in Tarle, *Napoleon's Invasion of Russia 1812* p.118
3   Quoted in Dubrovin, *Patriotic War in Letters of Contemporaries*, pp.71–73.
4   Bragin, *Kutuzov* p.59
5   Quoted in Tarle, *Napoleon's Invasion of Russia* p.126
6   Sergei Glinka, *Iz Zapisok o 1812 goda* pp.30–31
7   Baron Uxkull, *Arms and the Woman* p.74
8   Ibid, p.75
9   Ibid, p.75
10 Ibid, p.75
11 Ermolov, *Zapiski 1812* p.67
12 I. Radozhitsky, *Poxodnie zapiski artilerista s 1812 po 1816* (Moscow, 1835) I, pp. 125, 129.
13 Durova, *The Cavalry Maiden* p.142
14 Glinka's *Pisma* 18 August 1812 pp.40–41
15 Glinka's *Pisma* 20 August 1812 p.41
16 Quoted in Brett James, *1812* p.113
17 Quoted in Eugene Tarle's *Napoleon's Invasion of Russia* p.63

THE BATTLE OF THE SHEVANDINO
REDOUBT

'Here am I in a palace of greenery, lying outstretched on my coat … I feel a pleasant satisfaction', wrote Baron Uxkull on 3 September. After months of retreat a battlefield had finally been found and the Russians were excited by the prospect of finally making a stand, as Mitarevski recalled: 'With most of the army of Field Marshal Kutuzov having arrived, there spread the rumour that there was to be a general battle … [we wait] with impatient anticipation … from the general to the soldier.'

Baron Uxkull also knew the long awaited battle was imminent and wrote in his diary:

This evening I am submitting myself to the higher powers; I clasp my hands and pray fervently! May the Almighty grant victory to the Russian Army; may He give me strength and fortitude at the decisive moment; may He give me the courage to endure the blows of my fate, if I am put to the test; and finally may He protect my absent family and friends.[1]

At least three high-ranking officers, Kutuzov, Bennigsen and Toll, claimed to have chosen the rolling fields south of the village of Borodino for a battlefield. Writing to the Tsar, Kutuzov stated: 'the position … is one of the best to be found in the vicinity. The weak point of this position is on the left flank and I will try and correct it.' However, Bagration and Ermolov thought the position a bad one – Clausewitz agreed and had to admit that 'Russia is very poor in positions.'

The Russians drew up in front of the River Kalocha, which runs south of the New Moscow/Smolensk Road, until it reaches the town of Borodino when it flows under the road and then forks away to the north-east. In places the river was easily fordable, but in other areas the riverbank was 5 metres high. The town of Borodino, which was to mark the centre of the Russian position, was fortified with loopholes being cut into the houses. Just before the bridge over the Kalocha was a tributary stream called the Stonitz, which ran south of the main road. Farther up the hill, between the main road and the Stonitz was the village of Gorki.

About a mile or so on, on the opposite bank of the Kalocha were the villages of Dorodino, Fomkino and Akinshina. In the centre of the two Russian armies stood the village of Semenovkoe, which had been destroyed by the Russians to make an earthwork. This would become known as Raevski's Redoubt.

Further south, where the Semenovka stream forks into two, three more earthworks were to be built, known as Bagration's fleches. The 2nd Army's southern or left flank was anchored on the village of Utitsa, which was situated on the Old Smolensk Road, which ran from east to west. A large wood around the village also helped to protect this flank. The Russian's right flank was protected by the Moscova River, which flows north-east about a mile from the Russian position.

On the evening of 4 September, a pentagonal fortification, known as the Shevandino redoubt, was constructed on the Russians' left flank, by the River Kolocha. This redoubt was large enough to house the 12 guns of the 12th Battery Company, under the command of Lieutenant Colonel Vinsper, although according to Count Sievers it was the 9th Horse Artillery Company that occupied the redoubt. However, by midday on the following day, when elements of the Grande Armée began to appear, it was still not finished.

The popular theory as to why the Russians built this redoubt was that it was to be used as a forward observation position, but a regiment or two of Cossacks would have been enough to observe the enemy. Indeed that was one of their main duties. Moreover, why did the Russians put up such a fight on 5 September for an observation post? The Russians put a lot of effort in to building this redoubt at the expense of the other fortifications, and any regiment which garrisoned it would have been isolated and suffer heavy losses for no purpose. The clue is that before the battle, Kutuzov referred to the redoubt as being on his left flank and so it was almost certainly constructed to reinforce his left, as he had written to the Tsar, 'the weak point of this position is on the left flank and I will try and correct it.' Although at some point during 5 September, the Russian line was pulled back to the position it would hold on 7 September, the day of the Battle of Borodino. It was only then that it began being referred to as a forward observation position.

Neverovski's 27th Division, were deployed near the redoubt. The Odessa and Simbirsk Infantry Regiments being in the first line and the Vilenski and Tarnopol Infantry Regiments in the second line. The 5th, 6th, 41st, 42nd 49th and 50th Jager Regiments were deployed in a skirmish line from Aleksinki farm to the river Koloch, and from Dorodino to Dorodino Grove. To the north of Dorodino were the Kharkov and Kiev Dragoon Regiments and behind Dorodino were two squadrons of Ahtirsk Hussars. To the south of the redoubt was an eight-gun battery of the 9th Horse company, who were to support the Jagers in the town. On the right of the redoubt was a battery of 26 guns made up of part of the 9th Horse Company and the 21st, 23rd and 47th Light Artillery Companies. In reserve was Major General Duki's 2nd Cuirassier Division and further back was the 2nd Grenadier Division under Prince Karl von Mecklenburg. In the village of Semenovski was Major General Vorontsov's combined grenadier brigade, a total of about 18,000 men. The remainder of the Russian Army drew up along the Kolocha river.

On 5 September, Major General Count Sievers who commanded the rearguard of the 2nd Western Army took up position on the left flank. He would later report to Kutuzov, that the enemy 'appeared in large columns of cavalry, infantry and artillery and obviously revealed their intention to attack the left flank of the army.'

This was the French advanced guard under the command of Murat, marching along the Old Smolensk Road. They attacked and occupied the village of Akinshino, before proceeding to the town of Shevardino. Finding the Russians were preparing for battle Murat sent word to Napoleon, who hurried up to this advance position.

Meanwhile, Murat sent the 1/57th Infantry regiment to capture Dorodino, while another battalion of Compans' Division was sent to occupy the left bank of the Kolocha, near the town of Fomkino. The remaining regiments of Compans' Division were drawn up near Fomkino.

The 61st Line Regiment, four battalions of 57th Line and a combined battalion of Voligeurs under Compans were ordered to advance towards the Shevardino redoubt on the south-west side. The 25th and 111th Line Regiments were to attack the town, before attacking the redoubt on the left side. This force was to be supported by an artillery battery deployed at Dorodino, drawn from the artillery of the 1st and 2nd Reserve Cavalry Corps, part of the Guards artillery and 24 guns of Polish artillery. Also the artillery of Morand's and Friant's Divisions and 14 guns of Gerard's 3rd Infantry Division, in all about 200 guns also added their weight to the French bombardment of the redoubt and the forces surrounding it.

The 1st battalion, 57th Line regiment advanced towards Dorodino, and after a skirmish with the Russians jagers, was forced to retire. After receiving reinforcement from the 3rd Battalions and a company of the 57th Regiment, the 1st Battalion counterattacked. Second Lieutenant Andreev of 50th Jagers, whose company had deployed close to a wood recalls:

> Then an enemy column appeared on the field to the right of us … A column of the Tarnopol Regiment of our division, with music and songs (that is the first and last time I saw this), attacked. I saw the bayonet charge. The slaughter was short, and the colonel, their commander, was wounded … The regiment began to waver. His place was taken up, the regiment again made a bayonet charge and … drove away the enemy and relieved us.

The remainder of the 57th with the battalion of Voltigeurs also launched an attack, which in turn was met by the Russian jagers, supported by artillery. While they were distracted, the New Russia Dragoon Regiment encircled the voltigeurs, cutting them off from a small wood near to Dorodino, and from the 57th Regiment. Bruyer's 1st Light Cavalry Division charged the Russian dragoons and combined with the fire from the voltigeurs, forced them to withdraw.

After heavy fighting, which included house to house clearance, the French drove the Russians out of the burning town of Dorodino.

Farther to the north, on the Old Smolensk Road, Poniatowski's Polish Corps began to arrive and encountered some of Platov's Cossacks. However, this did not develop into a general engagement because Poniatowski was ordered south to join in the attack on the redoubt. After leaving a detachment on the Old Smolensk Road, Poniatowski pushed aside the Russian jagers in the brushwood, the Kiev Dragoons and the two squadrons of Ahtirsk Hussars, while Murat's cavalry kept communications open between Compans' Division and Poniatowski's Poles.

Later Sievers reported to Kutuzov: 'Colonel Emanuel with the Kiev Dragoon Regiment entrusted to him, twice attacked the enemy flankers and the supporting columns, and pushed them back.'

The Russian and French skirmishers and artillery began to exchange fire, whereupon

Two squadrons of the Ahtirsk Hussar Regiment, situated to cover the light battery under the command of Captain Aleksandrovicha, attacked one of the infantry columns approaching towards the battery, overthrowing it. Captain Bibikov ... stopped the enemy's flankers intending to turn the flank, all attempts by the enemy on the Elnin Road were in vain. The enemy passed in strong columns through the river Kolocha from the right of the position on the Smolensk Road, to the village and woods in front of where our jagers was situated. In order to support our jagers from the wood and village [who were] already withdrawing, I ordered the Novorossiiski Dragoon Regiment under the command of Major Terenina to enter the space between the wood and village and attack the enemy infantry columns that were supporting the tirailleurs ... The 1st squadron under the command of Captain Count Sievers attacked the first infantry column, the 2nd under the command of Lieutenant Stanukovicha the other [column]. The 3rd under the command of Major Borgraf protected these squadrons from enemy cavalry. The 4th under the command of Major Milfelda took the enemy tirailleurs in the rear. Every squadron enjoyed the greatest of success ...

The New Russia Dragoon Regiment overturned the enemy ... after the attack Major Terenin reformed the regiment quickly and again courageously attacked the advancing enemy cavalry, who were overturned, pursued [and] destroyed, but encountering the advancing infantry from the woods on all sides they were not supported by our infantry, who retreated from the woods and village towards the redoubt ... This attack covered the withdrawal of our infantry and drew off the guns from the nearest heights. The losses of this regiment in both these attacks were very considerable.[2]

By now more divisions of Davoust's 1st Corps had begun to arrive. Friant's 2nd Division was deployed to protect the left flank of Compans' Division, while Morand's 1st Division was to occupy the space between the Kolocha and the town of Shevardino and threaten the rear and right flank of Gorchakov's troops. It was supported by Gerard's 3rd Division positioned on the main road. Between the Divisions were skirmishers and behind Compans' was Girardin's light cavalry Division.

At about 5.00pm, Compans' 5th Division began its attack on the redoubt; the 61st Line Regiment, formed in columns of battalions, attacked the northern part. In front of the 61st was a skirmish line formed from three companies of the 2nd Battalion of voltigeurs. The other company occupied a hill, known as the Dorodino's Barrow, supported by a small battery of artillery of between eight and twelve guns.

Meanwhile the 57th, also in columns of battalions, and covered by the composite battalion of voltigeurs, attacked the south. The remainder of the Division, the 25th and 111th Line Regiments were to attack the Russians troops to the north of the redoubt. Under the heavy bombardment from the French guns the Russian artillerymen began to withdraw their guns accompanied by the 27th Division. Taking advantage of the withdrawal of the Russians, the French advanced. Major General Lowenstern ordered the Russians to return to the redoubt and they arrived just in time to stop the redoubt falling into French hands.

The French columns deployed into line and a heavy and lengthy exchange of musketry began. General Compans ordered a bayonet charge, but the noise of musket fire was such that nobody could hear him. Compans then galloped over to where the reserve was and led two battalions, in conjunction with 61st Regiment, in a bayonet charge on the redoubt.

When the French entered the redoubt, a hand-to-hand fight developed between the French and the Russian artillerymen who were still protecting their guns. At 7.00pm the redoubt was in French hands. Paskevitch was involved in this fighting:

> They attacked my left flank. I sent two Jager Regiments with 12 guns to the brushwood, near to a ravine, while the other two regiments of my division went to reinforce the jagers. They held on until evening, the enemy could not overthrow the jagers of my brigade, and although of the 12 guns of Colonel Zhiravski many were put out of action and half of the horses were lost, the artillery nevertheless was not withdrawn. The fighting had cost me about 800 men and my horse was wounded by a bullet.[3]

The sun was setting as the Russians launched a counter-attack, composed of the 2nd Grenadier Division and Combined Grenadier Battalion, supported by the 2nd Cuirassier Division. Three times the Russians recaptured the redoubt only to be forced out again. Though by this time there was nothing left of the redoubt itself, only hundreds of dead and wounded bodies marked where it once had stood.

> Lieutenant General Golitsin with all the cavalry of the 2nd Army was arranged in battle order, behind the batteries and the redoubt on the left flank. On account of reinforcements the enemy advanced, in spite of the actions of the artillery. The redoubt was abandoned by our battery of artillery at the same time as part of the covering infantry was withdrawn. Meanwhile the light artillery on the left side of the redoubt continued in action, the artillery of Major General Levenshtev, seeing the withdrawal of the battery's guns, without delay returned to the redoubt and withdrew the infantry battalions. The enemy was stopped for some time on

its approach, but having received reinforcements captured the redoubt. Although the infantry who defended it were not under my command, I tried to persuade and encourage them by my own example, and forced the infantry battalions to recapture the redoubt. The attack was supported by several grenadier regiments of the 2nd [Grenadier] Division which Lieutenant General Gorchakov himself led against the enemy. From my position I perceived the enemy's daring intention of attacking our infantry in the flank and rear with two strong columns that were quickly moving between the redoubt and the village [of Shevandino]. I rushed to the right flank of the cavalry line that was under my command [finding] two newly arrived cuirassier regiments deploying in front of the line. Their commander, the gallant Colonel Tolbruzin met me and I directed him to advance towards the already disordered enemy infantry column that was closest to him. In the first line of the Little Russia Cuirassier Regiment, he attacked one of the columns, and instantly overturned and pursued it as far as the enemy's battery, which this brave regiment seized, capturing the guns [and] presenting them to their commander. The Kharkov and Chernigov Dragoon Regiments were ordered by me to support the cuirassiers, these covered their right flank, which was threatened by the second infantry column. From the other side of the village appeared two squadrons of the Chernigov Dragoon Regiment under the command of Musin Pushkin, who attacked this column and overturned it, seizing two guns of the battery which the enemy had started to deploy to reinforce their infantry, but had not had time to fire one shot. Coming to a stop the cuirassiers and dragoon squadrons, having pursued the enemy, formed up, the enemy not daring to make the slightest attempt on these regiments.[4]

The Little Russia and Gluhov Cuirassiers attacked and pushed back the 25th Line, who began to retire. Cornet Dreyling of the Little Russia Cuirassiers recorded: 'Our regiment stormed the enemy battery of eight guns and beat it off. Four guns have been taken as trophies, the other four had been dismounted from the gun carriages and left in the place'.[5] Other accounts give the number of guns taken as between three and six.

As the fighting continued around the redoubt a gap opened up between Friant's and Compans' divisions, and in the growing darkness the Kharpov dragoons took advantage of this space and attacked the 111th Line. The dragoons routed some skirmishers, but while pursuing them were attacked and routed themselves.

During this time the Ekaterinoslav and Military Order Cuirassiers attacked the French to the south of the redoubt, probably forcing part of the 57th to form square, before attacking some Polish skirmishers at the edge of the wood. With the heavy firing from the Polish and French infantry and the French 1st Cavalry Corps advancing, the cuirassiers were driven off. At about 9.00pm the battle finally ended, with the French in possession of the Russian position. Neverovski:

At night I was ordered to abandon the battery and withdraw back to the army. In this battle I lost almost all my brigade chiefs, field and commissioned officers and my horse … was killed under me. The day before this battle I was given 4000 recruits to fill the division. I had 6000, and came out with three [thousand]. Prince Bagration sent me a note of gratitude and said 'You saved me.'[6]

While the battle for the Shevandino redoubt raged all afternoon and evening, the Russian Imperial Guard was involved in more peaceful activities, as Captain Pushkin of the Semenovski Regiment recalled:

The left wing under the command of Prince Bagration started a violent battle, which continued until night. While the battle was going on, in our camp we prayed for the blessings of God to be sent down to our troops and prayed for victory in the forthcoming battle.[7]

It is clear by Kutuzov's despatch of 5 September that he planned a defensive battle:

[We] will wait for the enemy's attack at the village of Borodino, where they will accept battle … In this battle order I intend to draw upon myself the enemy's forces and to operate in conformity with his movements. Unable to be at all points simultaneously, I must rely on the experience of Messieurs the Commanders in Chief of the Armies [Barclay and Bagration], and therefore I leave them to act at their own discretion to secure the enemy's defeat. I place my hopes in the Almighty and in the bravery and cool headedness of the Russian troops.

If, happily, the enemy forces are repulsed, I shall give my own orders regarding their pursuit. I deem it not superfluous to warn Messieurs the Commanders in Chief that the reserves should be husbanded as long as possible, for the general who husbands his reserves as long as possible is not yet defeated.[8]

Kutuzov would indeed leave many of the decisions to Barclay and Bagration. However, despite his advice to husband reserves, his dispositions made it necessary that these reserves would be used earlier in the battle than was intended, because Kutuzov had assumed that Napoleon would attack Barclay's stronger army, rather than Bagration's much weaker one.

It had been the practice for artillery officers to save their guns before they were overrun by the enemy, which meant that the guns were often withdrawn before the enemy came into effective range. Now, the commander of the artillery of the army, Major General Kutaisov, had a very different doctrine, and he lectured his artillery commanders about it:

Fire at a range of more than 1,000 metres is ineffective; at 650 metres it is effective enough; at 400 and 200 it is murderous; at the three latter ranges our new canister can be used. Consequently, when the enemy is at the first range, one should fire slowly, to have enough time to aim the piece more accurately and to make his movements difficult; at the second range, one is to fire faster, to stop or, at least, to slow down his approach, and at the shorter ranges, to hit as fast as possible, to overthrow or to destroy him ... In conclusion I say that there is nothing more shameful to an army than unnecessary waste of ammunition, which one must try to use so that each shot will cause the maximum damage to an enemy.[9]

With the Shevandino redoubt in enemy hands, the French could now easily deploy men on the fields opposite the Russian left flank by using the Old Smolensk Road, so Kutuzov ordered Bagration's 2nd Army to pull back. The much narrower Semenovka stream now marked the front of the Russian Army.

After the fierce battle for the Shevandino redoubt on 5 September, apart from some skirmishing on the left flank, the following day was an anti-climax. Mitarevski wrote: 'Early in the morning one could hear some firing on the left flank, but all day passed calmly, at least for us.'

It was only on 6 September that the Russians began strengthening their position where the Semenovka forks into two streams. They now started digging three earthworks known as the 'fleches'. These were in a V shape and had pits dug in front of them. Bagration's Army was given the task of defending these. Another earthwork, the Grand, or Raevski, redoubt was also constructed. The reason given for the late start to the construction of these fortifications were that they were waiting for tools to arrive, but there had been enough tools to construct the Shevandino redoubt.

To encourage his army Kutuzov decided to parade the Icon of the Holy Virgin of Smolensk around the army Glinka:

> The commander in chief ordered it to be carried all along the line ... The clergy accompanied it with chasuble censer smoke, glimmers of candles, and the air filled with singing and as the sacred icon passed ... the army of 100,000 fell upon their knees and bowed their heads ... Everywhere the sign of the cross was made, in places sobbing was heard. The commander in chief, surrounded by his staff, encountering the icon bent to the ground.

Another Russian officer, N. Sukhanin, was cheered by the effect:

> Placing myself next to the icon, I observed the soldiers who passed by piously. O faith! How vital and wondrous is your force! I saw how soldiers, coming up to the picture of the Most Holy Virgin, unbuttoned their uniforms and took [out their] ... last coin as an offering for candles. I felt, as I looked at them, that we would not give way to the enemy on the field of battle. It seemed as though after praying, each of us gained new strength; the live fire in the eyes of all the men showed the conviction that with God's help we would vanquish the enemy.[10]

Kutuzov then gave a rousing speech to the soldiers:

> 'Brothers and fellow soldiers,
> behold before you, in those sacred representations of the holy objects of our worship, an appeal which calls aloud upon heaven to unite with man against a tyrannous

troubler of the world. Not content with defacing the image of God, in the persons of millions of his creatures; this universal tyrant, this arch-rebel to all laws human and divine, breaks into the sanctuary, pollutes it with blood, overthrows its altars, tramples on its rites, and exposes the very Ark of the Lord (consecrated in these insignia of our church) to all the profanations of accident, of the elements, and of unsanctified hands. Fear not then, but that the God whose altars have been so insulted by the very worm his Almighty fiat had raised from the dust, fear not that He will not be with you! That He will not stretch forth His shield over your ranks; and with the sword of Michael fight against His enemies!

This is the faith in which I will fight and conquer! This is the faith in which I would fight and fall, and still behold the final victory with my dying eyes. Soldiers! Do your part. Think on the burning sacrifice of your cities – think of your wives, your children, looking to you for protection, think on your Emperor, your lords, regarding you as the sinews of their strength; and, before tomorrow's sun sets, write your faith and your fealty on the field of your country with the life's blood of the invader and his legions!'

The shout that followed this address assured the veteran [Kutuzov] that his brave troops only wanted the signal to be given, to realize on that spot his most devoted wishes for Russian safety and Russian glory.[11]

Glinka continues:

When the prayers finished, several heads lifted upwards and saw an eagle soar! The commander in chief looked upwards, catching sight of the eagle floating in the air and immediately bared his grey-haired head. The nearest to him gave a shout, 'Ura!' and this shout was repeated by all the troops.

The eagle continued to float, the 70-year-old leader accepting it as a good omen, stood bareheaded. This was a unique picture!

After the parade 'Everyone went away as though inspired and ready for battle, ready to die for his fatherland.'[12] However, not every soldier took part in the parade, many were deployed in a skirmish line to prevent Napoleon and his officers reconnoitring the Russians' position. Mitarevski had more pressing things on his mind than seeing the icon:

Biscuits, grits, beef and radishes were our daily food since Smolensk … other luxuries we never saw, tea was very rare, [we] scarcely had fresh rye bread, and white was even rarer. But without tobacco I was not able to manage. Smoking tobacco is the most simple little Russian pleasure and for that with joy I paid the sutler eighty kopecks assignat [paper money].

He set out to forage for something better. While both armies had been at Borodino they had eaten up all the forage in the neighbourhood, so he had to travel over a kilometre and even then , having

... stopped at several manor houses, all of them were empty and ruined under the general pretext of not supplying the French. I returned from foraging about midnight, finding all asleep, had a snack in a rough and ready fashion [and] also laid down to sleep.[13]

Despite referring to Napoleon as the Anti-Christ, some Russian officers were fascinated by him, and some of the younger officers crept forward towards the French lines to see if they could catch a glimpse of him. Meanwhile Glinka climbed to the top of the bell tower of Borodino church to see both armies. Looking towards the Russian side he could see in the distance the left wing, made up of the 2nd Western Army. Tuchkov had formed his corps near the village of Utisa in four lines. Konovnitsin's Division stood in the front and Count Stroganov's Grenadier Division behind. A strong chain of skirmishers from the 20th, 21st, 11th and 41st Jager Regiments were deployed in the coppice. On the left was the village of Semenovskoe, in front of which was an earth redoubt, which was protected by the Composite Grenadiers of Count Vorontsov and behind them, in the second line stood Neverovski's Division.

Prince Karl of Mecklenburg's 2nd Grenadier Division was deployed in two lines like 'four [living] walls', from the edge of the Semenovskoe village to the large battery. These grenadiers were supported by cavalry, in two lines. Then came the Corps of Count Sievers. The centre consisted of Doktorov's Corps. It deployed opposite Borodino in two lines of infantry, which was supported by the 3rd Cavalry Corps, which was also deployed in two lines.

To the right of Doktorov's Corps was Osterman's Corps, again in two lines. Behind them was Korf's Cavalry Corps. Baggovut's Corps formed the extreme right wing. The 1st Cavalry Corps was positioned behind the infantry of the right flank. There was also Platov with nine Regiments of Don Cossacks. This wing was commanded by Miloradovitch, under the overall command of the Barclay de Tolly.

Behind the centre was the 5th (Guards) Corps under the command of General Lavrov. This Corps was formed in three lines, the first two lines of infantry and the third cavalry. Five companies of horse artillery were positioned behind the 4th Cavalry Corps. The main reserve of artillery stood in front of the village of Psarev. All the Jagers were deployed to the front, lying down in the brushwood and occupying the various villages.

Kutuzov had set a trap by hiding a corps in the woods on the extreme left wing, which would emerge and surprise the French when they attacked. However, when Bennigsen saw this corps hidden in the woods, and not knowing of Kutuzov's plan, he ordered them into the open. Lowenstern informed Barclay de Tolly about Bennigsen's interference.

'That man will spoil everything' said Barclay de Tolly, 'He is jealous and envious. His conceit makes him think that he alone is capable of fighting battles and of bringing them to a successful close. He certainly has talent, but he wants to use it only for his own profit. The Common Sacred Cause is nothing to him, I regard him as a real pest for the army.'[14]

Looking across no-man's-land Glinka could see the French lines. At the extreme right was Poniatowski's 5th Polish Corps, then came Nansouty's, Latour-Maubourg's and Montbrun's cavalry, under Murat. Opposite to Bagration's fleches was Davoust's Corps, then Junot's and then Grouchy's Corps. Finally, the Viceroy's Corps formed the French left flank. Napoleon's Imperial Guard was deployed behind the right of Davoust's Corps.

Napoleon had crossed the Russian frontier with about 500,000 men, but on the eve of 7 September his army is estimated at between 130,000 and 188,000 men and 1,000 guns. Estimates also vary as to the numbers of the Russian Army. Glinka puts it at 113,500 men, not including the Opolchenye, plus 640 guns. A report dated 5 September puts the 1st Army's strength at 70,028, while another report on 6 September states 70,156. On 31 August the strength of Platov's Cossacks, including the Don artillery batteries, was put at 4,694, of whom about 1,000 were without horses. On 31 August the Moscow Opolchenye were said to muster 24,835 officers and men, although they had little or no training.

The strength of Bagration's army is less easy to estimate. On 31 August it mustered 34,925, but had been reinforced by 4,976 men, although it had lost about 140 men since then in rearguard actions. Then there was Karpov's Cossacks, who were with Bagration, whose numbers are unknown. In all, Kutuzov had about 134,500 officers and men. Although modern Russian historians give the figure as 155,200 for both armies.[15] Whatever the strengths of the opposing armies, the Russians themselves believed that they were outnumbered.

As darkness fell, Kutuzov feared there might be an attack on his right flank so he sent a strong detachment of Platov's Cossacks out to see if there was any movement from the French. Having scouted a large area they found nothing, except a ford over the river Kolocha, which might be of use to either side.

After the efforts of the day, the Russians began to prepare themselves for the battle that was sure to come the following day. They cleaned their uniforms as best they could. Glinka remembered that 'In the evening the officers put on … clean linen, the soldiers who had preserved for the event a white shirt did the same.' The soldiers of the Grande Armée did the same, because as one French general put it, 'one should always look one's best in front of the enemy.' The Russian officers took out their decorations to put onto their uniforms, for both friend and foe to see in the forthcoming battle. As the soldiers settled down for the night, many knew that it might be their last. Late in the night of 6–7 September Glinka sat down to write a letter.

All is silent. The Russians with a pure, faultless conscience silently sleep around the smoky fires … In the cloudy sky occasionally a stars sparkles, so all is quiet on our side.

Opposite us re the bright twinkling fires in the camp of the enemy; music, singing, trumpet calls clamour in all their different camps. Here, and exclamations is audible! There another! They truly welcome the journey in the service of Napoleon. Precisely as it was before the Battle of Austerlitz, what will be tomorrow? The wind extinguishes the candle and a dream closes my eyes, farewell.[16]

Not all the Russian line was silence. An anonymous captain, known only as Fritz, who was attached to Prince Karl of Mecklenburg's staff, spent some of the night with the Fanagoria Grenadiers:

> The soldiers were in fairly good order, and as they had had a rest during the last few days, they now sat, wrapped in their long grey [great] coats, round the fires – and often joined in chorus to sing the monotonous, melancholy, dirge-like, yet not unpleasing national songs that the Russian people are so fond of. This singing before the battle had a strange effect on me, and I listened to it for several hours until eventually I fell asleep, exhausted, besides my horse, an ugly though sturdy little chestnut, which I wanted to ride during the battle.[17]

That evening the Guard Jagers, who were stationed nearest to the enemy, were in a relaxed mood. Ermolov wrote: 'There was such carelessness in the outposts of this battalion that many soldiers were asleep, having taken off their uniforms.'[18]

Kutuzov spent the evening in an abandoned farmhouse in the village of Tatarinovo. After his staff left him alone he could be heard pacing up and down. Across no-man's-land, Napoleon also had trouble sleeping, not only was he worried that the Russians would once more slip away during the night, but he was also suffering from a bad cold. All the orders had been given, now all he could do, like the humblest soldier in his army, was to wait for dawn.

> The night passed slowly over the wakeful heads of the impatient combatants. The morning of the 7th of September at length broke, and thousands beheld the dawn for the last time. The moment had arrived when the dreadful discharge of two thousand guns was to break the expectant silence and arouse at once all the horrors of war.[19]

Notes

1 Uxkull, *Arms and the Women* p. 80
2 Sievers' report to Kutuzov quoted in *Otechestvennaya Voina 1812* pp.12–14
3 Quoted in *v Vospominaniya Sovremenailov* p.100
4 Sievers' report to Kutuzov dated 7 September 1812
5 Quoted in V.N. Zemtsov 's 'Compans' Division in the battle of the Shevardino Redoubt, 5 September 1812.'
6 *Zapiski, General Neverovski* p.79
7 *Dnevnik, Pavla Pushkin* pp.49–50
8 Bragin, *Kutuzov* pp.66–67
9 Quoted in A. and Y. Zhmodikov, *Tactics of the Russian Army of the Napoleonic Wars* pp.70–71
10 Sukhanin, 'Iz zhurnala uchastnika voiny 1812 goda' *Russkaya starina* 1912 p.281
11 Kerr Porter, *Narrative of the Campaign in Russia* pp.127–128
12 Sukhanin, 'Iz zhurnala uchastnika voiny 1812 goda' *Russkaya starina* 1912 p.281
13 Mitarevski *Vospominaniya o vonia 1812* p.57

14 Lowenstern, *Memoires du general major russe* p.269

15 Mikaberdze Borodino pp.50-53, Al'tsuller Borodino pp.22, 92, 160, and Valkovich *Feldmarshal Kutuzov,* p.66

16 Glinka, *Pisma* pp.70–71

17 Quoted in Brett James *1812* p.123

18 Ermolov, *Zapiski 1812* p.157

19 Kerr Porter, *Narrative of the Campaign in Russia* p.128

10

THE BATTLE OF BORODINO

As dawn broke on 7 September, men on both sides knew that the day they had been waiting for had finally arrived. Despite Woldemar Lowenstern's claim that the 'soldiers, officers and generals all burn with the desire to fight or die,' many dreaded the dawn, because they knew it might be their last.

To encourage his army, Napoleon, issued a proclamation:

> Soldiers! Before you, is the field you have so ardently desired! The victory depends upon you ... It will give you abundance, good winter quarters and a quick return to your country. Conduct yourselves as when at Austerlitz, at Friedland, at Vitebsk, at Smolensk, and the latest posterity will cite with pride your conduct on this day. They will say, 'He was in that great battle under the walls of Moscow!'[1]

Across no-man's-land the Russians could hear shouts of '*Vive l'Empereur*'. Shortly after, the outposts on the outskirts of Borodino reported that movement could be observed on the Russian right wing. The precise time is unclear, Colonel Bistrom in his report says it was 4.00am, but others state it was about 6 or 7.00am. Whatever the time, the alarm was given in the town of Borodino; but many of the Guard Jagers were still asleep in the houses within the town, others were taking a bath. So the jagers were slow to form up.

Suddenly from out of the fog emerged Delzon's Division on the outskirts of Borodino.

> The enemy was descending on the right side of the village in two columns, supposedly numbering 8,000. I was ordered by the Commander in Chief of the 1st Western Army to delay as long as possible [with] my regiment which occupied the settlement. In consequence of which I ordered Colonel Makarov [with the 3rd Battalion] ... to hold it. In execution of his orders Captain Petin with the 3rd

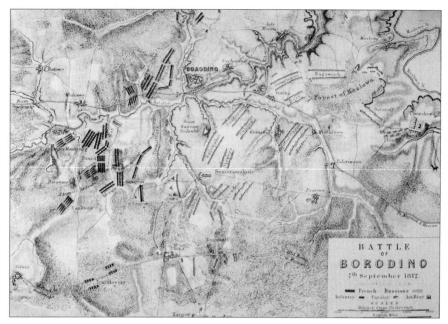

Plan of the battle of Borodino.

grenadier and the 9th Jager companies attacked the enemy with the bayonet, but by the superiority of the enemy's forces they were repulsed. Seeing the impossibility of overcoming such a numerous enemy, the above mentioned battalion was forced to retreat upon the 1st and 2nd, which was placed by me in fighting order and there were gathered the remains in reserve. The 2nd Battalion under the command of Colonel Rikter pursued the enemy, the 3rd Battalion meeting a violent battalion fire and from the 1st were despatched my skirmishers under the command of Staff-Captain Rall, which greatly assisted the retreat of the 3rd Battalion and the enemy was forced to withdraw ... [The enemy having] reinforcements the attack began again, but was met by the bayonets of the 2nd Battalion under the command of Colonel Rikter ... who courageously repulsed the enemy.[2]

Despite Colonel Bistrom's optimistic report, the Guard Jagers were driven back through Borodino. General Ermolov also recalls this action:

In less than half an hour, the entire regiment was driven back in confusion towards the bridge over the Kolocha. Clouds of enemy tirailleurs then fanned out along the left bank of the river. The 1st Jager Regiment, deployed by the bridge, swiftly counter-attacked, repulsed the enemy and rescued the Guard Jagers, who were immediately sent back to their division. Isolated from the rest of our forces, the 1st Jager Regiment was now in a dangerous situation and its commander ... was ordered to abandon Borodino, withdraw across the river [and] burn the bridge behind him.[3]

The attack was made by the French 106th Line of Prince Eugene's 4th Corps, however, encouraged by their success, many followed the Jagers across the bridge onto the
right bank of the Kolocha.

> Suddenly in Borodino the crackle of musket fire commenced, so that smoke from
> the firing began to cover the village. Shortly the departure [of our troops] from
> Borodino began in confusion ... this was in view of us and rather close, so that
> musket balls whistled about us, but with the smoke, dust and partly the fog it was
> difficult to see what was going on ...
>   ... The Jagers of the 24th Division [19th and 40th Jagers] attacked the enemy at
> bayonet point, driving them beyond the stream and pulled down the bridge. We
> artillerymen attest that the Guardsmen abandoned Borodino too quickly ... Every
> action and attack there and then was judged; even a successful artillery shot did not
> go unremarked ...
>   After the occupation of Borodino, the enemy advanced their batteries closer and
> began firing ball and grapeshot. In front was a violent exchange of musket fire and
> bullets in great numbers flew towards us.[4]

The 1st Jagers were ordered to attack the 106th Line on the right bank of the Kolocha.
The battalion commander M. M. Petrov of 1st Jagers described the action:

> When the Jagers of the Imperial Guard Regiment, having reformed upon a signal,
> marched from the Kolocha River to the rear of the 5th Corps, Colonel Karpenko
> then deployed my 1st battalion from column into line and brought up Major
> Sibirtsev's 3rd Battalion [formed] in column of attack at a distance of 15 paces from
> the rank of my battalion.
>   [There was a] mound ... in front of which the enemy troops stood, having just
> crossed [the river]. Colonel Karpenko with my battalion ... having run up at the
> mound, fired an aimed volley at the enemy with the whole line and while the
> smoke from the volley was still curling in the faces of their men, stricken and
> bewildered by the volley ... our jagers charged with the bayonet. Since the Jagers
> of the Imperial Guard intended to destroy the bridges after them [once they had
> crossed the river], they had removed about ten beams in the middle ... We pressed
> the French to the gap and into the slimy river.
>   At the same time our 3rd Battalion ... having half wheeled to the right, rushed
> from behind my [battalion] to the lower pontoon bridge, 40 paces from the upper
> one and also, after a volley from the front of the division, charged with the bayonet,
> so we slaughtered all the enemy troops [on the right bank] together with their
> general [Plauzonne] and [other] officers and having marched to the left bank of the
> Kolocha River into Borodino, drove the enemy from it.[5]

The 1st Jagers did not keep their prize for long because they were ordered to abandon Borodino and retire over the Kolocha once more, breaking up what remained
of the bridge. With the bridges at Borodino destroyed, Prince Eugene's corps turned

to the five bridges further south over the Kolocha that the French had built the day before, opposite General Raveski's Grand Redoubt.

At about the same time as Delzon's attack, a general bombardment had begun 'all along the line, between the village of Borodino as far as the extreme left'.[6] The French guns appear to have opened fire first and according to General Bennigsen, the guns of No. 4 battery in Raevski's Grand Redoubt were the first to reply, followed by the rest of the Russian artillery. Cannon balls showered down on both sides, Captain Biot of the Grande Armée wrote: 'Everything that fell beyond the second line went on to strike the third, not a shot was lost.' Baron Lejeune recalled how the Russian balls

> … furrowed our ranks with an infernal noise and an indescribable whistling. Misfortune dictated that, at this terrible outset, our reserve … cavalry were placed too close … We thus saw fall, without profit to the army, thousands of brave horse-men and excellent horses, which we could ill afford to lose.

Some shots even reached as far as where Napoleon was standing.

The French guns almost certainly had the same effect on the Russian lines. An officer in the 50th Jagers:

> The rumble of the guns at this point made such a noise that nothing else was heard until midday, the guns firing continuously. The smoke was such that it obscured the very sky. Our Jagers were little in the fighting of the morning against Ney, Murat and Davoust's Corps, our division was destroyed by the artillery.[7]

Not all French guns fired as successfully as these, shortly after the guns on Napoleon's right opened fired it was discovered that many guns had been placed out of range, and time was wasted repositioning them.

Bagration's Fleches

Before the battle the senior Russian officers, including Barclay de Tolly and Bagration, had argued with Kutuzov that Napoleon would attack the Russians' left flank; now with the majority of the army still on the right they were to be proved correct. Napoleon had deployed three entire infantry Corps against Bagration's 2nd Army, Davoust's Corps, supported by two Divisions of Junot's VIII Corps and General Ledru's Division of Ney's Corps, was to attack Bagration's Fleches. On Davoust's right was Poniatowski's Polish Corps, which was to attack the town of Utitsa, and on Davoust's left were the other divisions of Ney's Corps, which was ordered to advance on the town of Semenovskoe. It was while the 106th Line were fighting in the streets of Borodino that Napoleon ordered these three corps to advance.[8]

General Michael Worontsov's Division had been given the honour of defending the fleches. One battalion occupied each of the three fleches, while the remaining battalions were in support behind the earthworks. Twelve guns were deployed on the division's southern flank, and eight on the right, with other guns nearby. To the front of the fleches were deployed six battalions of the 6th, 49th and 50th Jagers in a skirmish line. Six more Jager battalions were deployed in the Utitsa woods nearby.

Davoust's Corp seems to have been the first to come into contact with the Russians, meeting the Jagers dispersed in the woods, who harassed the French columns. Upon emerging from the woods the French encountered the Russian guns.

> The execution wrought by our batteries was frightful and the enemy columns faded away perceptibly despite the continual reinforcements which arrived. The more effort the enemy put into the attack, the higher their casualties piled up.[9]

Despite this, the French were able to capture one of the fleches, but were driven out again. While trying to rally Compans' Division, Davoust's horse was killed under him, throwing the Marshal to the ground. A rumour quickly spread among the French that Davoust had been killed. Fortunately for the Emperor, Davoust was just badly bruised and was able to resume his position and the assault on the fleches continued.

> The whole of the French force was directed against our left flank, consequently on the fleches (defended by my division); more than a hundred pieces of artillery played some time upon us, and the greatest part of the best French infantry, under Marshals Davoust and Ney, marched straight upon us. Our fleches were stormed after a stout resistance, were retaken by us, stormed again by the French, retaken once more, and were at last lost again, because of the overpowering force employed against us.[10]

Lieutenant General Prince Eugene von Wurttemberg, the commander of the 4th Division of Baggovut's II Corps, described the loss of officers:

> Compans' 5th French Division entered part of the fortifications but could not hold it. The struggle for these fleches went on from 6 o'clock until 10 o'clock. By this time, Gorchakov, Sievers, Neverovski, Davout, Compans, Rapp (who had replaced Compans) and Desaix had been wounded and Reaumov killed. The bitterness of the fighting is witnessed by the fact that all the commanders on both sides had been hit.

Among the regiments which were called upon to assist Bagration was part of Major General Karl Sievers' 4th Reserve Cavalry Corps.

> The Novorosski Dragoon and the Ahtirsk Hussars Regiments were commanded by me to advance. The Novorossiki Dragoon Regiment under the commander of the regiment, Major Terenin ... courageously attacked the enemy and Major Terenin, setting a brave example, encouraging the lower ranks, and [although] being met by caseshot and musket fire they hacked their way through and overthrew the enemy's infantry columns. Captain Count Sievers ... and his squadron, with distinguished

bravery cut his way through the enemy's columns [and] reached the enemy's battery consisting of twelve guns. However, the regiment was unable to take away [the guns] because the enemy's cavalry, arriving with reinforcements of large numbers of infantry ... prevented this enterprise ... Captain Count Sievers was severely wounded by a bullet in the leg and a sabre cut in the head, [and his] horse was killed under him. The regiment under the cover of their flankers withdrew in order covering the withdrawal of the infantry.

[Meanwhile] the Ahtirsk Dragoon Regiment of Colonel Vasilchikov commanding the second squadron of this regiment deflected the cavalry, which circled in front of the fleches on the left flank, lready occupied by the enemy and with the two squadrons supporting them. Major Prince Kastriot rushed courageously on the enemy's cavalry, overthrowing them and after putting to flight the infantry occupying the fleches. Our infantry did not support this attack and Colonel Vasilchikov was forced to retreat to the rear of the fleches from where he blocked the enemy cavalry, which attempted several times to surround the fleches ... Major Duvanov with the 4th Squadron charged with distinguished bravery one of the the enemy's infantry columns, turned them, but was greeted by an intense musket fire from the other column and was severely wounded. Colonel Vasilchikov, with the 4th Squadron attacked the advancing enemy cavalry in the flank, turned them, pursued them as far as the enemy's battery [then] retreated with the regiment back to our battery.[11]

By now, Ney's Corps had come into action and General Duka's 2nd Cuirassier Division was sent to meet this new threat. General Alexander Tuchkov's 1st Brigade of the 3rd Division also became involved in this sector of the battlefield. Bagration appealed for reinforcements. Barclay ordered Baggovut's 2nd Corps to support Bagration, but it was on the Russian's extreme right wing and so it would take at least an hour and a half before the first elements of his corps would reach the left wing. Until then Bagration's 2nd Army would have to hold out.

Ney came up just after Davoust with his III Corps (10th, 11th and 25th Divisions) and their weight decided the contest for the three fleches. The troops then advanced against Semenovskoe but were vigorously opposed by Prince Karl von Mecklenburg's 2nd Grenadier Division and the 2nd Cuirassier Division. In this struggle Prince Karl and General Count St Priest were wounded, Grenadier Colonel Monakhtin, Prince Kantakusin and Count Buxhowden were killed. Here the fortifications were stormed and Prince Bagration mortally wounded, but they were retaken by Konovnitsyn's newly arrived 3rd Division, which had been sent up by Tuchkov I.[12]

Bagration was able to withdraw eight battalions of Raevski's Corps away from the Grand Redoubt and with the 2nd Grenadier Division and Neverovski's Division, Bagration led a bayonet charge which recovered the fleches.

About 10 o'clock in the morning all three redans (or fleches) at Semenovskoe were captured. So impertinently, so quickly that the Russians had no time to remove the guns. General Dufur (supporting Friant) charged across the ravine and approached even towards Semenovskoe. ... The French had split our army: but only for a short while! The enemy did not celebrate for long! The grenadier regiments of Kiev, Astrahan, Siberia and Moscow were already shouting 'Ura!' ... The [human] walls came nearer carrying muskets horizontal out in front ... they began the slaughter ... The grenadiers working the bayonet and the butt, driving out the French from the nest. But here Prince Karl of Mecklenburg was wounded ... Colonel Shatilov was also wounded and Colonel Buxhowden (of the Astrahan Grenadier Regiment) received three wounds.[13]

The French reformed for another attack. To meet this new threat the whole line advanced, according to D.V. Dushenkyevitch, a junior officer in the Simbirski Infantry Regiment in Neverovski's Division.

> Under cover of a small rising, in front of our flank the French placed a strong bat-
> tery with a great number of dense columns, they sent out skirmishers and all of a
> sudden, running out from behind the ridge, rushed on us, preceded by diabolical
> fire from their numerous artillery. The motherland began to groan beneath us, its
> faithful defenders.
>   In front of the regiment was a priest, in vestments with a cross in hand ... in
> everyone's eyes gleaming tears of pure faith and on the faces the readiness to kill and
> to die ... All of us began a bayonet charge; we overthrew their bayonets, then the
> artillery and cavalry of the French. This is not a battle but utter slaughter ... the field
> was ploughed up from ricocheting cross fire, cannon balls, grenades and caseshot
> smashing into the column or ripping into the ground in front of us.[14]

Glinka:

> The enemy columns swarmed into the fields, 400 guns protecting them. The
> caseshot of our guns could not stop them. They fall, close up and come on. Then
> Bagration leads the whole left wing in a bayonet charge, they come to blows, savage
> and fought to the point of exhaustion![15]

Impressed by their bravery Bagration is said to have shouted: 'Bravo! Bravo!' at the advancing Frenchmen.

An adjutant was despatched to try and hurry Baggovut to reinforce the desperate position. On reaching Baggovut the officer was asked: 'How are things going over there?' 'They could hardly be worse' was the reply. 'We are finished if you do not hurry up. Bagration's army has been pounded into the ground, and it's a miracle that Tuchkov is still hanging on'.

Things went from bad to worse; General Alexander Tuchkov seeing his brigade about to falter, seized a colour of the Revel Regiment and rushed forward shout-ing, 'Lads, follow me, forward!' He was killed shortly afterwards. The Russian attack failed and they were once more forced out of the fleches, but worst news spread among their ranks, Bagration had been wounded. On the Semenovskoe heights Bagration could be seen,

> [His] uniform was unbuttoned, his linen and clothes were soaked in blood, a boot was removed from one leg, a great red spot above his knee reveals the place of the wound. Hair a mess, face splattered with blood [and] patches of gunpowder, pale but calm … He is supported from behind … by the Preobrazhenski's Colonel Derhman … [Bagration's] left hand … rests on the shoulder of his adjutant, [with the other] he grasps the right hand … of General St Priest, and with a last farewell gives his last order. Exhausted by fatigue and loss of blood, Prince Bagration having forgotten the pain and the wound, listens to the distant roll of thunder. He wants to unravel the fate of the battle while it is still in the balance. Along the line the terrible message of the death of the 2nd [Army's] commander in chief is carried.[16]

At this moment Lowenstern, who had already been wounded several times during the battle, galloped up to the place where Bagration had been carried;

> I had the sorrow of seeing Prince Bagration seated on the grass, around [him] several medical officers and his ADCs. He was wounded, his leg was uncovered and Welje the surgeon of the Emperor, was busy working on him to extract a ball, which had entered the bone of [his] leg. He suffered a great deal, but with resignation and heroism.
>
> Upon seeing me, he asked me 'What's happened to General Barclay? Say to him that the salvation of the army is in his hands. All goes well until up to now'. With that Bagration was carried from the field, and with him the heart and soul of the Second Army, who believed that he had been invincible.[17]

With Bagration being carried from the field and the fleches once more in enemy hands, the 2nd Army began to falter and fell back. General Konovnitsyn took temporary command of the 2nd Army, before Kutuzov appointed Dokhtorov. In the heat of the battle, Dokhtorov received from Kutuzov a pencilled note instructing him to hold 'until the last resort', but with the army is such disarray he had no choice but to withdraw to a ridge behind the fleches.

Raevski's Grand Redoubt

The day looked black for the Russians, and by 12 o'clock Prince Eugene's Corps had reformed opposite Raevski's Grand Redoubt situated on Kurgan Hill. Napoleon now gave the order for Eugene to attack, because if this hill was taken then it would cut the Russian Army in two.

Unlike Bagration's fleches, only artillery was placed in the redoubt. Bagration having taken eight battalions of Raevski's Corps, Raevski had been forced to redeploy his men. He placed four battalions of General Paskevitch's 26th Division to the right of the redoubt, and four battalions of the 12th Division under General Vasilchikov to the left. The generals had orders that when the redoubt was attacked they should attack the French in the flank. Raevski was soon after reinforced by two battalions of the 19th Jagers, which he deployed in the ravine behind the redoubt.

Raevski had been wounded a few days before when he had stabbed himself in the leg on a Russian bayonet that had been left on a wagon. Although he could barely walk he refused to give up command of his Corps preferring to remain in the redoubt and direct operations. Morand's, Gerard's and Brusye's Divisions had formed up under the protection of the ravine between Borodino and the French battery, supported by a further two regiments Paskevitch:

> Seeing that the enemy was preparing to attack, we came out to them … In spite of the fire of the Russian artillery, the division moved forward. Although we were weaker than the enemy I managed successfully to hold their onslaught. Finally the superiority of numbers forced me to withdraw, in order to organise the regiments [which were] diminished by half.
>
> At the head of Morand's Division was the French 30th Line Regiment with General Bonami, which burst into the arena.[18]

According to Raevski,

> This was the decisive moment … upon the approach of the enemy within range my guns began to thunder out and the smoke hid the French so completely that we could see nothing of their array or ascertain what progress they were making. There was one of my orderly officers standing a little to the left of me, and after another volley he cried out, 'Your Excellency, save yourself!' I turned around and fifteen metres away I saw French grenadiers pouring into my redoubt with fixed bayonets. With difficulty I fought towards my left wing, situated in the ravine, where leaping on a horse and ascending to the opposite heights, watched as Generals Vasilchikov and Paskevich in consequence of my command rushed on the enemy at once. Generals Ermolov and Count Kutaisov arrived at this moment.[19]

Paskevitch continues:

> All the division supported him [Raevski]. At this time under cover of a battalion of the Ufa Regiment, led by Count Kutaisov, the division reformed and taking the 18th Jager Regiment, we fell upon the enemy.
>
> The fighting at the main battery was a terrible spectacle. The regiments of the 19th and 40th Jagers attacked the enemy from the left flank, General Vasilchekov with several regiments of the 12th Division attacked him from the right flank. The French 30th Regiment was almost destroyed. General Bonamy was taken into captivity. The rest of the regiment was routed …
>
> I took the rest of the regiments of the 12th Division, and set off for the lunette, in order to cut off the French troops and prevent them from taking the place.

Supported by a cavalry attack, by our powerful offensive movement Morand's Division was thrown into confusion. The retreat of the enemy at this point almost carried away his troops, which occupied the town of Semenovskoe. But the Viceroy of Italy managed to support Morand's Division [with] Gerard's and the battle was renewed.

Thus in a quarter of an hour the lunette was recovered. This fight was one of the most terrible and bloody in the course of all the Borodino battle; the corpses of the enemy blocked up the lunette in front of the fortification.[20]

While he was riding to the left wing, General Ermolov

… noticed its [the 2nd Army's] right wing on the heights, where General Raevsky's Corps was located. It was shrouded in thick smoke and the troops protecting the heights were in disorder. Many of us knew and, it indeed seemed obvious, that the loss of this vital point, as Bennigsen described it, would result in the most disastrous consequences for us. Therefore, I immediately rushed to this place. A minute lost could have been fatal so I ordered Major Demidov of the 3rd Battalion, Ufa Infantry of 7th Corps to follow me in open order hoping to halt the fleeing troops.

Our feeble fortification and handful of troops had long withstood the concentrated fire of superior enemy forces but there was not a single caisson for any of its 18 guns and their weak fire facilitated the French advance. Due to the limited space inside the fortification, only a small number of infantry could be deployed there at any one time and any troops outside the redoubt were mown down by canister and scattered. There were insufficient means to defend this point …

Approaching a small valley that separated us from the enemy occupied heights, I found the 11th, 19th and 40th Jagers acting as a reserve. Despite the steep slope, I ordered them and the 3rd Battalion of the Ufa Regiment to attack with the bayonet, the Russian soldiers' favourite weapon. The combat was fierce and terrible but continued for no more than half an hour; we faced a tenacious resistance, but seized the heights, recaptured the guns and not a single musket shot could be heard.[21]

General Wolzogen also witnessed the Russian attack:

The various columns approached the foot of the hill in even step to the beat of the drum and not a single cry arose from the troops. All of this so intimidated the French that we could clearly see that many men were fleeing from the ranks and that the garrison of the redoubt was diminishing perceptibly. The French kept up a fire on the advancing columns only from their cannon, which they had not managed to bring forward in any great quantity. Our troops reached the hill and then to a general 'Ura!' they carried the summit and the fortification.[22]

After the redoubt was recaptured all the French still in the redoubt were killed, except General Bonami. According to Lieutenant Colonel L. T. Rodozhitski:

When a Russian grenadier prepared to stab him, to escape he cried out 'I am the king!' then the man with the bushy moustache caught him by the collar, and dragged him to the commander in chief. Prince Kutuzov there and then congratulated the common NCO and rewarded him with the decoration of the Military Order of St George.[23]

Lowenstern also confirms Bonami pretended to be Murat to save his life. It is said that he had been wounded fifteen times; the grenadier who tried to bayonet him was Feldfebel Zolotov of the 18th Jager Regiment. News quickly spread that Murat had been captured, which no doubt boosted the morale of the Russian Army at this critical time.

Meanwhile, the remnants of the 30th Regiment were pursued by a squadron of Korf's Cavalry.

Ermolov continues:

> Having occupied the hill, I ordered the call to rally to be beaten and the wounded Colonel Savoini [of the Ladoga Infantry Regiment] appeared with a small number of officers and lower ranks. I feared that, if we were counterattacked, the enemy would bring strong forces against our depleted bands and deprive us of our recent success; so I despatched my adjutants with a few other officers to recall our troops and to clear the valley before us. Following this fierce combat, my battalions were reduced in strength and there was not a single caisson inside the earthworks, and the enemy were about to attack again. Still, wherever there was danger, one could find Barclay de Tolly. Scrutinising the action, he had dispatched a battery company and two infantry regiments so that I had all I needed and was prepared to face the enemy. At the same time, Barclay had managed to contain the attacks against our right by the Army of Italy.
>
> Having firmly established myself, I replaced our exhausted troops with fresh ones and moved them into reserve; Nikitin's three horse artillery companies had suffered disproportionately heavy losses and were moved back to their earlier position.[24]

While the remnants of the 12th and 27th Divisions were rallying, Likhachev's 24th Division was tasked with defending the battery itself. He deployed his division in two lines, the combined grenadiers and the Tomsk and Butyrsk Infantry Regiments extended from north to south, while the 19th and 40th Jager Regiments formed a skirmish line along the Ognick stream.

Among those killed retaking the redoubt was young General Kutaisov, whose body was never found, but his bloodstained horse was seen on the battlefield. General Kutaisov was later blamed for leaving his post and with his death effective control of the Russian artillery was lost. Kutuzov's adjutant, Golitsyn, commented:

> Our ignorance of Kutaisov's arrangements for the artillery meant that on every sector of the battlefield we had fewer pieces in action than the French, and that in some places ordinary field artillery was pitted against the enemy battery guns.

It is also worth mentioning that Kutuzov repeatedly said that, in his opinion, the deficiency accounted for our limited success.[25]

However it is highly unlikely that Kutaisov did not explain these arrangements to his battery commanders, and after his death batteries still continued to be deployed and ammunition supplied. Fortunately for the Russians, Prince Eugene did not have the resources at his disposal to launch an attack again immediately. Instead he once more tried to soften up the position with his artillery. Paskevitch:

> The Viceroy, not having the time to attack and to seize the lunette doubled the battery against the fortification and our troops. My division ... lost almost half of the troops under the terrible fire of the enemy artillery ... [The men] stood with extraordinary courage, showered in a hail of grapeshot, they suffered so great a defeat they were forced to withdraw from the first line, replaced by the 24th Division of General Lihadiev, taken from the centre, from the 6th Corps of General Doktorov.[26]

Mitarevski's artillery company was ordered to deploy near the Grand Redoubt:

> We occupying the appointed position ... covering the right wing of the lunette and prepared for action. Opposite us was a line of enemy guns to the right, which extended towards Borodino ... To the left, the end was not visible because of the lunette. Their guns were already in action [although] the French it seemed at first, took no notice of us ... The weather continued clear and fine, with a little wind, so that the smoke from the firing dispersed. I was unable to determine exactly what the distance between us and the enemy was, but we were able to observe all their movements: see as [they] loaded and sighted the guns, as [they] brought up the linstock towards the touch hole. To the right of us by the rising ground stood our artillery at work; below us, over the ravine where we formerly stood, there was also our artillery, amongst which were the other six guns of our company. From the left of us roared the artillery, but we were unable to see beyond the lunette. On the whole we saw nothing of what happened on our left flank. The rumble from the guns was so loud that not the musket fire, nor the clamour of battle, nor the moans of the wounded were heard. Commands also were impossible to hear and in order to give any orders near the guns, it was necessary to shout; all was lost in one long boom ... As soon as we opened fire the enemy poured shot and grenades at us ... Luckily the position of our guns were such that to our front stretched a slight rise, so that ... the enemy's projectiles mostly struck the rising ground and then richocheting flew over us, the grenades bursting far behind. But for this circumstance we would probably have been destroyed in half an hour. The position of our battery on the right side beyond the hollow on the rising ground was frightful, the artillery battery company first deployed there soon retired. Another took its place but before it was able to deploy and unlimber, hundreds of cannonballs flew there. The men and horses were literally butchered and splinters flew from the carriages and cassions ... The company abandoned this position, another one arrived and suffered a

similar fate … As for our company, despite its advantageous position, many men and horses were killed … The guns fell silent and the men repaired them … The general disposition of the artillery was, it seems, unsatisfactory. The lunette had enough room for 18 battery guns whereby all were under cover at the same time, bt it did not shelter the rest, maybe by reason of its state of destruction. It was impossible to supply the guns, but this has never been recognised. What could the companies do scattered on the hill to the right of us against fifty or even a hundred guns? If three or four companies could have been deployed and started fire at once, one might expected some success. There was enough space to deploy more guns and it is said that there were enough in the reserve. The use of the artillery in other places was probably the same. Like the Field Marshal, we had a reason to regret the death of General Kutaisov. It was noticeable that the enemy artillery was in great disorder … with the guns turned over and many taken away.

The infantry appeared for the most part to the rear of us, only partly in the hollow, in the ravine and in the cover behind the lunette … The company commander said 'Take care gentlemen, do not waste cartridges to no purpose, do not hurry and sight every shot.'

Mitarevski's luck ran out and he was wounded in the leg by caseshot. As he lay on the ground he could hear the caseshot flying over him and saw dust rise as it hit the ground near the infantry. On another occasion a cannon ball struck the ground near him, making a groove, before bouncing away.[27]

Meanwhile, General Wurttemberg was marching south with Baggovut's Corps.

Some cannonballs reached us even as we were marching through the woods but when we emerged from cover we found ourselves in the most dangerous of spots, right in the crossfire of the guns of the Viceroy and those of Semenovskaya. Shortly after this, General Barclay rode up with his entire staff to review the situation for himself. While he was speaking to me, death reaped a rich harvest among his staff, Barclay, ever the epitome of icy cool headedness and complete awareness, pointed to the Raevski battery and ordered me to advance in that direction. The 2nd Brigade was in the first line, the 1st was in the second line. The first was formed into open battalion columns, the second en masse.

We advanced to the drumbeat. Suddenly, we noticed a great commotion in the battery, but before we reached it and could see what was going on, we were assaulted from all sides by cavalry. They were received with effective fire and after several ineffective charges they fled.

Directly after this, Barclay rode up again, just as the enemy crater at Semenovskaya spewed fresh floods of lava at us. He told us that the battery had been retaken and, as a heavy mass of enemy infantry was advancing on the heights between the battery and Semenovskaya, he ordered me to attack this infantry and to push it back down into the valley behind it again.

I began to carry out Barclay's order to secure our left wing. It was like marching into hell. Before us was a mass of the enemy; the depth of their formation was unknown but their frontage alone was imposing enough. To their right hand side was a battery of artillery so large that I could not count the guns in it, but the French reports say eighty, and everywhere there were masses of enemy cavalry waiting to cut off our retreat. To guard against this threat, behind the Infantry Regiment Volhynia (which was deployed in line) was – at each flank – one battalion of the infantry Regiment Tobolsk en masse. The second rank was formed by the 2nd Brigade at some distance in columns.

We advanced towards the enemy through a hail of artillery fire. Generals Schroeder and Rossy were killed, hundreds of men in the Volhynia and Tobolsk Regiments were killed and wounded and within a very short time I had three horses shot from under me. As the last one fell, a battalion's adjutant who had just jumped from his horse to offer it to me, was also killed. The entire horrific, bloody scene was like a nightmare except for such events which convinced me that it was in fact reality.

Despite huge losses, my division continued to advance; the enemy infantry fell back before us without a fight while our dragoons charged to take the enemy battery in the flank. I now saw Barclay for the third time and must mention his utter resignation this day and the conduct of this most chivalrous of men who had been completely misjudged by Russian public opinion. He ordered me to halt and to deploy the 2nd Brigade more to the right hand side where Miloradowitch needed support. At this point, Miloradowitch's adjutant, Bibikov, rode up and asked me to ride at once to his commander. I asked him which way; he raised an arm to point it out and a cannon ball ripped it off. He pointed again with his remaining arm and said 'There! Hurry!'[28]

Northern raid

After the capture of Borodino by the French, several regiments of Platov's Cossacks had been posted in the woods to threaten the French left flank, 'repeatedly attacking ... overturning their cavalry ... and taking up to 200 prisoners of horse and infantry skirmishers'. But now, as the day was going badly for the Russians, Prince of Hesse and Colonel Toll remembered the ford that Platov's Cossacks had found the previous night, and suggested to Kutuzov that General Uvarov's 1st Cavalry Corps and Platov's Cossacks should make a flanking movement on their right. Kutuzov is reported to have said: 'Very well! Take it!'

Platov had to wait for Uvarov's cavalry to come up. Carl von Clausewitz, who was the quartermaster general of the 1st Cavalry Corps, recorded the failure of a Hussars attack at this time:

It was between 11 and 12 when he [Uvarov] reached the brook which flows by Borodino into the Kolocha. The village lay on his left, in which the troops of the Viceroy had established themselves; before him was the brook, which runs through swampy meadows. On his side of it stood a couple of regiments of cavalry, and a mass of infantry, which might be a regiment or a strong battalion. The French cavalry retired immediately over a dam, which crosses the brook at about 2000 paces from Borodino; the infantry, however, was bold enough to remain and form square with the dam in their rear. General Uvarov attacked; the Author [Clausewitz] suggested in vain that the artillery should first open up upon them; the Russian officers feared that they would then retire, and escape capture. The Hussars of the Guard were therefore advanced, and ordered to charge; they made three ineffectual attacks; the infantry (Italian troops) lost neither their composure nor their ranks, and returned a steady fire. The Hussars retired, as usually happens in such cases, some thirty paces, and withdrew out of fire. General Uvarov then discontinued these not very brilliant attempts, and caused the artillery to open [fire]; at the first discharge the enemy retired over the defile. The whole affair then came to an end.[29]

Uvarov gave the reason for the failure of his attack as the 'unfavourable position' for cavalry in his report to Barclay de Tolly. However, the Cossacks made a more effective attack upon Prince Eugene's Corps:

> General Platoff, with his 2000 Cossacks, was a quarter of a league to the right of Uvarov … He had at length found a passage and with his Cossacks was in the wood on that side. We saw, in fact, these troops so remarkable for wonderful transitions from the extremes of timidity to that of daring, careering about among the masses of infantry, without making any decided attack, as if skirmishing. The troops immediately in our front feared to be locked in the morasse, and made a side movement. The Cossack regiment of the Guard attached to Uvarov's Corps could stand it no longer; like a rocket and its tail, they were over the dam like lightning, and into the wood to join their brethren.[30]

Looking from the Russian lines Glinka recalled:

> The entire valley suddenly flushed brightly with Don Cossacks. They began making circles and flaunting their tricks. The French forward patrols quickly fled, the Cossacks sat on their shoulders! The French and Germans tried in vain to fend them off with their long swords and spurred their heavy horses [away]; yet, the Don Cossacks, braced to their saddles, flew like arrows on their small horses, circled around, rushed forward and stung them with their lances like incensed wasps. It soon began to resemble a hunt for hares. Russian soldiers standing near the Gorki heights … saw the Don Cossacks' valour and cheered them: they waved their hands, laughed aloud and yelled, 'Look at them, look at them! Well done Cossacks! Bravo Cossacks! Show no mercy to the French!'[31]

While the Cossacks galloped around the squares of Ornano's and Delzon's Divisions, the Viceroy sought shelter in a square of the 84th Regiment.

Meanwhile, Uvarov's cavalry remained motionless:

Uvarov unquestionably might have followed at this moment, but he had no desire to let himself be squashed in the defile, if repulsed, or to have to then make an unstructured retreat *en debandade,* as the Cossacks are accustomed to do on occasion. Having also despatched messengers in all directions to Kutuzov, Bennigsen and Barclay, he remained waiting for further orders. Before long the Cossacks of the Guard returned, and with a considerable deficit in killed and wounded.[32]

According to Platov's report: 'The enemy was situated behind the wood, and was overthrown … leaving in the place many dead, taken prisoner were in all more than 250 men of different ranks.' With the lack of support from Uvarov's cavalry, Platov had no choice but to retreat. When Kutuzov saw Uvarov later he said bitterly: 'May God forgive you.'

Although they did not know it, the attack had caused panic in the rear of the Grande Armée; Napoleon halted the attacks on the Russian lines, giving time for the Russians to reorganise their shattered forces. Ostermann-Tolstoy's IV Corps was sent to reinforce the left flank, but his Corps was on the right flank and would take time to march south. Two valuable hours had passed before the Cossacks were driven off and the French were ready to advance once more. It was not until about 3.00pm that another attack was launched. All this time the guns on both sides kept on firing, according to a Russian officer, 'The battle did not stop for a minute and volley fire from the guns continued all day.'

General Osterman-Tolstoy's Corps as it was marching south to take up its new position on the left wing had to run the gauntlet of the French batteries

> … exposed to the most murderous fire that I have seen. His Corps had almost disintegrated. As I [Lowenstern] talked to him, the cannonballs rained down in such numbers around and next to us and even in our group that at one moment all I could see was horses knocked over, men killed and all of us splattered with earth! … Although as brave as his sword, Count Osterman did not have the necessary qualities to be a good general. He is very indecisive and when he is in the thick of the action and has, above all, exposed all his men he believes that he has done everything and leaves the rest to chance … They are fighting, they are killing, for him that is the main thing … At that moment, he was more engaged than anyone. Those were his tactics, but no orders, no dispositions came from him and he did not leave any reserve.[33]

The French were also suffering, they were running out of infantry and were forced to use their cavalry to hold the line. The Russian cannonballs ripping through their formations. Among those mortally wounded was French General Montbrun who was practically ripped in two by a cannonball.

During the 'lull' in the battle because of Platov's raid, the 2nd and 3rd Cavalry Corps had also been sent south to reinforce the left wing. However, they were unable to deploy in time before the slaughter began once more, this time around the town of Semenovskoe, which was situated behind Bagration's fleches.

Kutuzov had responded to Bagration's appeal for reinforcements by sending the 2nd Brigade of the Imperial Guard, composed of the Lithuanian and Ismailovski Regiments, plus the Finlandski Regiments from the 3rd Brigade, three regiments of cavalry and the horse artillery of the Imperial Guard.

[The Lithuania Regiment] deployed on the ridge anchoring our left wing with orders to protect the batteries and defend the position. On the regiment's arrival there the enemy launched a strong attack on our battery and, upon being informed by Artillery Colonel Taube, I led the 2nd battalion of the regiment entrusted to me in a strong counter-attack, drove the enemy back. They were, however, soon reinforced and compelled our entire line to retreat fifty paces. The enemy showered us with cannonballs and canister and attacked the regiment with cavalry. My three battalions were arranged in squares awaiting the cavalry and despite being surrounded by superior numbers, they met them gallantly and courageously, allowing them to approach to close range before opening a battalion volley and yelling 'Ura!' They disordered and drove the enemy back to the heights, inflicting heavy losses both in killed and wounded. Our soldiers were so incensed that no prisoners were taken ... The enemy, having rallied on the heights, made a second attack on the regiment, but was met with equal courage and fled to the right, while the heights were occupied by the enemy skirmishers. To counter them I despatched Lieutenant Colonel Timofeyev with the 2nd Battalion to drive the enemy back and capture the heights. Although this was tackled with considerable success, the enemy was reinforced with several columns there who supported the skirmishers, which made it impossible for my regiment to capture the heights.[34]

The 1st and 3rd Battalions of the Lithuania Regiment were also deployed as skirmishers. Meanwhile the other regiment of the 2nd brigade was in action:

En route, we endured a heavy cannonade that inflicted considerable harm, but it could not contain the impetuousness of these courageous columns, rushing to their destination. Arriving there, we experienced the severity of the enemy canister fire ... Colonel Khrapovski, who remained in front of the troops to direct all movements, ordered the columns to deploy *en echeque*. In this position, the enemy tried in vain to defeat our regiment, increased the artillery fire, and although it devastated our ranks, it failed to produce any disorder among the men. The ranks were simply closed up again and the soldiers maintained their discipline as coolly as if they had been on a musketry exercise. Soon the enemy cavalry appeared to the right of us and forced the 1st Battalion's column to leave its position in *en echeque* and line up with the columns of the 2nd and 3rd Battalion; at the same time Colonel Khrapovitysky ordered the columns to form squares against the cavalry. The enemy cuirassiers made a vigorous attack but quickly paid a heavy price for their audacity. All the squares, acting with remarkable firmness, opened fire and fired a battalion volley from the sides of each. The enemy's armour proved to be a weak defence against our fire and gave them no confidence; the enemy cavalrymen quickly showed us their backs and fled in disorder. A fresher cavalry, consisting of Horse Grenadiers, tried to remedy the failure of the attack but was received in the same manner.[35]

Glinka continues:

In the smoke and horrors of battle the Izmailovski [Regiment] stood courageously ... The Saxon Cuirassiers, under the command of Thielmann, made haste and flung themselves on the right flank of the 2nd battalion of the Izmailovski ... all the battalion formed into square ... and opened such a battalion fire that the enemy recoiled and galloped under the blizzard of bullets! But the repulse did not stop the pressure! A cloud of bearskin caps swept up in the air. The Horse Grenadiers supported, following in the footsteps of the cuirassiers, and were also pushed aside and ran. Many pushed on forward regardless and died on the bayonets of the Ismailovski [Regiment].

During this time Nansouty's Corps rushed onto the field with specific orders to outflank and dislodge the Izmailovski and Lithuanian Regiments from their positions, in order to break our left wing. This raid was terrible ... The vast bulk of the French cavalry spread, like a sea, and our square emerged in the middle, like an island, with all sides lashed by copper and steel armour-clad waves. The riders were met and were seen off by the successful crossfire of the squares and the Russians' rain of lead finally penetrated and repulsed these *gens de fer*, these iron men, the French cuirassiers of Napoleon.[36]

Baron Uxkull, who had rejoined his regiment, took part in one of these charges:

For three hours we stood there motionless, looking, trembling, and losing patience. The shells hit and killed a great many horses, fewer men. At eleven o'clock the massacre grew general; the earth trembled, the air darkened.

Suddenly the noise stopped! The enemy cavalry, 25,000 strong, charged our columns and batteries. The reserves started moving. Our cavalry moved off, with Shevich at the head of our brigade to lead us to victory. Hurrah! We attacked! The earth trembled and groaned beneath the weight of the cuirassiers. There was a collision, but the dust prevented us from distinguishing our adversaries. It was the carabiniers and lancers. The carnage lasted five minutes. The horses trampled the dying and the wounded. The enemy had been repulsed, but we had scarcely formed our squadron when the fire from a disguised battery nearby decimated our ranks. The trumpet assembled us. There was a second attack, with less success. The enemy meanwhile had forced the left wing and we were despatched across the battlefield. The sight of the dead and wounded was frightful. A description of it all would be futile, since it would be too feeble.[37]

By now Chastel's 3rd Cavalry Division and the 7th Dragoons of La Houssaye's 6th Cavalry Division had joined the fray attacking Kapsevich's 7th Division. The Russian 2nd and 3rd Cavalry Corps had been positioned behind the 4th and 6th Corps, and now, to help the hard pressed infantry, Barclay ordered the 2nd Cavalry Corps to be committed. Major General Fedor Korf:

> The 2nd Cavalry Corps hurried there to reinforce the position, I saw them in the middle of a strong column of infantry on the left, cuirassiers and carabiniers, and to the right their horse grenadiers, under the protection of their battery, violently attacked our infantry … [They] had already forced our skirmishers to withdraw in disorder. I then ordered the Izum Hussars and the Polish Uhlan Regiments, under the command of Major General Panchulidzeva II, to advance at the trot and quickly attack the enemy's carabiniers and cuirassiers, but these regiments did not have time to reform before they were attacked by the enemy and were put in disorder.
>
> I then ordered the Pskov Dragoon Regiments to go to the right … the Moscow Dragoons stood behind in reserve. Colonel Zass, the commander of the Pskov Dragoon Regiment, saw that the enemy infantry and horse grenadiers were rapidly advancing and threatening the right flank of the Isum Hussars and Polish Uhlan Regiments, which had still not reformed … [The Pskov Dragoons] began to trot and attacked the enemy's cavalry, and despite the superiority of enemy forces, over-threw and put them to flight. After this attack Colonel Zass gathered the regiment under the fire of the enemy.[38]

This last attack gave the Isum Hussars and Polish Uhlans time to reform and attack the enemy heavy cavalry again:

> The enemy's cavalry until then in reserve approached and then Colonel Zass went into the attack with his regiment and also overthrew this cavalry and cut into the left flank of the enemy, which turned all its fire against the regiment. At this time His Highness Adjutant Prince Kudashev brought four guns of the Guard Horse Artillery into action, which immediately fired several very good rounds of caseshot, and the column was forced to give way. After this last violent attack, which ended about 5 o'clock in the afternoon, Major General Dorokhov, who had joined me with his cavalry… held the position. And the enemy after this did not venture to attack, but only fired caseshot with ferocity upon our cavalry who, however, stood unshakeable until night.[39]

Meanwhile a new attack was launch on Raevski's Redoubt by General Pierre Wathier's 2nd Cuirassier Division. They headed towards the Russian line on the left of Raevski's Redoubt towards General Dokhturov's VI Infantry Corps, which was situated in the Goruzka valley. Suddenly, to the surprise of the Russians, Wathier's 1st Brigade, formed from the 5th Cuirassier Regiment, wheeled to the left and entered Raevski's Redoubt.

General Defrance's 4th Cuirassier Division was meant to have supported Wathier's Division, but it was not close enough to aid the 5th Cuirassier Regiment, so the Regiment was forced out again by musket fire, a ball hitting Caulaincourt in the throat, mortally wounding him.

The 1st Cavalry Corps of General Nansouty occupied the space between the troops of Ney and one infantry square against the burnt village. This Corps (of two divisions of cuirassiers, one light cavalry and a brigade of Wurttembergers) fought the Russian cuirassier regiments, which once again endeavoured to take the position near the village of Semenovski. What a picture! The Semenovski redoubt was seized by the French in a minute. Kutuzov immediately ordered the deployment of a new flank battery of 25 guns. This meant that in conjuction with the other across the field, the French were in a crossfire to the front and rear. Meanwhile the Redan was again in Russian hands and Murat raced out in front, behind him a whole flood of his cavalry. He makes straight for the redans, but Golitzin with the cuirassiers around him go straight for the side and rear, where they are killed! What a crush! The horses trample the wounded men; the corpses are crushed under the wheels of the artillery, living walls of horses are knocked down... amidst the terrible cries and the bursting grenades, men are unthinkingly slashing with broadswords and sabres ... Our horse smash the French squadrons to pieces. They are blocked, turn, run ... One among them does not want to run! ... The horse under him turns, the brilliant horsemen calls, waving his sword, 'Frenchmen, towards me!, towards me!' In vain! He is surrounded ... Russian broadswords and sabres suspended above this soldier in fantastic clothes, he is recognised; 'This is him! The King of Naples! Catch him, catch hold!' There are joyful cries of 'He is ours!, He is ours! The king is in captivity!'

Murat nevertheless managed to escape.

The 33rd Line, its bristling bayonets raised fought with our horse, His and Her Cuirassier Regiments of the Imperial Guard ... pressed close to this unfortunate square. But already hurriedly advancing across the ravine and turning in column was the 48th Regiment (from Friant's Division). It hurried on to rescue the 33rd ... Seeing the importance of the position of Semenovskoe, Napoleon placed an enormous battery there under the command of General Sorbye and named it 'Adskoi'. He was confident that the Russians would begin a brutal fight for the village of Semenovski ... The Russians charge on this valuable position in huge masses. But the day fades, puffs of fire and smoke roll over the field, and a whole storm of case-shot comes whistling to meet them. There is no courage that could prevail against such a hurricane! ... under the French guns it is impossible for the Russians to move forward, but they are steadfastly determined not to withdraw.[40]

Finally the fight for the village of Semenovskoe had to be abandoned, and it was left in French hands.

A second wave of cavalry formed by General Lorge's 7th Cuirassier Division advanced towards the Russian lines; the Saxon Garde du Corps was ordered to attack the redoubt, while Zastrow's (Saxon) Cuirassier Regiment and Malachowski's 14th (Polish) Cuirassier Regiment and the 1st and 2nd (Westphalian) Cuirassier Regiments charged the Pernov and Kexholm Infantry Regiments and the 33rd Jagers. The

Russian infantry waited until the cavalry was about 60 paces from them and then fired a devastating volley, which caused the cavalry to flee in disorder.

This time the cavalry were supported by the remnants of Prince Eugene's Corps.

> The Viceroy with the Divisions of Gerard, Morand and Brusy assayed the lunette, and ordered the Cavalry Corps of Kolenkur (replacing Montbrun, who had been killed) to force their way through the fortification between the town of Semenovskoe and the main road.
>
> General Barclay ordered the 4th Infantry Corps of General Osterman to take the place of the almost destroyed corps. The Preobrazhenski and Semenovski Regiments ... and from the reserve advanced the 2nd and 3rd Cavalry Corps. Kolenkur broke through at the lunette from the rear, but he was killed. His troops drove away the regiment of the 4th Corps of Count Ostermann.
>
> The infantry divisions of the Viceroy attacked the fortifications from the front. The weakened division of Likhachev could not resist for long. Likhachev was seriously wounded, [and] taken prisoner. The enemy siezed the lunette, but the Russian troops occupied the heights behind the fortification, thus preventing any further success.[41]

General Likhachev was taken to see Napoleon, who offered him his sword back, but Likhachev refused to accept it and was led away into captivity. Meanwhile, Likhachev's Division had had enough:

> Raevski's Battery had been taken for a second time by the French, and General Likhachev, who had commanded, was wounded and taken prisoner. Those who had managed to escape this butchery found shelter in a ravine over which the caseshot of the enemy passed without doing them any harm. I was sent by the General in Chief, but I saw, to my great regret, that there was nothing that could have animated these men again. They had suffered too much and lost their spirits, choosing to die in this trap rather than to leave it.[42]

Lowenstern did not have the heart to make this Division attack again and as he rode away the French surrounded it. He would later write: 'I am unaware what became of the remnants of this division.'

Glinka continues:

> It is impossible to imagine the chaos and confusion unless you had seen it yourself. Of command and control there was no trace. Each regiment reformed itself and charged the enemy again at once. All the regiments were mixed up together, slashing and cutting at the foe in the midst of the ruins of our infantry, which was trying to reorganise itself as quickly as possible ...
>
> Suddenly, up charged a Saxon Cuirassier regiment that had broken through our left wing. They had assaulted our Guards infantry squares and had been repulsed, and were now trying to escape through our second and third lines.

It was not just the Saxon regiments that attacked the Lithuania and Izmailovski Regiments, as Glinka noted:

> Nansouty and Latour-Maubourg [Corps] charged in order to cut off the left wing from the centre of our main line. The Guard's squares repulsed the attack. Borozdin and Kretov, already wounded, with the regiments of famous names, Ekaterinburg and Military Order Cuirassiers, drove away the swarm of the enemy cavalry across the ravine. ...He, Ney, carried out Napoleon's plan with two corps of infantry and two of cavalry and led a huge attack on the centre of our line. Our columns received, came to blows and beat Ney.

However, according to Ermolov:

> Because of the terrain, the cuirassier regiments fought in isolation and, in general, our cavalry enjoyed certain local advantages but could not exploit them because of the hordes of enemy who came forwards again and again. Pursuing our depleted cavalry, the French appeared in front of our Guard regiments. The Life Guard Izmailovsk and Lithuanian regiments formed square, held their ground, but their vollies could not halt the enemy cavalrymen, many of whom found death on our bayonets, before heavy losses finally obliged the enemy to retreat.[43]

There was thick dust everywhere, no one could see more than ten feet and the opposing artillery batteries firing into the confused mass regardless of whether they hit friend or foe. General Dokhturov was everywhere, leaping into a square when threatened by cavalry.

The French cavalry were driven off for now, but the French artillery began to pound the Russian lines once more. The Guards' brigade would only have a brief respite:

> The enemy cavalry again resumed its charges but was destroyed by the cross-fire of these two battalions. The cavalry did not dare to harass our columns ... and contented itself with observing the site of its defeat from afar. The enemy artillery, however, continued to inflict horrible casualties on us and the approaching enemy skirmishers were driven back on many occasions.[44]

Utitsa

Early that morning Poniatowski's Polish Corps had advanced along the Old Smolensk Road, but it had been delayed by the woods, which were defended by Russian Jagers, and so it was not until about mid-morning that it began to make its presence felt.

General Sievers in his report states:

I perceived the intention of the enemy in the brushwood, several columns of infantry, with cavalry following under the cover of the tirailleurs, to turn our left flank … At this moment I took … two batteries and three light guns, and established them far in front of the position of the 2nd Army by the hillock near the woods [and] fired caseshot on these columns, which was so effective that the columns were overthrown and the enemy dared not repeat the attacks insteads they quickly organised their own battery. However … our battery and the other batteries on our left caused great harm both to the enemy battery and troops. The battery fired the last charges and in vain we endeavoured to obtain ammunition from somewhere or other. A diligent and efficient Lithuanian Uhlan Regimental clerk, who was attached to the regiment … brought one box. When the enemy made a new attempt on the battery, the guns operated again so well he was hastily forced to retreat in utter disorder. Despite the lack of cartridges I kept these five guns, under the protection of the jagers and infantry under the command of Major General Shahovsk and the Lithuanian Uhlan Regiment, until the evening.

According to Baggovut's report, Sievers' artillery was replaced by the heavier guns of No. 17 battery which were protected by the Brest Infantry Regiment, deployed in skirmish order.

The 1st Grenadier Division of Major General Stroganov of Tuckhov's Corps had been deployed behind Utitsa. With the aid of Sievers' battery, the Division repulsed three enemy columns which were advancing upon this position. According to General Wurttemberg,

Baggovut reached Tuchkov I at a very critical moment, just when Poniatowski and a Westphalian division were assaulting him. The 1st Grenadier Division (Stroganov) and the brigade of Count Ivelich, of the 17th Division, under Olsufiev, managed to stabilise the situation and push the enemy back to Utitsa.

Another Westphalian column had advanced into the gap between Konovnitsyn and Tuchkov I; it was counter-attacked by Prince Galitsyn's 1st Cuirassier Division and Colonel Oreus' brigade … The struggle was vicious, both sides fought extremely well. As General Count Vorontsov wrote 'My resistance was not of long duration, but it ceased only when my division existed no more.'[45]

Baggovut has also left us an account of this fighting:

Lieutenant General Tuchkov I informed me that the enemy forces were advancing against the hill on the left flank to occupy the heights. I sent the Belozersk and Willmanstrand Infantry Regiments with six guns of no. 17 Company … This detachment was commanded by Lieutenant General Olsufev.

This detachment arrived at the appointed place, [and] immediately Lieutenant General Tuchkov took command of it … The enemy, noticing this movement, opened a heavy fire on our battery, sending forward skirmishers under the cover of a strong column, trying to prevent us from occupying the heights … [but] the

Tsar Alexander I.

General Kutuzov. (Printed in *Otechyestvennaya Boina I Russkoe obshchyestvo*)

General Barclay de Tolly. (Printed in *Otechyestvennaya Boina I Russkoe obshchyestvo*)

General Peter Bagration. (Author's collection)

General Levin Bennigsen. (Printed in *Otechyestvennaya Boina I Russkoe obshchyestvo*)

Kutuzov as the commander in chief of the Russian Army, 1813 by I Terebenev. The eagle was seen flying over Kutuzov's head on the eve of the battle of Borodino. (Printed in *Otechyestvennaya Boina I Russkoe obshchyestvo*)

Raevski at the head of the Smolenski Infantry Regiment at the battle of Saltanovka, by N. Samokish, 1912. The other two officers are Raevski's sons aged 11 and 17. (Author's collection)

'Napoleon and his staff at the battle of Borodino', by Vassili Verestchagin. (Printed in *Otechyestvennaya Boina I Russkoe obshchyestvo*)

'The battle of Borodino', by P. Guesse. A wounded Bagration can be seen sitting in the foreground. (Printed in *Otechyestvennaya Boina I Russkoe obshchyestvo*)

'The attack of the Lithuanian Regiment of the Imperial Guard at Borodino', by N. Samokish, 1912 (Author's collection)

'French cavalry attacking the Grand Redoubt and the death of General Caulaincourt', by V Adam. (Author's collection)

'Council of Fili', by A. Kivshenko, 1880. (Printed in *Otechyestvennaya Boina I Russkoe obshchyestvo*)

'Napoleon on Sparrow Hill', looking towards Moscow, by Vassili Verestchagin. (Printed in *Otechyestvennaya Boina I Russkoe obshchyestvo*)

Political cartoon of a peasant who is said to have cut off his arm rather than serve the French, by Z. Daralianski. (Author's collection)

Political cartoon of a firing squad executing Russian incendiaries, by I. Ivanov, 1813. The caption read 'The spirit of the fearless Russian'. (Author's collection)

'Moscow on fire', by F. A. Clare (1768–1844).

Napoleon orders General Lauriston to conduct peace negotiations, by Vassili Verestchagin. (Printed in *Otechyestvennaya Boina I Russkoe obshchyestvo*)

Kutuzov receiving the news that Napoleon had left Moscow, by B. Zvorikin, 1911.
(Author's collection)

'To break through or retreat?' by Vassili Verestchagin. Napoleon's dilemma after the battle of
Maloyaroslavets. (Printed in *Otechyestvennaya Boina I Russkoe obshchyestvo*)

The Battle of Polotsk, by P. Guesse.

Russian Cossacks re-entering Moscow after the departure of Napoleon. (Printed in *Otechyestvennaya Boina I Russkoe obshchyestvo*)

'Don't touch them, let them come up', by Vassili Verestchagin. It depicts the partisans under Semyon Arkhipov. (Printed in *Otechyestvennaya Boina I Russkoe obshchyestvo*)

'Dreadful miseries of the French Army in Bivouac'.

'The Attack', by Vassili Verestchagin. (Printed in *Otechyestvennaya Boina I Russkoe obshchyestvo*)

'A halt for the Grande Armee', by Vassili Verestchagin. In reality the Russian Army suffered just as severely. (Printed in *Otechyestvennaya Boina I Russkoe obshchyestvo*)

The crossing of the Berezina, by G. S. Langley, 1827. (Author's collection)

Portrait of Ivan Galchenko of the Semenovski Regiment of the Imperial Guard, a veteran of the campaign, by P. Lebedyantsev, 1856. (Courtesy of the Borodino Museum)

Clockwise from above:
Portrait of Leotinus Shitikov
of the Jager Regiment
of the Imperial Guard, a
veteran of the campaign, by
E. Peitern, 1832. (Courtesy
of the Borodino Museum)

Portrait of Vasilisa Kozhina,
a partisan leader, by A.
Smirnov.

Portrait of Ivan Kondratov,
of the Semenovski
Regiment of the Imperial
Guard, a veteran of the
campaign, by E. Peitern,
1832. (Courtesy of the
Borodino Museum)

commander of the artillery of Lieutenant Shchepotev, with surprising composure, occupied the appointed place and operated with incredible success, so that there was no shot which did not injure the enemy and in the shortest of time the enemy column was repulsed ...

The enemy, seeing the failure of their infantry column, sent another, stronger than before, which certainly wanted to take our battery and their skirmishers were quickly at the foot of it. Lieutenant General Olsifev sent Lieutenant Colonel Kerna with a battalion of the Belozerski Infantry Regiment to overthrow the enemy. Supported by the Pavlov Grenadiers they resolutely rushed on the column and the enemy skirmishers with the bayonet, forced [them] to turn back and to look for an escape. Then the caseshot from our battery completed the utter destruction and finished this daring attempt. With both enemy attacks having failed, they were forced to retreat behind the wood and their battery was completely silenced.[46]

In this action Lieutenant General Tuchkov I was mortally wounded and the command passed to Lieutenant General Olsufiev, then to Baggovut.

On his march south, Baggovut had left Duke von Wurttemberg's 4th Division to stabilise the centre, now he was desperate to make use of this Division. Barclay de Tolly finally ordered Eugene von Wurttemberg, with the Kremenchug and Minsk Infantry Regiments, to join Baggovut, but only after Osterman's IV Corps had relieved him.

Major General Eugene von Wurttemberg arrived with two infantry regiments of Kremenchug and Minsk, which I placed between our left flank and the detachment of Major General Count Sievers, thus establishing communications between the two generals. The artillery arrived with them, six guns of the 4th Battery, relieved No. 17 battery and the other six guns I ordered to the detachment of Count Sievers.

During this time the enemy stretched from our left flank to the side of the detachment of Major General Count Sievers. I ... despatched a strong party of the Cossack Regiment of Major General Karpov [against] the enemy which was approaching towards the village ... The enemy ... immediately moved their guns forward, sent skirmishers out and opened fire on the Cossacks.

Meanwhile the enemy launched an attack on Major General Count Ivelich's Brigade. With the four companies of the Brest Infantry Regiment [he] took on an enemy column, fired a volley of musket fire, charged with the bayonet, but because of the superiority of the enemy guns his column was beaten back ... [and he] received a severe bullet wound in the shoulder.[47]

The 1st Grenadier Division's first line deployed its skirmishers, but with Poniatowski's 5th (Polish) Corps deploying on a small plain in front of the village of Utitsa, the Russians were ordered to withdraw and reform behind the 2nd Line. In their retreat the Russians set Utitsa on fire.

The enemy, exploiting his favourable position, began to set up his batteries, which included up to 22 guns. To counter them Lieutenant General Tuchkov immediately ordered six guns of the 1st Battery Company to deploy on a hill that overlooked the French batteries. The Leib Grenadier, Ekaterinoslav and St Petersburg [Grenadier] Regiments, led by Major General Fock, protected our guns.

A violent cannonade then opened up, and despite the superiority of the enemy fire, our battery continued to fire until it lost most of its men and having exhausted the greater part of its ammunition, was compelled to reduce its rate of fire, operating with four guns only.

While this was going on, the enemy, who knew the importance of the old Smolensk road which we protected, was receiving reinforcements continuously and finally managed to seize the hill where our battery was deployed. However, they were immediately vigorously attacked in the flank by Major General Tsvileniev, and in the front by Major General Fock, and repulsed with great loss.[48]

Another account concerning Stroganov:

[The enemy] attacked in close column, seeking especially to turn the battery which was placed on the left flank of the Grenadier Division, and which protected the regiments of St Petersburg and of Ekateringburg.

The heavy fire of our artillery and from our infantry could not stop the momentum of the enemy: They seized the hill and they prepared to continue on towards the left flank and on the rear of the Grenadier Division, but Lieutenant General Tuchkov I, who put himself in front of the Pavlov Grenadier Regiment ... attacked the French and at the same time ordered Lieutenant General Olsufiev, who had arrived with the Bielozersk and Willmanstrand regiments of the 2nd Corps, to [attack] ... the enemy who occupied the hill ... from the rear.

The St Petersburg and Ekateringburg Regiments, who were reinforced by the Grenadiers of the Guard and by Count Arakcheev's Regiment under the command of Major General Count Stroganov, supported this movement by attacking from their side.[49]

Major General Vartovski took over command of Ivelich's brigade and Baggovut ordered the Wilmanstrand and Ryanski Infantry Regiments with 500 men of Moscow Opolchenye to reinforce his brigade. With this additional strength Vartovski launched a counter-attack:

Two strong enemy columns with four guns penetrated the woods between our left flank and Count Ivelich's Brigade in order to completely cut off the latter from joining with me   A battalion of the Tauride Grenadier Regiment, situated there, encountered the enemy's heavy musket fire and ... came to a halt. Two companies acted as skirmishers and the remaining two companies withdrew to the road, which united us with the centre of the army. I was informed about this and sent word to commander Major General Shahovskago with the Minsk Infantry Regiment, ordering him to repulse the enemy … [they were] highly successful for the enemy immediately withdrew…

The enemy … decided finally to make a decisive attack on our left flank, organising a strong column of infantry and placing cavalry on its flanks … [They] charged our battery, commanded by staff captain Leskovim … but the brave Colonel Pishlitski with the Kremenchug Infantry Regiment … [led] a bayonet charge on the enemy … and in one minute the enemy was driven from the battery and his audacity was so punished by the Russian bayonet that the hill was covered with the bodies of the enemy, and the others sought safety in flight.[50]

The Moscow and Smolensk Opolchenye also took part in this fight. According to Glinka the Don Cossacks and the Opolchenye, or as he called them 'beards' to distinguish them from the clean shaven regular army, hid in an ambush, ready to strike the Poles in the flank, when they passed their position on the left.

The Polish Corps came nearer, the terrible roar of the battery in front of them. Everyone was firing. The main body charged, there was a whirlwind of caseshot in the air … a river of steel bayonets and sabres … the enemy intended to go around and suddenly … the high wood came to life and began to howl a storm. 7000 Russian 'beards' poured out in ambush, with a terrible shout, with home-made pikes, with domestic axes, they charged at the enemy, as if into a woodland thicket and cut the men like firewood![51]

Baggovut was in an exposed position, so he withdrew his men to Tsarevo hill, in line with the remnants of the 2nd Army. Shortly after,

Konovnitsin now rode up and suggested that Baggovut should resume his former position. Baggovut was furious, but burst out 'Very well, I'll take a handful of grenadiers and retake the bloody thing!' I asked for, and received, permission to lead the new assault, which cost the Kremenchug and Minsk infantry … hundreds of casualties. A Polish counter-attack threw us back on to Kern's brigade (previously Ivelich's) and I was lucky to escape with my life and to save the four guns that I had with me.[52]

All day the French Marshals had been appealing for Napoleon to release his Imperial Guard and if it made a decisive strike at the that moment in this sector of the battlefield he could divide the Russian Army in two and probably roll up the 1st Army. The Russians could not understand why Napoleon had not committed his guard either, but later that day he would say: 'People will be surprised that I did not commit my reserves in order to obtain greater results, but I had to keep them for striking a decisive blow in the great battle which the enemy will fight in front of Moscow.' Although there was to be no decisive battle for Moscow, Napoleon was correct in not committing his Imperial Guard, because before the year was out this would be practically the only force he would be able to count on.

The 1st Brigade of the Russian Imperial Guard was also not committed that day. Captain Pushkin of the Semenovski regiment wrote:

> Our brigade, regiments of Semenovski and Preobrazhenski, were under heavy fire from the enemy's battery over a period of 14 hours. The men stood firm with a calm composure, such as is fittingly possessed by elite troops. Towards evening, so much had already taken place that the bullets of the enemy muskets could fly as far as us, but in spite of this we retained our position and remained until night ... From my company we lost 35 men.[53]

Major General Lowenstern recalls that the Guards preserved

> ... a truly military bearing ... the shots were already working to devastating effect in their midst, but the men stood just as stoically and silently as before, with their muskets by their sides, and they coolly closed up their ranks whenever a missile claimed its victims.

It was not until about 4.00pm, when the French broke through the Russian lines and penetrated as far as Major General Grigory Rosen's Guard's Brigade, that the brigade finally took part in any fighting:

> Around 4 o'clock in the afternoon the enemy cavalry broke through to reach the columns of Major General Baron Rosen, who, however, charged with drums beating and met the enemy with bayonets, killing some cavalrymen while the rest fled. Shortly afterwards I received your Excellency's [Kutuzov's] order to shift these columns to the left and having occupied this position I was personally informed by Adjutant General Vasilchikov that the enemy skirmishers occupied the edge of the forest and harassed our cavalry and that the enemy was turning our left flank. A battalion of the Finlandski Regiment of the Imperial Guard, led by Colonel Zherve, was sent to support the cavalry and protect the flank. However, as the enemy skirmishers, lodged in the woods, began to inflict casualties on the columns of Major General Baron Rosen, I despatched the 2nd Battalion of the aforementioned regiment ... to drive the enemy back. Colonel Zherbe, with the battalion entrusted to him kept the enemy at bay through a chain of skirmishes, but half an hour later he reported that the enemy had entered the woods in two strong columns and, covered by the skirmishers, they were making a vigorous attack. Then Kryzhanovski having reinforced his battalion with skirmishers ... made a bayonet charge against the enemy skirmishers while Colonel Kryzhanovski approaching with the 3rd and 2nd Battalions ordered a bayonet charge against the enemy columns. Colonel Schtewen with the 2nd Battalion and Zherve with the 3rd Battalion charged with remarkable gallantry and shouting 'Ura!', routed the enemy, pursuing him to the edge of the woods, where they deployed skirmishers, who, in turn, came under fire from an enemy battery that was protected by the cavalry; this battery maintained a strong canister fire.[54]

It seemed that the hand-to-hand fighting would continue into the night, when abruptly, according to Colonel Wolzogen:

At five o'clock that afternoon (7 September 1812) the cannonade stopped and suddenly complete silence reigned in both armies ... A fairly general weariness had gripped the Russian Army. Many of the generals were dead or wounded, and almost all the regimental commanders too. As soon as I returned to the battlefield I had met a lieutenant with thirty or forty men behind the firing line, and when I ordered him to rejoin his regiment immediately he replied 'This is my regiment.' All the rest of the men were dead, wounded or missing.

Lowenstern:

Complete stillness descended. Only now we were able to calmly discuss the events of this memorable day. None of us considered the battle lost. Trophies were equal on both sides. It is true that the main battery (of Raevski) was in the enemy's hands but Barclay was still hoping to recapture it the following day as well as to recover the ground lost on the extreme left wing and launch an offensive movement.

Colonel Wolzogen continues:

Barclay instructed me to find Prince Kutuzov, who had not appeared in the battle-line all day, and report the situation of both armies (Russian) to him and obtain further orders. But he added, 'Get his reply in writing, because one has to be careful with Kutuzov.'

I rode a long way before I found the Prince. I eventually met him and his suite, who were so numerous that they looked to me like reinforcements on the Moscow Road about half an hour's ride behind the army. This suite consisted almost entirely of rich young Russian noblemen, who indulged in all kinds of pleasure and had taken no part whatever in the terrible and earnest event of the day. Colonel Toll was with them and busily eating a capon.

When I began my report with a description of the positions and state of the Russian Army and said that all important posts had been lost on the right wing and to the left of the high road and that the regiments were extremely tired and shattered, Kutuzov shouted 'With which low bitch of a sutler have you been getting drunk, that you come giving me such an absurd report? I am in the best position to know how the battle went! The French attacks have been successfully repulsed everywhere, and tomorrow I shall put myself at the head of the army to drive the enemy without much ado from the sacred soil of Russia!'

At this he looked challengingly at his entourage, and they applauded with enthusiasm. This disgraceful reception made me all the more angrier because I had only reported what I had seen with my own eyes during the turmoil of battle, whereas I know that Kutuzov had spent the whole day in the rear of the army among champagne bottles and delicatessen. However, I quickly regained my composure as I saw right through Kutuzov's sly, unfair motives in treating me as he had done. Certainly I said to myself, his associates will not realise the true state of the army and, so as not to be able to condemn his prepared bulletin on the battle as lies, will leave him in the belief that the Russians have won a glorious victory. Besides, he assumed correctly that Napoleon, as he had been unable to gain a decisive victory between six o'clock that morning and five in the afternoon, and had, rather, broken off the action, would not renew the battle; consequently the Russians would remain in control of the battlefield overnight. As I was convinced that I had correctly guessed at the motive for his fierce diatribe against me, I replied quite calmly that I must leave him to take my report how he chose. Meanwhile General Barclay wanted to know, by written orders, whether he was to continue the fight or what was to happen instead. At this Kutuzov took Colonel Toll on one side and talked to him. After a time Toll wrote out an order for Barclay which Kutuzov signed and handed to me. I rode back to Barclay at once and found him on Gorki Hill. The order contained an instruction that, as long as Napoleon did not reopen the battle, nothing should happen on the Russian side. Meanwhile Barclay should try to bring the army into line so that its right flank rested on Gorki Hill, with its left extending towards a strip of woodland beyond the old Smolensk road; this wood was to be held by Baggovut's corps … In addition, however, everything had to be prepared for the next morning, so that Kutuzov could attack the enemy.

Barclay shook his head and said to me that he did not know where he was going to find enough force for this. If we could attack the French on the spot and straight away, this might perhaps be feasible; but the next day the troops, who had exerted themselves for twelve hours without any food and would not get anything to eat during the night, would be so exhausted that further attack would be out of the question.[55]

So ended that bloody day; with the sound of the odd musket or cannon fire now and then, the combatants settled down to sleep where they could, with the prospect of the battle being renewed the following day.

Notes

1 Quoted in Robert Kerr Porter's *Narrative* p.129
2 Bistrom's report to Lavrov, in *Istoriya Leib Guardi Yegerskogo Polka* p.47
3 Ermolov *Zapiski 1812* pp.78–80
4 Mitarevski Quoted in *Vospominnaya o voine* 1812 p.65
5 Memoirs of M. Petrov in *The Goda 1812 goda vospominaniia voinov Russkoi Armii* pp.182–184
6 *Journal of Prince Eugene de Wurttemberg* p.12
7 Andeev of 50th Jagers in *Russkii Arkhiv* 1879
8 According to some historians this would be the first of eight such assaults on the fleches that morning. However the exact number of attacks will probably never be known.
9 Lowenstern to Kutuzov in *Borodino, dokumenty, pisma…* p.184
10 'Zapiski General M S Vorontsova' in *1812–1814* p.274
11 Wurttemberg, *Feldzuge des Jahres 1812* p.
12 Wurttemberg, quoted in Digby Smith, *Borodino* p.83
13 Glinka, *Ocherki Borodino Spazhniya* p.41

14 *Zapiski Duskenkyevitch* pp.113–114

15 Glinka, *Ocherki Borodino Spazhniya* p.17

16 Ibid, p.97

17 *Memoirs of General de Lowenstein* p.260

18 Quoted in *1812 v vosponinaniye* pp.102–103

19 Quoted in Beskrovny *Borodino, documenty, pisma* pp.380–381

20 Quoted in *1812 v vosponinaniye* p.104

21 Ermolov, *Zapiski 1812* pp.81–83

22 Wolzogen, *Memoiren des Koniglich Preussischen general der infantrie* p.141

23 I. Radozhitsky, *Pohodnie zapiski artilerista* pp.144–145

24 Ermolov, *Zapiski 1812* pp. 83–84

25 Quoted in *Borodino Dokumenty* p.343

26 Quoted in *1812 v vosponinaniye* p.104

27 Mitarevski in *Vospominaya o voine 1812* pp.63–66

28 Wurttemberg, *Feldzuge des Jahres 1812* pp.80–82

29 Clausewitz, *The Campaign of 1812* pp.162–163

30 Ibid, pp.163–164

31 Glinka, *Ocherki Borodinskago Srazhenie* p.359

32 Clausewitz, *The Campaign of 1812* p.165

33 Lowenstern, *Memoires du general major russe* p.263

34 Ivan Udom's report to Nikolai Lavrov, in *Borodino, dokumenty, pisma* pp.146–147

35 Colonel Kutuzov's report to Lavrov *Borodino, dokumenty, pisma* pp.148–150

36 Glinka, *Ocherki Borodino Spazhniya* pp.111–112

37 Uxkull, *Arms and the women* pp.84–85

38 Korf's report in *Otechestvennaya Voina 1812* pp.12–14

39 Ibid, pp.12–14

40 Glinka, *Ocherki Borodino Spazhniya* p.55

41 Quoted in *1812 v vospominanye sovremennila* pp.114–115

42 Lowenstern, *Memoires du general major Russe* p.268

43 Ermolov, *Zapiski 1812* pp.85–86

44 Colonel Kutuzov's report to Lavrov, in *Otechestvennaya Voina 1812* pp.12–14

45 Wurttemberg, *Feldzuge des Jahres 1812* pp.83–84

46 Baggovut's report in *Borodino, dokuments, pisma* pp.184–187

47 Ibid, pp.184–187

48 Stroganov's report in *Borodino, dokumenti, pisma* pp.151–152

49 Metternich, *Les Stroganov* pp.180–181

50 Baggovut's report to Barclay in *Borodino, dokumenti, pisma* pp.184–187

51 Glinka, *Borodino* pp.111–112

52 Wurttemberg, *Feldzuge des Jahres 1812* p.85

53 Dnevnik, *Pavla Pushkin* pp.50–53

54 Lavrov's report to Kutuzov

55 Quoted in Brett-James, *1812*, pp.132–135

11

AFTERMATH

The battlefield was strewn with the dead, dying and wounded. General Voronsov, whose Division had defended Bagration's Fleches, wrote:

> My brave division was entirely destroyed, and out of 5,000 men, not more than about 300, with one field officer ... remained untouched or slightly wounded; 4 or 5 of our divisions met with very nearly the same fate on the same ground.[1]

Raevski claimed that his corps 'had completely disappeared' and Lieutenant Andreev of 5th Jagers Regiment of Paskevitch's 26th Division lamented:

> Our division was destroyed by the artillery ... on the field I met our Major Burmin with 40 men. This was our regiment ... At 11 o'clock, the Division had been collected, about 700 men in total. The Odessa [Regiment] was commanded by a lieutenant, the Tarnopol, a sergeant major, and so on; in ours there was the colonel and three officers with me.

The Moscow Grenadier Regiment mustered 1019 officers and men before the battle but just 366, or about 37 per cent, after it.

The casualty returns for the Russian Armies show that there were 21,727 killed, wounded and missing for the 1st Army and for the 2nd Army a total of 38,569 casualties. This figure includes those that were killed or wounded on 5 September. True, some of the wounded and missing would rejoin their regiments, but this figure does not include Platov's Cossacks or the St Petersburg and Moscow Opolchenye. Ermolov wrote that 'the 2nd Army existed in name only'.

The Cossacks of the Guard, in contrast, which according to Clausewitz had a 'considerable deficit in killed and wounded' had just three killed and 30 wounded. In contrast the Preobrazhenski and Semenovski Regiments of the Imperial Guard who had hardly seen any action that day, but had been bombarded by the French artillery, suffered 155 and 121 casualties during the battle.[2] Unfortunately details of the casualties of the Grande Armée are not so easy to find, probably being lost in the retreat that followed.

Napoleon puts it at 40–50,000 Russians and 10,000 French casualties, whereas Kutuzov claims 25,000 Russians and 40,000 French. Modern studies have claimed 45–50,000 Russians and 28–35,000 French. The correct figure will never be known.

The Russian officer corps had suffered greatly; among them was Bagration, who would later die of his wound, Kutaisov and two Tuckhov brothers. The wounded Russian generals included Vorontsov, Neverovski, and Ostermann-Tolstoy. There had been few captured, Bogdanovich mentions fewer than 1,000, with General Likhachev being the only officer of note. Barclay, who had been in the thick of the fighting, remained unscathed.

The Grande Armée's officer corps also had heavy losses; Caulaincourt and Montbrun were killed and Marshal Davoust, Generals Grouchy, Nansouty, Latour-Maubourg, Friant, Rapp, Compans, Dessaix were wounded and General Bonami was captured.

Napoleon did not know it but by not destroying the Russian Army at Borodino, he had lost the best opportunity of winning the campaign. Russia could easily reinforce her army, but Napoleon was not in a position to recoup his losses. He would have to send messengers to France and his allies, who would then have to raise the troops and send them hundreds of miles before they could reach him. He could always retreat on his lines of communications and gather up the troops assigned to protect them, but this would show the world that he had been defeated. For all he knew, once he was in Moscow the Tsar would sue for peace and yet another brilliant campaign would have been won.

Although exhausted by the day's efforts, many were just glad to be alive. On the evening of 7 September Baron Uxkull had time to write in his diary:

> Oh, day of massacre! Oh! day of horrors! I'm still alive – and I prostrate myself to God for it. Jacques [his brother] what is he doing? Is he still breathing, or not? Perhaps he's wounded, and I'm far away from him, unable to bring him help! What cruel uncertainty![3]

Nadezhda Durova records:'A hellish day! I have gone deaf from the savage, unceasing roar of both artilleries.'[4] A Russian colonel said before he died:'We fought like lions, it was hell, instead of a battle.'

About midnight, news was brought from the Russian outposts that the French had abandoned the battlefield, and had withdrawn to where they had drawn up early that morning. Hope rose in some quarters that the following day would see the battle renewed and the Russians could retake their now abandoned fortifications. Ammunition was issued to some regiments as they prepared for another battle.

Kutuzov wrote to the Tsar that 'the Russian troops, so far from losing an inch of ground, defeated the enemy on every side with much greater loss than they sustained themselves.'[5] On hearing of this victory the Tsar gave Kutuzov a gift of 100,000 roubles and promoted him to field marshal. The common soldiers also received five roubles each.

Kutuzov held a council of war. As Bennigsen records: 'We were still not aware of the huge losses we had suffered during the day. We therefore considered for a while retaking our central battery during the night and continuing the battle on the morrow.'

Adjutants were sent out to discover the state of the army, and one Russian Officer, Frederich von Schubert, noted the result:

> As reports came in from the various corps and divisions, it became clear that we were missing up to 50,000 men. Many generals and commanding officers had been wounded or killed. The artillery was in the worst state; many of the horses had been killed, much of the equipment and vehicles damaged, the first line ammunition stocks were almost exhausted and the replacement parks were some days' march to the rear.[6]

Kutuzov, after listening to all the reports about the condition of the army, decided to give the order to retreat. Kutuzov's adjutant, Golitsyn, believed that he had no intention of fighting the following day before the reports were received but used the stated condition of the army as an excuse to withdraw.

> Kutuzov never intended to give a battle on the second day, his words were only a matter of policy. At night I and Toll made a tot r of the position, on which our exhausted warriors slept like dead, and he [Toll] reported that it was impossible to think of going forward, much less of defending the position, previously occupied by 96,000 men, with only 45,000, especially as Napoleon still had his entire Guard which had not fought at Borodino. Kutuzov knew all this, but he awaited this report and gave the order for prompt retirement only after receiving it.[7]

Surprisingly, Barclay de Tolly does not seem to have been invited to the council of war, because he wrote:

> At night I received an order, in conformity with which both armies were to retreat beyond Mozhaisk. I wanted to go to the Prince [Kutuzov] to beg of him to countermand this order, but I was informed that General Dokhturov was already on the march, and so I could do nothing but submit with a sad and heavy heart.[8]

The Russian soldiers' spirits were raised when Kutuzov promised that there would soon be another battle, this time to defend Moscow. On 10 September Kutuzov again wrote to the Tsar: 'I am currently at the village of Nara and am compelled to retreat further since the forces that were supposed to reinforce me have not arrived so far ... Rearguard actions take place daily.'[9] The lack of reinforcements was only an excuse to continue the retreat, because the Russian Army could not afford to be caught in such close proximity to the Grande Armée.

On 8 September, Napoleon ordered Murat with his cavalry to pursue the Russians, supported by the Corps of Poniatowski and Prince Eugene, who were marching on Borisovo and Ruza respectively in an effort to outflank Kutuzov. The Russians had left many of their wounded at Mozhaisk. Alexandre Bellot de Kergorre, an officer in the Grande Armée, described the grisly scene:

> Six hundred wounded Russians had fallen in the gardens and here they lived on cauliflower stalks and human flesh. Of this there was no shortage! In the first week I could give each man no more than half a pound of meat. Many of these wretches died. The others, as they recovered through Nature's care, went away, because they were not under guard. In fact, we could not guard them because then we should have to feed them.[10]

Platov commanded the rearguard, and as Clausewitz records:

> Thenceforward the retreat to Moscow was continuous, but very easy marches. Borodino is fifteen [German] miles from Moscow, and these were accomplished in seven marches; for on the 14th the army passed through the city.[11]

Prince Eugene von Wurttemberg recalls that only on 10 September was there any '*affaire de consequence*' near Krouiskoi, when General Miloradovitch – who had taken over the command of the rearguard – repulsed a French attack that tried to cut off the rearguard.

On the other hand, Ermolov remembered: 'Our army, pursued by the enemy and having its rearguard constantly engaged, could not find any suitable position in the places it passed through [to fight], as it approached the suburbs of Moscow'.

Prince Vasilchickov confirms Ermolov's view:

> We continue to retreat we don't know why. We lose men in the rearguard actions, and we lose our cavalry, which is barely moving. Thanks to the beast Sievers my regiment has been reduced to 400 men: other regiments fare no better. In brief, despite my best wishes and my disinclination to see the dark side of things, I believe that within two weeks we shall have no cavalry at all.

On hearing the news of Borodino, St Petersburg was illuminated with fireworks and a *Te Deum* was sung to honour Kutuzov's victory.

The dead and wounded remained on the battlefield. After the battle General Alexander Tuckhov's widow, dressed in black, scoured the battlefield looking for her dead husband's body, but it was never found. According to Glinka, 52 days after the Battle of Borodino long lines of fires were set alight to cremate the bodies of all ranks. The battlefield was said to have turned grey with the ashes. 'On 3rd December 1812 it was reported that all humans and horse corpses on Borodino field had been burnt, 93,999 men in total'.

A year later a British tourist, John Thomas James, toured the battlefield, which still showed signs of the battle:

On looking at the redoubts, these melancholy tokens were still more abundant: the interior was literally strewed with caps, feathers, scabbards, pieces of camp kettles, scraps of uniforms, both French and Russian mixed together in confusion, apparently in the place where each man had fallen.[12]

Notes

1 'Zapiski General M S Voronsov' in *1812–1814* p. 274
2 Valkovich and Kapitonov, *Borodino* pp.332–354
3 Uxkull, *Arms and the woman* p.89
4 Uxkull, *Arms and the Woman* pp.81, Durova, *The Cavalry Maiden* p.143
5 The *Russian Bulletin no.* 1
6 Quoted in Smith, *Borodino* p.129
7 Tarle, *Napoleon's Invasion of Russia 1812* p.149
8 Bragin, *Kutuzov* pp.87–88
9 The *Caledonian Mercury* 22 October 1812
10 Quoted in Brett-James *1812* p.142
11 Clausewitz, *Campaign of 1812* pp.172–173
12 James, *Travels in Russia* pp.262–269

COUNCIL OF FILI

After the heavy casualties of Borodino the army once more began its retreat, again pursued by the Grande Armée. Kutuzov maintained that Borodino had been a victory and promised another battle to prevent Moscow falling into Napoleon's hands.

Meanwhile, in Moscow, the civilians who had read about the Grande Armée's progress through Russia, began to prepare for the worst. Count Rostopchin's daughter Natalya, who in 1812 was 14 years old, describes the scene:

> My mother had sent me to father with a letter which she had just received and which required an immediate reply ... He stared sadly at me for a moment and then, picking up a dispatch, said 'Take your mother this letter from Barclay. Smolensk has fallen, and we shall soon have the enemy at the gates of Moscow'.
>
> The news of this frightful disaster spread instantly all over the town and produced general consternation. However, my father soon recovered his good spirits and, as always, tried to soften the unduly sombre colours in which the public saw this important event. In his public bulletins and in conversation with the people he stressed the prodigies of valour displayed by our generals and by our poor dear soldiers ... My father began to busy himself with putting the treasures of Moscow in a safe place. An enormous number of carts and horses were used to transport into the interior of the country the riches which were scattered in churches, convents, public libraries, and museums.
>
> Moscow soon began to empty. Every day one saw hundreds of equipages going through the streets, mostly full of women and children. However, the refugees occasionally included some young or old noblemen ... The crowds who collected at the barriers expressed their contempt for these *emigrés* in vehement terms, accusing them of cowardice and treachery. It was often difficult to repress these outbursts of patriotic indignation. And so, to escape the gibes and insults of the populace, men of all ages were seen to adopt the costume of their wives and mothers, hoping by means of this disguise to avoid any disagreeable comments.[1]

A French actress, Madame Louise Fusil who had been living in Russia since 1806 also recorded the feelings of the population of Moscow at this time:

> There was a continuous procession of vehicles, carts, furniture, pictures, belongings of all sorts. The city was already deserted, and as our [the French] soldiers advanced the emigration gathered pace ... As we feared a food shortage, everybody was making provision.[2]

Meanwhile, Rostopchin did all he could to reassure the inhabitants of Moscow that the city would not be surrendered, he issued propaganda posters and went about the streets 'I talked in a simple language' he records, 'telling them some good news or other, which later they disseminated through the city. Some believed me, others did not'.

One scheme Rostopchin took up was an idea proposed by a German of the name of Lippich, who persuaded him to finance the building of a balloon so that they could bomb Napoleon's army. Rostopchin paid Lippich at least 12,000 roubles to develop his invention and the Governor announced to the people of Moscow:

> The Emperor has confided in me the care of the construction of a balloon, which shall be sufficiently strong to carry fifty men and which can be directed with or against the wind. You will one day know what will result from this balloon, and you will rejoice at it; if the weather is fine tomorrow or the day after, I will make a trial of it at my own house. I inform you of it so that, in seeing it you may not think it proceeds from the scoundrel; it is on the contrary made for his ruin.[3]

Just over 100 years later, Zeppelins would be used in warfare and for transporting people from Europe to America, but when Rostopchin sent someone to Lippich's house on 6 September there was no balloon, no money and no Lippich; the whole business had been a smart confidence trick.

The same day Madame Louise Fusil, wrote:

> I left my lodgings on 6 September. Passing through the city, I was strongly impressed by the melancholy of the scene. The streets were empty, but now and then I met a passer-by, one of the common people. Suddenly I heard in the distance the sounds of mournful singing, and, coming nearer I saw a large crowd of men, women and children carrying holy images and following the priests, who were singing sacred hymns. It was impossible not to witness such a sight without tears, the people leaving the city and carrying away with them the treasures of their faith.[4]

The Englishman John James who would tour Russia in 1813 and spoke to many eyewitnesses, wrote:

> The demands for horses, mules, carriages were exorbitant beyond measure; on the last day four or even five hundred roubles were offered for horses to the first stage out of Moscow and repeatedly refused.

He also records that foreign residents who attempted to leave

> … unless under protection, would have been at the imminent peril of their lives …
> several were cruelly butchered by the peasants on the road, on no further ground of
> suspicion appearing than their ignorance of the Russian language.[5]

Prince Nikolai Boris-Galitzin, who had been wounded at the battle of Borodino
arrived at Moscow on 12 September:

> How different this great and imposing capital was from what it had been earlier!
> The streets, formerly so busy, were now all but deserted. The traffic had almost
> entirely stopped, the nobles and a majority of the inhabitants having moved out
> to the provinces. The few people one met in the streets looked more like souls in
> torment who appeared to have a presentiment of some great catastrophe. One had
> only to appear in military uniform to be accosted on all sides, questioned about
> events, the battle of Borodino, or the likelihood of a battle at the gates of Moscow.
> To all these questions I was hard put to find answers; nevertheless I took it upon
> myself to calm those who asked me whether they should hurry up and flee the city,
> by assuring them that as it seemed impossible that Moscow could be given up with-
> out the armies coming to grips again, there would be time to decide about leaving
> when the guns began rumbling. I admit that on this point I was under a complete
> delusion, fortified as I was by my knowledge of the order which had been issued to
> take the offensive on the morrow of Borodino. I could not conceive for a moment
> that Moscow would be sacrificed without firing a shot in its defence. This feeling I
> shared with all the members of the Army who, like me, did not know the outcome
> of the council of war held near Moscow, at Fili.
>
> Next day, 13 September, was a Sunday, and I went to the Kremlin, to the
> Cathedral of the Assumption. This was to be the last time Archbishop Augustin
> would celebrate the holy office there. But who could have foreseen that? The
> church was full. I can truthfully say that I have never attended a divine service
> at which every heart seemed to be so universally disposed to pray or where a
> more religious spirit prevailed. The truth is that misfortune teaches us to pray.
> The memory of this service, all sincerity and genuine fervour, will never leave
> me. The pontiff himself officiated with the most touching sincerity, and at the
> moment when, raising his eyes to Heaven, he pronounced in a voice filled with
> emotion the words, 'Lift up our hearts and give thanks unto the Lord', the eyes of
> all present filled with tears and turned spontaneously towards the only consola-
> tion of the afflicted.

The following day, Kutuzov arrived with the main body of the Russian Army and
began deploying before Moscow. A redoubt was ordered to be constructed on the
Poklonnaia Hill, and a battery was established near the road.

Duke Eugene von Wurttemberg, who commanded the 4th Infantry Division, witnessed the conflicting views on strategy – and the conflicting emotions:

Gradually more and more troops filled the valley between the Moskva and the heights of Vorobievo, and very soon they were jammed in confusion within the constricted area. General Barclay was not satisfied with the disposition of the troops, and staff officers were sent to reconnoitre the heights and to find a better position. General Konovnitsin and I accompanied them. All were of one opinion, namely that it was impossible to select a position there.

I took this news back to General Barclay. Kutuzov was sitting in an armchair, set on a small hillock beside the road and surrounded by innumerable generals. As far as I could gather, opinions were sharply divided. Barclay, who said little, held the correct view that where we stood was not the place to accept battle, and that we must either go forward or withdraw. Kutuzov, whose inward disquiet was apparent, listened in silence to many of the opinions expressed. In truth no less a decision was at stake than to rise boldly above all responsibility and, in spite of the views held by the Army and the nation, to yield the old imperial capital to the enemy after a battle which had been announced as won – after a retreat which had been voluntarily undertaken, and with an army which, it was claimed, again totalled 90,000 combatants, including militia and Cossacks.

This already tense moment, was suddenly interrupted by thunderous firing by the rearguard, indicating the enemy's approach. To most people the possibility of further withdrawal seemed to be ruled out by the demands of honour. In their view Moscow was the goal and the grave of the Russian warrior, as are the depths of the tomb to the wanderer on earth. The beyond lay in another world. In the local situation in which the Army found itself, a defeat was naturally to be assumed.

Kutuzov, who had promised not to give up Moscow without a fight, had arrived, or so it appeared.

Kutuzov and his generals retired to a small peasant's hut in the town of Fili, a village on the outskirts of Moscow, to discuss the forthcoming battle. Kutuzov knew that the Russian Army was not in a fit state to fight a major battle and that the ground itself was not good. If he gave battle and was defeated the war would be lost, but if he abandoned Russia's sacred capital without a fight the army would be saved, it could reorganise and might still win the war, if the Russian people held their nerve. Kutuzov opted for the latter option, but he could not be seen to abandon Moscow on his own authority, so put up a pretence that he still planned to give battle, and would let others appear to talk him out of it.

At about 5.00pm Kutuzov held a council of war, composed of Barclay de Tolly, Generals Platov, Bennigsen and Dokhorov, Lieutenant Generals Uvarov, Count Osterman, Raevski, Konovnitsyn, Major General Ermolov and Colonel Toll, with their adjutants were crowded into the small hut, as well as the Savostyanov family who lived there.

The first person to speak appears to have been Barclay de Tolly, who explained the state of the army:

Our current position is very unfavourable and, if we wait here for the enemy it will [be] very dangerous; considering that the French have superior forces, it is more than doubtful that we would be able to defeat them. If, after a battle, we still manage to hold our ground, we would have suffered losses similar to those at Borodino, and thus, would be unable to defend a city as extensive as Moscow. The loss of Moscow might upset the sovereign, but it would not be unexpected, certainly it would not incline him to end the war and would reinforce his resolute will to fight on. By saving Moscow, Russia will not avoid this brutal, ruinous war; but having preserved our army, the hopes of our fatherland would be preserved, and the war, our only means to salvation, would be continued on better terms. Our reinforcements, gathered at various places behind Moscow; would have enough time to join us. All recruitment depots have been removed to those regions. A new foundry has been established in Kazan and a new weapons factory has been set up in Kiev, in Tula, additional guns have been completed. The Kiev Arsenal has been evacuated, gunpowder, produced in factories, is being turned into artillery munitions and musket cartridges and stored deep inside Russia.[6]

Bennigsen, who arrived late, with the excuse that he was touring the army's positions but in reality had been finishing his dinner, writes in his memoirs:

> To my astonishment I learnt that it was a question of withdrawing from Moscow and of abandoning the capital to the enemy … General Barclay … assured us that, since the Battle of Borodino, our army was disorganised by the great losses that had been inflicted on us … He claimed that the positions that we occupied on the heights of Poklonnaya-Gora were bad; that we, being beaten, would then be destroyed … Whereas if we withdrew from Moscow and went along the Vladimir Road, we would remain true to the order of the Emperor and His government to continue the war. He added that His Imperial Majesty was prepared for the evacuation of the capital; he assured us that our Sovereign approved unquestioningly of our retreat and he employed all means to persuade the council to agree to this course …
>
> I began by asking had they properly considered the consequences of the evacuation of Moscow, the capital, the greatest city in our empire; or the immense losses that the civilian popuation represented, a crowd of individuals … Finally, with the shame of abandoning the capital without firing a shot, I demanded if the public would still believe that we had won the battle of 7 September, as had been published abroad. I asked if our … retreat should ever have an end. I added that I did not understand why they were so certain that we would be beaten and that we would lose all our artillery, after having received several reinforcements since the Battle of Borodino, an advantage that the enemy did not have; and that I thought, on the contrary, that we were still the same Russians who had beaten [the French] with so much bravery … The enemy had caused considerable losses on 7 September, yes, but those of the enemy were considerable in their turn, in soldiers, in generals and officers, and in consequence, if our army was disorganised since the battle, his own also had to be for the same reason.

Bennigsen proposed attacking the French; this was rejected by Barclay, 'We do not have enough troops for such an operation and we lose our communication with Kaluga, Tula, Riazan and Vladimir.'[7]

According to Wilson:

> Barclay spoke in favour of a retreat on Niznel Novogorod; Konownitsin for an offensive movement against the enemy before they could unite their three separate columns; Osterman and Ermolov leaned to that opinion; the Quartermaster General Toll recommended that a position should be taken in front of Moscow, with its right on Worobievo, and left on Woronovo, there being still sixty five thousand old soldiers in the army, which, including six thousand Cossacks, mustered ninety thousand men under arms, and which he rendered considerably more efficient by the support of the population; Bennigsen and Dokhtorov agreed with the Quartermaster General as to the defence of Moscow being a military as well as a patriotic duty, but preferred the position of Fili.[8]

The heated debate continued, Bennigsen arguing that the Russians could redeploy their army to a better position in front of Moscow, to which Kutuzov replied:

> I cannot approve of the count's [Bennigsen's] plan, gentlemen. Movements of troops in close proximity to the enemy are always risky, and military history affords many examples of disasters arising from them. For instance ... well, the Battle of Friedland, which, as I have no doubt the count remembers, was not ... completely successful owing to the change of the position of the troops in too close proximity to the enemy.[9]

This temporarily silenced Bennigsen. Platov, Dokhtorov, Uvarov, Konovnitsyn and Ermolov were in favour of defending Moscow, but Barclay, Raevsky and Osterman were for retreating. Finally after hearing all the arguments, Kutuzov indicated where the buck stopped:

> Well gentlemen, after all, it's me who will have to pay for the smashed pots. Some may disagree with me, but using the powers given to me by the Tsar and Fatherland, I order the retreat. Napoleon is like a stream we are as yet incapable of stopping. Moscow will be the sponge that will suck it in. As long as the army exists, we may still hope to win the war, but if the army is destroyed, that will be the end of Russia.[10]

The first thing Bennigsen did after the council of war broke up was to write a letter to the Tsar describing what had happened, and that he had nothing to do with the decision.

Upon hearing that Moscow was to be evacuated, a Russian officer wrote:

> I remember that when Lindel my adjutant, brought the order for the surrender of Moscow, everyone was siezed with consternation: many wept, others tore off their

uniforms and threatened to resign from the service after this humiliating surrender, or abandonment of Moscow. My General Borozdin definitely regarded the command as a piece of treason and did not move from the spot until General Dokhtorov arrived to replace him. By daybreak we were in Moscow. Its inhabitants, as yet unaware of the imminent misfortune, received us as deliverers, but when they learned the truth, swept after us almost in a body. This was no longer the march of an army, but the transportation of whole nations from one end of the world to the other.[11]

At 11.00pm that evening the artillery began to march through Moscow and were followed at 3.00am by the columns of infantry.[12]
Duke Eugene von Wurttemberg:

Count Rostopchin, Military Governor of Moscow, came up to me soon afterwards and said with great fervour, 'If I were asked my opinion, I would say "Destroy the capital rather than surrender it to the enemy!"' That is Count Rostopchin's view. As for the governor of the city who is called upon to look to its preservation, he cannot give such an opinion.

I was so struck by this thought that on my return to the divisional camp I passed it on to everybody round me. 'It is scarcely credible,' I exclaimed. 'It would be a gigantic task, but in this terrible crisis the proper expedient.' My companions at the time will confirm this incident. But I must admit that I soon changed my mind about believing any Russian had any share in the burning of Moscow, and, like General von Clausewitz, only reverted to that belief in more recent times.

During the night of 13–14 September the whole army received orders to march through the city in good order and in silence, and to take up position 14 km further on, near Panki.[13]

At 5.00am, the morning of 14 September, Rostopchin came to see Voronenko, the Superintendent of Police and ordered him to 'Go to the Wine Arcade and the Custom House … and in the event of a sudden entry by enemy troops, to destroy everything with fire, which order I carried out in various places to a certain extent.'[14]
Madame Fusil, who had been refused a pass to travel to St Petersburg:

We kept on climbing to the top of the house, where we could get a view over distance, and one evening we spotted the bivouac fires. Our servants came into our rooms in great alarm to announce that the police had been knocking at every door to urge the occupants to leave, as the city was going to be set on fire, and the fire pumps had been taken away. 'We do not want to remain here' they added. And in fact we learnt that the police had left, which was scarcely reassuring.[15]

Prince Nikolai Boris-Galitzin, had not heard of the order to abandoned Moscow:

On 14 September, a day to be remembered by Moscow forever, I rose early, mounted and rode quickly towards the Smolensk barrier to try and to discover what had been

decided. I was burning to take part in the battle which I assumed to be imminent.
I had still not gone through the barrier when I caught sight of General Kutuzov
from a distance; he was preparing to enter Moscow, escorted by his numerous staff.
Here was a most favourable opportunity for me to set at rest all my uncertainties, so
I attached myself to his suite.

We rode across Moscow in a melancholy silence, nobody expressing what was
in his thoughts, and each apparently absorbed in sombre reflections. The solemnity of this silent march, of which no one, except the Commander in Chief,
knew either the destination or the duration, had something sinister about it as
we passed through these streets, usually so thronged, now all but empty. Here and
there we encountered a few groups of inhabitants whose faces bore signs of anxiety and apprehension, and who received no replies to urgent questions some of
them addressed to us. Eventually, after riding for more than three hours through
Moscow's tortuous streets, we spotted in the distance the posts of a barrier. 'But
whichever barrier is that?' we asked in an undertone. 'It must be the Kolomna
barrier.' 'Where are they leading us to?' 'God knows!' Such were the questions and
exclamations that broke the gloomy silence which had presided over this march, so
impressive in its mystery amid the dangers threatening the capital. Here we found
the Governor, Count Rostopchin, whose impassive face gave nothing away. He
seemed to be expecting the Commander in Chief, and after exchanging a few
words with him in undertones, he returned into the city, and we ... abandoned it.
And from this moment we realised the sad truth: Moscow was going to be surrendered to the enemy without a defence.[16]

In silence, regiment after regiment marched over the wooden bridge that crossed
the Moskva river. Others paid a boatman a small fee to ferry them across. Even the
propaganda newspaper *Journal of Military Actions* reported: 'The army in the greatest of order and silence passed Moscow. A deep grief was written on the soldiers'
faces, and it seemed that each of them fed in the heart a revenge for the insult, as
though it had been caused personally to him.' Sir Robert Wilson described it as a
'funeral march'.

Baron Woldemar von Lowenstein was with Barclay during the evacuation of
Moscow, who 'remained in the saddle for eighteen hours and had all the parks and
wagon-trains file past him in the street. The columns of infantry and cavalry went by
one by one without a break.'[17]

Kutuzov was also watching the army march through the streets of Moscow:

Outside the gate Kutuzov was sitting in a droshky, buried deep in thought. Colonel
Toll drove up to the Russian general and reported that the French had entered
Moscow. 'God be praised', answered Kutuzov, 'That will be their last triumph.'

Slowly the regiments marched past their commander. How the faces of the
Russian soldiers had changed between morning and evening! In the evening anger
and grief burned in their eyes, their mouths uttered loud cries of 'Where are we
being led?' 'Where has he brought us?'

His right hand resting on his knee, Kutuzov sat motionless, as though seeing nothing, [and] hearing nothing, and pondering the announcement; 'The loss of Moscow is not the loss of the motherland'.[18]

According to Prince Golitsin, Kutuzov turned around and said to his staff, 'Who among you knows Moscow?' Golitsin said that he knew, to which Kutuzov replied: 'Lead me by a route where I will not meet anyone.' Kutuzov and his staff were led through the back streets to the Yauza Bridge.

Meanwhile, the French were getting ever closer, and Miloradovitch, who commanded the rearguard, had to defend the city until the Russians had passed. Bennigsen recalls:

> What might it not have cost us but for the presence of mind of General Miloradovitch, who commanded the rearguard and who, under enemy pressure, soon saw himself obliged to enter Moscow, where the streets were blocked by artillery, troops, wagons and horses, carts laden with provisions, hauliers and drunkards stretched out in front of the cellars, while enemy soldiers under the King of Naples' command on the one hand and, on the other, the Viceroy of Italy's advance guard on the road from Ruza, were entering the town almost at the same time as the last troops of our rearguard.
>
> In these critical and difficult circumstances, which could have cost our army very dear, General Miloradovich thought up an expedient which saved us in large measure from the losses threatening us. He sent a flag of truce to the King of Naples and proposed an armistice lasting several hours, so that he would have time to evacuate and surrender the city, adding that if the King of Naples did not agree, then he would make him pay dearly for the possession of Moscow and would not let him enter except over corpses and ashes. The enemy, who was anxious to preserve this great city and who was unaware that he would find there nothing but empty houses, except for the huts of the poorest inhabitants, consented without making difficulties. Both sides agreed not to engage in hostilities for several hours, to give us time to evacuate the city.[19]

Clausewitz, who was with the 1st Cavalry Corps that formed part of the rearguard records:

> General Miloradovich sent a flag of truce to the outpost with a request for an interview with the King of Naples, of whom it was known that he commanded the advanced guard. After a few hours the reply came that General Sebastiani was at the outposts. General Miloradovich was not satisfied, but nevertheless acceded, and a pretty long conference ensued, to which we of the suite were not admitted. Hereupon the two rode together a good portion of the way towards Moscow, and from their conversation the Author [Clausewitz] saw that the proposal of General Miloradovich had met with no difficulty. To some expressions of that officer relative to the sparing of the city as far as possible, General Sebastiani replied with the

utmost eagerness 'Monsieur, L'Empereur mettra sa garde a la tête de son armée, pour rendre toute éspece de désordre impossible etc'. This assurance was several times repeated. It was remarked by the Author as expressing a strong desire for the possession of Moscow in a complete state; and, on the other hand, the request of General Miloradovich was such as to militate against the notion of a Russian plan for its conflagration.[20]

A young junior officer, A. A. Shcherbin of the Quartermaster's department, was also with the rearguard as it marched through Moscow:

Miloradovich reached the head of the column when it was approaching the Kremlin. At that moment Nashchokin returned with news that the King of Naples had accepted the proposal and halted the advance. Miloradovich then went ahead of the infantry and rode with his suite to the Dorogomilov Gate, at a distance of seven and a half kilometres from which he ordered the rearguard to halt for the night. Riding through the Kremlin we saw two battalions of the Moscow garrison leaving with a band playing. Miloradovich addressed the garrison commander, Lieutenant General Brozin, as follows: 'What blackguard gave you orders that the band should play?' Brozin replied that when a garrison left a fortress on capitulation the band should play. 'It is thus laid down in the regulations of Peter the Great.' 'But where in the regulations of Peter the Great', retorted Miloradovitch, 'does it say anything about the surrender of Moscow?'[21]

Barclay had positioned his adjutants in various districts of Moscow with a Cossack escort to prevent any looting by the soldiers, but some officers decided to go home and save what they could from their homes, which resulted in several being captured along with the thousands of wounded in the hospitals. The prisoners were sent to France and paraded through the streets of Paris as a show of triumph, but there were all too few prisoners to show for the Grande Armée's suffering.

The Russians of course were also suffering from the loss of Moscow:

It would be difficult, indeed well nigh impossible, to describe our feelings after Moscow was abandoned, because interests and points of view differed so sharply.

Whereas one man grieved over the loss of his house, another regretted the loss of homes belonging to his parents or friends, while others – and they were the majority – were preoccupied with the humiliation at seeing this ancient capital occupied by foreigners. But quite spontaneously everyone forgot his personal concerns and thought only of the affront the enemy had just inflicted on us, and, far from being disheartened, we felt more passionately determined than ever to continue the war and to make every conceivable sacrifice. One felt as if a burden had been lifted. After the capture of Moscow we had the empire to save, not just a town; and from this moment everybody said; 'This war is only just beginning!'[22]

Wilson also confirms this change of attitude:

There was no more despondence, no more drooping, no more muttering of discontent: the hour of imagined shame and degradation had passed; confidence was restored. The soldier again exulted in the prospective grapple with the enemy, and planted his foot, and handled his arms, as if he were about to charge and penetrate the hostile ranks, and recover his burning lares.[23]

Meanwhile the last of the Russian rearguard were moving through the city, including Clausewitz of the 1st Cavalry Corps:

Moscow had nearly the appearance of a deserted city. Some two hundred of the lowest class came to meet General Miloradovich, and to implore his protection. In the streets some scattered groups were seen who contemplated our march with sorrowful countenances. The streets were also so thronged with the carriages of the fugitives that the General was obliged to send forward two cavalry regiments to make room. The most painful spectacle was that of the wounded, who lay in long rows near the houses, and had hoped to have been transported with the army. These wretched beings probably all perished.

We struck, in passing through the city, on the road to Riazan and took a position some 1000 paces behind it.

General Sebastiani had promised that the head of his advanced guard should not enter the city sooner than two hours after our departure. General Miloradovich was therefore much surprised having hardly taken up his position behind the city, to see two regiments of the enemy's light cavalry deploy before us. He sent immediately a flag of truce, and demanded a conference with the King of Naples. This time, however, the king also declined to appear, considering it perhaps beneath his dignity; and General Miloradovich was obliged again to content himself with General Sebastiani. He made the liveliest remonstrances against the too great rapidity of the pursuit, which admitted of easy reply, as from various causes we had taken much longer to defile than the French had anticipated. The conference however, led to the result that the two parties stood close opposite each other without coming to blows. We saw from this position how Moscow gradually emptied itself through the gates on either side by an uninterrupted stream of the light wagons of the country, without the first several hours being interrupted by the French. The Cossacks seemed rather to be yet in entire possession of these portions of the city, and the French advanced guard to occupy itself solely with the rearguard of the Russians. We saw also from where we stood wreaths of smoke rising from several places in the furthest suburbs, which in the Author's opinion were results of the confusion there prevailing.[24]

On 16 September, nine days after the Battle of Borodino and three after the decision was made to abandon Moscow, Kutuzov reported to the Tsar from the village of Gilino:

I could not venture another battle, which would not only have been ruinous to the army, but would had reduced Moscow to ashes. In this unpleasant situation, and after consulting with the chief generals, among whom were some of a different opinion, I was obliged to permit the enemy to enter Moscow, out of which all the wealth, arsenals and almost all the other property, imperial or private, had been previously removed, and no inhabitants remained in the town.

I must confess that the leaving of the capital is a circumstance of regret; but considering the advantages which may accrue to us ... I hope to compel him to leave Moscow, and to change his whole line of operation ... I am not far from Moscow; and having collected my troops, I can boldly await the approach of the enemy, and, as long as the army of your Imperial Majesty is entire, and animated with its known courage and zeal, the loss of Moscow is not yet the loss of the empire.[25]

As the Russians were marching away from Moscow, leaving the city to its fate, few of them noticed a rocket streaking across the sky. A sign from Voronenko, the Superintendent of Police for his incendiaries to begin their work.

Notes

1   Narichkine, *Le Comte Rostopchine et son temps* pp.141–142
2   Fusil, *Souvenirs d'une Femme sur la Retraite de Russie* pp.228–229
3   Quoted in Olivier, *Burning of Moscow* pp.29–30
4   Quoted in Varestchagin, *1812, Napoleon I in Russia* pp.193–194
5   James, *Journal of a Tour in Germany, Sweden, Russia, Poland during the years 1813 and 1814* pp.172–174
6   Quoted in Ermolov, *Zapiski 1812* p.170
7   *Memoirs du General Bennigsen* vol. 3 pp.90–93
8   Wilson, *Napoleon's Invasion of Russia* pp.163–164
9   Leo Tolstoy's *War and Peace* p.987 For his novel, Tolstoy researched the history of the campaign.
10 'Military Journal' quoted in Kutuzov, *Dokuments* pp150–151
11 Quoted in Tarle, *Napoleon's Invasion of Russia* p.153
12 *Memoirs du General Bennigsen* vol .3 p.94
13 Wurttemberg, *Les campagne de 1812* pp.98–100
14 Voronenko's report quoted in Tarle's *Napoleon's Invasion of Russia* p.170
15 Fusil, *Souvenirs d'une Femme sur la Retraite de Russie* pp.228–229
16 Quoted in Brett James, *1812* pp. 161–162
17 Lowenstern, *Memoirs du General Major Russe* vol. 1 pp. 279–280
18 Glinka, quoted in Brett James *1812* p165
19 *Memoirs du General Bennigsen* vol 3 pp94–95
20 Clausewitz, *The Campaign of 1812 in Russia* p.180
21 Quoted in Brett James, *1812* p.160
22 Lowenstern, *Memoirs du General Major Russe* vol. 1 pp.282–284
23 Wilson, *Napoleon's Invasion of Russia* p.171
24 Clausewitz, *The Campaign of 1812 in Russia* pp.180–183
25 Quoted in the *Edinburgh Evening Courant*

13

MOSCOW

Meanwhile, Napoleon had arrived at the gates of Moscow with the main body of his army. They marvelled at the city, with its spires with their rounded domes, reminding some of the tales of the Arabian Nights. Many believed that the war was practically over.

Napoleon stood on Vorob'yovi, or Sparrow Hill and waited for the delegation to come and surrender the city to him, as was the custom. He waited but no one came. Finally, his patience exhausted, Napoleon sent a detachment into the city. The streets were empty, only the movement at the windows suggested that some of the inhabitants had remained. These were mainly the poorest inhabitants and foreigners, who had nowhere else to go. Others had believed Rostopchin's propaganda that Moscow would be defended by the army. One of these was Elena Pokhorsky, a deacon's wife, who on hearing of the arrival of the French, shouted to her husband:

> 'Bonaparte has arrived! ... The sacristan's wife says so.' He burst out laughing. 'What a fool of a women you are! You believe the sacristan's wife and you will not believe the Governor. Here is the Count's poster. I have read it to you, haven't I? Well then. You would do better to prepare the samovar. Meanwhile leave me in peace. I am writing my sermon.'
>
> I served dinner. Suddenly we heard shouts in the streets. The deacon went to the window and looked out. Then he put his cup of tea down on the table, and I noticed that his hands were shaking. He was pale as if his face had been coated with flour. I said, 'My good man, what is the matter?' His tongue seemed to be stuck to his palate. He could only mutter 'The French!' and then sat down ... Bit by bit he regained his composure, and the colour returned to his face. Then he stood up, seized Rostopchin's poster, tore it into shreds.[1]

Others, like Prince Vasili Novikov's family, believed the rumour that the soldiers entering Moscow were in fact British troops and rushed to welcome them with 'two pots of butter and half a dozen loaves'. It was only then that they realised their mistake.[2]

In the confusion of that day some inhabitants could hear musket fire, which they believed was the beginning of the battle to defend the city. Andrei Karfachevsky was one of these inhabitants, who

> ... believed the battle had begun and, praying God to grant victory, hastened with their arms to the aid of their countrymen. Suddenly, however, there appeared in the Kremlin itself troops who ordered the running populace to throw away their weapons and say *pardon*. Anyone who resisted or who did not understand their language was stabbed and cut down mercilessly. It was then they guessed that this was our enemy, and all in fear and trembling ran for their lives, crying, 'The French are in Moscow!'[3]

As the French spread out into the city they began to loot the houses. The Abbé Surrugues saw that 'The soldiers did not respect the modesty of women, the innocence of children, nor the grey hairs of age.'[4] An anonymous eyewitness saw them searching on holy ground:

> Nothing so inflamed the greed of the plunderers as the Archangel Cathedral in the Kremlin, in the royal tombs of which they hoped to find enormous treasures. In this expectation the Grenadiers descended with torches into the vaults, and without compunction disturbed even the bones of the dead.[5]

That first evening some accounts record that a rocket streaked across the sky; this is usually interpreted as the sign for incendiaries to start setting fire to Moscow. As early as 24 August Rostopchin had written to Bagration declaring that the people of Moscow would 'burn the city to ashes, and Napoleon instead of booty, will get only the spot where the capital had been'. In later life Count Rostopchin would deny that he gave the order to set fire to Moscow, despite Eugene von Wurttemberg claiming Rostopchin thought they should do so.

Voronenko, the Superintendent of Police, also confirms that Rostopchin gave the order to set fire to the city. At 5.00am on the morning of 14 September, Rostopchin came to see Voronenko and ordered him, as mentioned earlier, 'in the event of a sudden entry by enemy troops, to destroy everything with fire, which order I carried out in various places to a certain extent.'[6]

Again as mentioned earlier ,Madame Fusil indicates that the police were apparently involved:

> Our servants came into our rooms in great alarm to announce that the police had been knocking at every door to urge the occupants to leave...And in fact we learnt that the police had left, which was scarcely reassuring.[7]

Not all the fires can be blamed on the Russians, according to one eyewitness known only as 'Mr C.', who was

… seated in his chamber the evening of the arrival of the French; where he heard the bustle of the military undisturbed at night, however two dragoons entered suddenly demanding, with pistols in their hands, whether any Russian soldiers were concealed. He replied that there were not. 'If you deceive us' they said, 'you will die.' They went upstairs to search, and presently returned, asking for some brandy and a pair of boots. These were given, and they went their way. Soon afterwards thick smoke began to make itself perceptible from the upper part of the house, and in a short time the whole burst into a blaze.[8]

The Duke of Wellington in his own analysis of the 1812 campaign points out that it was a common practice for soldiers to set light to the rag they used to wipe the gun oil off their muskets and use it as a touch paper. Once the soldiers could no longer hold onto this burning rag they threw it away.

With his house alight, Mr C.'s family sought refuge in another house, where about 100 others had also taken shelter.

It was hardly to be expected they should enjoy the sleep of this night unmolested, and they were visited successively by … several parties of marauders, of whom it can be only said that the first left nothing for their successors to deprive them of. Alarmed by the continued reports of assassination in the streets, he told us he never quitted the house except once during the six weeks of his abode; and then he had cause to repent of his temerity, being insulted by some of the soldiers, robbed of his coat, and congratulating himself that he had escaped with his life.[9]

The French believed that incendiaries were at work within the city, and anyone suspected was arrested or shot. In another example John James records:

A lady with her husband and daughter returned to an empty house and remained there for two days, not daring to stir out of doors. When being almost famished, the husband was obliged to go abroad with the hope of procuring provisions. In crossing the street he stopped, either from curiosity or some other trivial motive, and picked up a rocket case which was lying on the ground with the appearance of having been used in the conflagration; seeing, however, that he was observed by two French soldiers, he put it away in his pocket, perhaps in a somewhat hurried manner; they at the instant came up, and demanded in a threatening tone to see what it was he had concealed. On being shown, one of them accused him as an incendiary and without further parley took a step back, levelled his musket and shot him through the heart.[10]

His wife and daughter were taken to the palace of Count Rasumofski, where Murat was quartered and who had set up a haven for the poor unfortunates of the fire. They remained there until the occupation was over.

Not all the inhabitants tried to escape the fires; at least one old woman, by the name of Poliakov, did not want to leave her home, when some of her neighbours called on her to see if she wanted any help, they

… found her near the Icons, lighting her lamp. She was dressed as if for a Holy Day, all in white, with a white kerchief about her head. 'What is the matter Babouchka [old woman]?' I asked, 'Do you not know that your house is on fire? Let us pack up your traps and clothes as quickly as possible, and with God's help we may escape; we came to take you with us'. But she only replied 'Thank you, my pigeons, for remembering me. For my part, I have spent all my life in this house and I will not leave it alive. When it was set on fire I put on my wedding chemise and my burial garment. I shall begin to pray. And it is thus that death will find me.' We tried to reason with her; why should she become a martyr when the good God pointed out a way to escape? 'I shall not burn', she rejoined, 'I shall be suffocated before the flames can reach me. Go; there is still time. The smoke is already filling the room, and I have my prayers to make. Let us say goodbye, and then go. God bless you.'

Weeping, we embraced her. With tears in her eyes, she blessed us all. 'Forgive me.' she said, 'a wretched sinner, if ever I have done you any injury, and when you see any of my family, give them my last greeting.' We bowed before her as before one who was dead. The room was already filled with smoke.[11]

By now the fire was spreading quickly, although it had not reached the neighbour-hood where Madame Fusil lived, so she decided to go for an evening stroll:

When we left, our house was intact, and there was not even a suspicion of a fire in any of the nearby streets … We wanted to take the usual route along the boul-evard, but it was impossible to get through. Fire blazed everywhere, so we went up the Tverskoe, but there the flames were even fiercer, and the Grand Theatre, where we went next, was nothing but an inferno. A year's timber supply had been stacked against the walls, and the Theatre, built of wood, fed this terrible fire. We turned right, as that seemed less on fire, but when we got half-way along the street the wind drove the flames with such violence that they joined the other side and formed a canopy of fire. This may seem an exaggeration, but it is nevertheless exactly what happened.

We could go neither forward nor sideways, and we had no option but to retrace our steps. However, the fire was gaining every minute, and sparks dropped just by our carriage. The coachman, sitting sideways, held the reins convulsively, and his face, turned towards us, expressed extreme fright. We shouted to him 'Nazad!' (Turn back!). This was difficult, but impelled by fear he managed to summon up enough strength to turn his horses. He set them at a gallop, and we reached the boulevard once more. We took the route back to our district, looking forward to being able to rest our eyes which were sore with dust and the heat of the flames.

I shall never forget my impression when I saw what awaited us. The house, to which we expected to return peacefully, and where, only an hour before, there had been no sign of a spark, was on fire. This can only just have happened, because the people inside had not yet realised the fact. It was the cries of Madame Vandraminy's little girl which brought them running. This child had lost her head and was shout-ing, 'Save mama, save everything. Oh, my God! We are lost!'[12]

By the night of 15/16 September, the fire had spread to the neighbourhood of the Kremlin where Napoleon had made his quarters. Fearing for his life his marshals forced him to leave the building. He had no option but to walk through burning streets to the Petrovsky Palace. 'We were besieged by an ocean of flames,' wrote Count Segur.

It was this night that the retreating Russian Army first saw a glow in the sky, a German captain in the Elizabethgrad Hussars recalls:

> It was during the night of the 15–16 September that we first saw an immense glow on the horizon, indicating that a great fire had broken out in Moscow. Although the swarm of refugees had gradually scattered along various roads and into different neighbourhoods, we were still surrounded by many hundreds of people of every age, sex and rank. When these poor wretches, who had often been able to save only a tiny part of their belongings, saw the fiery glow of their blazing home town in the night sky, they began wailing and complaining. The women in particular showed this by violent outbursts of grief, whereas the men often did no more than clench their fists and swear bitter revenge on these insolent enemies of their motherland on whom they now laid the blame for the downfall of their proud city. The glow was so bright that it almost lit up the road, and we were able to travel almost the whole night through, since sleep was out of the question and we could maintain our horses on full rations of fodder.[13]

The following evening the fire was just as bright. At 3.00am, the morning of 17 September, a merchant by the name of Marakuyev saw

> … from the direction of Moscow a strong glow, very different from the ordinary glow; on the horizon the sky was like a burning pillar which seemed to be wavering or trembling … I beheld it, speechless, numbed with fear, pity and dreadful uncertainty.

The fire was so intense that ashes from it fell on the retreating Russian Army and the refugees, another blow to their morale. Sergei Glinka, who belonged to one of the militia regiments, recorded: 'Quickly our soldiers turned to look at Moscow and exclaimed sadly "Mother Moscow is burning". Overcome by a heavy and deathly grief I threw myself to the ground and my hot tears mingled with the dust.'[14]

To Lieutenant Radozhitsky of the artillery, the fire was seen by the superstitious people as 'the triumph of the Antichrist, soon to be followed by the Final Judgement and the end of the world'. While General Lowenstern claimed that at night even though he was 20 to 30 km away from Moscow he could still 'read without difficulty the letters and the newspaper that I had received'.[15]

The Russian General Benkendorf looked on the more positive side of Moscow in flames, proclaiming the flames were 'more fatal to Napoleon than to Russia'.[16] The fire lasted six days before it burnt itself out, by which time three-quarters of Moscow was in ashes, and with it the provisions that were stored in the city. Explosions could be heard within Moscow because the French were demolishing houses that were likely to collapse.

Meanwhile, the drunken soldiers of the Grande Armée continued to plunder the ruins of Moscow. Andrei Karfachevski, who worked for the post office in the city, described the thoroughness of the effort:

The fires went on for six whole days and nights, so that it was impossible to tell night from day. All that time pillage continued: the French entered houses and, committing gross acts of violence, took from their owners not only money, gold and silver, but even boots, linen, and – most ludicrous of all – cassocks, women's furs and cloaks, in which they stood on guard and rode on horseback. It was not uncommon for people walking in the street to be stripped to their shirt, and many were robbed of boots, overcoats, frockcoats. Anybody who resisted was beaten savagely, often to death; and in particular many priests of the churches here endured severe tortures at the hands of the French seeking to extract from them information on where the church treasure was hidden. The French seized merchants and peasants, judging from their beards alone that they were priests. In short, their treatment of the inhabitants was most inhuman, and they made no distinction: any man they came across, whether official or peasant, they put to work. They made him carry sacks of stolen property and barrels of wine, dig potatoes in the vegetable gardens and then peel them, chop cabbage and drag from the streets the bodies of men and horses ...

After pillaging churches they stabled horses, slaughtered cattle and lodged wounded soldiers there; and having stripped the sacred icons of their frames they bayoneted them and poured filth on them; they also committed other abominations which the tongue cannot mention. In the houses of merchants and gentlemen property which had been in store rooms and basements and cleverly walled up with bricks so that it was quite impossible to perceive that there was a hole was discovered by the French. Not even property buried in the ground escaped discovery; under vegetables and courtyards they prodded the ground and pulled out chests.[17]

The inhabitants of Moscow were not all passive spectators to the plundering; given the opportunity they fought back:

From time to time Frenchmen would come up to us, go round everybody, and take anything they came across; and everybody gave away his property, if only to keep his head on his shoulders. You see they had muskets and swords and we had our bare hands. Then again, on our side, nearly all the people were women, old men and children, so we had perforce to bear it. However, when one of the French on his own or two of them together looked in on us, we received them in our own way. I recall seeing one dashing young lad going along in search of gain. He did not touch us, but went on and started to take someone else's things. All at once several men set on him and then the fun began: our people shouted and he shouted – begging for mercy. But how could he expect mercy when the people themselves were homeless and starving and were now, on top of everything else, being robbed? I saw them drag the wretched Frenchman off somewhere, and afterwards return without him. 'We finished him off,' they said, 'We strangled him and put him down a well.'[18]

Anna Grigorievna, a shopkeeper, also remembered an incident (amongst several, it seems, at the same place) when the Russians exacted some revenge :

> My father stayed in our cellar alone with the women. As ill luck would have it, an enemy soldier forced the door. Over his shoulder he carried a huge cudgel. He brandished it in his left hand and with his right seized my father by the throat. I rushed at the brigand, snatched his cudgel, and caught him by the nape of the neck. He dropped, whereupon everyone fell upon him, killed him in an instant, and dragged his body off to the pond. We had thrown quite a few uninvited guests into this pond and two wells. Sometimes four or five arrived together. They rummaged all over the place, but we did not move. They could see for themselves that there was nothing to take, and if they took it into their heads to do us harm, we knew how to bring them to reason. Not one of them went out alive. All this sickened me, but the instinct for self preservation is uppermost. If we had let them go after beating them, you can see that they would have gone away in a fury and returned in a band to exterminate us to the last man. And so we had no pity. To the death!

As the occupation continued food began to run low; Mr C:

> Meat, which had been abundant during the first week, was not now to be had. They doled out day by day to each a small allowance of flour from the household store, which they kneaded into paste and baked themselves over their fires. This supply began at last to fail, without the possibility of it being replenished from any quarter; for the present those who had ventured to market were being beaten and robbed of their provisions. Carts and horses had ceased their visits, so that no grain was to be produced. Feeling themselves deprived, therefore, of every other resource, they were driven to forage accompanied by the French soldiers, in the gardens of the neighbourhood, digging for potatoes and roots or whatever they could find: yet even this mode of subsistence was precarious, and their work was often interrupted by the incursion of the Cossacks. In a half starved condition, without a single change of clothes or linen, this gentleman passed the greater part of the time the French stayed at Moscow.[19]

Like any occupied country or city, some of the population inevitably collaborated with the victors. Some women turned to prostitution for food; Captain Vionnet, who served in the Grande Armée, wrote: 'they included some honest women who were nearly dying of hunger and were obliged to surrender themselves … to the first comers.'

A puppet Russian government was set up by Napoleon from prominent citizens who remained in the city, whether they wanted to or not. 'Inhabitants of Moscow,' began a French proclamation,

> Your miseries are great, but His Majesty the Emperor and King desired to put an end to your sufferings. Terrible examples have shown you how he punishes

disobedience and crime. Severe measures have been taken to put an end to disorder and restore general security.

A paternal administration, composed of men chosen from among you, will govern your municipality. The administrative body will care for you, your needs and your interests …

Several churches of different sects are open, and divine service is there celebrated without obstacle.

Your fellow citizens are daily returning to their houses and orders have been given that they shall have the aid and protection due to their misfortune.

Such are the means by which the government hopes to re-establish order and mitigate your misfortunes. But to attain that end you must unite your efforts with theirs, you must forget, if possible, the evils you have endured, you must cherish the hope of a less cruel destiny, you must be convinced that an inevitable and infamous death awaits all those who make any assault upon your lives or your property, and especially you must believe that your welfare will be cherished for such is the will of the greatest and most just of all monarchs.

The members of the new government were to be distinguished by a red scarf, which was worn in 'a form of a cross', the mayor was also to wear a white belt. There were to be two general commissioners and twenty magistrates who were to be assigned to different areas of the city and to be distinguished by a white band on the left arm. All but a few probably realised that this was a mere puppet government.[20]

On 13 September, Rostopchin had lost no time in sending a messenger to Alexander to inform him of the fall of Moscow, prompting the Tsar to send Prince Volkonsky to the army to find out about the situation. The same cannot be said about Kutuzov; almost a week passed before he sent a message informing the Tsar of Napoleon's entry into the city.

On 23 September the American John Quincy Adams, who was then in St Petersburg, recorded in his journal

… rumours that the French are in possession of that city. These rumours have been prevailing these three days and with them other reports, that the French had been repulsed and the Emperor mortally wounded. Mr Harris paid us a visit in the evening and told us that official accounts were now received that the Russian Army had retired behind Moscow, 16 km on the road to Kazan, and that Moscow had been surrendered by a sort of capitulation to the French; that the King of Naples [Murat] with 8,000 men took possession of the city on the 15th or 16th of this month and that the Emperor Alexander was informed of it three days afterwards. The French Emperor with his great army had not entered Moscow, but was still in pursuit of the Russians. There has been no battle since that of the seventh, which Prince Kutuzov reported as a splendid victory, for which he was made a field marshal and received from the Emperor a present of one hundred thousand roubles. The result of this great Russian victory was to put the French in possession of Moscow.[21]

Those who were caught spreading this 'false' rumour were ordered to sweep the streets of St Petersburg. However the rumours continued, but still there was no official declaration that Moscow had been captured. Finally at the end of September Alexander was forced to issue a proclamation:

It is with a heavy heart we are compelled to inform every son of the country, that the enemy entered Moscow on the 3rd [15th] of September. The glory of the Russian empire, however is not thereby tarnished. On the contrary, every individual is inspired with fresh courage, firmness and hope, that all the evils meditated against us by our enemies will eventually fall upon their own heads. The enemy has not become master of Moscow by overcoming or weakening our forces; the Commander in Chief has found it expedient to retire at a moment of necessity, in order, by the best and most effectual means to turn the transient triumph of the enemy to his inevitable ruin. However painful it may be to Russians to hear that the original capital of the empire is in the hands of the enemy of their country, yet it is consolatory to reflect that he is possessed merely of bare walls, containing within their circuit neitheèr inhabitants nor provisions. The haughty conqueror imagined he would become the arbiter of the whole Russian empire, when he might prescribe to it such a peace as he should think proper; but he is deceived in his expectations: he will neither have acquired the power of dictating, nor the means of subsistence …

Russia is unaccustomed to subjection and will not suffer her laws, religion, freedom and property to be trampled upon. She will defend them to the last drop of her blood. Hitherto the general zeal against the enemy clearly evinces how powerfully our empire is guarded by the undaunted spirit of her sons.

Thus no one despairs; nor is this a time to despair, when every class of the empire is inspired with courage and firmness, when the enemy, with the remainder of his daily decreasing forces at a distance from home, in the midst of a numerous people, is surrounded by our armies, one of which stands before him and the other three are endeavouring to cut off his retreat to prevent him receiving any fresh reinforcements …

Almighty God! Turn thy merciful eye to thy supplicating church. Vouchsafe courage and patience to thy people struggling in a just cause so that they may thereby overcome the enemy and in saving themselves may also defend the freedom of kings and nations![22]

As the war progressed anti-French feeling increased – the German poet Ernst Moritz Arndt who spent the summer of 1812 in St Petersburg records that Madame de Staël's lover and her son went to see Jean Racine's *Phèdre,* performed by French actors at a St Petersburg theatre:

The two of them came back quite soon and rather disconcerted. They explained that at the beginning of the play there had been so much noise and roaring in the theatre and such abuse of the French and the French play by the Russians that the performance had to be stopped. And that is what happened in fact; this was the last time the French actors played that summer in St Petersburg, and public hatred and contempt was so bluntly, so roughly expressed that at the beginning of the next winter they had to leave the city.[23]

Others refused to speak French, the language of the Russian court. For many, their hatred turned upon the Tsar, who they blamed for Russia's misfortunes. This prompted Catherine, Alexander's sister, to write to the Tsar, on 19 September:

> I cannot restrain myself any longer, notwithstanding the pain which I am forced to inflict on you. The capture of Moscow has caused extreme irritation. Dissatisfaction has reached the highest point, and your person is far from being spared. If such things reach even me, you may judge the rest for yourself. You are loudly blamed for the misfortune which has overtaken our Empire, for the general devastation and the ruin of private persons, and, finally, for having dishonoured the country and yourself. It is not one class that brings these charges against you, but all classes. Not to mention what is being said about the way we are carrying on the war. You are chiefly attacked for violating your word to Moscow ... abandoning the city. It looks as though you have betrayed the city. You need not fear a catastrophe of a revolutionary kind. But you can judge for yourself the state of affairs in a country whose head is despised. There is nothing that people would not do to restore our honour, but, considering their desire to sacrifice everything for the Fatherland, they ask 'What good will that do if everything is destroyed, spoiled, by the incapacity of our leaders?' The desire for peace is, fortunately, far from universal, because the feeling of shame caused by the loss of Moscow engenders a desire for revenge. People are blaming you, and blaming you loudly. I think it is my duty to tell you this dear Friend, because it is extremely important. What should you do is not for me to say, but do save your honour, which is being attacked. Your presence may incline minds towards you; do not neglect any means to achieve this end, and please do not think that I exaggerate. No, unfortunately I speak the truth, and my heart bleeds for you; I owe you a great deal, and I would give my life a thousand times to save you from the situation in which you now find yourself.[24]

Catherine was not the only one to recognise the hostile feelings towards the Tsar. Countess Edling, one of the ladies in waiting, wrote after the royal retinue had attended a *Te Deum* at the Cathedral of the Virgin of Kazan in St Petersburg to celebrate the anniversary of his coronation.

> I shall never, as long as I live, forget those moments when we were mounting the steps of the Cathedral. Not a single greeting was heard. We could hear our own footsteps, and I had not the slightest doubt that the least spark would have been enough to cause a conflagration. I glanced at His Majesty and understood what was going on in his mind. I felt my knees giving way under me.[25]

Alexander has been much criticised by historians for his weaknesses, and remembering that both his father and grandfather had been assassinated this tension may have broken a lesser man. But Alexander held firm, writing to his sister on 30 September in reply to her letter:

> At St Petersburg I found everyone bent on old Kutuzov being given the chief command, that was the general cry. My knowledge of the man made me against it at first, but when, in his letter of 5th August, Rostopchin informed me that all Moscow wants Kutuzov to command, considering Barclay and Bagration both incapable of the post, and meanwhile, as if on purpose, Barclay only commanded blunder on blunder round Smolensk. I could not do otherwise than yield to the general wish, and appointed Kutuzov. I still believe at this moment that in the conditions then obtaining, I could not do otherwise than out of three generals, alike unfit to take the chief command, fix my choice on him for whom the general voice was given.[26]

In those days of uncertainty no one knew what the future held for Russia. How long would the French occupy Moscow? Would Russia come to terms with Napoleon? What had become of the Russian Army?

Notes

1 Quoted in A. N. Rambaud, 'La Grande Armée a Moscow', in *Revue des Deux Mondes,* 1873 p.204
2 Quoted in A. A. Orlov 'Britons in Moscow, 1812' in *History Today* vol 53
3 Quoted in Brett James, *1812* p.170
4 Varestchagin, *1812, Napoleon I in Russia* pp. 203–204
5 Ibid, pp. 198–199
6 Voronenko's official report to Moscow Administration quoted in Tarle's *Napoleon's Invasion of Russia* p.170
7 Fusil, *Souvenirs d'une Femme sur la Retraite de Russie* pp.228–229
8 James, *Journal of a tour...* p. 178
9 James, *Journal of a tour...* pp.179–180.
10 James, *Journal of a tour...* pp.183–184
11 Varestchagin, *1812, Napoleon I in Russia* p.200
12 Brett James, *1812* pp.181–182
13 Ibid, p.175
14 Ibid, p.165
15 Radozhitsky, *Poxodnie zapiski artilerista* p.172
16 *Zapiski Benkendorfa 1812* p.63
17 Brett James, *1812* pp.186–187
18 Quoted in Garin, *Izgnanye Napoleona iz Moskkvy* (Moscow, 1938) p.48
19 James, *Journal of a tour...* pp.179–180.
20 Leo Tolstoy's, *The Physiology of War* pp.89–90
21 *Journal of John Quincy Adams* p.404.
22 The *Caledonian Mercury* 22 October 1812
23 Brett James, *1812* p.70
24 Tarle, *Napoleon's Invasion of Russia* p.180
25 Bragin, *Kutuzov* p.100
26 Tarle, *Napoleon's Invasion of Russia* pp.180–182 and Henry Havelock *Scenes of Russian Court Life* pp.111–113

14

THE NORTHERN FLANK

Marshal MacDonald's Corps had crossed the River Nieman at Tilsit to protect the northern flank of Napoleon's main thrust. Fearing that he might be outflanked, Napoleon also sent Marshal Oudinot's II Corps to support MacDonald.

On 11 July Oudinot attacked the fortress of Dunaburg. Major General Ulanov, the commander of Dunaburg:

> At noon the enemy appeared on the heights of the fortifications about 2 or 3 km from the Kalennen Gate … [and] at 4pm attacked the bridge of the fortress higher up towards the hills and continued the engagement from six o'clock in the evening until ten.
>
> Although the enemy made great exertions to penetrate into the fortress, he was constantly repulsed by a sharp fire from the battalions in reserve, and a constant discharge of artillery from the fortress and the vicinity. He, nevertheless, harassed us during the night by his sharpshooters, and this morning, at break of day, the cannonade was renewed. Yesterday I am inclined to believe, the loss of the enemy was considerably greater than ours, the exact number of which however, on account of the unceasing cannonade, I have not had time exactly to ascertain.[1]

On 16 July the 1st Russian Army continued its retreat from the camp at Drissa. Barclay feared that the enemy might make a thrust towards St Petersburg and so detached Wittgenstein's I Corps, with orders to place his corps between the River Druia and Drissa and so cover the road to St Petersburg. The same day Russian Army Headquarters issued the following report:

> The enemy having directed a great force against our right wing, the first army has put itself in motion to oppose it. Count Wittgenstein, whose corps was posted on the right bank of the Dwina, being informed that two French regiments of cavalry had approached Druia, sent Major General Kulnev across the river with the Grodno

Regiment of hussars and a few squadrons of Cossacks. Kulnev attacked the French cavalry with complete success. The two regiments of the enemy were completely cut up, and their commander, Brigadier General St Genie, with several officers and 200 privates, were made prisoners.

On the first of this month, Marshal Oudinot's corps in front of Dunaburg at four in the morning commenced an attack upon the bridge. They were repulsed by the garrison. According to the latest accounts from Major General Ulanov, the attack was renewed on the 14th, but the enemy were again repulsed with loss.[2]

On 19 July, the Prussians, under General Gravert, which formed part of Macdonalds' X Corps, forced General Lewis to withdraw to Riga. However, the Prussians advanced towards Riga to lay siege to the port. The garrison made several sallies to try and break the siege, but with mixed fortunes.

At the end of July, General Gravert was taken ill and handed his command over to General York. Meanwhile, the remainder of Macdonald's Corps remained inactive at Jakobstad. Without their support the Prussians could only shadow Riga. The inhabitants of the town did not know that, and on 24 July Rear Admiral Martin of the Royal Navy reported to London:

> The alarm here among all classes has been very great. Thinking that the enemy would push forward with his whole force at a moment when least expected and this, after much wavering and contradictory orders, induced the General [Essen] to direct the extensive suburbs on this side of the river to be set on fire at 11 o'clock last night, forgetting, I fear, that the inhabitants had been lulled into security in the morning by being given to understand the place would not be immediately destroyed. The consequence has been most shocking and the scene of uproar and confusion beyond anything I can describe for the inhabitants were taken so much by surprise that some were actually burnt to death in their beds. The whole of the suburbs are now already consumed, the houses on the opposite side of the river were burnt three days ago … The initiation produced in the public mind by this punitive measure is, I am sorry to say, very great and will no doubt be manifested in the most resentful manner when the enemy invest the place.
>
> The suburbs had a population of 15,000 souls and many families have wandered into the woods, while others are floating about the river on stages, with their effects in the most deplorable state.[3]

The garrison appears to have received little intelligence on the events of the campaign. Martin continues, 'It is extraordinary their General [Essen] seems so uninformed of what is passing he has no knowledge of anything beyond the limits of his own command.'[4] Over the next few months the city heard unconfirmed rumours that the Russian 1st and 2nd Armies had united at Vitebsk and then routed Napoleon's Army at Borodino.

On 31 July, six Russian gunboats manned by Royal Navy crews and several ships of the Royal Navy at Riga were reinforced by 102 Russian gunboats, with their

280 guns and 5,000-strong crew. These ships could support Riga, but not attack the French inland, so in early August it was proposed that a strong naval force should land an Anglo-Russian force on the Heel of Danzig, and so threaten the port of Danzig.[5] On 22 August the force sailed for the Heel, arriving a few days later. HMS *Meteor* was to bombard Danzig itself and it was hoped that this would be mistaken for the beginning of a Swedish invasion or at least distract the French forces in the north of Russia.[6]

Once the force arrived off Danzig and HMS *Meteor* had fired a few shots into the town, it was decided not to land the 8,000 men, but occasionally to land a few hundred men at a time for exercise. The inhabitants were told to stay indoors while the troops were on shore. Finally on 16 September, having achieved very little, the force sailed back to Riga. Even so, on 24 September General Essen wrote to Rear Admiral Martin, the commander of the force:

> The expedition to Danzig which your Excellency has conducted with so much judgement has been … very advantageous to the interests of this country and particularly to the city of Riga in arresting the march of the enemy's troops, which were advancing towards it, and I can never sufficiently repeat to you, Sir, that the judgement with which they were executed has acquired you the gratitude of all those who wish success to the common cause.[7]

Despite the somewhat oleaginous praise, it is doubtful this attack made any impact on the campaign.

Meanwhile, Wittgenstein decided to advance and confront Oudinot. Their forces clashed on 28 July, and the French were driven back by the Russian advance guard. Another clash between the 30 July–1 August had the same results. The Russian bulletin dated 31 July reported:

> Yesterday and today Lieutenant General Wittgenstein defeated the corps of Oudinot near Dworzhbibova, between Polotzk and Sebetch. The advance guard and the reserve of Count Wittgenstein pursued the enemy closely. A large part of the baggage of the French had already been taken by the Russians.
>
> The next day, he intended to pursue the enemy, and after passing the Dwina with or without opposition from Oudinot's Corps, it was his intention to turn upon MacDonald to relieve Courland and Livionia.
>
> At the time of departure of the courier the Russians had taken 3,000 prisoners and two pieces of cannon and were continuing in pursuit of the enemy.[8]

On 2 August, a Russian force under General Berg defeated several French divisions. Far from pressuring the force protecting St Petersburg, the French were being forced back on Polotsk, a town just south of where the Polota stream joins the River Dwina. Like most towns in Russia it was formed from wooden huts and a bridge over the Dwina linked the town with the village of Little Polotsk on the west bank. To the east of Polotsk is the village of Spas and north of that the Prismenitza estate.

A crescent-shape forest was nearby, which partly enclosed a flat marshy plain, with the land rising towards the Polota. Running north-east of Polotsk through the forest was the St Petersburg road.

Oudinot appealed to Napoleon for reinforcements, which prompted the Emperor to send Saint Cyr's Bavarians to his aid. On 4 August, already hungry and with dysentery spreading through their ranks, the Bavarians received orders to join Oudinot at Polotsk. Still the skirmishing continued, the Russians usually having the upper hand.

The *Edinburgh Evening Courant* published the following information they had received from Riga:

> The General Count Wittgenstein has on the 11th August and 12th August at Dworjakora, between Polotsk and Sebesch, totally defeated Marshal Oudinot's Corps and pursued him to Polotsk, where he will be under the necessity of returning back over the Dwina; 3,000 men, two pieces of artillery and the greatest part of the baggage, have fallen into the victor's hands. Count Wittgenstein is now in pursuit of MacDonald, to liberate Courland and Livionia, from their oppressors. This victory has inspired our troops with redoubled courage, and their ardour for the liberty of their native country is great, and as this ardour goes hand in hand with valour, no army scrapped together from several nations, and differing in their religion, manners and opinions, shall dare to oppose our disciplined troops who are animated by patriotism, and not compelled by force, and whose most ardent desire is to be revenged of their enemies. The enemy is on the western bank of the Dwina, at a distance of 21 km from the fortress of Riga, his force is estimated at about 15,000 men. General Grandjean's Corps is at Jacobstadt, on the western side of the Dwina, and is endeavouring to throw a bridge across the said river at Kreutzberg. Riga is in a most excellent state of defence, and has certainly no danger to fear. The commandant, General Essen, has detached a number of troops to attack the right wing of the Prussian Army, and cut off the Prussian General Cravert from Mittau in which place there is but a very inconsiderable garrison.[9]

On 12 August Count Wittgenstein wrote to the Tsar:

> I have received information from my advanced posts that the enemy was making every effort from Polotsk to carry them, and by prisoners and deserters, that the French Grande Armée was constantly receiving reinforcements of Bavaria and Wurttemberg troops.
>
> I accordingly detached four squadrons under the command of Major Bedragni whom I directed to observe every movement of MacDonald's army and give me notice thereof. I advanced against Oudinot's corps, which I met on the evening of the 10 August 4 km from Rochoaova.
>
> Having immediately made the necessary arrangements, I yesterday vigorously attacked him with the help of God.
>
> After eight hours constant fighting the enemy was routed and pursued by his Majesty's brave troops, until night came on.

We have taken three officers and 250 soldiers. The loss of the enemy in killed and wounded has been considerable. Their cuirassiers, particularly, have suffered much in consequence of their attempts to take our guns. I caused them to be pursued by the hussars of Grodno, who distinguished themselves on this occasion. We have lost 400 men in killed and wounded, among whom we have particularly to lament the death of the gallant Colonel Dennissen.[10]

Although it was not until 15 August that the Bavarians arrived at Polotsk. The following evening Oudinot and Saint Cyr held a council of war to discuss their strategy. Early in the morning of 17 August, Wittgenstein attacked along the St Petersburg road and drove the Bavarians from Prismenitza and launched an attack on Spas, which was on the right of the allied positions. By 11.00am they were in possession of the town, except for the church and monastery. The Bavarians counter-attacked and the village changed hands several times. Finally, towards evening the Russians were repulsed and Wrede's Bavarians were masters of Spas. At about 6.00pm, having failed to turn the Allies' right wing, the Russians switched their attack towards the centre commanded by the French Division of General Legrand, but were repulsed. Towards night Wittgenstein withdrew his men to the line of the trees.

With Oudinot and St Cyr wounded, Wittgenstein expected the French to withdraw. However, although Oudinot himself retired, St Cyr remained at his post and decided to launch an attack the following day, but considering the exhaustion of his men he decided to attack at about 4.00pm. In the meantime he evacuated his wagons to the west bank of the Dvina and a truce was agreed so that both sides could bury their dead.

As the monastery clock struck 4.00pm (some sources say 5.00pm) a Bavarian cannon fired as a signal for the whole allied line to advance. Wittgenstein and his staff were at Prismenitza and were totally surprised by this attack, believing that the allies had been withdrawing. The Russians quickly recovered and laid down a heavy fire, the attack began to waver, but with the loss of Prismenitza, Wittgenstein knew that the day was lost and he ordered a withdrawal. The Russians had lost about 5,500 men to the Allies' 3,500.

On 17 August Lieutenant General Wittgenstein wrote to Alexander and tried to make the best of his defeat:

> I remained with the corps close to Polosk, I resolved to make a movement for the purpose of observing the corps under Marshal MacDonald. Meanwhile Marshal Oudinot had, exclusive [of the] reinforcements of Bavarian troops under the command of General Wrede, received a further reinforcement of the same troops under the command of General Deroy. Then, at 4 o'clock in the afternoon of the 18th, he [Oudinot] attacked me at all points with five divisions of infantry, commencing the attack with a most heavy cannonade from all his artillery. This was one of the bloodiest, most severe and obstinate battles fought on both sides. Your Imperial Majesty's valiant troops without regard to the enemy's number, which was triple their own, confronted them everywhere with their usual courage and animosity, drove back

their batteries and their strong columns on several occasions, obliging them to retire into the town and they even fought in the very streets. The pitch black of night compelled us to put an end to this exceedingly fierce and desperate action; after which the enemy withdrew into their entrenchments. Whilst I, according to my plan, after leaving my vanguard there, marched with the body of the army on the Schesch road to the village of Belofoe. In the battle the losses in killed and wounded were great on both sides. We have taken prisoner two lieutenant colonels, fifteen officers and about 500 soldiers. We have also taken two pieces of heavy artillery. The cuirassier regiment had taken fifteen pieces, but we could not bring all off for want of horses and the difficulty of getting them over the ditches which separated us.

The enemy has certainly lost three times the number in killed and wounded that we have; for as they threw themselves with their columns of infantry on our batteries, each time they left the greater part of their men dead on the field. On this day the cuirassier regiment cut to pieces two whole columns and during the whole progess of the action, that regiment everywhere proved to be of the most distinguished value. Neither is our loss trifling; Major Generals Berg and Gamen have each received a wound. Major General Kosatschkovsk is wounded by a musket shot and Colonel Brovlav by a cartridge ball. The enemy is thrown into great confusion by the battle. On the 17th Marshal Oudinot himself was wounded in the shoulder and on the 18th so was the next senior commander of the Bavarian troops [Deroy]. The French General Gouvion St Cyr took the command in his place and I hope that he will not be able to undertake anything of consequence. I shall now observe the road to Pskov on all sides, and wait to see what progress the Grande Armée will make.[11]

After the Battle of Polotsk both sides settled down to a period of inactivity, patrols clashing with each other every now and then. Disease and hunger ravaged the ranks of the Franco-Bavarian force, while Wittgenstein could easily gain reinforcements, among them the St Petersburg Opolchenye.

On 14 September, the St Petersburg Militia, after receiving what was described as five 'summer days training' marched out to join the army after being reviewed by his Majesty the Emperor, and receiving the blessing of the Archbishop.

These troops retain their national dress; they wear round hats, embellished with a cross, and an inscription 'for our religion and native country' they are armed with good muskets and bayonets, and have battle-axes at their sides. These troops are inspired with the most lively enthusiasm; and when the Emperor arrived to conduct them to the city gates, he was received and accompanied with the most cheerful huzzahs.[12]

Although poorly trained and armed with muskets, pikes and axes, they would distinguish themselves in the forthcoming battles against Napoleon's veteran regiments.

Lieutenant General Thaddeus Steingell's corps also joined Wittgenstein about this time. His corps had been released from garrisoning Finland, after promises from

Sweden that it would not take advantage of the situation to regain the province, which had been lost to Russia after the Russo-Swedish War (1808–1809).

On 15–16 October, Wittgenstein again advanced on Polotsk, while a force of 12,000 under Lieutenant General Steinhall attacked the French under Strohl at Disna on the 16th. After heavy fighting, Strohl was forced to withdraw. Two days later Wittgenstein attacked the Allies at Polotsk. Among the attackers were the St Petersburg Opolchenye, tired from their long march but full of enthusiasm, supported by the Voronezh Regiment. Rafail Mihailovich Zotov was a junior officer in one of these Militia regiments:

> The forward columns advanced along the main road, as the shots began. This was the beginning of a bloody day. The enemy outposts, which did not expect so strong an attack, were shattered and quickly retreated ... Detachments of cavalry, both ours and enemy's, dashed past us constantly... we looked at all this with curiosity not thinking about any participation ourselves and not even imagining that the battle had already begun.
>
> We soon entered the wood, the mud was awful, hardly passable, the horses were unable to convey the guns and we, it goes without saying, began to drag them ourselves.

For four hours they dragged the cannon to the battlefield, hearing the noise of battle in the distance:

> We imagined that the city would be captured without us and that we would be too late ... About 12pm we finally arrived at the edge of the wood, delivered our guns close to the bushes and rested. Here for the first time in my life I saw the terrible action of the main body of the army. An unfortunate horse not far off had both front legs torn off. It was impossible to look at this poor animal without the greatest pity, that with despair was licking the fresh blood from the wounds ...
>
> They did not give us a long time to rest. The Voronezh Regiment, which formed our first line, moved forward, but we remained for a time in reserve. Noticing our column's recent appearance from the wood, the enemy directed fire on it from several guns of the brick battery (they had converted the brick works into a strong field fortification, making use of the bricks by lining the trenches and parapets).
>
> Suddenly shots buzzed above our heads and dug into the ground behind the column. We all, as if directed by a magic baton, squatted ... Someone's adjutant came galloping up and ordered the colonel to advance to reinforce the Voronezh Regiment ... [The colonel] led us toward the enemy. This first attempt was very unsuccessful; we did not get far ... We did not have time to cover a hundred metres before three batteries, from God knows where, began to greet us from different sides with both ball and caseshot! We advanced for about five minutes with something like intoxication, almost unconsciously, then suddenly, what triggered it I do not know, the entire front did not stand, we rushed back in confusion. Not until the edge of the wood did we all halt, bewildered, and we began to look at each other.

This first sally did not flatter anyone. The colonel flew into a rage, swore and beat the soldiers with his sword and ordered 'Halt! Reform!' Somehow all of us came to our senses, feeling ashamed, and we returned to duty. All excitedly began to encourage the soldiers and again the entire front advanced regularly and resolutely. Again they started to shower us from the batteries, but this time the hearts were strengthened, and all the Druzhina [militia unit] heroically slowly advanced. To the left of us we saw the Voronezh Regiment withdrawing silently and in good order …

We noticed in the distance the enemy advancing. We stopped and began firing. About a quarter of an hour it continued and here for the first time I heard the music of Charles XII. The whistle of bullets about the ears did not now produce such a big impression. But the enemy's actions were very effective. Every moment soldiers and officers were knocked out from the front rank and others took their place.

Meanwhile the enemy came closer and closer to us; our shooting, it seemed, was not particularly deadly. Suddenly the colonel ordered 'Stop firing!, Officers to the front! Charge bayonets, quick step, march! Ura!' Finally we felt that we were on our own ground. A terrible and pleasurable moment! We quickly walked towards the enemy, then instead of the quick step we were running at the enemy, who, not resisting and not waiting for us, started to run as fast as their legs could carry them, exactly as we had recently retreated.

For a minute the colonel stopped us, reformed, ordered us not to run but to proceed as evenly as possible – and not being able to see the enemy, who were hidden by the brick trenches, we decided to storm them. Cheered by our success we ignored the shots and bullets and our initial fears and chatted among ourselves, … and with the Druzhina shouted 'Ura!' set off towards the brick trenches … I remember that at that moment a glorious Udryadnik was nearby me, loading his musket … he was struck by a bullet directly on the forehead between the eyebrows just as he bit a cartridge in order to pour [the gunpowder] in to the priming pan – and he fell backwards still holding the unopened cartridge in his lips. I, who had so recently been almost in tears when touched by the suffering of the dying horse, burst out laughing over the cartridge sticking out of his mouth and all those around me, soldiers and officers ,shared my laughter. Strange, human nature …

We soon reached the brick trenches. There we imagined there would be slaughter and bloodshed! Our expectations were not fulfilled, we reached the trenches very cheaply [in casualties]. Before we reached them, our fine artillery, which we recently had dragged through the mud with such enthusiasm,… paid us back for our labour. From the outset it had turned its fire on these batteries and trenches … Neither guns nor soldiers were there. All we could see was … the terrible effects of our artillery. In fact this was partly because of the enemy's unusual idea of constructing parapets from bricks. As a temporary protection against infantry, they could serve well enough, but under the first intense effects of artillery those same bricks, crushed by 12 pounder shots, scattered into smithereens and killed their own soldiers. We saw the proof of this as we entered into the abandoned trenches. The heaps of enemy bodies lay throughout the entire area of the former factory. We were very sure that in death, all of them were completely innocent.

Be that as it may, we captured these trenches and were very pleased with our exploits. Here we rested for a quarter of an hour. It seems the colonel did not have further instructions and did not know what to do next.

The day was clear and bright. The dense clouds of gunpowder smoke rose majestically above the combatants. Echoes of Russian 'Uras!' were heard constantly! The masses of cavalry rushed along the plain backwards and forwards. To the right of us a country church, converted into a strong fortress, was armed on all sides with numerous artillery pieces. To the left was quite a large lake and behind it an immense field. Ahead of us was the town of Polotsk – the object of our labour and blood. Before it ran the small Polota Stream, which flowed in a deep and steep ravine over which there were only two bridges, along the Sebezhskoi Road and from the side of Vitebsk. For some time we admired this splendid picture, not understanding what masses moved around us. Where and for what are they directed? … At length we caught sight of a column advancing. We left the trenches. This was the 6th Druzhina advancing to experience the enemy's fire for the first time . To their credit it should be said that there was some bewilderment and timidity visible on the faces of the soldiers and officers, but they courageously went forward and they were not going to withdraw in our opinion.

But at this moment we forgot our basic training and we saw ourselves the victors over the Bavarian columns, which had run from our bayonets, and the conquerors of the brick trenches. That is why we encouraged those passing by and (guiltily!) even laughed at some, particularly at one officer from Germany who was very amusing. On the right flank of his platoon when he heard the bullets whistling about him, he brushed them off every time by hand and at the crash of a ball squatted almost to the ground. For a long time we had done the same but now this all seemed to us very funny. 'What are you doing here?' some angry adjutant shouted at us, catching sight of us in our quiet observation, 'The Voronezh Regiment again attack a superior enemy and you stand here and lay down your arms.' Our Colonel answered him and after a short explanation about further actions, he formed us in a dense column and ordered us to the left, where we could see in the distance a violent exchange of fire.

After about half a kilometre we were [coming up on] the Voronezh [Regiment] … [there] we came across the fine sight of a Bavarian column, which was apparently twice as strong as the Voronezh, but they pressed on in a most careless manner. On the road we were greeted with some caseshot from an enemy battery and this compelled the colonel to deploy us in line again in order to offer a smaller target. Soon we were formed up with the Voronezh Regiment and our arrival gave them heart. We joined their right flank … we stood on the spot and the Bavarians moved nearer and nearer to us. We suddenly saw that after ceasing fire they were coming at us with bayonets. Their impudence surprised us. The Colonel immediately … gave the order 'Charge bayonets' and without waiting for the enemy to reach us, ordered a quick and full attack. The customary 'Ura!' resounded and our front advanced. The officers withdrew from the front line and went around their platoons encouraging the soldiers not to be afraid. This time the Bavarians were not cowed and came on us with daring. In a few minutes both fronts came together – and the hand-to-hand fighting began.

Our soldiers were stronger, courageous, but less experienced. In the heat of the fight the enemy disrupted our line in different places and twenty Bavarians suddenly burst through our section. An officer's sword was not an equal weapon to their bayonets. One officer, Leont'ev, was the first victim of this inequality. Several bayonets in the chest threw him down unconscious. (He has since recovered and said that it was the most unpleasant feeling, three cold thrusts into the chest). Our Lieutenant Colonel, an honourable 60-year-old man had earlier been wounded in the leg by caseshot but still stayed in front and was knocked down by a blow from a butt [of a musket] in the head. After falling to the ground he abused the Bavarians with strong Russian words and lying on the ground defended himself with his sword against the bayonets.

All this lasted no more than two minutes, the Bavarians who had broken through were all beaten and the line, as far as possible, closed ranks, and after a few minutes more all the Bavarians were overthrown. Not listening to the commands, our bearded heroes were allowed to run after them and continued to stab them. A big effort and even blows were necessary for the Colonel to stop and reform these brave men, especially as at that moment a commander of the line, Kor-de Battail, sent the cavalry (the Yamburg Dragoons) to complete the defeat of the retreating Bavarian columns.

Stopping again, the Colonel waited for instructions for further action and received an order to reform us into a dense column, [and] to withdraw with the Voronezh Regiment ... to the reserve and to send from the regiment and from the Druzhina a platoon only ... to observe the enemy ...

From the Druszhin, I and Groten [another officer] with about 90 men as skirmishers ... crossed ourselves, and began to go forward ...

Across the whole 10 km extent of the plain on which the battle raged no one noticed us. The fighting boiled to the right of us as we approached the chains of enemy skirmishers, and engaged them in an amicable fire fight, not doing much harm to each other. My comrade was the son of a rich merchant and during a lull he asked me if he were killed to take his wallet and gold watch ... a bullet hit him straight in the forehead and he fell near me. With bitter tears I looked at him and forget his request. A detachment of two soldiers carried him to our column. This incident hit me hard and distressed me; I broke into a run to get to all the skirmishers and explained to them that it was vital to pay the enemy back for the death of our comrade.

They followed my wishes and we rushed forward with fury and killed the little group of enemy skirmishers. Breaking through ... their line, we reached as far as some battery, from which we did not receive fire, but as in the front of the battery there was a ditch and palisades we asked for advice from an old army NCO, 'What are we to do?' 'We, sir are too few; we will be killed here in vain. Return to our column' he replied ... I obeyed him and fairly quickly we began to withdraw back the way we had come.

Suddenly seeing in the distance a black mass of enemy cavalry bearing down on us, we immediately turned to the right and they reached as far as the empty brick trenches ... Here our rear was protected, but instead of taking refuge behind the trenches and hiding, we drew up in a group in front and waited for what was to happen. In two minutes the cavalry, which we had seen from a distance, came up to us. They were French cuirassiers. The sun struck directly onto their armour, horse-tails fluttered from their helmets, the earth shook from the clatter of their horses, quite simply, this was a magnificent sight. I would have paid a lot for this show. All this huge mass (not knowing where it was directed) rushed past us, without paying us the slightest attention, except for an occasional contemptuous glance. But it seemed to me just not right to see the enemy and not to shoot at them. I gave the order to our troops and they set about doing it. These sudden shots amazed the cavalrymen. They received them in the flank and many straightaway fell from their horses. However, they continued on their way, threatening us with their broad-swords. We continued to answer them with bullets, feeling very pleased that we had managed to kill about fifty of the enemy, which drew no response against us because they had another destination.

Their entire column had already almost passed, when suddenly we saw with ae certain uneasiness that the rear squadron had stopped and turned towards us, and begun to surround our small group. We nevertheless continued to shoot. Cursing us hard, they all came closer and closer upon us. In a few minutes I noticed that our firing began to abate. 'Why are you lads not shooting?' Some soldiers answered me, 'But sir, your honour, all the cartridges are gone!' and I could see at once that our position was very bad. The cuirassiers finally completely surrounded us and their commander shouted to us that we should surrender. I communicated the offer to my soldiers, but a large part answered me 'We will not give up to the infidel alive. Perhaps God will help and will come to our rescue.' I yelled my refusal, the last cartridges were quickly spent. Then the cuirassiers hacked their way through us and the slaughter began. Escape was just about impossible and everyone sold his life as dearly as possible and died very contented if he managed to plunge his bayonet into the side of a cuirassier. I think that this game continued about half an hour.

My small group was thinning out moment by moment and soon I remained alone, leaning on the brick parapet. Several times an enemy officer shouted to me, ordering me to surrender, but I answered them by profanities. Finally reaching me the gave me ... the first two blows by a broadsword to the head, but I did not fall, ... [I] remember that I wounded one in the thigh and jabbed the point [of my sword] into the side of another; and one of them, I don't know which paid me for it with a pistol shot, then another, one grazed me on the neck, and another hit my leg. I then fell, and blows and profanities rained down on me like rain. I was wearing a frockcoat, uniform and waistcoat and on top of all this was a haversack. All this was hacked to pieces like chopped cabbage. Of all the blows only two on the head were powerful, one in the arm was just a scratch and one horseman stabbed me in the back with the point of a broadsword. All the other blows did not even make a hole in my clothes. Believing me completely hacked to pieces they finally left. Sensing that they had left us, I opened my eyes. A river of blood flowed from my head and made me feel a kind of of pleasant warmth. The instinct for self preservation sprompted me to try to stop the blood running. Collecting all the strength, I untied my scarf, wrapped it around my head and lay down on the bricks, committing my fate to the Most High. Whether weakened from loss of blood, or from weariness of all this day's work, I felt sleepy. I shut my eyes and fell asleep. [13]

While Zotov lay there asleep, the French cuirassier were attacked by the Voronezh Regiment and two Druzhins to their left, a twelve-gun battery to the right and the Yamburg Dragoons struck them in the rear. Under this pressure the cuirassiers broke, pursued by the dragoons. The Druzhins advanced to the brick trenches, where they found Zotov and carried him to a doctor. The Russians made about seven assaults on Polotsk that day but after heavy fighting were repulsed leaving the Bavarians still in possession of several redoubts.

The following day, Wittgenstein, knowing that Steingell's force would arrive, began to bombard Polotsk. It was not until the afternoon that Steingell finally arrived, and realising that the Russians were advancing on several fronts, St Cyr decided to withdraw. However, fierce fighting continued into the evening through the burning streets of Polotsk. Finally St Cyr was able to withdraw from the town, but he had to leave many wounded behind, who were captured by the Russians.

On 20 October the Bavarians fought a rearguard action, which beat off Steingell's attacks. The losses on each side were about 8,000 troops. St Cyr could not afford to lose this number and his army was reduced to about 15,000 men; in contrast the Russians still had about 40,000 men in theatre.

St Cyr had been wounded and General Legrand, the next senior Frenchman, assumed command, but General Wrede was unwilling to obey his orders since he was junior in rank and decided to withdraw from the campaign. The Russians pursued Legrand's force, until Wittgenstein was ordered to march south to intercept Napoleon at the Berezina, driving the II and VI Corps with him.

If Napoleon had meant for MacDonald and St Cyr to threaten St Petersburg, Wittgenstein had prevented this. In fact in those dark days of the summer of 1812, Wittgenstein's army gave the populace of Russia something to celebrate. Following his successes, during the spring of 1813 Wittgenstein would succeed Kutuzov as the commander in chief. However, this position would eventually prove to be beyond his military talents.

Notes
1 The *Edinburgh Evening Courant* 17 August 1812
2 The *Edinburgh Evening Courant* 17 August 1812
3 Rear Admiral Martin, 24 July 1812, BL Add ms 41,366 f.70–71
4 Ibid
5 The British contingent consisted of 430 Royal Marines plus seamen.

6   The ships log for HMS *Meteor* records 'Employed bombarding the town of Danzig' on 1 September 1812, but not how many shots were fired and the damage these caused,. TNA Adm 25/3916

7   General Essen to Rear Admiral Martin, BL Add ms 41,366 f.230

8   The *Edinburgh Evening Courant* 17 August 1812

9   The *Edinburgh Evening Courant* 3 September 1812

10   Quoted in the *Edinburgh Evening Courant* 26 September 1812

11   Quoted in *The Times* 28 September 1812

12   *Windsor and Eton Gazette* quoting a St Petersburg source dated 15 September

13   Zotov, *Razskazi o pohodah* pp. 475–482

15

THE SOUTHERN FLANK

On 1 July, Schwarzenburg's Austrian Corps of about 34,000 men crossed the river Bug at Drogichina. His orders were to occupy Brest Litovsk, Kobryn and Yanov, and so protect the southern flank of the Grande Armée's main thrust and to divide the 2nd and 3rd Russian armies, which were separated by the Pripet Marshes. Estimates vary as to the size of the marshes, but even today with some of the land being reclaimed it is still known as the largest swamp in Europe. It is partly covered by forest and has very few roads and even fewer villages. The careless traveller who strayed from the roads could be sucked into the marsh. It was a home to wolves and like most swampy areas to thousands of mosquitoes, which must have plagued the soldiers incessantly.

The following day Reynier's VII (Saxon) Corps of 21,000 crossed the Russian frontier at Belostok and moved towards Slomin. His orders were to confront General Tormassov's 3rd Western Army of about 46,000 men. Although its headquarters were at Lutzk and it was superior in numbers to the Saxons, the Army was dispersed over almost 300 km along the southern Russian border.

Like the other two Russian armies the 3rd Western Army was also ordered to retreat, which prompted Major General Vasili Vasilivich Vjazemsky of 13th Jager Regiment, to write on 12 July: 'In our army everyone is surprised and cannot guess the manner and method, which the Sovereign has taken, to begin a war of retreat, to let the enemy into the country. All this is a mystery.'[1]

Leaving part of Sacken's Corps to watch the Galician border, Tormassov at first tried to unite his army with Bagration's by marching towards Minsk, but he soon found that this was impossible. However, by retreating and so concentrating his forces, Tormassov soon found that he outnumbered the Saxons. On 15 July Reynier's Corps arrived at Nieswicz, which would be their most eastward position because they seem to have advanced too far into Russia and so were ordered to retrace their steps and support the Austrians, who had arrived at Slomin on 10 July.

On 18 July, the Russian advance guard under General Lambert marched out of Vladimir-Volinsk, advancing along both banks of the River Bug to confront the

Austro-Saxon force. On 23 July, the Russians quartered at Brest Litovsk, before continuing on towards Kobryn, where on 26 July, Tormassov found General Klengel's Saxon brigade quartered. He decided he would attack the Saxons on the following day.

On 27 July Major General Vasili Vasilivich Vjazemsky wrote:

> At 7am the corps set out towards Kobryn … Major General Chaplitz, command-ing our advanced guard, attacked the enemy cavalry, and cut his way through them. Some of them escaped into the place and some into a small wood. The 13th Jagers Regiment were ordered to attack the Saxon infantry. This regiment bravely fought for more than two hours … [The jagers had] about 900 men and two guns, the Saxons … more than 3,000 and eight guns. About 9 hours later our corps appeared on the Divinski Road … The 13th [Jager] Regiment was supported by the Pyazhski Regiment, but the 13th had already taken the eight guns, the commanding general, about 20 field and commissioned officers and about 1,000 soldiers. At the same time with a division I by-passed the place on the right, with de Lambert on the left and the remaining troops in front. This victorious engagement ended at 12 o'clock midday. From the enemy we captured 8 guns, four ensigns, 1 general [Klengel], 53 field and commissioned officers, 2,500 private soldiers, plus a great number of horses and weapons. We killed about 1,300 of the enemy. On our side two officers were killed and about 109 wounded, about 100 [other ranks] were killed and about 100 wounded.[2]

In fact, only 1 officer and 108 Saxons were killed and 164 wounded. The Russians lost 74 men killed and 181 wounded. Although this had been a minor affair in which most of the Saxons had surrendered, when the inhabitants of St Petersburg heard about this battle on 9 August, a *Te Deum* was held in the Imperial Chapel. In the evening the sky was lit up with fireworks to celebrate the first major Russian victory of the campaign.[3] Tormassov was awarded the St George's Cross second class.

The Saxons retreated to Slomin pursued by the Russians under Count Lambert and Major General Chaplitz. This defeat prompted Reynier to appeal to Schwarzenburg, who was then near Minsk, and to Napoleon for reinforcements. The latter reluc-tantly issued orders for Schwarzenburg to retrace his steps and support the Saxons. Meanwhile the Saxons retreated to Ruzany near Slonim to await the arrival of Schwarzenburg.

On 8 August, the Austrians joined the Saxons and with Schwarzenburg in over-all command, they were able to launch an offensive once again. On 9 August, Schwarzenburg fell upon Chaplitz's detachment at Revantshy and the following day Lambert was also attacked at Prushany. Both detachments retreated towards the town of Gorodetschina, where Tormassov arrived on 11 August. Although now only 18,000 strong and outnumbered by more than two to one, Tormassov decided to await the Austro-Saxon advance.

The following day the attack came. The Austrians drew the Russians' attention to their front, while the Saxons made a flank attack. Unbeknown to the Saxons, the

Russians' flank was protected by a swamp and they spent most of the day negotiating this obstacle, all the time being fired upon by the Russian guns. During the afternoon a brigade of Austrians were sent to their aid, but still the Saxons could not break through.

Schwarzenburg's frontal attack fared no better and the engagement developed into a series of skirmishes and artillery duels, rather than a general engagement. The fighting ended at nightfall, the Russians having lost 950 men, the Austrians lost 1,360 men and the Saxons 950 men. Despite being in a strong position, Tormassov decided to withdraw to Kobryn.

On 15 August, the Austrian advanced guard clashed with Chaplitz at Novoselki, while Tormassov continued his retreat to Divinu. On 23 August, Tormassov crossed the River Kovel and continued to retreat to Lutsk, arriving on 29 August. During his retreat Tormassov was able to recall some of his detached troops. The town was in a strong position protected by the Pripet Marshes, so it was here that Tormassov decided to await Admiral Chichagov's Army of the Danube, which had been released from fighting the Turks by the Treaty of Bucharest. Meanwhile the Austro-Saxons took up position on the river Stir, also to await reinforcements.

For two months both armies had been operating in the Province of Volhynia and had foraged for supplies, which by now were almost exhausted. This prompted Major General Vasili Vasilivich Vyazemsky of 13th Jager Regiment to write on 16 August: 'The soldiers have a lot of meat and also have vodka, but oats are in terribly short supply ... Our troops have suffered since the spring and the enemy have found everything ... The land is devastated.'[4]

To add to both sides' miseries, the very hot weather and long marches meant the troops were now exhausted. The Russians left camp in the afternoon and marched through the night to avoid the worst of the heat. By August, the heat of July had given way to heavy rains, which caused sickness on both sides.

The rain also slowed down the Army of the Danube. On 3 September Tormassov reported that:

> I have received information from the first column of the Army of the Danube, which is under the command of Lieutenant General Voinov, that by reason of the heavy torrents of rain, which have continued for twelve successive days, he has experienced some difficulty in crossing the river Pruth, owing to the waters being so high. But he was hopeful of soon joining the army under my command.[5]

On 14 September, the day Napoleon entered Moscow, Chichagov's army finally joined Tormassov at Lutzk. According to the Count de Rochechouart, a Frenchman serving with Chichagov's Army:

> These two army Corps formed together an effective force of 75,000 men, of whom 20,000 were excellent cavalry ... the first [army], under the Admiral, consisted of veterans returned from the provinces on the Danube and the 22nd Regiment of Chasseurs, who had accompanied all our expeditions to the Circassia. It was to

oppose the Austrian army of Prince Schwarzenburg; the second corps, consisting
of less seasoned troops under General Tormassov, was to remain in Volhynia, awaiting events.[6]

Another Frenchman in the Russian Army, Count Langeron, confirms Rochechouart's
view, describing Chichagov's Army as 'excellent soldiers who had made war on Turkey
and sustained several very active campaigns despite the dangers of an unhealthy climate. Our generals and our officers had in seven or eight campaigns acquired much
experience.'[7]

On 20 September, a detachment under General Lambert crossed the river Stir and
surprised a force of allied cavalry under the command of General Zechmeister, as
Langeron recalls:

> Count Lambert with part of the cavalry passed the Stir … [and] met several of
> the enemy's party, and surrounded them. The men, disguised in enemy uniforms,
> deceived by subterfuge the enemy's pickets, and at dawn attacked the sleeping
> enemy cavalry of 900. They dispersed them, killed many and wounded more of
> them. 200 were taken into captivity, together with one field officer, eight officers
> and all three standards of the Regiment of Prince O'Reilly.[8]

These standards would be later sent back to Vienna, as a mark of respect to the
Austrian Emperor.

On 23 September, while Tormassov remained at Lutzk, Chichagov crossed
the Stir in several places to launch an offensive against the now outnumbered
Schwarzenburg, who also had received reinforcements of a newly formed Polish
Division under General Antonie Kosinski. Kosinski's men, apart from a regiment of
infantry, were poorly clothed and armed. Later that day the Saxons were attacked
at Lokachei.

Chichagov had planned to trap Schwarzenburg's force against the Pripet Marshes
or the River Bug, but Schwarzenburg fell back in three directions: the Polish Division
to Vladimir-Volinsk, the Saxons to Tyrisk and the Austrians to Kobel. The Russians
attacked the Polish Division at Vladimir-Volinsk, cutting them off from the Saxons
and forcing them to retreat to the fortress of Zamost.

While pursuing the Allies, Langeron wrote: 'The ground here is utterly ruined.
The Germans show themselves to be robbers.' On 29 September, another action took
place near Luboml, this time between Lambert and the Austrian General Bianchi,
where the Austrians were driven back. Langeron continues:

> Schwartzenburg continued to retreat on the Lubomel, where he took up a suf-
> ficiently strong position, having the town to the left, his right to the Opalin Road
> and the woods to his front covered by a marsh. During his retreat, he had broken
> the bridges and dykes. The Russians attacked both wings, which were forced to
> retreat. That night Schwarzenburg retired on the Bug, which he crossed at Wlodawa
> on a bridge of boats. It was here that the Russian advanced guard caught up with

Schwarzenburg. Our chasseurs fired a fusillade in the sands which bordered the Bug, close to the head of the bridge that the enemy had constructed and which protected his crossing … In the morning of 1 October Lubomel was occupied by Colonel Vassiltchikov with his regiment of Viatka … The Admiral [Chichagov] rested at Lubomel several days to await Tormassov's army.

Lambert, Lanskoi and Langeron made a forced march by Doubok, Zbourai and Oltutsch towards Brest Litovsk. In 2 days they covered 106 kilometres. The cavalry of Lambert and Lanskoi, 9,000 strong, halted in the village of Zbouray. It was hot and we were fatigued, we gave hay to the horses and all of the men lay on the sand. We did not think that we would meet the enemy. A half squadron of Austrian hussars of the Barco Regiment, commanded by Captain Miklosch, detached for foraging, arrived unexpectedly in the village and were deceived by the red uniforms of the hussars of Little Russia, which it took for the Saxon hussars. They advanced at a walking pace until in the midst of the sleeping Russians; they realised their mistake, but they had no escape route, they were in the middle of us. The noise that they made awakened our men, one reached for his pike, another his sabre, others for their pistols. Miklosch attempted to defend himself, he was wounded from a sabre cut. Three hussars were killed and the others surrendered.

I arrived an instant after, and I ordered the hussars to be well treated, but this was a pointless order to give to our men. When the prisoners were Austrian, and especially Hungarian, our soldiers conducted them to their bivouacs, shared with them all that they had and treated them like brothers in arms, but there was not any quarter given to the Polish and [they] showed a great deal of animosity against the Saxons.[9]

During the night of 10 October, Schwarzenburg decamped and his columns marched out of Brest, guides with lanterns leading the way. The following day, the Russian Corps, under General Osten Sacken, caught up with Schwarzenburg between Brest Litovsk and Kobryn while crossing the river Muchavietz. The Austro-Saxon force turned and faced the Russians, who were defeated. The Russians, this time under General Lambert, were again defeated two days later at Biala Podlaska, halting their advance. Despite these victories Schwarzenburg's force continued its withdrawal; all this time he does not appear to have been kept informed of the Grande Armée's movements. Nor had Admiral Chichagov been informed of events concerning other Russian armies either.

On 29 September the former spy, Prince A.I. Chernyshev, arrived with orders for Tormassov to join the main Russian Army under Kutuzov and for Chichagov to leave part of his force to observe Schwarzenburg and march to join Wittgenstein's army, to cut off Napoleon at Borisov. With the recall of Tormassov, the two Russian armies became one, known as the 3rd Western Army.

To keep the Austro-Saxons occupied, Chichagov ordered Prince Chernyshev to take a body of cavalry to threaten the Duchy of Warsaw and operate in Schwarzenburg's rear. Fearing such an attack, the Austrians withdrew behind the river Bug to cover Warsaw. Shortly afterwards Chernyshev was ordered to rejoin Chichagov. By now,

Schwarzenburg had received reinforcements, and so the balance of power swung back in favour of the Allies.

On 4 October, the Austro-Saxons crossed the Bug at Brest Litovsk. The following day the Russian advanced guard attacked a detachment of Austrians at Kobrin and forced it to retreat to Pruszhani. A week later the Russians again attacked the Austro-Saxon Army at Brest Litovsk, but Schwarzenburg decided to retreat rather than give battle.

On 30 October, Chichagov belatedly set off north to join Wittgenstein. According to Langeron: 'The Tsar had calculated that Chichagov would be at Minsk on 21 October, he only was there on 17 November.'[10]

Schwarzenburg had sent an adjutant to Napoleon to seek instructions, but the adjutant had returned on 12 October without any orders. On discovering that Chichagov's army was marching north, Schwarzenburg decided to follow him. Reynier had argued that the Allies should first defeat Osten-Sacken, who Chichagov had left behind to shadow the Allies. However, Schwarzenburg ignored this advice and set off in pursuit, Reynier's Saxons setting off a few days later. Osten-Sacken in turn set off in pursuit of the Allies.

The Russians quickly caught up with the Saxons and clashed on 8 November near Porosovo, and then again on the 13th at Lapenica. Reynier withdrew to the town of Volkovisk, where he decided to make a stand. Upon hearing that he was being pursued by the Austrians, Chichagov sent Chernyshev with a regiment of Cossacks to destroy the bridges over the rivers Nieman and Zelva, and so prevent the Austrians from crossing. Finding his way blocked and receiving news that Reynier had been attacked, Schwarzenburg decided to retrace his steps and march to the assistance of the Saxons.

On the night of 14/15 November, Sacken attacked Reynier. The fighting continued the following day, all the time the Austrians getting closer. On 16 November Schwarzenburg fell upon the Russians' rear. Despite being evenly matched and suffering a similar number of casualties Osten-Sacken retreated to Kobryn, pursued by the Saxons, who captured many stragglers.

On 25 November, Schwarzenburg received orders to march north once more and confront Chichagov again, which probably saved Osten-Sacken from complete destruction. By now, rumours were rife that something dreadful had happened to the Grande Armée. This was confirmed in early December. On 22 December a ceasefire was agreed between the Russians and Austrians, the latter retreating to Warsaw. The Russians were enraged by Schwarzenburg's actions; they had been told by the Austrian Chancellor, Metternich, that they were unwilling allies of Napoleon and would only half heartedly support his campaign in Russia. Certainly Napoleon was pleased with Schwarzenburg's performance during the campaign and on the Emperor's suggestion he was promoted to field marshal.

The Saxons crossed into the Duchy of Warsaw on 25 December; it would not be until October 1813 that they finally changed sides.

Notes

1 http://www.museum.ru/1812/Library/ver/ver_win.txt
2 http://www.museum.ru/1812/Library/ver/ver_win.txt
3 *Journal of John Quincy Adams* p.396
4   http://www.museum.ru/1812/Library/ver/ver_win.txt
5 Quoted in the *Caledonian Mercury* 5 November 1812
6 *Memoirs of the Count de Rochechouart* p.144
7 *Memoirs du Langeron* p.7
8 Ibid, pp.7–8
9 Ibid, pp.9–10
10 Ibid, p.19

16

TARUNTINO

The unthinkable had happened: Moscow had been abandoned to Napoleon, the Anti-Christ. The Russians considered themselves fugitives in their own country; according to Baron Uxkull:

> We're swinging and changing direction. Kutuzov is still cheerful and confident. What will the end of all this be? We lead the life of animals. Our food is repulsive, our bed is the earth, our pleasure is sleeping, and with all this no hope for the future. What a situation![1]

On 18 September Kutuzov wrote to the Tsar from Podolsk:

> Last night my rearguard followed the army on a forced march … having left a party of Cossacks behind them, who were to make a feigned movement towards Kolomna, as if the army had likewise made its retreat towards there … This affords me an opportunity of positioning the army so that tomorrow, after having made a flanking movement of 20 km on the Kaluga Road and with a strong contingent on the Moscow Road, we will threaten the rear of the enemy.
>
> I hope that, in consequence, the enemy will endeavour to give me battle; from which, being in an advantageous situation, I may expect the same result as at Borodino.[2]

Kutuzov knew that that Russian Army was in no fit state to fight and needed time to reorganise and bring its regiments up to strength. By using the Cossacks to screen his movements, he was able to break contact with the Grande Armée and march south about 10 km from the city upon the Old Kaluga Road, to threaten Moscow if necessary or block any movements south into the more fertile lands. According to General de Lowenstern: 'The infantry were exhausted, but nobody quit the ranks and I have seen with my eyes several soldiers drop stone dead from fatigue.'

On 25 September at Podolsk, Baron Uxkull was confident: 'The army is beginning to pluck up its courage again. The enemy is getting weaker day by day, and our reinforcements are reaching us in small detachments.' The same day, the 1st and 2nd Western Armies were reorganised into one, under the command of Barclay de Tolly. Shortly afterwards news came of the death of the Bagration, who had died on 24 September from the injury he had received at Borodino. Bagration had been greatly loved by the Russian soldiers and this news came as a blow.

Rumours began to spread that there was to be an armistice, which prompted Baron Uxkull to write in his diary on 29 September:

An armistice is being discussed; that would be bitter. Our motto must be: either exterminate them or perish, for the enemy is a hydra that sooner or later will be reborn if a single head is left … Napoleon made a tremendous mistake in venturing as far as the centre of Russia. Everyone is beginning to appreciate the wisdom of this retreat that has been so criticised. Barclay has fallen back, a great deal of wrong has been done to this man.[3]

Barclay de Tolly had had enough, depressed since Kutuzov had been appointed commander in chief and tired of his reports and opinions being ignored, he returned to his estate.

On 2 October, the Russian Army set up camp at Taruntino, with the rearguard commanded by General Miloradovitch at Voronovo. It would be at Taruntino that the army would rebuild itself. To encourage his men, Kutuzov rode from regiment to regiment saying:

'I saw your tears, heard the grumbling to destiny and know the burning desire of brave comrades to die for every step of native Russian land, and this is the place where all the world will see a striking example of the sacred love and steadfast devotion of the Russian troops to God, Sovereign and Fatherland! At this point we revived the heroic and at the same time the Christian exploits worthy of our ancestors! Here will be reborn the great times of Pozharski, Palitsun and Minin! Here, friends, we will rally our noble desire in a united effort and refuse everything except glory, victories and death! Win!' … 'Death or Victory' barked Ataman Platov. 'Death or Victory' we repeated. The old man [Kutuzov] began to cry … and departed, and we also began to cry.[4]

Captain Skobelev wrote to his friend:

In three days we have made a new Moscow. Just not of stone … Except for the sentries and the vanguard, all the army has been employed on the construction of batteries, entrenchments and traps. Regiments every day increase [in strength]. From the Don, a great crowd of Cossacks has arrived to help, noblemen, the old and the young arrive hourly to join the regiments.[5]

This was the arrival of 22 regiments of Cossacks, which according to one source, 'in some platoons ... were grandfathers and grandchildren, the first with whitened hair, the others in adolescent years'. From their outposts the French could clearly hear new recruits being put through their paces; but despite all these reinforcements in October the army still had only about 78,400 men.

While the Russian Army was reorganising itself, other forces, mainly the Cossacks and the local peasantry, were besieging Moscow. There would be no mercy for any French foraging party which fell into their hands. On 18 September at Stupia, Uxkull witnessed a grisly scene:

> Approaching a village in order to get some supplies, I saw a French prisoner sold to the peasants for twenty roubles; they baptised him with boiling tar and impaled him alive on a piece of pointed iron. What horror! Oh, humanity, I groan over it. The Russian women kill with hatchets the prisoners and marauders who pass by their houses. But measures have already been taken to stop this barbarity. The saddest thing of all is that our own soldiers spare nothing. They burn, pillage, loot and devastate everything that comes to hand. All around, for a circle of 100 km, you can see immense fires that indicate the road taken by the enemy troops and our own, since we have vowed to leave nothing for the enemy. Bread, fruit, animals, everything is wiped out. The wells and streams are ruined and the foragers do not dare show themselves for fear of being clubbed down by the peasants.[6]

Among those on the forward position was General Benkendorf, who recorded that Colonel Ilovaiski had orders to apprehend all enemy foragers and by doing so 'increased the temerity and the vigilance of the Cossacks and reduced the morale and the resistance of the French day by day'.[7]

> My camp had the air of a den of thieves, it was filled with armed peasants with all manner of booty from the enemy; helmets, cuirasses, shakos and even the uniforms of the different arms and nations, mixed in grotesquely with the beards and the villagers' costumes. A society of rogues was thriving, unceasingly haggling for the pillage that was produced daily in the camp. They continually source ... goods of all kinds from jewels ... to old clothes ... from the soldiers, from the officers, from the women and the children of all the nations leagued against us. The peasants were adorned with clothes of velvet or old embroidered jackets. Gold and silver circulated in this camp in great abundance ...
>
> The peasants followed the parties of Cossacks everywhere and ... [took] all the booty, cattle, poor horses, wagons, arms and uniforms of the prisoners ... Often it was impossible [to stop a prisoner being] dragged away by the fury of the peasants excited [to acts of] vengeance by the thought of the ashes of their huts and the desecration of their churches.[8]

Soldiers also plundered the prisoners, and market stalls were set up at Taruntino to sell off their ill gotten gains.

One day orders came for Benkendorf to disarm these peasants:

> Because of false reports owing to the foul slanders I received the order to disarm
> the peasants and to execute those who were convicted of revolt. Astonished by this
> order, so contrary to the noble conduct and obedience of the peasant, I responded
> that it was impossible for me to disarm the hands that I had armed myself, and who
> served to crush the enemy of the Fatherland, that I was not able to give the name
> of rebels to those who sacrificed their lives for the defence of their churches, of
> their independence, of their women and their homes, but that the name of trai-
> tor belonged to those who …dared to slander those more zealous and those more
> genuine defenders. This response had a dramatic effect, calmed the misgivings that
> some sought to give the Emperor and perhaps making me an enemy of some of the
> schemers of Petersburg.[9]

Benkendorf did not know that there had been many peasant uprisings, demanding
more rights. These had to be put down by using badly needed troops. Some peasants
traded with the French in Moscow, and it was only the fact that they were plundered
of their wares that put a stop to this practice, rather than any patriotic feeling.

Many soldiers of the Grande Armée fell into the hands of the Russians. Baron
Uxkull described their fate:

> The number of prisoners is immense and these poor people can scarcely drag
> themselves along; they are escorted by Cossacks, who kill them with lances the
> moment they no longer have the power to walk. The prisoners tell stories about
> their Emperor amusing himself in Moscow, and how they are soon going to St
> Petersburg. As proof, they show military bulletins full of lies. This arrogance is the
> most absurd and miserable thing in the world. But such is the character of that
> nation; it is manifested everywhere. Among the prisoners can be seen Bavarians,
> Spaniards, Italians, Saxons, etc. What an enormous army, that of the Allies. It is said
> that twelve peoples are fighting against us. It is like a crusade. But our hour will
> come. It is true that the Gauls inundated the Roman Empire; and the Slavs will one
> day swallow up the French Empire.[10]

Some prisoners who fell into the hands of the Russian soldiery were treated less
harshly, and some were even offered the opportunity of serving in the newly formed
Russian German Legion.[11]

Not all foraging parties were stopped, as this extract from a letter written by a
steward of an unknown estate near Moscow shows:

> The French came to us, and took from us hay, oats, bread and some cattle; however,
> we have got still sufficient for the winter. In some of your estate they have committed
> great depredations; about three weeks ago they came to us again with the intention
> of burning our village, but with the assistance of God and your peasantry we have
> killed them all, like so many starved dogs. We found in their baggage many church

ornaments, a priest's surplice and a string of pearls. I have given all these to our church; we want nothing belonging to the French, we are contented and must not provoke divine vengeance.[12]

It was not just the French who seized provisions from the local population, the Russian Army also demanded supplies for the ever-growing camp at Taruntino.

By the end of the French occupation of Moscow, Cossacks were launching raids into the city. It was even alleged that Alexander Figner, who later became a partisan leader, tried to assassinate Napoleon while in the Kremlin, but was disturbed by a soldier of the Imperial Guard.

With the Grande Armée besieged in Moscow, and most of the city destroyed by fire, Napoleon was desperate for peace. Major General Tutolmin, the director of the Foundling Hospital in Moscow, had asked for a guard to protect the hospital, which favour the Emperor had granted. Now, on 18 September, he wanted the favour returned, and invited the General to the Kremlin. Tutolmin entered the room and the Emperor asked:

> I should have desired to deal with your city as I dealt with Vienna and Berlin, which to this day have not been demolished. But the Russians have left this city nearly empty, and have committed an unprecedented act. They have deliberately set their capital on fire to cause me temporary inconvenience, they have destroyed the work of many centuries … I have never waged war in this manner. My warriors are capable of fighting, but they do not burn cities. Beginning with Smolensk, I have found nothing but ashes.

After complaining about Rostopchin, who Napoleon saw as responsible for the fires, he asked Tutolmin if there was anything he wanted. Tutolmin replied that he would like to send a message on the condition of the hospital to Maria Feodorovna, the Dowager Tsarina, who was its head. Napoleon consented to this, but asked the general to add to the missive:

> The Emperor Napoleon groans at seeing your capital almost entirely destroyed by means which, he says, are not those that one uses in real war. He seems convinced that if no one interferes between him and our August Emperor Alexander, their former friendship would soon resume and all our misfortunes would cease.[13]

The letter was sent immediately to St Petersburg, escorted part of the way by French cavalry to make sure the message arrived safely. However Napoleon was so eager for peace that when on 20 September a Russian nobleman named Ivan Yakovlev appealed for a pass to leave Moscow, it was granted on condition that he would take another letter to the Tsar himself. After setting down the facts of the fire of Moscow, Napoleon continued:

> I have waged war on Your Majesty without animosity: a letter from you before or after the last battle would have halted my advance and I would have liked to be in

a position to sacrifice the advantage of entering Moscow in return for it. If your Majesty still retains some remnant of your former feelings for me, you will take this letter in good part. In any case, you cannot but be grateful for my having informed you about what is happening in Moscow.[14]

Napoleon chose not to remember the envoy from the Tsar, whom he had interviewed at Vilna shortly after the invasion had begun, when he declined Alexander's peace overtures. By revealing the state of Moscow he revealed how weak his position was, albeit claiming that the 'supplies were in the cellars that the fires could not reach'. Napoleon was confident that Alexander would make peace, and his reputation would thus be enhanced by his conquest of Russia.

Whether Alexander ever received this letter is not known, but on 3 October, angered by not receiving a reply to either letters, Napoleon held a council of war at the Kremlin, where he stated his intention to burn the rest of Moscow and then march on St Petersburg. The marshals pointed out that the Grande Armée was in no condition for such an undertaking and for the most part had become an ill-disciplined mob. Moreover, winter was coming. Napoleon was silent, and must have known the truth himself.

That afternoon, Napoleon summoned Caulaincourt and requested that he take a letter to Alexander personally, but he refused, saying that it would be useless and show how weak their position was. Lauriston was then chosen as the peace envoy; at first he also refused but then was ordered to go to the Tsar, with the entreaty: 'I must have peace, I need it absolutely, I must have it at all costs, save my honour.'

On 4 October, General Lauriston was sent to discuss peace terms. He arrived at one of the Russian outposts later that evening. After some discussion a private meeting between him and Kutuzov was arranged on the fringes of the Russian Army.

Probably exaggerating his own importance, Sir Robert Wilson claims that he was summoned by General Bennigsen, and other Russian officers, to prevent this meeting taking place, because they feared that Kutuzov was about to conclude an armistice. Writing in the third person Wilson claims to have quickly returned to Kutuzov's headquarters:

The Marshal, [Kutuzov] on seeing him enter, looked already embarrassed, but asked 'whether he had brought any news from the advanced guard?' After some slight conversation on that subject, the English General intimated a wish to confer with the Marshal alone …

The English General said that 'he had returned to headquarters in consequence of a report, an idle one he trusted, which had reached him that morning.' That 'it was, however, a mischievous report, causing much excitement and uneasiness; and therefore that it was desirable at once to put an end, under the Marshal's own authority, to the scandal.'

The Marshal's countenance confirmed the allegation; but the English General proceeded with as much courtesy as possible to communicate the rumour, and afford [an] opportunity for the voluntary cancellation of the arrangement, without any humiliating or irritating *eclairissement*.

The Marshal was confused, but in a tone of some asperity replied that he was commander in chief of the army, and knew best what the interests confided to him required; that it was true that he had agreed to give General Lauriston, at the request of the French Emperor an interview during that night, under the circumstances reported, in order to avoid notice which might be accompanied with misrepresentation or misunderstanding of motives; that he should keep his engagement, hear the propositions which General Lauriston was empowered to offer, and determine his future proceedings according to their nature …

The English General having patiently listened to all the explanations of the Marshal asked him 'if such was his final determination?' He said 'Yes – irrevocable'; and he expressed his hope that the English General would on reflection acquiesce in its propriety and taking into consideration the state of the Empire, and the fact that although the Russian Army was becoming numerous, it was still far from being efficient in proportion, that he would in this instance suffer his affection for the Emperor and Russia to prevail over his well known hostile feelings to the Emperor of France.

These last expressions were uttered in a very sarcastic tone, and he seemed to think, or to desire, the conference terminated.[15]

Wilson even went as far as calling into the room several Russian generals to get Kutuzov to change his mind. Wilson was too thick skinned to see that Kutuzov wanted the 'conference terminated' because of this upstart General, poking his noise into the Field Marshal's business; rather, he saw it as proof that Kutuzov was about to make peace with the French.

In the end, Kutuzov agreed to postpone the meeting and invited Lauriston to a meeting at his headquarters. Lauriston was blindfolded and led to Kutuzov's hut, which he entered at 11.00pm and found Wilson and a group of Russian generals. A little while later the generals withdrew leaving Kutuzov and Lauriston alone.

Although he was not present at the time, Count de Langeron records the scene:

This meeting took place at the headquarters of Kutuzov, He put his mind (and he was intelligent) and that astuteness which eminently distinguished his character, to gaining the best advantage. He was surrounded by his staff. He received Lauriston politely, but coldly. He took the letter that Napoleon had written to the Emperor Alexander and those addressed to himself, and he placed them on the table, without reading them.

Kutuzov then reminisced about Lauriston's time in St Petersburg, how he had stayed at Kutuzov's home, the weather and the state of the roads. Finally Lauriston interrupted this small talk and said:

'Napoleon desires to see an end to the cruel war.' At this Kutuzov snapped 'Finished? … but it has not begun for us'…

The astonished Lauriston, after some words on the position of the armies, complained of the barbarity of the Russian peasants, who sacrificed to their rage and with an extraordinary cruelty all the French who fell into their hands. Kutuzov responded 'Our peasants … they think of the old invasions of the tartars, of the barbarians, that their ancestors had destroyed.' At this mention of barbarians, Lauriston protested. Kutuzov resumed 'But our people, seeing 600,000 enemy coming amongst them with sword and flame could justifiably compare them to barbarians who formerly did the same.' Finally Lauriston insisted on a decision. Kutuzov said that he had not the power to make one, but that he would send a courier to the Emperor. Lauriston demanded that to save time the courier should pass by Moscow. Kutuzov refused. He gave his parole.[16]

While Kutuzov was meeting with Lauriston, Bennigsen, who according to Wilson had asked him to stop any negotiations with the French, was having his own meeting with Murat. It was not just the generals who fraternised with the enemy, according to Baron Uxkull:

We are holding some hills and a vast plain divided by a river. Our pickets and outposts are on one side, the enemy's on the other. To pass the time we get together at one place or another; we amuse ourselves playing cards, smoking or drinking.[17]

On 5 October Kutuzov wrote to Alexander about the Lauriston visit:

At last he [Lauriston] came to the real point of his mission, that is to say he began to talk about peace, saying that the friendship that had existed between Your Majesty and the Emperor Napoleon had unfortunately been broken by purely external circumstances; the present moment offered a good opportunity for re-establishing this friendship. 'Must this strange war, this unique war, last eternally, then? My master the Emperor has a sincere desire to end this dispute between two great and generous nations, and to end it for ever.'

I replied that I had no instructions on this subject and that at my departure to join the armies even the word peace had not been mentioned once; moreover, I had no desire to communicate one iota of all this conversation to my Sovereign, regardless of whether all the words that I had heard from his mouth came from him, as the result of his personal reflections, or of whether they had a higher source; that 'I would be cursed by posterity if I was regarded as the prime mover in any kind of settlement, for such is the prevailing frame of mind of my nation.' At this moment, he handed me a letter from the Emperor Napoleon, a copy of which is enclosed, and asked me to request your Majesty's authorisation for him, Lauriston, to go to St Petersburg with it; and proposed an armistice (which I refused him) while waiting for a reply. Then he impatiently calculated the time it would take for a reply to arrive.

I promised to comply with his request, which amounted to making the Emperor Napoleon's desire known to Your Majesty.

Unfortunately, both the copy and the original of Napoleon's letter to Alexander does not appear to have survived. Napoleon was probably relieved when Lauriston recounted what had happened at the meeting, assured that his letter would be passed to Alexander and peace would no doubt follow. However upon reading Napoleon's letter, Alexander exclaimed: 'Peace! But we haven't waged war yet. My campaign is only beginning.'

News spread around the Russian Army that there was to be an armistice. However, they need not have worried, it was only a ploy by Kutuzov to keep Napoleon in Moscow for a few more weeks until winter set in. Upon hearing of the negotiations the Tsar was angry and wrote to Kutuzov:

> At the very moment of your departure for the armies that were entrusted to you personally, you knew of my firm and insistent desire to abstain from all negotiations and all relations with the adversary that might have tended to produce a peace.
>
> But today, after these events, I must repeat with the same firmness that the rule established by me must be respected strictly and resolutely in its entirety.
>
> On the same occasion, I learnt with extreme displeasure that General Bennigsen has had an interview with the King of Naples and, what is more, without any urgent motive.
>
> Pointing out the unseemliness of his behaviour, I demand you to exercise strict and effective supervision to prevent the other generals from having meetings, and if the possibility of such communications should arise, I ask you to see that they try to avoid them by all possible means.[18]

While Napoleon was waiting for a reply the days were getting shorter and colder. He sent the wounded from Borodino back down his lines of communication and began to prepare to leave. He must have known by then that he was facing defeat in this campaign. Napoleon set the day when he would leave Moscow for 19 October, which was changed to the 20th, still hoping that Alexander would make peace.

On 17 October Baron Uxkull wrote: 'There is word of an attack we are going to undertake tomorrow. The French are exhausted from hunger and fatigue. All peace proposals are being rejected.'

After much persuasion by General Bennigsen and Colonel Toll, Kutuzov reluctantly agreed to an attack on Murat's position. Kutuzov had wanted to wait a few more weeks before ending the truce, so when he visited the regiments, which he assumed would be on the march by now, he found them still in their bivouacs and flew into a rage. The generals who were meant to have been organising the attack were nowhere to be seen, the horses of the artillery had been sent to forage for provisions, and those infantry regiments who had set off had to be recalled.

The French – who had received intelligence of the attack and had been in arms all day – believed the information was false, and once more settled down believing that the truce was still intact, and that a peace would shortly be signed.

That evening, according to General Lowenstern, Kutuzov

> … visited the position of the army and the entrenchments which had been built. It was at this moment that an eagle flew about him and was not startled by the

occasional lightning without thunder. We were astonished because lightning was a very rare phenomenon at that time of year. He regarded this eagle and the lightning as a good omen, and this occurence was communicated by word of mouth to all the army who interpreted it as forecasting a very happy result.

With this good omen, it was decided that the attack should be made the following day. During the night the corps set out to take up their positions. The attack would begin at daybreak on 18 October, when three cannons would fire as the signal to launch the attack. The attacking force was divided into five columns. The first under General Orlov-Denisov, with 10 regiments of Cossacks and the 20th Jager Regiment with between 12 and 20 guns was to turn the enemy's left and attack them in the rear. The second column under Baggovut with the 2nd and 3rd Corps and 60 artillery pieces was to support Denisov. The third column under General Ostermann-Tolstoy with the 4th Corps and 12 guns was to plug the gap between Baggovut and the remainder of the army. The 4th Column under General Dokhturov composed of the 6th Corps and about 34 guns, and the 5th Column commanded by General Raevski and formed from the 7th and 8th Corps and 46 guns, were to cross the Nara river at Taruntino and march via Vinkova and Czerniecznia to engage the French frontally and so keep them occupied while the other columns attacked their left. The advance guard was commanded by General Miloradovitch with the 2nd and 4th Cavalry Corps. The 1st and 2nd Cuirassier Divisions and the 5th Infantry Corps formed the reserve. General Bennigsen was in overall command.

A Polish deserter came to Orlov-Denisov, offering to capture Murat in return for 1,000 roubles. The Russian staff agreed and despatched the Pole with two regiments of Cossacks, and the threat of death if he led them into a trap. After some thought these two regiments were recalled, because it was feared they might be discovered and alert the French to the forthcoming attack.

Things seemed to be going well when at 1.00am Eugene von Wurttemberg's 2nd Corps captured an enemy battery of fourteen guns near Teterinki on the enemy's left. However, the 2nd and 4th Corps got lost in a dense wood, which separated the Russians from the French, in the darkness. Orlov-Denisov does not seem to have waited for the signal to attack, but launched his Cossacks into the fight as soon as they were ready. At daybreak the French were awoken by the sound of hooves galloping towards them.

These belonged to the Cossacks of the Imperial Guard, the Ataman's Regiment and Colonel Sisoev, who threw the French cavalry into disorder and captured several pieces of cannon.

The enemy's cavalry, who had just discovered that some extraordinary movements were in progress within the wood, was beginning to mount when the shot fell among them, and at the same instant Orlov Denisov presented himself behind their extreme left and dashing upon them before any formation could be completed, threw not only the cavalry, but the whole left, into general confusion.[19]

Orlov-Denisov account records 'They took many guns and boxes of ammunition …
[and] prisoners and these actions contributed greatly to the enemy's defeat.'

The Polish troops quickly recovered from this initial shock and began to form
up. When Prince Eugene von Wurttemberg's 2nd Corps managed to arrive at the
rendezvous more or less on time, he found that it was difficult to deploy his men,
because they had emerged from the wood in front of an enemy battery. As the 6th
Corps advanced about 1,000 paces, the battery inflicted heavy casualties upon them.
Meanwhile, General Baggovut's Corps also emerged from the woods and found the
French waiting for them. Baggovut quickly deployed his Jagers and twelve pieces of
artillery in front of the wood, but he was hit by a cannon ball and killed.

Prince Eugene:

General Baggovut with the 4th Jagers was confronted with the sight of the enemy
en masse and one of the first shots of the battery near to Teterinki cost him his life.
This accident ruined all the co-ordination in the movements of the 2nd Corps. The
jagers scattering in skirmish line and attacked in the confusion with great daring,
but as they were ill supported they suffered great losses and a battalion of the 48th
had almost entirely been annihilated by the French Carabiniers …

On the left of the 2nd Corps, Frisch's battery had moved forward and maintained a vigorous cannonade against those of the enemy. The Kremenstruck and
Volhynia Regiments took up position within range to support our pieces, but the
17th Division remained inactive in the wood.

The 4th Corps appeared at this time and advanced in concert with the 2nd and
3rd Corps towards the position the enemy had just left and the head of the army
under the direct orders of the Marshal [Kutuzov] reached Czerniczia. General
Wassiltchikov was beyond Ivankovo and still lightly engaged with the enemy's
rearguard.

While this was going on Count Orlov-Denisov had already attacked at a little after
8am. Despite all the slowness of our movements he himself nevertheless had successfully completely surprised the division of cuirassiers placed near Dmitrotvskoie
and spread terror at the rear of the enemy camp. The rest of the division formed up
by the 1st and 2nd Carabiniers and the 1st Cuirassiers were drawn up behind the left
flank of the Poles, and it was precisely at this time that I came out from the edge of
the wood opposite the flank with the Tobolsk Regiment and three pieces of light
artillery, the rest of the battery and the Krementschuck and Volhynia Regiments;
losing some time in the wood we finally followed the direction of the Jagers and the
17th Division.[20]

Miloradovitch's Corps was also met by the enemy infantry when it emerged from the
woods. Miloradovitch ordered his cavalry to charge, which cut off a Polish column
from the rest of the army. Usually, the Polish infantry would have been annihilated
in this situation, but according to P. H. Grabbe, 'At that moment Miloradovitch was
recalled by Kutuzov and everything stopped because of the absence of the commander'. This allowed the Poles to retreat into the woods.

Wilson also witnessed the cavalry battle:

> The Cossacks, especially those of the Guard under Orlov-Denisov, intrepidly attacked even the cuirassiers endeavouring to form a screen for the columns gliding along the skirts of the wood to gain Spass Kouplia.
>
> Charges were mutually given and repulsed, and there never was a cavalry combat in modern warfare where the antagonists continued so close and commingled for such a length of time. Had it not been for the cuirass before and behind, the Cossack spear would infallibly have pierced every horseman.[21]

The Cossacks were close enough to the cuirassiers that 'during the whole time they not only dealt blows, but pelted hard words at each other.'[22]

Wurttemberg continues:

> Fearing for his left flank, Bennigsen sent the 3rd Corps to protect it. Meanwhile the fight between the Cossacks and the Cuirassiers continued. At about 9 o'clock the Tobolsk Regiment arrived and gave a volley at point blank at the mass of the 1st Cuirassier Division, which was routed, pursued by Cossacks. It was only when they reached the main road that the cuirassiers rallied.[23]

The Tobolsk Regiment then supported the skirmish line of the 4th Jagers, who were driving back the Polish infantry. Murat's force began a general retreat, but the Russian troops were too exhausted to pursue. Colonel Toll managed to deploy a battery which was able to bombard the retreating French.

The Cossacks had still not finished their attack, as Eugene von Wurttemberg recalls:

> The Cossacks also passed the ravine and attacked the 6th Regiment of Cuirassiers in front of Bogorodskoie who on this occasion put up an admirable resistance. The 20th Jagers Regiment, which had slipped into the ravine to take the enemy cavalry in the rear was surprised as soon as it appeared and had several men cut down. The Tobolsk Regiment on the contrary, always in good order, was limited to supporting the Cossacks and did not suffer losses. The cavalry of General Muller-Sakomelski proceeded to the right in the direction of Dmitrotuskoie to Spass Kouplia and had only a light engagement with the French cavalry that covered the march. The King of Naples had arrived at Spass Kouplia and had taken up a new position with his Corps, covered by strong batteries. It was at this point that our pursuit ended. The remainder of the 2nd Corps, of which General Olsouvief had taken command, came to rejoin me at Bogorodskoie. The other corps remained in the rear. Our reward came to about 1,000 prisoners and about 30 pieces that the Cossacks had carried off.[24]

Despite pleas from General Miloradovitch and Ermolov to attack, Marshal Kutuzov, had remained with the main body of the army, 'a passive spectator of all these handsome feats of arms', at one point even having breakfast with General Platov and his staff. Kutuzov then mounted his horse and rode over to Ermolov and wagged a finger under his nose, saying,

> You have no need of those words, 'let us attack, let us attack' ... you do not under-
> stand that we are calling upon [soldiers that] are still not ripe for that; that combined
> movements are still beyond our ability and that in general we do not know how to
> manoeuvre ... Today proves it and I regret having lent a favourable ear to the plans
> of General Bennigsen.[25]

By being present on the battlefield, Kutuzov could claim that he was in command of the army and in his report to the Tsar he claimed the credit for this victory.

Murat, whose adjutant had been killed, had lost 2,500–3,000 men, 28 guns and the 1st Cuirassier Regiment had lost a standard. However, the Russians had little to be proud of; despite their initial success, they had achieved very little, according to Lowenstern:

> General Bennigsen was strongly indignant about the Prince's [Kutuzov's] indeci-
> sion and his indifference. He had done almost nothing the whole day. Bennigsen
> greeted him coldly and demanded permission to retire for several days because he
> had received a severe contusion ... we returned to headquarters and the army to its
> positions, all dissatisfied at having been the quiet spectators of the day.[26]

The following day a *Te Deum* was sung and news of the victory was sent to St Petersburg. The battle had not been a decisive victory, as the Russians had hoped, but nevertheless it was seen as the first clear victory over the French and bolstered the morale of the Russian Army.

Bennigsen, still indignant, wrote to his wife on 22 October:

> I can hardly control myself! What results might have been achieved by that magnificent,
> brilliant engagement. If I had only received reinforcements ... Instead, before the eyes
> of the entire army, Kutuzov forbade sending a single man to assist me; those were his
> own words. General Miloradovitch, who commanded the left flank, burned with the
> desire to assist me, but Kutuzov forbade him ... You can imagine at what distance our
> old man was from the battlefield! His cowardice exceeds the proportions permissible
> even for cowards, he gave the greatest proof of it at Borodino, and for that reason he has
> covered himself with contempt and become ridiculous in the eyes of the whole army.[27]

Bennigsen had no power base within the army when he wrote to the Tsar complain-
ing about Kutuzov's conduct. The letter was forwarded to Kutuzov, who ordered Bennigsen to leave the army.

Kutuzov had not wanted a general engagement; if the Russian Army had been defeated then all the achievements of the campaign would have been lost. So despite its victory, the Russian Army remained at Taruntino for several days after the battle, waiting to see what would happen next.

Meanwhile cannon fire could be heard in Moscow, and a little later an adjutant came galloping up to Napoleon with a message that Murat had been attacked. Napoleon now knew with absolute certainty that there would be no peace treaty and that he would have to retreat.

Napoleon had already been making preparations for his army to leave Moscow on 20 October, but now he brought the departure forward by 24 hours.

Notes

1 Uxkull, *Arms and the Woman* p.88
2 Kutuzov, *dokumentov* vol. IV part 2 pp.16–18
3 Uxkull, *Arms and the Woman* pp.91–92
4 Skobelev letter viii in 1812 god v vospominainiyakh I rasskazazakh sovremennikov pp.163–166
5 Skobelev letter xii in 1812 god v vospominainiyakh I rasskazazakh sovremennikov pp.170–172
6 Uxkull, *Arms and the Woman* pp.88–89
7 Zapiski, *Benkendorfa 1812* p.66
8 Ibid, pp.69–70
9 Ibid, pp.70–72
10 Uxkull, *Arms and the Woman* pp.91–92
11 The Legion was raised in July 1812 and in 1813 mustered eight infantry battalions, two hussar regiments a company of jagers and artillery. However, it took no part in the 1812 campaign.
12 James p 179 *Journal of a tour...* p.238
13 Quoted in Olivier, *The Burning of Moscow* p.101
14 Quoted in Olivier, *The Burning of Moscow* pp.108–109, and Tarle, *Napoleon's Invasion of Russia* pp.209–210
15 Wilson, *The French Invasion of Russia* pp.183–185
16 *Memoirs de Langeron* p.32 Langeron claims that Kutuzov told him what happened at the meeting when they met in Vilna.
17 Uxkull, *Arms and the Woman* pp. 92–93
18 Tsar to Kutuzov 21 October 1812, Kutuzov, dokumentov vol. IV part 2 p.68
19 Wilson, *The French Invasion of Russia* p.200
20 Journal of Eugene de Wurttemberg pp.19–24
21 Wilson, *The French Invasion of Russia* p.211
22 Ibid, p.211
23 Journal du Prince Eugene de Wurttemberg pp.19–24
24 Ibid, pp.19–24
25 *Memoirs of General Lowenstern* pp.303–304
26 Ibid, p.304
27 Quoted in Tarle, *Napoleon's Invasion of Russia* p.228

17

THE BATTLE OF
MALOYAROSLAVETS

Just after midnight on 22 October, the guerrilla leader Seslavin came galloping up to a Russian outpost. He was taken to several Russian generals, including Ermolov:

> Hiding in the woods near the road some 4 km from Fominskoe, Seslavin saw Napoleon with his enormous entourage, followed by his Guard and numerous troops. As they passed, he captured several prisoners and brought us the most intelligent of them, a non-commissioned officer in the Guard, who told us the following 'We abandoned Moscow four days ago, Marshal Mortier and his detachment have blown up the Kremlin walls and joined the army ... Tomorrow, Imperial headquarters will be in Borovsk, and then will head to Maloyaroaslavets.' General Dokhturov was immediately informed.[1]

A messenger was despatched to Kutuzov. On arriving at the cabin where the Field Marshal was staying, the hussar, named Bologovsky, reported to General Konovnitsin, who then entered Kutuzov's room. Shortly afterwards Bologovsky was called in and Kutuzov said to him: 'Tell me, my friend, what are these events you have brought me news about? Has Napoleon really left Moscow and is he, indeed, retreating? Tell me quickly, my heart is pounding with impatience.' Bologovsky confirmed the news, at which Kutuzov began to cry with joy, knelt on his bed and prayed to the icon which was hanging on the wall, 'God my creator. At last you have heard our prayers. From this moment Russia is saved.'[2] The Cossacks were the first to enter Moscow, although a small garrison had been left by Napoleon to demolish what remained of the city. Benkendorf recorded the scene:

> The Grande Armée of Napoleon had quit Moscow and General [Winzingerode] had trustworthy intelligence that the garrison which had been left in the Kremlin

was also preparing to leave and had mined those ancient walls to leave behind a trail of more devastation and sacrilege.

The General determined to save the Kremlin and proceeded himself to our outposts, which had already penetrated far enough into the interior of the city to encounter the French who were close to the Government House. The General approached, making a gesture with his handkerchief ... like a bearer of a flag of truce and he was coming forward to warn Marshal Bertier who was at the Kremlin, when a drunken hussar threw himself on the General and led him away a prisoner; our Cossacks were too far away to help.

At two o'clock in the morning a horrible explosion accompanied by an illumination told us the of destruction of the Kremlin and the deliverance of Moscow.[3]

Winzingerode was led away into captivity.

On 22 October General Benkendorf entered the city:

This ancient capital is all smoking ... We cleared a path through the bodies of men and beasts, the debris and the ashes obstructed all the streets. The churches are pillaged and all blackened by smoke, and only serve sadly as markers for finding one's bearings in this immense devastation.

The populace of the city who had remained during the occupation now set out for revenge on those soldiers of the Grande Armée who had been left behind. This crowd was surging towards the Kremlin to see what had happened to the palace, when the Cossack Regiment of the Guard arrived and forced the crowd back for their own safety because the walls of the Kremlin were still likely to collapse. Benkendorf was able to proceed into the Kremlin, entering the fourteenth-century Cathedral of the Assumption, where for centuries the Tsars of Russia had been crowned.

I was seized with horror at seeing this revered church that even the flames had spared, had been desecrated by the unrestrained soldiery. I was persuaded that the state it was in ought to be hidden from the eyes of the people. The relics of the saints were defaced, their tombs filled up by filth, the ornaments of the tombs were pulled off; the images which decorated the church were defiled, torn up, all this had been provoked by the greed of the soldiers ... The altar was thrown down, casks of wine had flooded these sacred floors and the bodies of men and horses tainted these vaults ... All the rest of the Kremlin had become the prey of the flames or had been shaken by the explosion of the mines; the arsenal, the church of Ivan the Great, the towers and the walls, all were a pile of stones.

Benkendorf then proceeded to the Foundling Hospital, which Napoleon had promised to protect.

Several hundred children which had been admitted by the enemy had died of hunger, a quantity of women and Russian wounded ... had found shelter and several

thousand French sick had been abandoned. All asked for bread, but the devastation
of the neighbourhood of Moscow did not allow me to provide immediately for a
need so pressing. The corridors [and] the courtyard of this enormous building were
filled with dead, the victims of destitution, of sickness and of terror.

Other large buildings were encumbered with Russian wounded, who had
escaped from the fire, and were barely existing, without help, without food, surrounded with corpses and awaiting the end of their sufferings.[4]

On their departure the French had set alight to what remained of Moscow, instead of
trying to put out the flames the peasants tried to pillage what was left. Consequently
the following day Benkendorf returned with three battalions of infantry and with
difficulty restored order. He also had to place guards on the Foundling and Galitzin
Hospitals, to protect the 2,000 wounded Frenchmen that lay within the buildings
from the mob who demanded revenge.

The crowd also demanded vengeance against French collaborators. The civilian 'Mr
C.' who had been appointed a member of the provisional government of Moscow by
the French now found himself being accused of being a collaborator.

On the return of the Russian police, no argument that he could urge was held [to
be] a sufficient justification for such conduct. It was necessary, in compliance with
such feelings of the time, that the utmost abhorrence should be shown against every
person who bore the slightest mark of connection with the enemy and to have
merited their confidence was the highest crime. For this he was condemned by the
unanimous voice of his tribunal and the punishment awarded was that he should
be obliged to labour half an hour (pro forma) on the public works with a badge of
infamy affixed to his arm; after which exposure he was thrown into prison for three
months and ever more forbidden to quit the city of Moscow.[5]

With the French gone, the inhabitants who had fled Moscow began to return. Among
those was Sophia Alexandrovna, who on 9 November wrote to Grigori Korsakov:

I have been back in our unhappy Moscow for five days now. Oh, Grisha my dar-
ling, you would not believe what has become of Moscow, it is unrecognisable, and
one cannot look upon these ruins without weeping. Only the walls of the stone
houses are left, and only the stoves sticking out of the wooden ones. Imagine what a
miracle it was to find Mamma's house still in one piece, and even more miraculous
Matushka's wooden one, in which we are now living. As for the settlement, it is as
if it never existed – burnt to the ground and in ruins, and we are left with nothing.[6]

Meanwhile Napoleon was heading south towards the Province of Kaluga. From there
he could either divert to Smolensk where he had ordered a magazine to be established,
or march to the Ukraine, which still remained untouched by the ravages of war.

On 23 October, Uxkull wrote: 'Moscow has been retaken. The occupiers have
turned their backs; we are in hot pursuit! The weather seems to be backing our efforts;

it's severely cold and snow is already covering the fields.'[7] The same day, upon hearing the news of Napoleon's route, Kutuzov despatched General Dokhturov to march to cut the French off at Maloyaroslavets, a small town of 232 houses with a population of about 1,500. Wilson describes Maloyaroslavets:

> Built upon the side and summit of a lofty hill, rising immediately above the Luzha (which the enemy called the Lutza), and over which river is a bridge distant about a hundred yards from the ravine …
>
> The ground on both flanks of the town, ascending from the river, is woody and steep, and the ground on the left is intersected with very deep fissures and ravines, so as to be impracticable for artillery movement from the bank of the river.
>
> The whole town is built of wood; near the summit of the hill there is an open space like a Grand Place; and near the ravine, at the bottom are a church and a couple or more houses that command the approach.[8]

Although the town had been intially nearer to the Russians, the French had a four-day head start. However, Prince Eugene's IV Corps, which formed the advance guard was allowed to rest on 22 October and heavy rains turned the roads to mud, so slowing Napoleon's artillery and the 40,000 or so carriages that accompanied his army.

At 4.00pm, Dokhturov's force arrived near Fominskoie, where Cossacks reported a strong force of French occupying the town. Dokhturov decided to wait for reinforcements, but that evening the Cossacks reported that the French were on the move once more. Dokhturov retired beyond Maloyaroslavets, and ordered the wooden bridge over the River Luzha to be destroyed. However, the destruction of the bridge did not prevent the French, under General Delzon, occupying the town that evening.

Early in the morning of 24 October, Dokhturov, seeing that only two battalions occupied Maloyaroslavets, attacked with the 6th and 33rd Jagers. The Italians, outnumbered two to one, were driven to the northern end of the town, where they occupied a group of buildings by the Luzha, including the Nicholas Chernostrov Monastery. Here they made a stand, being bombarded by Russian artillery. Under this bombardment the Italians managed to build a temporary bridge, which allowed the 2nd Brigade of Delzon's Division, plus two guns, to cross and reinforce the battalions.

This force counter-attacked and pushed the Russian jagers aside, until they in turn were reinforced by the 1st Jager Regiment, who regained much of the town. By now Dokhturov's 6th Corps had deployed across the Kaluga road, forming the centre and left wing. On the right wing was General Dorokhov's Division. The 19th Jagers were also thrown into the fight for the town. While the regiment was advancing, a priest, Father Vasili Vasilkovski, with a cross in his hand encouraged the advancing Jagers, despite being wounded in the head. For this he was awarded the St George Cross 4th Class, the first priest to receive such an award.

The Jagers were supported by the eight guns of the Imperial Guard's Horse Battery, which occupied a hill overlooking the bridge and began to bombard it.

Meanwhile, the 7th Horse Artillery Company occupied the cemetery near the town, from where its guns could also fire upon the bridge. The French suffered heavy casualties from these two batteries while trying to cross the bridge. Delzon, whose men still held onto part of the town, wanted to send the 1st Brigade of his division into the fray, but Eugene preferred to wait for the rest of his corps to arrive before launching another attack.

A battalion of the Wilmanstrand Infantry Regiment was also committed to fight for the town, which further pressurised the French who were desperately holding the end of the town. At about 8 o'clock Eugene de Beauharnais finally ordered the 1st Brigade of the 13th Infantry Division to support the 2nd Brigade of the Division. Although suffering heavy casualties from the Russian artillery, the brigade crossed the river and attacked the town on the western side, expelling the Russians once again.

The artillery of the 13th Division deployed as a counter battery, which prompted General Ermolov to bring up the 32nd Battery Company. This battery deployed on the heights overlooking the bridge.

At about 10.30am Eugene then threw in the 14th Infantry Division. The Russians in turn committed the 1st brigade of the 7th Infantry Division under Major General Talyzin. After a heavy bombardment the Libav and Sofia Infantry Regiments advanced on the French, supported by the Jagers. With only the sounds of their drums beating, without firing a shot they forced the French out of Maloyaroslavets and drove them towards the river.

> The very militia who had just joined (and who, being armed only with pikes, formed a third rank to the battalions) not only stood as steady under the cannonade as their veteran comrades, but charged the sallying enemy with as ardent a ferocity.[9]

Only the French who occupied the Monastery stopped the pursuit of their comrades.

Eugene threw the 2nd Brigade, 14th Infantry Division in the fray to recapture the town, which by now was in flames. Again the town changed hands, so the Tomsk and Polotsk Infantry Regiments were ordered to advance. By now, 18,000 French and Russian troops were battling in the small town and after heavy fighting the French were once more driven out, with heavy losses. The see-saw battle continued throughout the day, with General Pino's 15th (Italian) Division, being sent in.

At midday, General Raevski's 7th Corps arrived on the battlefield, but it was not until about 2.00pm that Kutuzov gave the Nizhni-Novgorod and the Oryol Infantry Regiments of Paskevitch's 26th Division orders to advance. By then the town was once more in the hands of the French and Italian forces. The Ladoga and Poltava Infantry Regiments, also of the 7th Corps, advanced towards the village of Spasskoi, held by Italian troops. Spasskoi was taken, as too was most of Maloyaroslavets.

The Jagers of the Italian Imperial Guard and the 2nd Brigade of the 15th Division rushed forwards at bayonet point and saved the situation. The remainder of the infantry of the Italian Imperial Guard crossed the river to act as a reserve. Two battalions of the Jagers of the Italian Imperial Guard advanced on Spasskoi and attacked the Russian right wing, putting the Russian skirmishers to flight.

The Italian jagers were stopped in their tracks by a hail of caseshot from a Russian artillery battery. Before they could recover, the Italians were attacked by the Lagoda, Poltava, Smolensk, Narva, Aleksopolsk and Novo Ingermanland Infantry Regiments and forced to retreat. The Italian infantry barricaded themselves in Spasskoi, while the Italian Guard Jagers reformed and counterattacked, once more overthrowing the Russians.

At 4.00pm, Lieutenant General Borozdin I's 8th Corps arrived, followed by the remainder of Kutuzov's forces and deployed on both sides of the Kaluga Road, about 2 km from Maloyaroslavets. They begun constructing four earthworks, where Kutuzov planned to place his artillery batteries. At one point during the battle, Kutuzov is said to have mounted his horse and advanced closer to the fighting. Despite pleas from members of his staff and musket balls whizzing over his head, he wanted to see for himself how the battle was going. Upon hearing that some French troops were still in Maloyaroslavets, Kutuzov decided to send Raevski's Corps to support Dokhturov, whose Corps had suffered heavy casualties.

The 27th Division of Raevski was divided in two, the Odessa and Simbirsk Infantry Regiments was sent to the right wing, while the Tarnopol and Vilensk Infantry Regiments were sent to the left. At about 5.00pm, Marshal Davoust's 1st Corps and the 1st and 2nd Cavalry Corps began to appear on the battlefield, closely followed by Napoleon's Imperial Guard. By this time the sun had set, but the musketry and cannon fire continued on both sides.

The Russians were once again forced out of Maloyaroslavets, this time by Compans' Division of Davoust's Corps. Seeing this, Kutuzov ordered the 3rd Infantry Division of Lieutenant General Stroganov's 3rd Corps to reinforce Raevski's and Dokhturov's Corps, while Lieutenant General Konovnitsin was ordered to retake Maloyaroslavets. The 2nd Grenadier Division was ordered to retake the town of Spasskoi.

The Russians succeeded in their objectives, but were again forced to withdraw because of a French counter-attack. Dokhturov had deployed a line of skirmishers but being informed that more French had crossed the river, reinforced his line. The Moscow Infantry Regiment, supported by the Ufa Infantry Regiment and the 3rd Battalion of the Polotsk Infantry Regiment, was sent to the left wing to recapture the wood near the river, which had been occupied by the French. However they could not prevent General Gerard's Division from crossing the river.

By now there were enough French infantry in Maloyaroslavets that they could consolidate their position. There now began another artillery duel, which lasted until about 10.00pm. Firing could still be heard until 11.00pm, but the last attack was by the Astrakhan Grenadier Regiment, on the left flank, which entered the town and set fire to the remaining houses still untouched by the fire, before withdrawing again.

How many times the town was taken and retaken is uncertain, Lowenstern states seven times; while Uxkull says: 'the French had taken the town eight times, but they were always driven off again by our gallant grenadiers and chasseurs. Finally, on the ninth try, they were totally beaten back and our people remained masters of the town.'

Uxkull was mistaken, it was the French who still occupied what was left of Maloyaroslavets when the battle finished. He continues:

The sight there was indescribable. The cannon shells were shattering the walls of houses, which were burning and collapsing. The streets were filled with corpses and the wounded. The hubbub was frightful ... Throughout the night we were disturbed by bombs and rockets. I was exhausted with hunger and fatigue. My greatcoat was pierced through by two bullets, and my grey [horse] was scarcely breathing.[10]

General Lowenstein also recorded the heavy street fighting during the battle, and that: 'The stubbornness was so great that we did not take any prisoners. The Generals Delzon and Levie were killed, Generals Pino, Fontana and Gifflenga wounded. Our loss was very great.' Another Russian source states the number of prisoners 'did not exceed 200 men for the fierce fighting of our soldiers during the numerous storms of the town did not allow for mercy to the enemy'.

General Eugene von Wurttemberg noted that 'the field of battle, especially inside the town and the bank of the Luzha presented a horrible appearance.' The French still occupied Maloyaroslavets, but General Delzon and his brother were both killed along with about 4,000 other casualties. An official report put the number of Russian casualties at 6,887 men. 7,000–8,000 killed or wounded is probably nearer the mark, including Dokhturov, who was mortally wounded.[11]

With the battle over, the Russian officers tried to persuade Kutuzov to renew it the following day, but as General Lowenstern put it, Kutuzov 'preferred to construct bridges of gold for the enemy's retreat, whereby the enemy would be allowed to leave Russia'. The Russian Army withdrew to a safe distance from Maloyaroslavets, but it still held the Kaluga Road.

General Eugene von Wurttemberg's 2nd Corps had set off from the camp at Taruntino early in the morning of 24 October towards Maloyaroslavets, but did not arrive until late that night, so bivouacked near the battlefield. The following morning

The enemy noticed it and threw grenades into the bivouac of the 4th Division which killed several men and caused confusion. Although busy reforming the troops, I received orders to retreat and the 2nd Corps marched about 3 km and was placed behind the little river of Kortuka to the right of the army.[12]

Kutuzov wrote to the Tsar:

I intend to inflict tremendous damage on Napoleon by a parallel pursuit and finally cut his line of operations. This offers me various advantages: (1) I shall reach Orsha by the shortest route if the enemy begins to retreat in that direction. If however, Napoleon turns to Moghilev. I shall completely cut him off from that city. (2) I shall cover the country from which the Army obtains supplies.[13]

That night, Napoleon, who had arrived too late to take part in the battle, called a council of war, where the basic decisions about the retreat were made. Orders were issued that the Grande Armée should begin its retreat towards Smolensk, which would mean marching over already ravaged ground.

On 24 October 1812, a General Order had been issued

> ... to all generals of corps, all the chief Cossack regiments and also all the partisans informing them of the great successes the Cossacks had achieved who every day take a number of pieces of cannon from the rear of the enemy, which, weakened, harassed and worn down, is now reduced to the most deplorable state.

It also ordered them to look out for Napoleon, who was described as

> ...short and compact, hair black, flat and short, the beard black shaved up towards the ear, the eyebrows strongly arched, but contracted towards the nose, – the nose aquiline, with perpetual marks of snuff, – the countenance gloomy and violent, the chin extremely projecting, always in a little uniform, without ornaments, generally wrapped in a little grey surtout ... and continually attended by a Mameluke.[14]

It was rumoured in the Grande Armée that Platov had promised the hand of his only daughter in marriage to any Cossack who captured Napoleon.

On 25 October, the day after the battle, Napoleon with a small party of his staff rode out in front of Maloyaroslavets to reconnoitre the position. Napoleon's party saw some horsemen approaching that they mistook for French cavalry because 'they were arranged in pretty good order'. On the Cossacks drawing closer they realised their mistake, apart from Napoleon who took some convincing.

Fortunately for Napoleon, the Cossacks did not recognised him and were finally repulsed. They retired to the opposite bank of the Luzha, covered by a battery of Don Cossack artillery. This incident, known as the 'Emperor's Hurrah', left Napoleon badly shaken and that evening he asked his doctor to prepare a bottle of poison, which he would wear around his neck in case he was ever captured. That day the Grande Armée, now less than half its original strength from when it crossed the border just five months before, began its retreat.

Notes

1 Ermolov, *Zapiski 1812* pp.182–183
2 Quoted in Bragin *Kutuzov* pp.112–113
3 *Zapiski Benkendorfa 1812* p.76
4 Ibid, pp.79–80
5 James *Journal of a tour...* pp.179, 181–182
6 Quoted in *Moscow* ed. Laurence Kelly p.191
7 Uxkull, *Arms and the Woman* p.98
8 Wilson, *The French invasion of Russia* pp.223–224
9 Ibid, p.225
10 Uxkull, *Arms and the Woman* pp.96–97
11 The official figure was 19 officers, 45 NCOs, 1,294 privates and 6 noncombatants killed, 1 general, 136 officers, 153 NCOs, 2924 and 17 noncombatants wounded and 31 NCOs, 2248 privates and 13 noncombatants missing.
12 *Journal de Prince Eugene de Wurttemberg* p.23
13 Quoted in Bragin, *Kutuzov* p.120
14 Quoted in Spring, *Cossacks* p.49

18

PURSUIT

The Grande Armée, the victors of numerous campaigns with the battle honours of Austerlitz, Jena, Friedland and Wagram on their eagles, now experienced a new aspect of warfare, retreat. Napoleon began to retrace his steps along the Mojaisk Road, while the Russians took the Medyn Road. The roads would cross each other at Viazma, so the Grande Armée needed to out-march the Russians if they were not to be cut off. The Russian Army was eager to be at Viazma first. On 30 October Chicherin wrote: 'Some of his [Napoleon's] force are already being beyond Viazma, we have to cover 40km in order to cut them off. I burn with impatience. I should like wings to be attached to our army.'[1]

A problem for the Russians was that many of them were newly conscripted and the forced marches quickly exhausted them. Eugene von Wurttemberg wrote: 'The distance that we covered daily depended rather on the physical state of the troops than on any order received to advance [to a specific location].' Even the Russian Imperial Guard suffered. Captain Pushkin, of the Semenovski Regiment, remembered: 'For a long time our men did not receive permission to cook soup.'

Finally the Russian Army arrived at Viazma. Eugene von Wurttemberg:

> 1 November … [we] arrived at 4 o'clock in the evening at the same moment as General Paskevitch, whose division followed close behind the Cossacks of General Platov. The enemy marched in extreme disorder and an attack would have yielded perhaps a hundred pieces of artillery and many prisoners. General Paskevitch assisted me with a will and our divisions were drawn up in order of battle, but it was impossible to involve General Korf [cavalry].[2]

Wurttemberg decided to wait for reinforcements before he attacked, so letting this part of the Grande Armée pass; the remainder would not be so lucky.

On 2 November after his regiment were finally allowed to cook some soup, Captain Pushkin recalls:

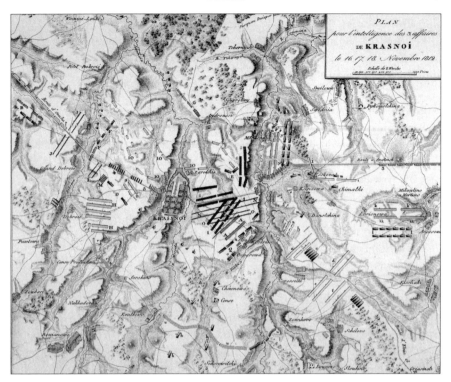

Plan of the battle at Krasnoe.

> We did set out until 10am … During the course of the whole day we could
> hear explosions of ammunition wagons and from time to time cannon fire. With
> the approach of night the Cossacks, in one of their celebrated nocturnal sorties,
> descended on the French …
>
> 3 November. The cannonade of the advance guard situated near Viazma … began
> at 7am. Our orders are to prepare [for battle], in spite of this we set out only at 12
> o'clock for Viazma. At dusk we had a short rest, and after that continued the journey
> along the country roads all in the same direction. Darkness and cold made it a very
> difficult campaign. We did not halt until 11pm.[3]

Although the Semenovski Regiment was only 8 km from Viazma, it would take no
part in the forthcoming battle.

That day the Russians caught up with the Grande Armée near Viazma.

> Early in the morning … the cavalry of Miloradovitch moved to reach the high road
> leading from Fedorovskoie to Viazma: when it arrived near Moksimova at about
> 8am, the Viceroy and Poniatowski had already passed this point, but the advance of
> Davoust was still approaching.
>
> Miloradovitch charged down upon it, threw the enemy into confusion, formed a
> cheval upon the road, and opened [fire with] his guns, which he had established on
> the heights, upon the broken column.

Platov, hearing the cannonade, commenced his attack upon the rear guard in Fedorovskoie, and in this attack he was supported by the cavalry of Paskevitch.

The enemy contained Fedorovskoie for some time but was at last overpowered and vigorously pursued by the cavalry.

The Viceroy, informed by the cannonade of the danger to which Davoust was exposed, immediately faced about and returned with two Italian Divisions and the Poles to extricate him, because ... he never deserted a friend. On arriving near Messoidowo he formed his troops on the adjoining high ground, and opened fire with his guns, which enfiladed the Russian left.

The rest of his corps, consisting of the division Pino and the [Italian Imperial] Guards, had been left at Viazma 'to co-operate with the corps of Ney in resisting the Russian Army, if it should advance from Biskovo on that city'; and they were ordered 'to make the best disposition that their means might permit for that object, and to secure the ... retreat of the Viceroy and Davoust'.

The whole force of the enemy amounted to at least forty thousand combatants.

Miloradovitch with the Cossacks could not bring more than twenty five thousand into action.

Davoust, on seeing the Viceroy prepared to assist him, threw forward a cloud of tirailleurs, and moved on with his main body. The Russian cavalry, posted on the road and on each side, could not withstand the united cross fire of the Viceroy, of Davoust's artillery, and of the light troops: but one of the batteries was withdrawn with great difficulty. The regiment of Kharpov's dragoons that had passed beyond the main road was also obliged desperately to cut its way through the enemy to rejoin the Cossacks.

It was not until near ten in the morning that Prince Eugene von Wurttemberg arrived with his infantry division ... Without pausing he attacked the enemy ascending the heights to carry a Russian battery, which still continued to fire, though from a position of the most imminent jeopardy.[4]

Eugene von Wurttemberg takes up the narrative:

The Cavalry Corps of General Korf deployed to the right and that of General Wassiltchikov to the left ... General Wassiltchikov charged with the regiments of Kiev (dragoons) and Askhitir (Hussars) against the head of the enemy column and Colonel Joussefovitch with the dragoons of Kharkov attacked the rear. The enemy, surprised at the outset, nevertheless put on a bold front after several strong batteries were established in front of the 13th Division of the Corps of the Viceroy. He stopped the remainder of his corps as well as part of that of Prince Pontiatowski which preceded it and extended his line on his right, while Marshal Davoust ... marching behind the Corps of the Viceroy turned the head of his column to the right. Colonel Joussefovitch, who had passed between the corps of the Viceroy and Davoust, found his way blocked ...

The Russian cavalry, deprived now of the means of penetrating the enemy column, fiound themselves hurled back on the defensive and lost many men to bullets. They began little by little to lose ground and the 17th Division, which arrived at this time with its artillery, was drawn up with them. The skirmishers followed closely and increased the pressure on the Russian troops. The enemy had not, for all that, any other objective but to retreat. Ccontenting himself with this success the Viceroy began to leave on the Viazma Road. Meanwhile Marshal Davoust did not think to hasten his march to overtake the Viceroy's corps. General Platov, close to his right side with Cossacks and the Jagers of General Gogel and General Paskevitch's brigades, over-threw his rearguard with the light infantry of the 26th Division and two regiments of dragoons. General Miloradovitch recalled the cavalry and the 17th Division and began a very lively fire against the divisions of Davoust. Still delayed on the main road, his corps became confused and suffered a complete rout …

Seeing that the enemy had no other intention but to retreat. It appeared to me essential [to work against] his communications and instead of placing me behind the cavalry as had been judged necessary at first, I continued the march of my detachment as far as a little wood, between Federovskoie and Viazma and established myself on horseback on the main road. Immediately after, it could have been 8.30, the head of the column of the Viceroy appeared in front of the Volhynie Regiment, which was covered by a light battery … these troops did not notice us at first … because they were marching with confidence. The head of the artillery of the Polish corps, Pelletier, fell into our hands and the column was showered by a hail of bullets; they were terror stricken and dispersed into the fields …

Meanwhile General Miloradovitch ordered me … to leave my position on the main road and take up a new one along this road … to the left of the 17th Division. He had warned me at the same time that an enemy corps was marching from Viazma to support the troops.

My Jager regiments were at this time already well advanced beyond the main road but withdrew upon seeing the enemy and took station in the woods mentioned above. The 4th Division was positioned to their right with a strong battery on a height. The cavalry of Vassiltchikov took up a position behind the 4th Division. The main road was thus a few hundred paces before our front.

The Viceroy's Corps, encouraged by the apparently favourable circumstances and keenly aware of the necessity of covering the march on the main road of Davoust's Corps, which was sharply pressed by Generals Platov and Paskevitch. Davoust was no longer master of his movements. [The Viceroy] advanced to attack my detachment and stubbornly tried to carry off the battery in front of the 4th Division. The latter believed it was their duty to withdraw because of the lively tiraillade to which they were exposed. My ADC, Captain Wachten, went to reassure the leader of this battery and led a battalion of the Tobolsk Regiment to its support. The Krementsch and Volhynie Regiments meanwhile were involved to the left in a very close fire fight, which sustained the loss of 13 officers on this occasion … The enemy gave up the attack …

I … [then] concentrated on the pursuit of the enemy by advancing a battery and in giving a hand to General Paskevitch who marched on my right, still on the heels of Davoust's Corps. The Viceroy's Corps was supported near the village of

Rskawetz by a brigade of Ledru's Division that Marshal Ney had sent to the action and the 14th Division of the French 4th Corps … In the meantime the Russian 4th Corps had reached the suburbs of the town; the 23rd Division attacked Rskowetz's position and the 11th engaged farther to the left with Marshal Ney's Corps who had stopped behind the Ulitza in order to help the withdrawal of the Viceroy. The enemy troops were no longer thinking therefore but were in a headlong retreat. The 14th Division of General Broussier followed his corps through the town and was pursued at bayonet point by General Paskevitch with the 26th Division.

Bennigsen records that Miloradovitch ordered Viazma to be captured:

The order was executed by Pernov's regiment … who bayonet charged and after a fight lasting a half an hour drove the enemy with losses from Viazma, of which the greater part of the houses were consumed by flames.[5]

Kutuzov added in his report to the Tsar:

The battle continued until the enemy retreated into the town, from whence he was driven with the bayonet by the 11th and 26th Divisions … The infantry regiment of Pernov, which was at the forefront of the columns, was the first to enter the town with colours flying and music playing, and made a road for the rest of the troops over the dead bodies of the enemy.[6]

For its actions that day the Pernov regiment received the honour of carrying the colours of St George.

Eugene von Wurttemberg continues:

Davoust left Viazma … pursued by Cossacks until daybreak. Marshal Ney passed the town … and stopped afterwards to form the rearguard from what he [could] save of the remainder of the 14th Division …

The 17th Division had few losses, but the loss of the jagers and of the 4th was considerable. They exceeded 1,000 men of all ranks. The peasants who formed our third rank had besides profited from the leisure that they were granted for transporting the wounded and had not rejoined us, so that the 4th Division saw itself reduced after this affair to about 1,600 men.[7]

According to General Lowenstern, while this fighting was going on Kutuzov did nothing:

He could hear the cannonade as distinctly as if it were taking place in his own antechamber, but despite the insistence of all the higher officers, he remained a mere spectator of that battle which could have brought the destruction of the greater part of Napoleon's army and the capture of the Viceroy … At headquarters, everyone was burning with impatience to give battle to the enemy; the generals and officers protested and set fire to their tents to demonstrate that they were no longer needed; everyone awaited the signal to battle. The signal did not come. Nothing could compel Kutuzov to act; he even grew angry with those who pointed out to him the extent of the enemy's demoralisation and he chased me from his study for telling him … Kutuzov kept stubbornly to his plan and advanced parallel to the enemy. He refused to take risks and preferred to expose himself to the censure of the entire army.[8]

So there would be no general engagement and the Grande Armée was allowed to escape, but not before they had suffered 4,000 killed and wounded and 3,000 prisoners, compared with the Russian losses of 1,800 casualties.

The losses of the enemy at the affair at Viazma during this march showed that a phenomenal number of wounded and of sick had remained in the rear and the majority had frozen during the night of 4 November to 5 November. This day the advanced guard marched as far as Zaroubej. All the road was covered with corpses, the majority being frozen. For the enemy troops, harassed by fatigue and lack of provisions, the frost of the nights completed their loss.[9]

Acccording to Eugene von Wurttemberg, the Russian attitude and circumstances were very different:

Every bivouac was on the contrary for us a kind of celebration. The soldier, naturally satisfied at the happy results of these efforts, expressed his satisfaction in accents of cheerfulness; besides we were all the time very well equipped with provisions, above all of meat, and our only regret was that were not supplied two days. The revengefulness of the Russian soldier decreased since he considered his enemy an object worthy of his pity. Kind by nature, he immediately ceased mistreating the unfortunate victims of the hated ambitions.[10]

The same day as Wurttemberg wrote these words, 4 November, Uxkull expressed a very different view of the campaign:

Men and horses are dying of hunger and exhaustion. Only the Cossacks, always lively and cheerful, manage to keep their spirits up. The rest of us have a very hard time dragging on after the fleeing enemy, and our horses, which have no shoes, slip on the frozen ground and fall down, never to get up again. The artillery especially is suffering a lot.[11]

On the following day Uxkull, again wrote in his diary:

We are going back along the same road we marched on this summer. What a contrast, and all in the space of a few months! We are doing 32 to 42 km a day, moving towards Polotsk at this great pace. The life I'm leading and my clothing are too unusual not to say something about them. My underwear consists of three shirts and a few pairs of long socks; I'm afraid to change them because of the freezing cold. I'm eaten up by fleas and encased by filth, since my sheepskin never leaves me. During the day it's underneath my greatcoat, and during the night it serves as a blanket. The food I eat is disgusting; since we lack everything, we grill the meat in the fire and swallow it, half raw and blackened by smoke, without salt or bread. Only hard liquor keeps us going.[12]

Meanwhile it was getting colder, in what would prove to be the coldest winter in living memory. When warned about the Russian winter Napoleon had, almost incredibly, dismissed it as being the same as in France, but on 4 November Eugene von Wurttemberg noted that the first snows of winter started to fall. On 7 November Baron Uxkull wrote:

How cold the nights are! We can't sleep, so we sit around a warm fire to warm ourselves, but our backs are ice cold; then we turn around to warm up the back side. The most disagreeable thing is the smoke; the wind drives it into our eyes, which give us a lot of pain. But this gypsy life does not prevent anyone from being very happy. We all get together around the camp fire, chatting, singing, playing pranks and all in the best of tempers.[13]

On 8 November, Chicherin wrote while at the village of White Holm:

The French continue to escape, and we after a day's rest at Viazma continued to advance by forced march. At this moment we are situated 90 km from Medini on the road to Yelnye. It has already been snowing for three days and although I sit in front of a large campfire, my hands are completely stiff with cold.

The following day he wrote: 'Billets – understand? Billets! Not bivouac, not camp, but genuine billets, a mansion, paradise! In a narrow hut, where we crowded so that it was impossible to turn, but where on the other hand it was warm.'[14]

If the suffering of the Russian Army was bad, then that of the Grande Armée was of course far worse. Count Platov:

The retreat of the French is a flight without example, abandoning everything that demands carriage; even their sick and wounded. The traces of this fearful career are marked with every species of horror. At every step is seen the dying and the dead, not merely the fallen in battle, but the victims of famine and fatigue. In two days … the full amount of the dead could not be ascertained for the nature of the warfare did not allow these calculations; no prisoners were taken, as it was a regular system with the Cossacks in their battles never to burden themselves with men as prisoners.

On 8 November D'Aistedt wrote to Count Charles Nesselrode, on the Elno Road about 34 km from Dorogobouje:

It was 15 degrees of frost, the ground is covered with snow, but nothing stops the army, which follows with swiftness and with all its train, the enemy, who abandon daily their cannons, their sick, their stragglers for quickening their flight … [the enemy's] cavalry being exhausted as their teams, whereas the Russian cavalry iis at full strength; and there are 20,000 Cossacks on all the roads both in front and in the rear.[15]

Several eyewitness accounts talk of cannibalism within the ranks of the Grande Armée; General Kreitz while marching between Viazma and Smolensk claims to have seen several Frenchmen in a wood eating one of their comrades. On 11 November, a Russian officer by the name of Voieykov wrote: 'Hunger has compelled them to eat horses' carcasses and many of us have seen them roasting the flesh of their compatriots. The Smolensk road is covered at every step with dead men and horses.'

On 9 November, the Corps of the Viceroy of Italy was held up at the river Vop, near Dorogobuzh, while his sappers tried to build a bridge, with Platov's artillery firing upon them. The bridge soon collapsed because of the sheer weight of traffic. This forced the Viceroy's Corps and the many stragglers to ford the almost frozen river. The *Journal of the Russian Army* records that Platov had

… overtaken four divisions of the French army under the command of Beauharnais [the Viceroy] upon the road from Dorogobugth and Doughovtchshstchina [and] … charged through this body dividing it into two parts with great slaughter and the capture of sixty two pieces of ordnance … part of the remains of this corps fled in the direction of Doughovtchshstchina closely pursued by Cossacks and light cavalry. General Platov had expectations of coming up with these divisions and of taking Beauharnais himself.

Unfortunately for Platov's Cossacks, the Viceroy escaped.

The same day, Napoleon entered Smolensk, where he had hoped to spend the winter and reorganise his forces, but the city was in no condition to quarter an army for the winter. Napoleon had ordered the garrison to establish a magazine for 100,000 men, but few provisions had been collected. One commissariat officer had believed that the provisions would not be needed since victory was certain, and so had sold the oxen to the Jewish community, who in turn sold them to the Russians. He was arrested and sentenced to death, but reprieved at the last moment when he begged Napoleon for mercy. Other oxen and wagons full of provisions had been captured by Cossacks, who were also able to rescue General Wintzingerode.

The thought of waiting for what little provisions had been collected to be distributed was too much for the starving soldiers of the Grande Armée. They plundered the magazines and houses of any food they could find. Nothing was left for the straggling soldiers outside the city, whose officers were doing their best to restore some kind of order.

During the early part of November, not knowing of the true state of the Grande Armée, the inhabitants of St Petersburg were apprehensive, fearing that Napoleon would march on their city. Many had abandoned the city, or were preparing to do so, but they soon realised the truth.

Other towns were liberated by the Russians; the inhabitants of Chaus, whose village had been occupied since July, began to hear rumours that the French had been defeated. Then,

> There were advanced parties of Cossacks ... [then] our regiments, with music, songs and drumbeats; all [our] hearts began to beat faster. Many of the generals and officers, by the invitation of my father, visited our house, in which beforehand we had prepared breakfast.

Napoleon stayed at Smolensk until 14 November when he continued his retreat. The Grande Armée had looked upon Smolensk as the end of their sufferings, but now with the temperature -23.75°C (-10.75°F), they were forced to carry on their march. If their retreat had been bad up to then, from now on it would be agony.

However, Alexander was furious with the lack of success during the pursuit and on 11 November he wrote to Kutuzov criticising his strategy:

> I see that the hope of erasing the general sorrow over the loss of Moscow by cutting the enemy's road of retreat has completely vanished. Your incomprehensible passivity after the fortunate engagement of Taruntino has cost us the gains it promised; your unnecessary and pernicious retreat to Goncharov after the battle of Maroyaroslavets destroyed all the advantages of your position; you could have forced the enemy to hasten his retreat near Viazma, and thereby cut off at least three of his army corps: those of Davout, Ney and the Viceroy, which were fighting near that city.[16]

Clausewitz saw only too well that Kutuzov was trying to save his army from the severe winter and that the Russians were suffering just as badly as the French:

> The winter in all its hostility, on shattered powers, physical and moral, an army led from bivouac to bivouac, suffering from privation, decimated by sickness, its path strewn with dead, dying and exhausted bodies, – they will comprehend with what difficulty each motion was accomplished, and how nothing but the strongest impulses could overcome the inertia of the mass. Kutuzov saw his army melting in his grasp and the difficulty he would have in bringing any considerable portion of it to the frontier. He saw that the result of the campaign must in any case be a colossal one; he foresaw with much acuteness the total destruction of his army ... Kutuzov determined not to throw his whole strength upon his adversary, but to follow his unceasingly with great and small detachments, to harass and exhaust him. This he deemed sufficient for his object.[17]

Among those suffering was Baron Uxkull, who wrote in his diary on 11 November: 'I've got a high fever. Really, what a sad life we lead. We've turned into cattle. These blasted camps are soon going to do me in. Our situation gets worse from one day to the next, and there's no hope of its soon ending.'[18]

Captain Skobelev, who was a member of Kutuzov's staff, also complained: 'We sometimes do not have firewood, in order to cook our Kasha [gruel] … loaves are not supplied; … [there is] nobody to buy [food] from – the sutlers seldom reach us, only appearing with provisions [that] the troops at the rear buy up.'[19]

The pursuit was left mainly to the Cossacks and the light cavalry, who hovered around the Grande Armée's flanks, waiting for an opportunity to attack. Robert Kerr Porter records in his history of the campaign that while it continued its long retreat 'every surrounding track, whether wood or open ground; swarmed with Cossacks and light troops to harass the enemy and destroy the bridges in his path.'

On 11 November, Captain Pushkin observed a column of prisoners escorted by some Cossacks:

> Today on our arrival we saw a great number of prisoners, which evoked a deserved sympathy. They were half-naked, several of them inform us that for 12 days they had nothing to eat. Exhaustion had not given them the opportunity to [forage] … [and] the brutality of their escort … I saw one killed from a haemorrhage, and a comrade of his lying with him by the side of the pool of blood quietly waited, until death saved him from torture.[20]

The weather and the Russian Army were not all that the remnants of the Grande Armée had to contend with. A few days before the Battle of Borodino, Bagration had ordered Colonel David Davydov to attack the enemy's lines of communications. He only had 150 Cossacks and 50 Hussars for this purpose but this small force soon began to prey on the enemy with good results and grew into a much stronger force. In October 1812 Kutuzov ordered Platov to

> Try and gain a march over the enemy in such a way that with your main forces you can make suitable attacks on the retreating heads of his columns, combined with constant night alarms. The same orders have been given to General Orlov Denisov to perform similar operations on the left of the high road. This kind of pursuit will bring the enemy into an extreme position and will deprive him of the major part of his artillery and baggage wagons.[21]

At first the members of the Grande Armée had been surprised by the courtesy shown to them by the Russian serfs. In return for their kindness the French soldiers had plundered these serfs and turned them into groups of partisans seeking revenge. The Partisan leader, Colonel Denis Davydov, instructed these groups to

> Receive them in a friendly way … Do plenty of bowing (because not knowing Russian, bows will be better understood) and bring out all you have in the way of food, and especially drink. Put them to bed drunk and when you see that they are properly asleep, grab all their weapons, which are usually stacked in the corner of

the hut or outside in the street, and do what God has ordained against enemies of Christ's church and your motherland.

Once you have wiped them out, bury their bodies in the animal barn or in some inaccessible place in the woods. In any case, take care that the spot where they are buried will not stand out because of recently dug-up earth. Cover it with a pile of stones, logs, ashes or whatever. As for all the military booty, such as uniforms, helmets, belts and so forth, either burn it or bury it in the same type of place where you bury the bodies. Take this precaution because otherwise another band of robbers [French] will be sure to dig in the freshly moved earth, naturally hoping to find money or valuables there. But when they uncover instead the corpses of their comrades and their belongings, they will be sure to turn on you and burn down the village.[22]

Amongst the guerrilla leaders was Stephan Eremenko who had been a private in the Moscow Infantry Regiment and had been captured at Smolensk, but managed to escape and formed a band of 300 men. Another soldier turned guerrilla was Trooper Samus, of the Ekaterinoslav Hussar Regiment, who had been captured at Borodino and who also had escaped and gathered about him 3,000 partisans and imposed strict discipline on them. Sometimes, it was said, that Samus' band even dressed as French soldiers, to outwit the soldiers of the Grande Armée. However, not all guerrilla leaders were military men; a peasant, Ermolai Vasilyev, commanded a band of 600 peasants. At least two women, Vasilia Kozinov and a peasant called Praskovya, formed a band of guerrillas. The latter killed a French colonel with a pitchfork.

Among the most famous partisans was Alexander Figner, who was renowned for his brutality towards French prisoners. Denis Davidov records:

> I had often been told that Figner was a barbarian, but I never quite believed that he would go so far as to slaughter unarmed enemies, especially as our country's fortunes were now improving and it seemed to me that there was no room for feelings of revenge when our hearts were so full of overwhelming joy. Yet as soon as he learned about my prisoners, he came running to beg for permission to have them shot by some new Cossacks of his who had not yet properly been 'blooded'. I cannot express what I felt at the apparent contradiction between these words and Figner's handsome face and pleasant expression.[23]

Fortunately for Davidov's prisoners, he refused to hand them over to Figner.

On 13 November, Wilson wrote about some of these guerrilla bands' activities:

> At Viazma, fifty French, by a savage order, were burned alive. In another village fifty men had been buried alive; but these terrible acts of ferocity were minor features – they ended in death with comparatively little protracted suffering …
>
> Sixty dying naked men whose necks were laid upon a felled tree, while Russian men and women with large faggot sticks, singing in chorus and hopping around, with repeated blows struck out their brains in succession.[24]

In another incident Wilson records:

> The clinging of the dogs to their masters' corpses was most remarkable and interest-ing. At the commencement of the retreat, at a village near Selino, a detachment of fifty of the enemy had been surprised. The peasants resolved to bury them alive in a pit: a drummer boy bravely led the devoted party and sprang into the grave. A dog belonging to one of the victims could not be secured; every day, however, the dog went to the neighbouring camp, and came back with a bit of food in his mouth to sit and moan over the newly turned earth. It was a fortnight before he was killed by the peasantry, afraid of discovery.[25]

On occasions the Russians also fell foul of these partisans, as Denis Davydov wrote in his diary:

> Local volunteer militia groups habitually barred the way. In every village the gates were closed: young and old manned them with pitchforks, pikes, hatchets and sometimes firearms.
>
> As we approached each settlement, one of us had to ride and parley with the inhabitants, telling them that we were Russians, that we were coming to help them and to protect the orthodox churches. Often the reply came in the form of a shot or an axe thrown at us. Providence saved us from these missiles.

Not all the serfs were as brutal towards the soldiers of the Grande Armée, Chicherin acknowledged that

> The inhabitants of this province [Smolensk] are not ruined. They all voluntarily … arranged for them [the French] magazines of forage and rations [in order to] preserve a part of their houses and cattle. Several of us severly reproached these unfortunate peasants, because they received the French well … The inhabitants and the mercenary landowners remained on their property in order to avoid complete ruin … they opening their barns; shedding insincere tears and talking about patriot-ism, and their loyalty to the Fatherland.[26]

The pursuit of the Grande Armée continued. On 21 November Glinka wrote in another letter:

> All these days the weather was mostly stormy and rainy. The frost reached about 20 degrees. We pass along country roads, our artillery cutting through the tracks in deep snow. The infantry and cavalry penetrate the dense woods and march about 40 km a day. Do not forget that that is on a winter's day.[27]

The same day, Chicherin wrote: 'Yesterday we covered only 16 km towards Krasnoe and stopped here [Shchelkanov] about 37 km from Smolensk. On arrival we learnt that our battalion is appointed to guard the headquarters.' Chicherin was chosen to be the duty officer, but he was embarrassed by this honour, because he looked like a 'scarecrow'.[28]

The Grande Armée's brief stay at Smolensk had allowed part of the Russian Army to overtake it and on 16 November, General Tormassov with a large force took up position to the north-east of Krasnoe, which overlooked the main road from Smolensk. A smaller force under Lieutenant General Prince Dimitri Galitzin positioned itself to the south east along the Krasnoe-Elnia Road, with two battalions in the town of Uvarovo. They awaited the arrival of the French, who would be caught in the crossfire.

Prince Eugene von Wurttemberg was also present: 'As soon as the head of the [enemy] column arrived within grapeshot range, it was overrun and a terrible panic initially seized it and was dispersed in an instant. It was the most beautiful moment for the Russian cavalry.' Unfortunately, Eugene does not go into detail about what the Russian cavalry achieved, but continues:

> General Paskevitch … advanced at this moment on my right with a strong battery and with the infantry of his division. The enemy column, although meaning to rally, being in this way under a cross fire of the more terrible kind abandoned before long all resistance and looked to their safety in flight … [We were] approached by a new enemy body that was considerably stronger, from which we received a few cannon shots. My stronger battery responded immediately, and again struck terror into the column, which followed the example of the first … The artillery took advantage of every favourable moment for overpowering them, but without cavalry we were unable to take prisoners. We heard a cannonade at this time and the fire of the skirmishers on the right …
>
> In effect the Viceroy of Italy whose advance guard I had dispersed acknowledging the impossibility of clearing the way [for the] army by the main road, tried to pass to the right of General Paskevitch …
>
> Now the 12th Division was placed to encounter the Viceroy as well as the cavalry under the orders of General Uvarov, whose several regiments made a handsome charge, brought back several thousand prisoners and forced the Viceroy to turn back.
>
> The French held out until night when they made a dash for the woods, which lay on their right, and were able to slip away.[29]

On 17 November, it was Davoust's corps' and Napoleon's Imperial Guard's turn to run the gauntlet of Russian fire along the main road near Krasnoe. The Imperial Guard was first and upon hearing of their approach Davydov records:

> We jumped on our horses and again appeared on the main road … The enemy, noticing our noisy crew, cocked their guns and went on proudly marching without accelerating their step. No matter how hard we tried to detach at least one private from these closed columns, they remained unharmed, as though made of granite, disdaining all our efforts.

I shall never forget the unhurried step and awesome resolution of those warriors, for whom the threat of death was a daily and familiar experience. With their tall bearskin caps, blue uniforms, white straps, red plumes and epaulettes, they looked like poppies on the snow-covered battlefield. If only we had had a few squadrons of horse-drawn artillery and regular cavalry (who God knows why, were trailing behind our army), then the enemy's leading and following columns would not have been able to retreat with such small losses as they sustained that day.

Having only Cossacks under my command, we bustled in turn around the enemy columns, capturing supply wagons and artillery, and the platoons that lagged behind, but failed to make the slightest impression on the columns themselves. Colonels, officers, sergeants, many privates rushed at the enemy, but all in vain. The columns moved on, one after another, driving us off with shots from their muskets and jeering at our futile attempts to raid them ... Napoleon and the Guard passed through our Cossacks like a hundred-gun warship through fishing boats.[30]

The Russians were unable to penetrate the columns of Napoleon's Old Guard, but the Young Guard would not be so lucky. To protect his flank Napoleon ordered the Young Guard to take Uvarovo to cover Davoust's, and if possible, Ney's retreat.

According to General Bennigsen:

Two weak battalions of the Young Guard advanced to cover the main road, the one in front of the position occupied by General Tormassov and the other in front of that of Prince Galitzin. The first was attacked by a battalion of our chasseurs of the Guard and the second by a battalion of our regiment of Reval. The two enemy battalions ... [were either] killed or taken and the rest dispersed.[31]

The Young Guard had driven a Russian detachment under Galitzin from the Uvarovo and a counter-attack was not long in coming. According to Sir Robert Wilson when General Bennigsen ordered the town to be recaptured, Galitzin was

... determined to recover Uvarovo, when a column of the voltigeurs of the Imperial Guard attempted to oppose the march of the division.

This column charged by two regiments of cuirassiers, formed square and beat off the assailants; but two pieces of cannon being brought up to play on an angle which they perforated, the attack was renewed, when the whole were either killed or taken.

Uvarovo was immediately evacuated and the enemy's first line, which had moved forward to support the voltigeurs, fell back on seeing their fate; but in its retreat it was shattered by the grape of a company of flying artillery directed by the brave Colonel Nitchin.[32]

Nearby Napoleon's 3rd Regiment of Grenadiers a Pied were also heavily involved in the battle and being overrun, it ceased to exist. Meanwhile, fearing that the main Russian Army would surround him, Napoleon could not wait for Davoust and Ney's Corps and so continued his march westwards.

On 18 November, Kutuzov reported to the Tsar:

General Miloradovitch commanding the advanced guard with the 2nd light corps of infantry, and the 2nd of cavalry, perceiving the corps commanded by Marshal Davoust advanced near Krasnoe, detached thither Lieutenant General Prince Galitzin. The enemy conceiving himself turned on all sides, began to defend himself. Our artillery made a terrible carnage in the enemy's ranks. Napoleon himself was an eyewitness of the battle, and not waiting for the issue, he fled with his whole suite to the village of Liadam and abandoned the corps of Davoust.

The battle lasted the whole day; the enemy were completely defeated and dispersed in the neighbourhood of the wood, for a distance of 5 km along the banks of the Dnieper, thus the corps of Davout has been completely destroyed. The loss in killed and wounded is immense. We have made prisoners two Generals, 58 officers of different ranks, 9,170 prisoners other ranks, 70 cannon, three standards and taken the baton of Marshal Davoust.[33]

Despite all the odds Davoust's Corps managed to get past the Russians and after suffering heavy losses, the Young Guard was forced to abandon Krasnoe and Ney to his fate. Ney had only left Smolensk that morning so a large gap had developed between his corps and that of Davoust and it would not be until the following day before Ney would reach Krasnoe, who was pursued by the Russian advance guard under General Miloradovitch.

During the cold morning, Ney's Corps struggled up the hill, but they did not notice the Russians who were drawn up there. Suddenly,

Forty pieces of cannon loaded with grape, simultaneously ... vomited their flames and poured their deadly shower on the assailants.

The survivors intrepidly rushed forward with desperate energy – part reached the crest of the hill, and almost touched the batteries. The Russians most in advance, shouting their 'huzza', sprang forward with fixed bayonets, and without firing a musket.

A sanguinary but short struggle ensued: the enemy could not maintain their footing, and were driven headlong down the ravine.

The Uhlans of the Guard at the same time charged, swept through the shattered ranks, and captured an eagle.

The brow and sides of the hill were covered with dead and dying, all the Russian arms were dripping with gore, and the wounded, as they lay bleeding and shivering on the snow, called for 'death', as the greatest mercy that could be ministered in their hopeless state.[34]

Sherbinina described this part of the battle:

This was not a battle, but annihilation of the enemy columns with artillery fire. No other effort was made. It was assumed that Ney's remaining troops would surrender; therefore, the cannonade ceased before darkness fell, and many enemy guns were captured.[35]

Later on 18 November, Kutuzov wrote a second report, this time about the rear guard under Marshal Ney:

> In order to obtain a certain victory over Marshal Ney, and to cut off entirely his communication with the rest of the army, I reinforced General Miloradovitch with the 8th Corps, gave him orders to prevent the Marshal's advance, and to take a position near the villages of Syroherenic and Tcherniska. Major General Lourkouski perceived the enemy advancing about three in the afternoon. The thickness of the fog prevented him from ascertaining his numbers, who kept marching forwards until they were close to our batteries.
>
> The enemy attempting in vain to pierce through our lines, received at a distance of 230 paces a general discharge of musketry and of 40 pieces of cannon, the effect of this fire upon the enemy was extremely fatal. Finding he had no hope of escaping he at length sent a flag of truce to General Miloradovitch. At midnight the whole corps d'armes of the enemy, amounting to 12,000 men, was obliged to lay down its arms. All their artillery, in number 27 pieces of cannon and the baggage and military chest, were the fruits of our victory.
>
> In the number of prisoners are above one hundred officers of different ranks. Marshal Ney was wounded, but saved himself by flight and was pursued by the Cossacks beyond the Dnieper. The losses of the enemy are enormous; according to the report of prisoners, four Generals of Division were wounded. We have not lost above five hundred men killed and wounded.
>
> The army is at Krasnoe, and the advanced guard at Dovbrovna, from whence we shall follow the movements of the enemy.[36]

Ney's corps managed to hold out until dark, when Miloradovitch sent a flag of truce to Ney, asking for his surrender, but the Marshal refused. According to Wilson, the Russian General sent two flags of truce, both of which were detained by Ney fearing that they would report back that the remnants of Ney's men were preparing to leave.

Ney's corps gave the appearance that it was setting up camp, so that the battle could continue the following day. But Ney sent out scouts to find an escape route. Sherbinina continues:

> Only one general of the main headquarters guessed that Ney would break through. It was [General] Oppermann. On 19 November Oppermann arrived at a small hut that General Konovnitsin occupied, and where I was also billeted. He named a place on the Dnieper about 13 km from Krasnoe, where Ney would certainly cross the river and break through; so he advised [Konovnitsin] to occupy this location at once. Konovnitsin agreed with him … He went to the commander in chief and informed him about Oppermann's views, but no decision was made. To Oppermann's credit,

he correctly determined the enemy's plan. It is known that Ney took advantage of the increasing frost and, having spread hay on the ice, crossed the Dnieper.[37]

As the remnants of Ney's Corps silently crossed the river Dnieper, which was frozen by a thin layer of ice, a cannon fell through, which forced Ney to abandon his artillery and the wagons he still had with him. Before the last of Ney's men were across the river, a detachment of Cossacks fell upon their rear and took several hundred prisoners.

Platov with his Cossacks set off in pursuit, Ney's men tried to keep to the woods that bordered the road to Orsha, so hindering any Cossack attack. At about 3.00pm on 20 November, the French came to the end of the wood, and they were still a long way from Orsha, where they believed Napoleon was. The night was dark and Ney was able to proceed without being attacked by Cossack patrols, but to their horror they saw many campfires in front of them. They advanced silently on the Russian encampment, expecting at any moment to be discovered, however the French discovered that it was just a ploy by Platov to delay their movements. Many Frenchmen lost their way in the darkness, which prompted Captain Pushkin of the Semenovski Regiment of the Imperial Guard to write:

> 19 November. [We had to take] precautionary measures concerning French deserters, wandering in the woods bordering our camp, In the course of the day we caught about 1,000 souls, supposedly almost all of them of Marshal Ney's Corps, which has already lost about 9,000 prisoners on the day of the battle of Krasnoe.[38]

Meanwhile two Polish messengers, which Ney had sent, had arrived safely at Orsha, where they found the remnants of the Viceroy's Corps. Prince Eugene immediately called his men to arms. Retracing their steps Eugene's Corps managed to link up with the remnants of Ney's Corps. On hearing the news that Ney was still alive, Napoleon was overjoyed and the two corps, now united, were able to fend off any Cossack attack and so were able to continue their retreat.

Notes

1   Dnevnik, *Aleksandr Chicherina* p.45
2   *Journal de Eugene de Wurttemberg* p.26
3   Dnevnik, *Pavla Pushkin* p.68
4   Wilson, *The French Invasion of Russia* pp.243–244
5   *Memoirs of General Bennigsen* pp.137–138
6   The *Morning Chronicle* 8 December 1812
7   *Journal de Eugene de Wurttemberg* pp.27–29
8   Quoted in Tarle, *Napoleon's Invasion of Russia* p.261
9   *Journal of Eugene von Wurttemberg* p.28
10 *Journal of Eugene von Wurttemberg* p.28
11 Uxkull, *Arms and the Woman* pp.99–100
12 Ibid, pp.99–100
13 Ibid, pp.99–100
14 Dnevnik, *Aleksandr Chicherina* p.42
15 *Lettres et papiers du Chancellor comte de Nesserode* p.116

16 Quoted in Tarle, *Napoleon's Invasion of Russia* p.235

17 Clausewitz, *The Campaign of 1812 in Russia* pp.213–214

18 Uxkull, *Arms and the Woman* p.101

19 Skobelev letter 22 in 1812 god v vospominainiyakh I rasskazazakh sovremennikov pp.186–187

20 Dnevnik, *Pavla Pushkin* p.70

21 Quoted in Spring, *Cossacks* p.47

22 Davydov, *In the service of the Tsar* p.88

23 Ibid, p.134

24 *General Wilson's Journal* ed. by Brett-James pp.71–72

25 Wilson, *The French invasion of Russia* p.260

26 Dnevnik, *Aleksandr Chicherina* p.47

27 Glinka, *Pisma* pp.171–173

28 Dnevnik, *Aleksandr Chicherina* p46

29 *Journal of Eugene von Wurttemberg* p.31

30 Davyov, *In the service of the Tsar* p.142

31 *Memoirs of General Bennigsen* pp.144–145

32 Wilson, *The French Invasion of Russia* p.270

33 The *Morning Chronicle* 17 December 1812

34 Wilson, *The French Invasion of Russia* pp.278–279

35 Zapiski, *Sherbinina* pp.49–50

36 The *Morning Chronicle* 17 December 1812

37 Zapiski, *Sherbinina* pp.49–50

38 Dnevnik, *Pavla Pushkin* p.71

19

CROSSING THE BEREZINA

While Ney was fighting at Krasnoe, the remnants of the Grande Armée struggled onwards towards their next major obstacle, the Berezina river. Many succumbed to the worsening weather and lack of food. On the evening of 19 November, Glinka found time to write another letter to his friend:

> It is hardly possible to see such horrors that are represented here daily to our eyes ... One of our preachers recently called the French an inhuman people ... [They] seek food in manure heaps, eat cats, dogs and horses ... [even] devour themselves, they do not shudder at all and with great composure argue on the taste of horse's or human meat! But they perish like flies in the very late autumn! The corpses' faces were terribly disfigured. The rage, despair, furious and other wild passions were deeply embodied on them. It is clear that these men perished in a minute of frenzy, with a gnashing of teeth and froth on the lips ... Those who have not entirely lost their senses continually beg to eat and they were fed until they could not eat any more warm food – and die! But the greater part of them are absolutely terrified; they wander like the blind. Yesterday I saw one, who in the heat of battle, with the greatest of composure wound a ball of thread and to myself I imagined that he [thought he was] sitting in his mother's home. But yesterday night was for me the most terrible! Wishing to dry ourselves a little, we entered an *Izbi* [peasant's hut] ... [filled with] hundreds of ... ghosts making terrible cries ... One Frenchman ... breaking open the skull of a recently dead comrade, said to me 'Take me, I can be useful to Russia, I can bring up children.'[1]

General Wittgenstein's force, which had been guarding the route to St Petersburg, and Admiral Chichagov's Army, which had joined the 3rd Western Army, were ordered to prevent Napoleon from crossing the river Berezina. They do not seem to have been informed about the Grande Armée's condition or strength and for all they knew Napoleon's army was still intact.

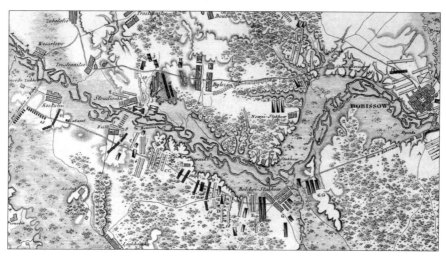

Plan of the battle of Berezina.

On 15 November, Admiral Chichagov's Army crossed the River Nieman and the following day Chichagov occupied Minsk, where he found a large magazine of supplies and a hospital with about 8,000 sick. The Russians remained at Minsk for two days to refresh themselves and decided to seize the town of Borisov, with its bridge over the river Berezina.

On 22 November after heavy fighting the Russians entered Borisov, where they found a letter saying that Napoleon would be there the following day. The Russians began making preparations.

All the corps (except Chaplitz's detachment which remained at Brili, near Veselovo, 10 km to our left) assembled on the right [actually left] bank of the Berezina, to right and left of the bridgehead …

We had to stay on the [right] left bank of the Berezina; this bank is high and dominates both river and town. We needed to cut the bridge, establish our numerous guns on the heights, send a strong force of Cossacks in front of Borisov on the route along which the French Army was retreating, so that we should receive warning of its approach and line of march. We should also have sent out bodies of cavalry along the left [right] bank of the river in both directions, prepared a bridge ready to throw across the Berezina at the spot where Count Wittgenstein would arrive, so as to facilitate a junction with him without loss of time. Above all we should have allowed nobody to establish positions in Borisov and remain bivouacked in the bridgehead. Finally, we could have burnt Borisov, though I admit that this useful step would have been very cruel.

The Admiral did none of these things. As he disliked bivouacs, he took up quarters in the best house in Borisov. He allowed, indeed he ordered, all the generals to lodge there too – I was weak enough to do the same. He packed in the whole headquarters, all the Army's baggage, the ambulances, the mobile church, the offices of the general staff, the engineers, and the artillery. He cluttered up this small town to such an extent that not a single room remained unoccupied by a crowd of people and vehicles blocked every street. And all this took place by our outposts on the road along which we expected the enemy, and which had only a weak line of Cossacks as protection.

Yet we had learnt that Kutuzov had already passed Smolensk and Orsha, and that Napoleon must be two or at most three marches from us. Nothing could upset the Admiral's calm. It was useless to point out anything to him or to offer advice, without exposing oneself to a very tart rebuff, a scornful silence, or outrageous rudeness.[2]

On the 23rd Chichagov held a council of war, but there was still no news of the Grande Armée's approach, so the officers dispersed to their quarters. Chichagov did send the advanced guard, commanded by Major General Count Pahlen II, towards Bohr to discover the whereabouts of Wittgenstein's Army, also unknown to the Admiral. Pahlen clashed with the advanced guard of Marshal Oudinot's Corps under Dombrowski at Doshnitsi. The Russians were forced to retreat.

Meanwhile, Count Louis Victor Leon de Rochechouart, the previously quoted Frenchman on Chichagov's staff, was having his evening meal along with the rest of the senior Russian officers at Borisov:

In the middle of dinner we saw some Russian hussars belonging to the advance-guard dash up, their horses white with foam. They shouted '*Frantsusyi!*' [The French!] and headed for the bridge ...

The number of refugees increased from one minute to the next, yet the same soldiers had fought bravely two evenings before. Instead of running to my lodging and ordering my servants to cross to the far bank, I tried to stop the fugitives ... Panic-stricken and drunk with fear, if I may express it thus, they shouted, '*Frantsusyi! Frantsusyi!*', being quite unable to say anything else. A few guns, followed by their ammunition wagons, rushed through the town at a gallop, knocking down or crushing everything in their way. One had to follow the torrent, so I headed for the bridge and there found Madame de Lambert, bareheaded. She had managed to halt a few of her husband's hussars and had said to them in Russian, 'Children, are you going to abandon your wounded general?' They dismounted and carried their commander on their shoulders. Four mounted hussars, leading their comrades' horses, headed the procession to clear a path and protect the wounded man until he reached the far end of that interminable bridge.

I took advantage of the escort to cross the Berezina in the middle of the throng, and after risking being crushed or hurled into the river a score of times, I reached General de Langeron's bivouac. There I waited in vain for my horses and carriage. I hadn't even a coat.

The Admiral was just sitting down at table with his officers and had been obliged to leave the meal when it was served and, like me cross that damned bridge on foot. It was all over in half an hour; that is to say, out of 10,000 men and twelve guns forming the advance guard, only a thousand men and two guns crossed. The rest were captured or scattered. Fifty French *chasseurs* of Legrand's division, fortified with a stiff brandy ration, had surprised the look out posts of our advance guard in front of Loshnitsa. They charged fiercely and swept them as far as the square in this little town, thereby causing a panic, which routed the entire corps. Poor Count Pahlen was unable to muster a hundred men to charge the French *chasseurs*. He had been commanding this division since the previous evening only and, unrecognised by his soldiers, was dragged along against his will by the fleeing mob. He reached our bivouac in an indescribable state of despair.

As soon as the Admiral got to the far bank, fearing at any minute to see the Grande Armée arrive on the scene – he did not know its strength – he had the bridge cut in two places, so making communications with the other bank impossible.[3]

Langeron puts the attack at 1pm:

At one o'clock on 23 November we heard sharp firing – two or three miles from the town. This was our advanced guard, which had been attacked by Oudinot's corps. In a moment it was repulsed and dispersed and had to retire to Borisov in complete disorder. The French arrived on their heels. Nobody expected them. We were dining quietly. The carriage and wagon horses were neither harnessed nor bridled. I was the only person who, foreseeing some catastrophe, had my horses harnessed. I had three vehicles: a calash and two little carts. In one were all my office papers and a very large sum of money from the Army's treasury destined for the purchase of the troops brandy ration. The other contained some provisions. I lost the latter and was very glad not to have to mourn the loss of the former. The two vehicles I saved were riddled with bullets.

By this time bullets were whistling through the streets. Our men – cavalry, infantry, gunners with their guns – were fleeing helter-skelter for the bridge, pursued by the French who were yelling in a really frightening manner. You can imagine the confusion and disorder which now reigned at Headquarters, which had been so rashly placed by the forward posts. Each man ran away, abandoning horses and vehicles, and many of them their dinner too – and this was not unwelcome to the French. The Admiral's meal was already on the table, and was captured, along with his silver plate, his belongings, his clothes and his portfolio.

We incurred enormous and irreplaceable losses. Our wounded and sick were left behind with the hospital equipment and they all perished. The rich church was lost. The records of the engineers, which contained all the most valuable plans from the Turkish wars and other maps prepared by our staff officers – there was no other copy in existence – were left in vehicles which fell into French hands. Many officers and servants could not escape and were taken prisoner. The disaster was complete. The Admiral, partly on foot, partly on horseback, managed, just as we did, to reach the heights on the right [left] bank of the Berezina, where our troops were bivouacked.[4]

Despite the panic the Russians managed to destroy the bridge at Borisov, so preventing any further pursuit, but more importantly they had destroyed a vital crossing point for the Grande Armée.[5]

This meant that the only crossing point over the Berezina was about 16 km north of Borisov near to Veselovo, and so Chichagov sent a strong detachment under General Chaplitz to observe this crossing, while another force under General Joseph O'Rourke, a Russian officer of Irish descent, was sent south to another crossing point at Lower Beresino. The other divisions of Chichagov's Army were spread out along the west bank of the Berezina to observe any possible attempts to cross.

Reports began to arrive that a large enemy force was at Lower Berezino about 26 km from Borisov. Chichagov quickly set about concentrating his army and marched to meet this new threat, leaving Langeron to guard the vicinity around Borisov in case any attempt was made to rebuild the bridge. Little did the Russians know that this large force was a diversion and the force was composed largely of camp followers, who were ordered to make as much noise as possible.

With Chichagov marching towards Lower Berezino, a large force began to appear on the opposite bank not far from Borisov:

> I having before me at one km more than 100,000 enemy and the Admiral left me 1,200 infantrymen, 300 Cossacks and 36 pieces of large artillery, more cumbersome than useful ...
>
> I have never in any circumstances of my military life, passed a day more cruel than that of 25 November, when I was with my 1,200 infantrymen at the head of the bridge of Borisov; Napoleon who had seen our army march on our right, and who had been able to judge the few forces which had remained with the general, which he was opposed, could have avoided making a laborious march, and of risking a hazardous crossing; he could quite simple force that of the bridge of Borisov and march on Minsk, I myself waited that every instant.
>
> I employed my Cossacks and my poor exhausted soldiers to maintain all the night fires the length of the Berezina, to 4 or 5km distance to the right and left of the bridge, a trick of war much used, which is known, but which always deceives the enemy; perhaps even in this circumstance, Napoleon, [would be] deceived by it. From his side he was to light fires on his left ... which deceived me also; I believe that he wanted to force a crossing at Oukoloda, 5 km to my right, but I was soon undeceived, the noise of cannon, of the carriages, the hubbubs which announced always the march of the columns, especially during the night, taught me that Napoleon proceeded to Veselovo on his right.

Early in the morning of 26 November Napoleon had arrived at Studienka, where he intended to cross the Berezina. Unfortunately for Napoleon, thinking that the river would be frozen and that his army would easily be able to cross the 300-foot wide river, he ordered all his bridging equipment to be burnt. Even nature herself seemed to be against him because no sooner had the bridging equipment been destroyed then the weather became warmer and the frozen Berezina became a river once more.

Napoleon ordered General Eble to build two bridges, one for vehicles, the other for those on foot. The pontooniers set about demolishing the houses in the local villages for materials and they worked in freezing water. At about 1.00pm on 26

November, the first bridge was finished and French troops began to cross. Two hours later the second bridge was also completed. Oudinot's Corps was the first to cross and began driving the elements of Chichagov's Army back, until they were reinforced by Chaplitz's Division, but Oudinot had to protect the bridgehead while the remainder of the Grande Armée crossed.

The warmer weather that had thawed the Berezina also turned the ground to mud, which slowed down the Russians:

> The Admiral began to fear he had made a wrong manoeuvre. In the evening, he learned with certainty that this fatiguing march had been greatly to the advantage of Napoleon … In spite of the terrible roads we returned to the bridgehead, but with men and horses tired out, and we left many stragglers, occupied for the most part in dragging the cannon and wagons out of the mud where they had stuck.[6]

Langeron also mentions that the Russians were exhausted by this time and not in the best of humour:

> The unfortunate 30,000 men he [Chichagov] dragged with him covered in 30 hours 57 km in the month of November in a land half frozen and came back to the head of the Borisov bridge on the 26th in the evening and already in the darkness, weary, weakened and cursing the Admiral aloud with reason.[7]

On 27 November, while Chichagov's Army had returned to the area, his men were so exhausted that they spent all day resting. Langeron, who was still at Borisov received an order to march to assist Chaplitz:

> I marched to the assistance of Chaplitz with 24 cannon of 12 pounders and 900 men. I arrived before night had put an end to the fighting; It cost us 500 men, the brave General Ivanov, chef of the 10th Regiment of Chasseurs was wounded. During the night I withdrew myself onto the little heights, close to a hamlet situated at the entrance of the Stakow Wood, which the enemy occupied in entirety, as well as the town; they took up position less than four km from Borisov. They rested there very peacefully during the day of the 27th.
> The troops that had fought against Chaplitz were Oudinot's Corps, the remainder of that of Dombrowski, the battalions spent … several days beforehand by Bronikowski from Borisov to Veselovo, of the Swiss Regiments, which fought admirably, and the cuirassiers. All these troops were … at that time the best in Napoleon's Army. They were well dressed, were well nourished and had not suffered from the deprivations which had weakened the Grande Armée in the retreat from Moscow.
> Our outposts were placed in the wood 20 paces from those of the enemy. And on the main road, instead of outposts, they had every battalion in dense columns. These battalions were so close to my outposts I believed at first that they were Russians. I myself advanced towards them to visit the posts; I was in the uniform of a general, and nevertheless not one of the enemy soldiers made the least movement against

me, although I was not more than about five or six paces from their front, they rested all weapons at the arm, and two or three officers advanced to talk to me.

This peace lasted all the day of the 27th and a part of the morning of the 28th.

Meanwhile Napoleon was busy supervising the transfer of the majority of his army to the west bank of the Berezina, including his Imperial Guard.

Wittgenstein's Army had also arrived in the vicinity on the eastern bank. Marching along the Veselovo Road he came across General Partouneaux's Division of Victor's Corps, which had taken the Borisov, rather than the Studienka Road. General Partouneaux's Division was surrounded and on 27 November was forced to surrender after several hours' fighting. Hearing the gunfire, some of the remnants of the Grande Armée stormed over the bridge in an effort to escape. At 4.00pm part of the larger bridge collapsed causing further panic in the ranks.

By the evening of 27 November, most of the Grande Armée had crossed, leaving only the remnants of Victor's Corps as a rearguard and the stragglers on the eastern bank. They knew that Victor would have to make a fighting withdrawal if he was to survive the Russian attacks the following day.

By this time Platov's Cossacks had also arrived in theatre and began rebuilding the bridge at Borisov, meaning that Chichagov's and Wittgenstein's Armies could co-ordinate their actions. The two generals agreed that at daybreak on 28 November Wittgenstein would attack the eastern bank and Chichagov the west bank. However, the following day the Russians awoke to find that the warmer weather of the past few days had passed and had been replaced by a 'blinding snow storm' that lasted throughout the day.[8]

Nevertheless, at daybreak Chichagov marched with all his force to Stakov. He had divided his army into five columns, plus an advanced guard under Chaplitz. General Alexander Rudzevich, who commanded the first column was supported by the columns of Generals Peter Kornilov and Vasili Meshcherinov. They were supported by the Pavlograd Hussars and two regiments of dragoons. A fourth column under the command of General Afanasii Krassovski was composed of two Jager regiments and two regular cavalry regiments, plus a regiment of Cossacks. Its task was to protect Chaplitz's right flank. The fifth column was commanded by Chichagov himself and formed from Woinov's and Pahlen's Divisions, plus eight other infantry regiments. There was also a reserve.

Krassovski marched to the bank of the Berezina overlooking where the French were crossing and with his artillery began to fire on the bridges and its causeways. Meanwhile, Rudzevich's column attacked the advanced posts of the Grande Armée, which put up a stiff resistance.

Chaplitz, with his troops shouting 'Ural' and the drums beating the charge also attacked the French. They marched through a large wood and when they came to a clearing the French 'opened a blazing fire which smashed the trees and maimed in the like manner a great number of our soldiers. Chaplitz advanced nevertheless.' The Russian infantry had deployed in skirmish order better to navigate their way through woods and

... advanced into the wood from two sides of the road and dispersed in to skirmish line. This was the only kind of fight that the terrain permitted, this was also where the French soldiers had the advantage on ours, being less laden down, more accustomed to act alone and deployed better, our loss was therefore in effect greater than those of the enemy.

The firing lasted until the evening without a single moment of respite, it was terrible; the musket shots were repeated by the echoes that the woods always returned several times; sometimes our soldiers fought individually with the bayonet, but we were not able, during the whole day, to win an inch of the enemy's terrain, nor they of ours.

All our infantry was employed and already, towards 3 o'clock in the afternoon, there remained no more than a single battalion in reserve.

The enemy also employed all those who were still able ... to carry arms. Marshal Oudinot having been wounded, was replaced by Marshal Ney, commanding those who remained of his army Corps and Prince Poniatowski's ...

These two corps had no more than 3000 or 4000 men in a fit state to fight. To our left, in the middle of the wood a little closer than a kilometre from the road, were two little clearingss of about a hundred metres square.[9]

General Ermolov, who had also recently joined Chichagov with a detachment from Kutuzov's Army, recalls:

[Our] light guns, equal in numbers to the enemy guns, were deployed to the fore, while battery guns, placed behind, fired at the enemy infantry massed in the clearings ... It was soon noted that the enemy forces were increasing, exhausted troops being replaced with fresher units and our troops driven back. Attacks were resumed frequently and with increasing vigour.[10]

Suddenly, the Russian infantry were attacked by General Doumerc's Division of cuirassiers, who were formed in small detachments so were more manoeuvrable than the Russian cavalry who were 'preserved in perfect order ... [and so were] useless because of the forest'. The Russian infantry did not have time to form square, the traditional defence against cavalry, and so were cut to pieces. A panic ensued, which spread to the other elements of the Russian Army. Langeron continues:

The French General Doumerc came upon this division with his two regiments of cuirassiers, a charge most certainly quite unexpected in the terrain where they were and which had for us a disastrous result. In the opening between the trees and the brushwood, he reformed his cuirassiers at the entrance of the two little openings, forming them up as quick as lightning and smashed the columns, they sabred more than 600 men, and made as many prisoners ... The regiment of St Petersburg Dragoons, which came to the assistance of the infantry, caused some losses. This desperate charge afforded great honour to General Doumerc and to his cuirassiers. It is a very fine feat of arms, and in general the whole affair was glorious for the French, who were very inferior to us in number.

On our right, the brigade of General Gangeblov, commanded by General Rudzewitsch and composed of two regiments of chasseurs, the Crimean and Kouban (12th and 22nd), were placed close to the river, these chasseurs were wonderfully valorous; they were almost destroyed. Out of 4000 men, they were reduced to 700, and there remained few officers who were not wounded. The 22nd lost all its field officers, these two regiments accustomed to fighting individually on the line of Kouban and against the Circassians, were excellent skirmishers; ... [and] caused the greatest losses to the enemy.[11]

The Russians were retreating in disorder, but according to Sir Robert Wilson:

Chaplitz, at the head of two squadrons of hussars of Pavlograd, opportunely checked their career, and gave time to rally the infantry; but the enemy, by advancing the two corps, had gained the side of the wood nearest Stakhow, whence they could not be dislodged, and where they continued for the remainder of the day.[12]

According to Rochechouart it was not just the regular cavalry who helped restore order:

When we reached the edge of the wood, three squadrons of cuirassiers charged us; they sabred and put to rout our grenadiers, but our Cossacks stood their ground and enabled us to rally the main body of the army.[13]

Despite this setback, for six hours Chichagov's and Oudinot's artillery had bombarded each other at terrifyingly close range, causing thousands of casualties on each side. Those who were killed on the bridges were rolled off into an icy grave by their comrades.

Oudinot had been wounded during the battle and his plan was taken over by Marshal Ney, and with the help of Napoleon's Imperial Guard he was able to punch his way through the Russian line. This allowed the remnants of Junot's, Eugene and Davoust' Corps to continue their retreat along the Zembin Road towards Vilna.

Victor's Corps was also putting up a stiff resistance, although General Dandel's Division had to re-cross the Berezina to reinforce Victor. The Russian attack on the right bank began at about 10.00am and was composed of two columns under Generals Egor Ivanovich Vlastov and Burhardt Maximovic Berg. About midday, a third column under General Alexander Borisovich Foch was also thrown into the attack.

Ermolov recorded events:

The advance forces of Count Wittgenstein arrived before 10am, but limited their actions to exchanging artillery fire. Around 1pm, his entire corps had finally concentrated; the enemy withstood the devastating fire of his batteries for a brief period and sweeping all obstacles aside, Wittgenstein's troops occupied the elevated ground on the right bank, inflicting terrible losses on the enemy troops fleeing into a depression. Everyone was gripped by desperation and confusion reigned everywhere.[14]

Wilson also confirms that the battle started at 10.00am:

Vlastov about ten o'clock in the morning arrived and formed up in front of Victor's position; thence he directed an attack on the enemy's left with the hussars and Cossacks, but this was foiled by Fournier at the head of his cavalry, who was, however, repulsed when pursuing his success, by the Russian reserves.[15]

Having tried to turn Victor's left flank, Wittgenstein now attacked his right, which was composed of a brigade of Baden troops, who were slowly pushed back. Wilson continues in his own curiously constructed style.

Diebitch having established a battery of twelve guns against the enemy's right flank, the shot plunging upon the mass gathered around the bridges [which] caused a frightful scene of terror, struggle and carnage. Overset carriages blocked up the bridges, horses in herds without riders flew wildly about, bearing down all in their way, numbers of men and women who attempted to pass the river perished, numbers were driven into the stream [sic] by the pressure of those who were farthest distant; numbers were thrown down, trampled upon and suffocated. It was a pandemonium of horrors.

Victor and his gallant band nevertheless undauntedly continued their resistance and made repeated sallies against the Russians as they encroached on his position. Notwithstanding that the Russian artillery was overwhelmingly superior, and 36 guns kept incessantly pouring their fire nor was it till nightfall (at that season and latitude soon after two in the afternoon) that Victor was forced to make a conversion and approach his bridges with his host, not conquerors but enobled by their valour and to take the rank amongst the proudest for the Russians had also fought with great bravery and in no way favoured the enemy's success by any want of energy on their own part.[16]

During the day, one of the bridges had collapsed leaving only one bridge as an escape route. After the heavy traffic of the day the remaining bridge was eerily silent during the night because the remainder of Victor's Corps and the stragglers refused to leave their campfires during the freezing night.

By the dawn of 29 November all the organised units of the Grande Armée were across the Berezina, leaving only the stragglers on the eastern bank, who began crowding onto the bridge, but with the Russians close behind them. At about 9.00am, fearing that the Russians would also cross the bridge, General Elbe had no choice but to blow up the remaining bridge. There was a cry of despair from those stranded on the right bank.

Langeron mistakenly believed that it was the Russians who burnt the bridges:

Wittgenstein advanced and burnt the remaining bridge, the other already having been cut and many people perished. On the left [right] bank of the river a crowd of unfortunates were stranded, deathly sacrifices ... The light artillery of Wittgenstein rained shells on the multitude of carriages crammed close to the bridge, one may imagine the horrible disorder that soon reigned, the cries of the unfortunate servants, vivandières, sick, wounded, women, children, French and foreigners, emigrants from Moscow, who followed the army, crushed under the wheels of the carriages, between the coaches, mutilated by the shell fragments or perishing under the lances of the Cossacks. They rushed on the burning bridge, and were then consumed by the flames and engulfed by the waters.[17]

Nevertheless, as Rochechourt wrote, 'the French army was able to cross the Berezina, the last river wide enough to check its progress.'[18]

Rafail Zotov of the St Petersburg Militia had still not fully recovered from the wounds he had suffered at Podolsk but decided to rejoin the army. Upon hearing from some Cossacks that Napoleon was about to fall into Wittgenstein's hands, he quickened his journey to arrive in time to play a part in the Berezina battle. Unfortunately for Zotov, his battalion, which by now mustered only about 200 out of its original 800 men, was in Wittgenstein's rearguard and all they could hear was cannon fire in the distance. He recalls feelings of disappointment and frustration among the Russians:

> Towards evening everything stopped. All our Corps assembled at bivouacs lit up by bonfires and there the discussions, quarrels and conjecture began. What does it all mean? How did they allow Napoleon to cross? Why did they allow him even to erect the bridges? Why did Chichagov's Army not force them into the river, when they began to cross? When Kutuzov was on his heels why did he not get to the river in order to drive him in?
>
> All this occupied our thoughts almost the whole night,. All of we important and learned people naturally condemned Chichagov first, then Kutuzov and finally even Wittgenstein. All the Berezina business seemed to us feeble, limp and dirty. God deliver us from such opinions![19]

On 29 November, Chichagov wrote to the Tsar to explain why the French had succeeded in crossing the Berezina:

> The corps of Oudinot and Victor that formed part of it were composed of soldiers who had not suffered that much as they still were provided with both artillery and cavalry. The Guard of Napoleon is likewise in a tolerable condition.[20]

It is true that both Oudinot's and Victor's Corps had not suffered as much from the adverse conditions. The latter's corps had only advanced as far as Smolensk, but Chichagov's Army was made up of veterans. Wittgenstein attempted to turn the day's events to his own advantage, when he also wrote to the Tsar: 'Today I compelled him [Victor] to cross the river near Studenkia, where after having passed it, he burnt the bridges.'[21] Clausewitz's analysis was the most succinct:

> Wittgenstein and Chichagov were both afraid of him [Napoleon] here, [just] as Kutuzov had been afraid of him, his army, and of his Guard. No one chose to be defeated by him. Kutuzov believed he could obtain his end without that risk. Wittgenstein was reluctant to impair the glory he had acquired, Chichagov to undergo a second check.[22]

The French continued their march towards Vilna, but they had left behind their wounded, many of whom died of exposure. Martos, an officer in Chichagov's army, wrote:

> Towards the evening that day, the vast plain of Veselovski presented a horrifying, unbelievable spectacle: it was littered with carriages and carts, mostly broken, piled one on another, carpeted with the bodies of dead women and children who had followed the army from Moscow in an effort to escape the misfortunes that had befallen that city and to accompany their countrymen, whom death later struck down in different ways. The fate of these unfortunates, hemmed in between two opposing armies, was inescapable death; many were trampled by horses, others crushed by heavy vehicles, struck by a hail of bullets and cannon balls, drowned in the river during the crossing, or stripped by the soldiers, thrown naked into the snow where the cold soon put an end to their agonies ... According to the most moderate estimates, up to ten thousand people were lost in this way.[23]

Count de Rochechouart of Chichagov's army:

> Nothing in the world [could be] more saddening, more distressing! One saw heaped bodies of men, women and even children; soldiers of all arms, all nations, choked by the fugitives or hit by Russian grapeshot; horses, carriages, guns, ammunition wagons, abandoned carts. One cannot imagine a more terrifying sight than the appearance of the two broken bridges, and the river frozen right to the bottom. Immense riches [from Moscow] lay scattered on this shore of death. Peasants and Cossacks prowled around these piles of dead, removing whatever was most valuable. I found my servant rummaging in the coffers of a carriage. He told me he was trying to restock my wardrobe with shirts, handkerchiefs, stockings, etc., since through his own fault he had let everything be captured.
>
> On the bridge I saw an unfortunate woman sitting; her legs dangled outside the bridge and were caught in the ice. For twenty-four hours she had been clasping a frozen child to her breast. She begged me to save this child, unaware that she was offering me a corpse! She herself was unable to die, despite her sufferings, but a Cossack did her this service by firing a pistol in her ear so as to put an end to her appalling agony.
>
> Both sides of the road were piled with dead in all positions, or with men dying of cold, hunger, exhaustion, their uniforms in tatters, and beseeching us with take

them prisoner. They listed all their attainments, and we were assailed with cries of 'Monsieur, take me along with you. I can cook,' or 'I am a valet,' or 'I am a barber. For the love of God, give me a piece of bread and a strip of cloth to cover myself with.' However much we might have wished to help, unfortunately we could do nothing.[24]

Many had just enough strength to cross the bridges before collapsing. Skobelev recalls the scene on the left bank of the Berezina and beyond:

> The Berezina is loaded with wagons and bodies … It is forbidden for us to take water from the river … the roads are encumbered with wagons loaded with the goods of Moscow and church plate … Going further towards Vilna we were obliged to witness all the horrors of what happens to a Godless people – Bonaparte and the French, our villains. There was not a day that we did not cry, seeing the misfortunes and troubles of our cruel enemy …
>
> Suddenly seeing a whole camp of dead soldiers and amongst many hundreds of hardened [corpses] ten or so moving, hearing us moving around, begging for help and food, but already lacking the strength to speak. They managed only an incomprehensible murmur [we could] scarcely hear '*Duipen!*' [drink] and several had even learnt to say '*Kleb!*' [bread]. But to assuage [such] grief was impossible and turning away to look elsewhere we only found the same half frozen forms, wrapped in skins torn from dead horses … [and for a cap] trousers taken from a dead comrade wrapped around the head. Fortunately most of them wandered, with neither memory, nor thoughts, nor senses! Several gathered with their last ounce of strength and stretched out by a fire, to begin to warm themselves, and burnt together with the brushwood and firewood …[25]

Another eyewitness recalls:

> An uncontrollable feeling of horror seized our hearts. Imagine a wide sinuous river, covered as far as our eyes could see with human corpses; some were just beginning to freeze. Here was the empire of death in all its horror … The first thing that caught our eye was a woman who had fallen half through the ice and had frozen in; one of her arms was cut off and hung loosely, with her other arm she held a suckling baby. The little thing had wound itself around its mother's neck; the woman was still alive, she was staring at a man who had fallen through the ice but was frozen to death; between them on the ice, another dead child was lying … The wind and the frost were extremely cruel, all the roads were covered with snowdrifts, crowds of Frenchmen were staggering about on the nearby field. Some tried to light fires, others were cutting up horses and chewing the bones. Some roasted them, some tried to eat the raw flesh. Soon I noticed piles of frozen or freezing bodies.
>
> That day was painful beyond anything I can remember. The little village was crowded with our own and French wounded and prisoners whose number

became so great that there was almost no room for them. It was horrifying to
see them: adults and children, all together, men and women, with feet wrapped
in straw, wearing some indescribable rags, without shoes, with frozen faces, with
hands gone white.[26]

During their retreat the Grande Armée were given orders to shoot any Russian prisoners who lagged behind. The prisoners were not even allowed to start fires once
they had halted. This had increased the Russian Army's desire for revenge, but now
seeing these horrors, according to Langeron,

> Pity replaced this desire for revenge, which was certainly cruel and unjust but was
> perhaps excusable in view of the evil inflicted on their country and of the memories
> of an invasion reminiscent of the most barbarous times. Soon they looked in silence
> and with indifference on the victims offered to them by fate, and they shared their
> bread with them – a useless, even a cruel act of humanity, since it served merely to
> prolong the frenzied agony of these wretches.[27]

Those who were captured were led away:

> The Russian Army marched in the middle of the road in close columns, and on
> the two sides of this road marched also, or rather crawled along in two columns,
> the enemy without arms, both treading under their feet the dead who strewed the
> way. Every minute, one could see hundreds of these fugitives fall down; those who
> had reached the end of the physical strength necessary for wrestling against death
> … falling down and expiring … We still saw on the decomposed figures of all these
> corpses the expression of their character and the impression of the moment when
> they had died. One was dead with arms outstretched towards the sky, without doubt
> imploring heaven to his last breath, another joined hands in the posture of a man at
> prayer, a third raised a fist in front of him with the air of despair or menace or rage,
> of which to be sure, Napoleon was the object, for the magic of the man was still as
> powerful as ever.[28]

A new division, under General Loison, which Langeron estimated at about 10,000
strong, set out from Vilna to reinforce the Grande Armée, but with the temperature at
-18°, within two days 7,000 men had been lost to the cold.[29]

It took two days for the Russians to repair the bridge and set up pontoon bridges
and cross the Berezina. However, by now there was no other Russian force to stop the
Grande Armée, except for the Cossacks and light cavalry who all the time hounded
the retreating soldiers. Lord Cathcart, the British Ambassador to Russia wrote to the
Foreign Office in London:

> The French march at night and halt during the day in hollow squares; surrounded
> by Cossacks, their supplies must be very precarious and numbers are said to be
> found dead of cold and famine on every ground their army quits.[30]

The Russian Army's condition was by now more or less as bad as that of the Grande Armée. With the weather getting colder, Kutuzov issued a proclamation to encourage his men:

> After the extraordinary successes we have daily achieved over the enemy, every-where, we have now only to pursue him swiftly and then, perhaps, the soil of Russia which he had dreamed of subjugating will be bestrewn with his bones. And so we shall pursue him tirelessly. Winter is coming with its blizzards and frost, but has it any terrors for you, children of the North? Our steel hearts fear neither the inclemency of the weather nor the wrath of our enemy: they form a reliable bulwark for our country against which everything is crushed. You will be able to stand temporary privations should this occur. Good soldiers are distinguished by their staunchness and patience; the veteran will set an example to the novices. Let everyone of you remember Suvorov, who taught us to bear cold and hunger when victory and the glory of the Russian people were at stake.[31]

In one of the coldest winters in memory, the Russian Army could only march 16–17 km a day and had to rest two days in five. Some squadrons of cavalry had no more than 20 or 30 men in a condition to fight. The horses were in an even worse state; Lowenstern described their suffering: 'Our horses were in a bad state and almost all suffering from sores, so much so that the stench was appalling and one could smell a cavalry regiment a long was off.'[32] He also records the agonies of his men.

> After the crossing of the Berezina, a terrible frost set in. I was unable to remain on my horse for more than ten minutes, and, as the snow made it very hard to walk, I alternately mounted and dismounted, and allowed my Hussars to do the same. To keep my feet from freezing, I stuck them in the fur caps of the French Grenadiers [of the Guard], which littered the road. My Hussars suffered terribly … The Sumi regiment had no more than 120 horses capable of charging … Our infantry was obviously disorganised. Nothing makes a man so pusillanimous as cold; when our soldiers managed to get under a roof somewhere it was absolutely impossible to get them out. They preferred to die. At the risk of being burned, soldiers sometimes crawled into the large Russian stoves. One had to see these horrors with one's own eyes to believe them … Only vodka sustained our strength. We suffered no less than the enemy.[33]

Sir Robert Wilson witnesses the Russian Army's sufferings at this time:

> The Russian troops who were moving through a country devastated by the enemy suffered nearly as much as they did from want of food, fuel and clothing.
> The soldier had no additional covering for the night bivouacs on the frozen snow; and to sleep longer than half an hour at a time was probable death. Officers and men, therefore, were obliged to relieve each other in their snatches of sleep, and to force up the reluctant and frequently resisting slumberers.

Firing [fires] could scarcely ever be obtained; and when obtained the fire could only be approached with great caution, as it caused gangrene of the frozen parts; but as water itself froze at only three feet from the largest bivouac fires, it was almost necessary to burn before the sensation of heat could be felt.[34]

Being quartered in a village could also be dangerous, as Fedor Schubert recalls: 'We took quarters in villages completely devastated and infected by typhus. The number of sick increased immediately in an alarming manner and in spite of all the unsparing care ... few sick had the fortune to recover.' By now, the Russian Imperial Guard had not received any bread for twelve days, but they were better off than the line regiments who had not received it for a whole month. On 30 November, Uxkull complained: 'I'm frozen through and half dead with hunger.'

Only the advanced guard seems to have been issued with food, given to them by the local inhabitants and Cossacks who had taken the food from the surrounding villages. The rearguard also seems to have obtained some food, which was sold to them by the various sutlers who followed the army and grew rich on their takings. According to Wilson, 'above ninety thousand perished', whereas Clausewitz adds that 'the Russian Army marched out of Taruntino 110,000 strong, and entered Vilna 40,000. The rest had remained behind, dead, wounded or exhausted.'[35]

On 28 November Chicherin wrote:

When we set out from [St] Petersburg, in our company were about 160 men. Wounded and killed at the Battle of Borodino [we] lost no more than 10 in the company. But now barely 50–60 soldiers remain.[36]

By the end of the campaign some regiments mustered just 150 men.

Fodder was in short supply for the horses, so that they were so weak they were unable to pull the artillery. 'Our horses suffered greatly from want, except for the poor [quality] country oats, they did not have any hay and fed only on juiceless straw.' No fodder was to be found in the towns and Radozhensky blamed the inhabitants for their 'devotion to the French'.[37]

Another Russian source states that

The loss of cavalry horses in the Russian Army appears to be nearly equal to that sustained by the French. None but the Cossack horses which are accustomed to be in the open air in all changes of weather and seasons ... can hold out in such a campaign at the present.[38]

As a consequence of these losses, for the third time in 1812 an Imperial decree was issued conscripting more serfs for the army. Among them would be a member of the Nazarov family. After some discussion it was decided that Pamfil Nazarov, who was the only unmarried member of his family eligible for military service, should go. He was marched to the rendezvous in the provincial capital at Tver. In a large building he was left standing in just a shirt with the rest of the recruits. After being stripped and examined by a doctor his forehead was shaved, the sign of a new recruit, and he swore an oath of allegiance to the Tsar. He was taken to lodgings for the night.

The following day the recruits had to say goodbye to their families. 'I ran to my mother,' wrote Nazarov, 'She caught me in floods of tears … [I] persuaded my mother … instead of crying, that she say a prayer to God.' At this he was marched away knowing that he would probably never see his family again. Because of his height, Nazarov was chosen to join the Finlandski Regiment of the Imperial Guard, but it would not be until 1813 that he would join his regiment at the front.[39]

On 3 December, Napoleon wrote his 29th Bulletin at Molodetschno, in which for the first time he declared that the Grande Armée had suffered a terrible disaster. It was also from there that Napoleon decided to leave his army and travelled to France, so that he could be in Paris before the news of the disaster became general knowledge. Early in the morning of the following day the Russians entered the town, to discover that they had narrowly missed him. Langeron arrived shortly afterwards:

> I entered one of the first houses in the town and the caretaker of the little man-
> sion where Napoleon had billeted said to me that he had arrived the day before at
> 4 o'clock in the afternoon, that he had not gone to bed, [but] had written until 2
> o'clock in the morning and had taken to horse. He [Napoleon] left his army and
> goes to Paris.

Langeron also found that the French had had time to plunder the town, and in the churches

> … the sacred vases pulled out of the sanctuary had served to perform foul deeds, the
> Holy water had been spilt on the pavement and trampled underfoot …
>
> The villains – without principles, without morals, without religion – in a word
> the pupils of the revolution, were ready to finish their guilty and sorrowful exist-
> ence, and several had died in the same church, close to the altar which they had
> desecrated, and their lack of remorse made them even more more criminal in the
> eyes of God.[40]

With Napoleon no longer with the army, what little semblance of order disappeared. Even Napoleon's Old Guard now became an undisciplined mob.

> In the first four days of the pursuit, we counted the cannon, the caissons and the
> carriages abandoned, but after Smorgoni, which we entered on 7 December, their
> number became so considerable that no one was concerned about making an
> account on the way from Smorgoni to Vilna; when we arrived on the 11th we
> found more than 500 cannons and 3000 to 4000 caissons, wagons, carriages etc.
>
> The corpses also multiplied in the same proportions; one might estimate more
> than 100,000 men … As far as Smorgoni, Napoleon's Guard, always privileged
> and well groomed by him, suffered less than the other corps and preserved a kind
> of organisation. But when their Emperor had left, they shared the privations and

disasters of the rest of the remnants of the army, and by the number of bearskins that we found on the road we learnt that these Guards were not immortal.[41]

By now all the Russians cared about was their own survival; Captain Pushkin:

5 December … This march is extraordinarily tiring, many in the regiment dropped behind and five died.

6 December. Still very cold … Had lodgings in Galitsi. We were 23 officers in one room and all without dinner since our wagons were not able to arrive in good time owing to the bad roads. The soldiers as well are almost without quarters and dinner. Today there are less men than the evening before; many froze to death.[42]

Pushkin could no longer go on, but fortunately he managed to obtain a lift on a sledge with other officers for about a week.

The *St Petersburg Gazette* on 11 December reported:

The progress of the Russian Army in the pursuit of the enemy becomes every hour more rapid and remarkable; every step it advances is a victory, and destructive to the enemy … Russia now exhibits an exalted aspect to the whole world and we can boldly assert that all nations, not even excepting those unhappy slaves of despotism, who through pusillanimity and weakness have been armed against her, await victories, in hopes, through them, of obtaining peace and happiness. On the one side we see a valiant army, whose regiments are unbroken and whose warriors are animated with a lofty feeling of vengeance for their homes, for the plundering of their towns and villages, vengeance for inhumanity. Glory inspires them, they know no weakness, feel no sufferings; and even if, in their rapid pursuit of the enemy, they may at times be exposed to some unavoidable wants, they bear them with courage, because they see victory before them. On the other side appear the ruins of an immense army, in which numerous foreign nations were united together to destroy a powerful nation in the bosom of its native country. They were encouraged by the idea of the result, but this result was a mirage. One single heavy blow threw this immense host into confusion. They fly, pursued by fear and terror. They are followed by hunger, having no food; they are in despair, and forced to eat dead horses – forced to do what their polished contemporaries can scarcely believe – feed upon the bodies of their own dead brethren.

The roads by which they fondly dreamt to retire in triumph, laden with booty, are covered with their dead bodies. Their sick and wounded are thrown aside by them on their march, and left a prey to famine and the cold. All these unfortunates, condemned to perish far from their own countries, curse, in different languages, ambition as the cause of their destruction; and those who still remain under the colours of the broken legions follow them without courage – without hope. Worn out with sufferings, they have lost all confidence in fortune and in their generals. Their cannon are taken in hundreds. They themselves surrender in whole detachments. At the first shot they either throw away their arms, or fight out of mere desperation.

Such is the condition of the two armies, which are now to decide the fate of many nations.[43]

The days of shame were over, now the Russian people celebrated. One anonymous eyewitness recorded in St Petersburg:

> The successes of our armies have spread the liveliest of joy throughout this city. Te Deums are performed daily to celebrate our victories, and religious processions made to impress upon the minds of our citizens. To so high a pitch is public confidence raised that the Emperor has deemed it proper to order the archives, regalia etc., which had, during the first alarm, been removed to Archangel, to be brought back in great pomp …
>
> It is said by the clergy that the enemy's ruin was entirely owing to the profanation of Moscow, that the saint of that city, the holy Sergius had appeared to several persons of rank, declaring that he would inflict vengeance upon the invaders for their temerity, and that he delayed until the winter had commenced, when he delivered them to the sword of the faithful and pious Russians.[44]

There was even a rumour in St Petersburg that Napoleon had been killed, which prompted the guns of the city's fortress to be fired in celebration. However, on 9 December news was brought that Napoleon was still alive, but had abandoned the remains of his army.

On 11 December, Admiral Chichagov was just 21 km from Vilna. By now both sides looked to Vilna for their salvation, both sides wanted to spend the winter there, but only one side would be able to do so.

Notes

1   Glinka's Letters 7 November 1812 pp.165–166
2   *Memoirs of Count Langeron* pp.50–54
3   *Memoirs of the Count de Rochechouart* pp.152–154
4   Brett James, *1812* pp.250–252
5   Some secondary sources state that the Russians retook Borisov before destroying the bridge but this does not appear to be the case.
6   *Memoirs of Count Rochechouart* p.157
7   *Memoirs of Count Langeron* p.65
8   *Memoirs of Count Rochechouart* p.158
9   *Memoirs of Count Langeron* pp.73–74
10 Ermolov, *Zapiski 1812*
11 *Memoirs of Count Langeron* pp.73–74
12 Sir Robert Wilson, *The French Invasion of Russia* p.333
13 *Memoirs of Count Rochechouart* pp.157–158
14 Ermolov, *Zapiski 1812*
15 Wilson, *The French Invasion of Russia* p.333
16 Ibid, p.333–334
17 *Memoirs of Count Langeron* pp.9–10
18 *Memoirs of Count Rochechouart* p.158
19 Zotov, *Razskazi o pohodah 1812…* pp.85–86

20 The *Morning Chronicle* 31 December 1812
21 Ibid
22 Clausewitz, *The Campaign of 1812 in Russia* p.211
23 Quoted in Tarle *Napoleon's Invasion of Russia* p.275
24 Quoted in Brett James, *1812* pp.260–261
25 Skobelev letter xxviii pp.198–200
26 Martos quoted in Tarle, *Napoleon's Invasion of Russia* p.277
27 *Memoirs of Count Langeron* pp.89–94.
28 *Memoirs of Count Langeron* pp.89–94.
29 *Memoirs of Count Langeron* p.94
30 Cathcart to the Foreign Office TNA FO 65/80 11 December 1812
31 Quoted in Bragin, *Kutuzov* p.120
32 *Lowenstern Memoires du general major russe* vol. 1 pp.352–356
33 Quoted in Tarle, *Napoleon's Invasion of Russia* p.276
34 Wilson, *The French Invasion of Russia* p.352
35 Wilson, *The French Invasion of Russia* p.353, Clausewitz, *The Campaign of 1812 in Russia* p. 213
36 Dnevnik, *Aleksandra Chicherina* p.63
37 I. Radozhitsky, *Poxodnie zapiski artilerista* p.284
38 The *Morning Chronicle* 3 February 1813, letter dated 25 November 1812
39 Quoted in Spring, *Russian Grenadiers and infantry* p.12
40 *Memoirs of Count Langeron* pp.95–96
41 *Memorirs of Count Langeron* pp.98–99
42 Dnevnik, *Pavla Pushkin*, p.79
43 The *Morning Chronicle* 18 January 1813
44 Letter dated 27 November in *St James Chronicle* 2 January 1813

20

RUSSIA IS SAVED!

On 8 December, Napoleon was seen pacing up and down in a tavern. He had long since abandoned his familiar grey greatcoat and hat in favour of warmer clothing. He went unnoticed by the other customers in the tavern until an officer of his Imperial Guard came in and saluted him, and ordered the customers to take off their hats in his presence. The landlady, who had not allowed him to go near the roaring fire, now offered him a seat so that he could warm himself before continuing his journey to Paris. This belated show of respect was very different to the reaction he had received almost six months before, when he had first arrived in Vilna.

Not far behind, the remnants of his Grande Armée began to appear. Countess de Choiseul-Gouffier, who had welcomed the sight of Polish troops entering Vilna in June, now saw the return of the Grande Armée.

> We soon had a spectacle that excited pity and secret terror, the remnants of that army so triumphant and formidable six months earlier, whose rapid march and destiny had been like that of a brilliant meteor. During three or four days the streets of Vilna were filled with a throng of men, I cannot say soldiers, since it was impossible to recognise them as being such under the grotesque garments that covered them. One had thrown away his helmet and was muffled up in a woman's velvet hood and black satin mantle, under which you could see his spurs. Another had enveloped himself in the ornaments and vestments of the church, stoles, chasubles and altar clothes all piled one upon another to keep out the cold, from which nothing could really protect the men. Those more fortunate in their booty had thrown about their shoulders ladie's fur dressing gowns with the sleeves tied about their necks. Still others trailed woollen blankets after them, or like shades from that place from which one never returns, they walked on in grave clothes and winding sheets. These sombre liveries, these gloomy tokens of death, figured in that historical *masquerade,* the expiring glory of a great conqueror.

Infantry, horse and artillery, no longer recognising authority, without any order
or discipline and almost without arms, their faces blackened by the smoke of the
bivouac, deprived by starvation and physical suffering of nearly every sentiment
except that of courage, which never deserted a Frenchman, marched in confusion,
imploring help and pity. My father gave shelter to a number of them.[1]

Originally the Grande Armée had planned to take up winter quarters in Vilna, but
this was now impossible, and they would have to continue to retreat into Germany.
But many had had enough, their only aim was to get to Vilna, and they could go no
further.

The King of Naples was kind enough to assure me, through his secretary, that the
town would not be defended and that I had nothing to fear. The King left that
evening. The soldiers were lighting fires in the streets to keep themselves warm.
The Town Hall Square resembled a Teniers painting. One could see a thousand men
scattered among the flames and leaping sparks, and also the Town Hall with its col-
onnade which still bore some festival decorations: Napoleon's cipher appeared to be
covered with a veil as one looked at it through the clouds of smoke rising to the sky.
The night effects had a Rembrandt touch among them.
   In the university courtyards opposite the castle the Emperor's carriages were
being burnt all night, as well as a pile of other things, tents, camp-beds, etc.[2]

The Russians were still of course on the heels of the Grande Armée. There was no
need for scouts to find the enemy, or maps to figure out where they were going, all
the Russians had to do was to follow the trail of destruction, which became worse the
nearer they got to Vilna.

Overturned wagons, cannons, kegs of powder, carriages etc., were scattered about
all along the road. On both sides of the road you could see poor wretches either
dead already or in the throes of death, wearing the most grotesque clothing and
in the saddest situation. We passed by all these phantoms, all these corpses, without
feeling or a shudder, we were so accustomed to the horrors of this destructive war.
From Osmian to Vilna 6000 corpses were counted. Passing by a tavern I saw inside
a heap of dead bodies, all naked, piled up one on top of the other, and living people
were sitting on their comrades, gnawing away at the flesh of their companions and
roaring with pain like savage beasts. Oh! humanity Where hast thou hidden! But
what advantage that the cold is so intense that the air cannot become infested so
quickly; otherwise plague would surely be upon us. For eight days we watched all
this, and for eight days I was surrounded by these terrors; for eight days I couldn't
shut my eyes; these scenes will never be erased from my memory. How cruel man
becomes the moment he loses his compassion and pity! The Cossacks continue
playing tricks on these wretches.[3]

Chicherin of the Russian artillery confirmed this scene of horror:

[We] covered 30 km, the weather was foul, the going was very difficult. As the passing horror enveloped us – the sight of the piles of frozen dead bodies, heaped on top of one another, frozen in a pose, the expression of the agonising death pangs [on their faces] – I turned away from the dead bodies. In all the men's faces was engraved their suffering, it was heart rending … in vain the eyes searched for a less sorrowful sight, in order to give them a rest, to fix one's stare at a remote field, pleased to see at least a little space covered only by snow, free from the terrible corpses.

All the country is ruined, burning … from the coaching inns, stationed along the road, only the ruins of the ovens remain, close to which are hundreds of skeletons, the pitiful remains of the unfortunates … Seeing these homes stiffened the heart, so that in the end I ceased to feel anything at all. [4]

All the time the Russians were getting closer to Vilna. On 9 December, the day after Napoleon's short stay in the town, the *Journal of Military Operations* announced:

The partisan Colonel of the Guard, Sesslavin, reports that having come up with the enemy's cavalry, he immediately attacked them, they were overthrown and he entered Vilna as it were on their very shoulders. In this attack he took six pieces of cannon and one eagle. Having afterwards joined the detachment under Major General Lanskoi, an attempt was made to carry the town itself; but finding themselves too weak for the enemy's infantry, dispersed throughout the houses, they were obliged to wait for the arrival of the advanced guard of Chichagov's army.

Admiral Chichagov reports on the 10th of December that Major General Tschabitz, regardless of all obstacles and profiting from the disorderly flight of the enemy, had pursued them into Vilna, taking 31 pieces of cannon; and that the suburbs had been occupied and piquets posted round the body of the town, under the orders of Major Generals Orourka and Laskine.

Viscount Cathcart, writing to the Foreign Office in London, takes up the story:

The advanced guard of the several Russian columns arrived in the immediate neighbourhood of Vilna nearly at the same time, and the retiring army was compelled to continue its retreat from that town almost without halt.

It is said that an Aide de camp of Marshal Davoust was sent to order the rearguard to defend itself before Vilna as long as possible; but instead of the French rearguard, this officer found the Russian advanced guard, which made him prisoner, having already demolished or sent to the rear the whole of the French rearguard. [5]

Admiral Chichagov's army continued to pursue the remnants of the Grande Armée through Vilna. Meanwhile Platov's Cossacks and two regiments of Russian cavalry, supported by the Cossack artillery, tried to cut their retreat off by occupying the Kovno Road. The slaughter among the Grande Armée was terrible and 1,000 soldiers were captured.

Countess de Choiseul-Gouffier:

Next morning I was woken with the news that the Cossacks were in Vilna. I got up, went to the window, and saw the last Frenchmen disappearing from the square … At eleven o'clock we heard the shouts of '*Hourra!*' and I recognised, from their pointed caps, [and] their long lances, my old acquaintances, the Cossacks, who galloped through the street and even out as far as the hills near the town, pursuing the wretched remnants of the French Army.

Many more prisoners and a great deal of booty were taken. The Jews behaved barbarously, and handed over the weakened, defenceless French to the Russians. The women were no less cruel and massacred these poor soldiers by hitting them with the heels of their slippers. Blood and water flowed under the carriage gateways.

I tried to go out on foot (my father had taken his horses) and this walk made me very depressed. A few feet away a Frenchman was knocked down and robbed. I sent my servant to help, but in vain. I saw terrifying corpses in the streets, seated on the ground, leaning against the walls, preserved by the cold, their limbs shrunken and stiff in the position in which Death had overtaken them. They had died of hunger, of pain and without physical or spiritual help. One dared not look at these poor creatures, and when one accidentally met these pitiful objects one averted one's eyes involuntarily.[6]

On 8 December, Kutuzov had issued a proclamation to the people of Lithuania offering them an amnesty for supporting Napoleon:

The destruction of the allied army is complete, you have seen the march and progress of the innumerable battalions; you now see its miserable remains flying before a victorious army. At this solemn moment, when we come to restore to you order and tranquillity, to plant again the victorious Russian eagles in those provinces which have for some time past suffered under the power of the enemy, remember your duty, and the sanctity of your oaths. Think of your own welfare and that of your children – recollect that an aggressor who neither could protect you nor keep the false promise which he made … would willingly have plunged all of you without a thought into the abyss of misery, that he might save himself and some of his confederates by flight. Even should false conceptions or a momentary delusion have seduced some among you, their future conduct may yet erase their fault, for the compassion of his Imperial Majesty, my most gracious lord, is boundless and to me, forever bound by happy ties to the province I have formerly governed, it gives new life to be by providence appointed the bringer of such great magnanimity. Show yourselves worthy of the grace bestowed on you, and you may be assured of continued peace for your families.

You shall again see commerce flourish, its springs so long dried up re-opened; an outlet for your products is again assured; your provinces shall become the habitation of happiness and plenty again. You have seen false greatness vanish before the course of justice, which God particularly protects. Your fellow citizens return crowned with a palm of victory. Prove yourselves worthy of them, you may yet do something for your native country and the cause of honour. What a delightful destiny! Hasten to fulfil it.[7]

On 11 December, the day after the town had been 'liberated' by the Russians, Count de Rochechouart arrived at Vilna.

When the temperature was 29° Reaumur, I entered Vilna [in a carriage]; ... it went forward amid human remains frozen on the road and hundreds of horses that had died of hunger and cold, or had broken their legs, for they were not rough shod; our servants walked in front, thrusting to the right, or left, the obstacles in the way.

We were assigned rooms in a suitable house, but they were already occupied by French or Polish officers, wounded or sick; the proprietor preferring to house four of the Tsar's aides de camp, rather than dying enemies, had them carried to a convent, and gave us their rooms, well warmed, an inestimable luxury in that temperature.

It is impossible to imagine the state of Vilna during the four days after our arrival; we found sick and wounded prisoners – Frenchmen, Poles, Germans, Spaniards, Italians and Portuguese, crowded into the various convents and monasteries. It was necessary to house everybody. Happily, the French Government had accumulated immense stores of provisions, which they had not been able to use, being so closely pursued by the Russians. These were distributed among all. The frozen snow which covered the streets deadened the sound of the vehicles that were constantly passing, but did not prevent our hearing the cries of the wounded asking for food, or the drivers urging on their horses; in short, we did not know where to hide to get an hour's sleep.[8]

As the days passed, more and more Russians entered Vilna. On 12 December Baron Uxkull arrived.

We've finally arrived. What happiness! What joy! Our quarters are good, and we have been given a month of rest. You must never despair in this life, for the more critical or unhappy the situation, the closer the moment approaches that will end our miseries. Our entry, which was supposed to represent a triumph, looked more like a masquerade. The costumes of various regiments were really burlesque, and the Emperor, who had arrived a day earlier and before whom we paraded, couldn't stop himself from laughing.[9]

On 14 December Kutuzov again wrote to Alexander:

After the capture of Vilna, I employed every possible means to re-establish order, and to inform myself of everything; but the lack of time prevents me from presenting your Imperial Majesty in this report a detailed inventory of all we have found here, especially the quantity of provisions of every sort. Similarly, the number of prisoners is so great that it will take a considerable amount of time to make an exact account.

During my stay here, the Chief of the Staff, General Stavrakov and Major General Besrodni, have collected from the different magazines of the town, fourteen *tschetwert* [a *tschetwert* is about 100 kg] of barley, five thousand *tschetwert* of biscuit and flour, an immense number of uniforms, muskets, pouches, saddles, great coats and other articles and equipment.

We have made prisoner seven Generals – viz., Viver, Gousse, Normand, Gouliot, Le Fevre, Fvanovski and Sajoutschik – 10 staff officers, 224 superior officers, 9,517 soldiers; and 5,130 sick were found in the hospitals.

A great number of prisoners continue to be taken in the neighbourhood and several magazines have been taken, which we have not had time to certify. As soon as the reports are drawn up I shall be delighted to submit them to your Imperial Majesty.[10]

At least some of these prisoners were taken to Vorenezh in Russia. An anonymous letter was printed in the *St Petersburg Gazette*, describing their state:

A few days since a large party of French prisoners of war, among whom were several staff and other officers, passed through our town on their way from Kursk to Saratov. These prisoners, who are merely covered with rags and barefooted, are provided here with warm clothing and covering for their feet against the present cold weather. It is worthy of remark that some of them would not at first accept this benevolent supply, regarding it as an ominous symbol of their fate, their commanders having in their march into Russia instilled into them a belief that the Russians sent all their prisoners of war to hard labour in Siberia for life. But after having convinced themselves thatr this is not true and that on the contrary they will be taken to places where they are certain to be supported and supplied in the best manner, they now receive every gift with pleasure.[11]

On 16 December, Chicherin was nearly at the gates of Vilna and all he could think of was the luxury of sleeping in a bed. However, on 17 December Kutuzov and Grand Duke Constantine were due to enter Vilna. The latter, never a person to miss an opportunity to have a parade, ordered that the Russian Army should enter the city in triumph. Chicherin recalls that his regiment, along with the Russian Imperial Guard,

… were all ordered to be dressed in clean [uniforms] and in good repair and to observe on the march the greatest order and so on. Finally we entered into Vilna! … At 2 o'clock in the afternoon we made a festive entrance. My heart beat. I forgot about everything. 'At last' – I thought – 'I will have a rest from all the misfortunes of camp life, a good dinner, visit the theatre, walk in the boulevards, I will put my wardrobe in order.' All these plans completely filled my mind … So here it is, this Eden, this refuge of peace, this dwelling place of rest.

The parade lasted until about 3 o'clock and all the participants were unsurprisingly 'numb with cold'.[12]

After the parade, Kutuzov was surrounded by the Russian soldiers and according to Captain Pushkin, 'a mighty "hurrah" resounded in the air and our old general shed a few tears ... The end of the campaign which has glorified us forever has come, our native land is saved.'

After being dismissed from the parade Chicherin, discovered that 'for seven copecks it was possible to get an excellent cup of coffee ... what nice bread! What excellent coffee! Six cups, seven loaves, swallowed in one minute. Here a bed was straightaway supplied and bed curtains drawn.'[13] Pushkin also looked forward to his bed, but after all the rigours of the campaign, he found his bed too soft to sleep in, and so ended up sleeping on the floor.

Also on 17 December, Alexander issued a proclamation to the Russian Army:

Your courage and your endurance have been crowned by a glory that posterity will never forget. Your name and your deeds will be handed down from mouth to mouth by your sons to their children and to their children's children to the last generation. You have made your way over their bodies and their bones to the borders of the realm. Now you will step over those borders, not in order to make conquests or to bring war into the land of your neighbours, but in order to secure a desired and enduring peace. You are Russians, you are Christians! As such, need you be reminded that it is the soldier's duty to be courageous in battle and gentle on the march and in the land of the enemy? That is demanded and expected by your orthodox religion, by your Fatherland and your Tsar.[14]

That evening Kutuzov attended the theatre, according to an anonymous letter written by an inhabitant of Vilna.

In the evening the opera of the benevolent land was performed at the theatre. The conclusion of the piece, which the Commander in Chief honoured with his presence, was distinguished by an expression of the gratitude of the inhabitants of this city towards the illustrious hero who delivered them from the enemy. On the stage was displayed a transparent picture, with the portrait of the victorious Field Marshal, and the inscription 'To the deliverer of his country' above an eagle holding a scroll, with the name of the Emperor Alexander. The verses which were sung on this occasion were received with the loudest applause.[15]

After issuing his proclamation, Alexander decided to rejoin his army at Vilna. At the village of Michaelesckhek, about 74 km from the city, he was met by a crowd of people cheering him enthusiastically with shouts of 'Long Live the great monarch Alexander I.' A delegation from Vilna offered him bread and salt, the traditional Russian welcome. The people accompanied him to Vilna, which he entered on 22 December. On 24 December, according the *St Petersburg Gazette*, the population of Vilna did their best to show their loyalty to the Tsar:

Early this morning, it being his Majesty's birthday, he was pleased to attend the parade of the guards, and after returning to the palace, he received the congratulations of the military and civil officers. When his Majesty went to church to hear the holy liturgy, the town corps of this city, with their colours, stood before the palace, and when the colours were saluted a joyful hurrah was raised. The dinner table for his Majesty was on this solemn day laid at the house of the Field Marshal General, with whom it pleased his Majesty to spend the evening.

Whilst the cannon were firing during dinnertime, the joyful acclamations and hurrahs intermingled with the thunder of the artillery throughout the city. The inhabitants embraced each other as in the holy Easter Feast, and loudly expressed their heartfelt joy and the most lively satisfaction. In the evening this general solemnity was concluded with several illuminations, one of which, at the Town Hall, is deserving of particular description. In this, Minerva was portrayed, standing with her sword on a serpent with several heads and driving away the enemy before her; above the spread eagle appeared in effulgence the cipher of his Majesty's name 'Alexander I'. In the theatre before the close of the piece, a transparent picture of his Majesty was placed in view, before which this happy people, singing solemn songs with great feeling, expressed their grateful thanks for the delivery of this part of the country.

Captain Pushkin:

On 24 December for the Sovereign's birthday the town was magnificently illuminated in the evening. These were the same ornaments which had been used at the time during the festivities arranged for Napoleon with some essential changes, the letter N replaced by the letter A. The Russian double headed eagle replaced the French one headed eagle. The joy and rejoicing was evidently universal. The field marshal put on a ball, which finished at 4 o'clock in the morning. Two enemy standards, very opportunely received from General Platov of the advanced guard ... as trophies, were laid down at the feet of the Sovereign, when he entered the hall and there and then His Majesty placed on Prince Kutuzov the Order of St George 1st Class.[16]

The day he arrived at Vilna, Alexander wrote to Kutuzov.

I am impatiently looking forward to seeing you, to tell you personally how greatly the new services you have rendered to your country, and, we may add, to all Europe, have strengthened the respect I have always had for you. Wishing you well as ever.

A few days later, according to Sir Robert Wilson, he had an audience with the Tsar and discussed Kutuzov being awarded the Order of St George First Class, in which Alexander allegedly told Wilson:

I know that the Marshal has done nothing he ought to have done – nothing against the enemy that he could avoid; all his successes have been *forced* upon him. He has been playing some of his old Turkish tricks, but the nobility of Moscow support him, and insist on his presiding over the national glory of this war. In half an hour I must therefore (and he paused for a minute) decorate this man with the great Order of St George, and by so doing commit a trespass on the institution; for it is the highest honour and hitherto the purest, of the empire. But I will not ask you to be present – I should feel too humiliated if you were; but I have no choice – I must submit to a controlling necessity. I will, however, not again leave my army, and there shall be no opportunity given for additional misdirection by the Marshal.

He is an old man, and therefore I would have you show him suitable courtesies, and not refuse them when offered on his part.

I wish to put an end to every appearance of ill will, and to [treat this day] as a new departure, which I mean to make one of gratitude to Providence and of grace and will.[17]

While the Tsar attended the ball in his honour, tens of thousands of soldiers of both sides were dying in the houses and streets of Vilna. The French hospitals had been poorly equipped through lack of money, and those supplies which had been collected, according to Countess de Choiseul-Gouffier, had been 'sold to the paper makers [the Jews] and the soldiers were bandaged with wadding and hay. I have these details from the hospital director.'[18]

Count de Rochechouart visited St Basil's Monastery, which had been converted into a hospital, to see if he could find anyone he knew:

A dreadful scene met our eyes at a monastery that had formerly belonged to the Monks of St Basil; not only the dead, but the living, were being thrown out of the windows on every storey, to make room for the sick and wounded Russians, who were arriving in crowds. 'Be it so, as regards the dead', I exclaimed, 'but we cannot allow it to be done to those who are crying for mercy as they fall.' The sufferings of the unhappy men who were still living were increased by the terror of such a barbarous act. Saint Priest [the Tsar's Aide de Camp] stopped this inhuman execution in the name of the Tsar, and I ran to find a detachment of the Imperial Guard. Thus reinforced, it was easy for us to restore order in this hospital, and to arrange for those who were still alive to be placed again in the rooms, rather close together, it is true, but it was necessary to shelter both friends and enemies. Finally, two Government officials were ordered, in the name of the Tsar, to have blankets, provisions and medical stores distributed to the wounded foreigners, who overwhelmed us with thanks.[19]

Little had improved a week later when Sir Robert Wilson visited the hospital.

The hospital of St Basil presented the most awful and hideous sight: seven thousand five hundred bodies were piled up like pigs of lead over one another in the corridors; carcasses were strewn about in every part; and all the broken windows and walls were stuffed with feet, legs, hands, trunks and heads to fit the apertures, and keep out the air from the yet living.

The putrefaction of the thawing flesh, where the parts touched and all the process of decomposition was in action, emitted the most cadaverous smell.

Nevertheless in each of these pestilential and icy repositories three or four grenadiers of the Guard were posted, inhaling the pestilential effluvia.

On the English General [Wilson] making the Emperor acquainted with this inconsiderate 'employment of his finest troops' he went himself to the convent and inspected the chambers, speaking the kindest words to the unfortunate inmates, and giving the requisite directions for their treatment. The Grande Duke followed his example, but caught the epidemic, from which he with difficulty recovered.[20]

During his stay in Vilna, Alexander often went to the hospitals to make certain the French wounded were being well treated. On hearing this Countess de Choiseul-Gouffier asked him if he was ever recognised:

'Yes' said he, 'in the officers' ward, but generally they have taken me for the Aide de Camp of General St Priest'. The emperor related a story in this connection which touched him very much, and me equally. A Spanish officer lay dying on his bed of straw. He had finished dictating a letter to his comrade, when General Saint Priest, followed by the Emperor, approached to speak to him, 'Monsieur' said the Spaniard, with a feeble voice, addressing Alexander, who he took for the Aide de Camp of the Russian general, 'have the goodness to take charge of this letter. It is the last farewell which I address to my wife in Spain.' 'I will send the letter' said the Emperor. He then had all the Spanish prisoners assembled, and sent them at his own expense by sea to their native country.

The picture which the Emperor drew of the French hospitals which he visited in the university building made us shiver with horror and froze the blood in our veins. 'It was in the evening' said his Majesty, 'one single lamp lighted the high vaulted room, in which they heaped up the piles of corpses as high as the walls. I cannot express the horror I felt, when in the midst of these inanimate bodies I suddenly saw living beings. And now,' he continued, 'nobody will follow me in my visits to the hospitals. My young people, who are enchanted to go to a duel or in assault, hastened to find some plausible reason for not accompanying me when I go to do my duty'.[21]

In these filthy conditions the sickness, almost certainly typhus, spread to the local population. On 30 December Wilson was still at Vilna and noted in his journal:

Sickness has made very serious progress in this city. In fifteen days nine thousand prisoners have died, and in one eighteen hours, seven hundred [died]. The mortality has extended of course to the inhabitants. The physicians have ordered straw to be burnt before every house, but the pestilential atmosphere is not to be corrected by such palliatives; and as if fate resolved to spread the contagion to the utmost, there has been a thaw for the last twenty-four hours.

In the spring Vilna must be a complete charnel house. All the carcasses which are removed from the streets and hospitals are laid at a short distance from the town in great masses; and then such parts as the wolves have not devoured during the winter will throw pestiferous miasma back upon the city, which, from [its] position, is always shrouded in vapour. I rode yesterday round the town to look at the camp which the enemy proposed to trace, and in all directions I saw mountains of human bodies, and carcasses of beasts. Disgusting as the sight was, I could not help occasionally stopping to contemplate the attitudes in which those who had been frozen had died. The greater part happened to have been writhing with some agony at the instant their hearts' blood congealed; some were raised upon their hands with their heads bent back and their eyes uplifted, as if still imploring aid from the passer-by.[22]

Countess de Choiseul-Gouffier continues:

We could not stir into the streets without encountering the dead bodies of French soldiers, either frozen to death or murdered by the Jews, who had killed them to get their watches, money or any other article which they had about them. The slightest thaw showed traces of blood on the pavements and even in the main entrances of some of our houses. Jewish women and even children were seen robbing the dead soldiers, or if they were not quite dead, killing them by kicks from their iron bound shoes.

The bodies of these unfortunates were to be seen, frozen still in the attitudes in which death found them in, some sitting, some bent forward with their faces in their hands, others leaning against a wall with their fists closed in a menacing attitude. One would have thought them asleep, but it was the sleep of death.

In the search made by the police in the town and its environs the bodies of about four hundred French soldiers were found. In entering our country the French had brought disorder and pillage, in quitting it they left disease and death. The contagious fever, known as hospital fever, broke out and caused unheard of ravages, destroying a large part of the population on the path of the Grande Armée. The hospitals of Vilna were infected and a great number of the inhabitants of the town fell victims to this new scourge; and still the French prisoners wandered freely about the city. Nothing can ever efface from my memory these walking spectres. I can see them still with worn, emaciated features and eyes of which only the whites could be seen, as they sat and warmed themselves at the fires which were kindled before our houses to keep away infection. I have often seen them searching in the rubbish of the street for something to satisfy their hunger, which was not the least of their sufferings ...

One day I was going out to a convert where my aunt was abbess they had given me a quantity of cakes, gingerbread etc. At the door I saw several prisoners who asked for charity, and I gave them all the cakes. They fell upon them with such voraciousness that I was frightened ...

I had taken into my house one of these poor creatures, whose mental faculties had been destroyed by suffering. As I asked him if he wanted anything, he answered with a wan smile 'I need nothing, I am a dead man.' It was impossible to get any other answer from him. I cannot tell you how that smile haunted me. The poor man escaped one day and no one ever knew what became of him.[23]

Among those found amid the French wounded was a former cornet in the Nezhinsk Dragoon Regiment, who had deserted when the Russians were retreating. Like most Polish deserters he had enlisted in the Grande Armée. He was court martialled and shot for desertion on 30 December.

On 11 January 1813, Ernst Moritz Arndt, the German poet, arrived at Vilna and found little had changed:

The town looked to me like some Tartar hell. Everywhere is frightfully dirty and smells; greasy Jews; some unfortunate prisoners, most of them wounded or convalescent, crept miserably around; every street was wreathed in acrid smoke and steam, because people had set fire to all sorts of inflammable materials, even dung heaps, in front of each house, in order to disperse the pestilential air from the many hospitals and infection centres …

I met a fine young man to whom I spoke and put several questions. He came from Brabant and was senior surgeon for French prisoners, who were lodged in a religious establishment. I accompanied him as far as the entrance hall of distress, saw the whole churchyard of the convent full of corpses, and turned back. He told me he had between fifty and eighty deaths every day out of two thousand patients in the hospital. This would soon reduce his work.

As I approached the town gate I met fifty or sixty sledges, all laden with bodies which had been removed from the hospitals and public places. They were driven as one drives firewood and were stiff with the frost and as withered as palings, and would provide a poor meal for the worms and fishes, because many of the bodies were thrown into holes which had been hacked in the ice.[24]

The dead were thrown into large pits, at least one containing over 7,000 men, another 2,000. Amongst this horror some of the Cossacks set up stalls from which they sold the items they had pillaged, including jewellery, gold, silver and even children who had been found wondering amidst the husk of the Grande Armée. Countess de Choiseul-Gouffier

These poor little creatures, passing from the maternal breast to the strong arms of their strange protectors, having only voices enough still to cry, could not even tell the names of their parents, who had perished, no doubt in the retreat.[25]

Not all the Russians had the luxury of quartering in Vilna – the Grande Armée still had to be driven from Russia's soil. On 14 December Chichagov's Army, now only 20,000–25,000 strong, marched out of Vilna to continue its pursuit. The same day the town of Kovno was re-occupied.

As early as September General Essen at Riga had reported:

The Prussian officers whom I have made prisoners tell me that they are restrained from quitting the service by the threats that their families would be imprisoned, their property confiscated and themselves outlawed. Both officers and men have likewise long arrears of pay, which are withheld to bind them to the service.[26]

On 25 December, negotiations began between the Prussian General Yorck and General Diebitch, and other Prussian officers in Russian service, near Tauroggen. On 30 December after much discussion Yorck signed the Convention of Tauroggen, which declared that the Prussian Corps would no longer take an active part in the campaign. Whether Yorck acted alone or with the consent of King Frederick William III of Prussia is not known, but following this act Napoleon had no choice but to evacuate East Prussia. It would also lead to Prussia declaring war on France in 1813.

Meanwhile Marshal MacDonald's force had marched to Tilsit, where he waited for General Yorck's Prussian Division. For five days he waited, until he heard that Yorck had made a separate armistice with the Russians. After this 'act of treachery', as he described it, MacDonald proceeded to Konigsburg, where he linked up with Marshal Ney.

If the Russian soldiers thought they were going to spend the winter in Vilna, they were sadly mistaken. Alexander was keen to continue the war into the Duchy of Warsaw and Germany. On 1 January a proclamation by Kutuzov was read to the Russian Army:

Brave and victorious soldiers! At last you have reached the frontiers of the Russian Empire! Everyone among you is a saviour of our country. Russia hails you by this name! Your impetuous pursuit of the enemy, and the extraordinary labours you have accomplished in this campaign have astounded all nations and covered you with immortal fame … Let us cross the frontiers and endeavour to complete the enemy's defeat on his own ground. But let us not follow the example of our enemy in committing acts of violence and savagery unworthy of a soldier … Let us be generous, let us carefully distinguish between the enemy and the peaceful population. Our just and kind treatment of the population will clearly demonstrate that we do not strive to enslave them and win a futile glory, but that we are trying to liberate from misery and oppression even those nations that had taken up arms against Russia.[27]

Prayers were said and although many companies were completely wiped out and many battalions less than fifty strong, the same day, to shouts of 'Ura!', the Russian Army crossed the Nieman River, and Russia's War of German Liberation had begun.

Notes

1   Memoirs of Countess de Choiseul-Gouffier, p.121
2   Brett-James, *1812* pp.280–281
3   Uxkull, *Arms and the Woman* 3 December p.105
4   Dnevnik, *Aleksandr Chicherina* p.67
5   Viscount Cathcart to Foreign Office, TNA FO 65/80 17 December 1812
6   Brett-James, *1812* pp.280–281
7   The *Edinburgh Evening Courant* 28 January 1813

8   Memoirs of the Count de Rochechouart p.165

9   Uxkull, *Arms and the Woman* p.105

10 *The Times* 18 January 1813

11 *St Petersburg Gazette* 25 December 1812

12 Dnevnik, *Aleksandr Chicherina* p.68

13 Ibid, p.68

14 Uxkull, *Arms and the Woman* p.107

15 The *St Petersburg Gazette* 14 January 1813

16 Dnevnik, *Pavla Pushkin* p.82

17 Wilson, *The French Invasion of Russia* pp.356–357

18 Memoirs of Countess de Choiseul-Gouffier, p.122

19 Memoirs of the Count de Rochechouart p.166

20 Wilson, *The French Invasion of Russia* p.357

21 Memoirs of Countess de Choiseul-Gouffier, p 148

22 Quoted in Brett James, *1812* p.284

23 Memoirs of Countess de Choiseul-Gouffier, pp.126–128

24 Quoted in Brett James, *1812* pp.285–286

25 Memoirs of Countess de Choiseul-Gouffier, pp.128–130

26 Despatch from General Essen at Riga 6 September 1812 quoted in the *Caledonian Mercury* 22 October 1812.

27 *Pohod Russkoi Armii protiv Napoleona v 1813* p.13

RUSSIAN ARMY – JUNE 1812

1st Western Army

Commanded by Barclay de Tolly

1st Infantry Corps
Commanded by Lieutenant General P. Wittgenstein

5th Infantry Division
Commanded by Major General G. M. Berg
1st Brigade
Sevski and Kaluzhsk Infantry Regiments
2nd Brigade
Perm and Mogilev Infantry Regiments
3rd Brigade
23rd and 24th Jager Regiments
5th Field Artillery (5th Battery, 26th and 27th Light companies)
2 Combined Grenadier Battalions

Cavalry
Rizhsk and Yamburg Dragoon Regiments
Grodno Hussar Regiment
Rodionov 2nd, Platov 4th and Celivanov 2nd Don Cossack Regiments
1st Reserve Artillery Brigade
27th and 28th Battery, 1st and 3rd Horse, and 1st and 2nd Pontoon Companies.

2nd Infantry Corps
Commanded by Lieutenant General Karl Gustav Baggovut

4th Division
1st Brigade
Tobolsk and Volhynia Infantry Regiments
2nd Brigade
Kremenchug and Minsk Infantry Regiments
3rd Brigade
34th and 4th Jager Regiments

4th Artillery Brigade
4th Battery, 7th and 8th Light Artillery Companies

17th Division
Lieutenant General Zakhar Olsufiev III
1st Brigade
Ryazan and Brest Infantry Regiments
2nd Brigade
Belozersk and Willmandstrand Infantry Regiments
3rd Brigade
30th and 48th Jager Regiments
17th Artillery Brigade
17th Battery, 32nd and 33rd 32nd Light Artillery Companies

3rd Infantry Corps
Commanded by Lieutenant General Nikolay Tuchkov I

1st Grenadier Division
1st Brigade
Leib Grenadier and Count Aracheev Grenadier Regiments
2nd Brigade
Pavlov and Yekaterinoslav Grenadier Regiments.
3rd Brigade
St. Petersburg and Tauride Grenadier Regiments

3rd Division
1st Brigade
Murom and Revel Infantry and 1st Combined Grenadier Battalion
2nd Brigade
Chernigov and Selenginsk Infantry Regiments and the 2nd Combined Grenadier
3rd Brigade
20th and 21st Jager Regiments
3rd Artillery Brigade
1st Battery and 6th Light Artillery Company

4th Infantry Corps
Lieutenant General Alexander Osterman-Tolstoy

11th Division
1st Brigade
Kexholm and Pernau Infantry Regiments
2nd Brigade
Polotsk and Yeletsk Infantry Regiments
3rd Brigade
1st and 33rd Jager Regiments
11th Artillery Brigade
2nd Battery, 3rd and 4th Light Artillery Companies

23rd Division
1st Brigade
Ekaterinburg and Rylsk Infantry Regiments
2nd Brigade
Kopor Infantry and 18th Jager Regiment
23rd Artillery Brigade

44th Light Company

2nd Combined Grenadier Brigade

1st Combined Grenadier Battalion (6 companies from the 1st and 2nd Combined Grenadier Battalions of the 17th Division)

2nd Combined Grenadier Battalion (7 companies from the combined Grenadier battalions of the 11th and 23rd Divisions.)

5th Infantry Corps

Commanded by Lieutenant General Nikolay Lavrov

1st Brigade

Preobrazhensk and Semeovski Regiments of the Imperial Guard (3 battalions each)

2nd Brigade

Izmailovsk and Lithuanian Regiments of the Imperial Guard (3 battalions each)

3rd Brigade

Jager and Finland Regiments of the Imperial Guard (3 battalions each)

Guard Artillery Brigade

His Majesty Grand Duke Mikhail Pavlovich's 1st Battery Company, Count Aracheev's 2nd Battery Company

Major General Kaspersky's 1st Light Company

Captain Gogel's 2nd Light Company

Guard Equipazh's Artillery

2 guns assigned to the 1st Light Company

1st Combined Grenadier Brigade

1st and 2nd Combined Grenadier Battalions of the 1st Division

1st and 2nd Combined Grenadier Battalion of the 4th Division

1st Cuirassier Division

1st Brigade

Chevalier Guard and Horse Regiments

2nd Brigade

His and Her Imperial Majesty's Cuirassier Regiments of the Imperial Guard and Astrakhan Cuirassier Regiment

Horse Artillery Brigade of the Imperial Guard

1st and 2nd Horse Batteries

6th Infantry Corps

Commanded by General of Infantry Dmitry Dokhturov

7th Division

1st Brigade

Moscow and Pskov Infantry Regiments

2nd Brigade

Libau and Sofia Infantry Regiments

3rd Brigade

11th and 36th Jager Regiment

7th Artillery Brigade

7th Position Battery, 12th and 13th Light Artillery Companies

24th Division

1st Brigade

Ufa and Shvan Infantry Regiments

2nd Brigade

Butyrsk and Tomsk Infantry Regiments

3rd Brigade
19th and 40th Jager Regiments
24th Artillery Brigade
24th Battery Company 45th and 46th Light Artillery Companies

1st Reserve Cavalry Corps
Commanded by Lieutenant General Fedor Uvarov
1st Brigade
Dragoon and Uhlan Regiments of the Imperial Guard
2nd Brigade
Cossack and Hussar Regiments of the Imperial Guard
3rd Brigade
Elisavetgrad Hussar and Nezhinsk Dragoon Regiments
Artillery
2nd Horse Artillery Company

2nd Reserve Cavalry Corps
Commanded by Major General Fedor (Friedrich Nicholas Georg) Korf
1st Brigade
Moscow and Pskov Dragoon Regiments
2nd Brigade
Izum Hussar and Uhlan Regiments
Artillery
6th Horse Artillery Company

3rd Reserve Cavalry Corps
Commanded by Major General Fedor Korf
1st Brigade
Courland and Orenburg Dragoon Regiments
2nd Brigade
Irkutsk and Siberia Dragoon Regiments
3rd Brigade
Mariupol and Sumsk Hussar Regiments
Artillery
7th Horse Artillery Company

Irregular Forces
General of Cavalry Matvei Platov

Separate Units
Ataman commanded by Colonel Stepan Balabin II
1st Bug Cossack Regiment commanded by Esaul Stepan Zhekul.
1st Bashkir Regiment Cossack Regiment
1st Teptyarsk Cossack regiment

1st Brigade
Adrianov II', Chernozubov VIII, Vlasov III 's Don Cossack Regiments and
Perekop Horse Tatar
2nd Brigade
Ilovaisky V and Grekov XVIII's Don Cossack Regiments
3rd Brigade
Denisov VII and Zhirov's Don Cossack regiment

5th Brigade
Kharitonov VII's Don Cossack ant the Simferopol Horse Tatar Regiment

Artillery
2nd Don Cossack Artillery
Reserve Artillery
Total of 10 artillery companies with 120 guns.

1st Artillery Brigade of the 1st Division
1st and 2nd Light Companies
3rd Artillery Brigade of the 3rd Infantry Division
5th Light Company
2nd Reserve Artillery Brigade
4th and 5th Horse Artillery and 29th and 30th Battery Artillery Companies
3rd Reserve Artillery Brigade
9th and 10th Horse Artillery Companies and 4th Pontoonier Company
4th Replacement Artillery Brigade
22nd Horse Artillery Company

2nd Western Army

Commanded by General Peter Bagration

7th Infantry Corps

12th Division
1st Brigade
Narva and Smolensk Infantry Regiments
2nd Brigade
New Ingermanland and Aleksopol Infantry Regiments
3rd Brigade
6th and 41st Jager Regiments

26th Division
1st Brigade
Nizhni Novgorod and Orel Infantry Regiments
2nd Brigade
Ladoga and Poltava Infantry Regiments
3rd Brigade
5th and 42nd Jager Regiments
26th Artillery Brigade
26th Battery Artillery and 47th Light Artillery Companies

8th Infantry Corps
Commanded by Lieutenant General Mikhail Borozdin I

2nd Grenadier Division
1st Brigade
Kiev and Moscow Grenadier Regiments
2nd Brigade
Astrakhan and Fanagoria Grenadier Regiments
3rd Brigade
Siberia and Malorossia Grenadier Regiments

2nd Artillery Brigade
11th Battery Company and 21st Light Company

27th Division
1st Brigade
Odessa and Tarnopol Infantry Regiments
2nd Brigade
Vilna and Simbsk Infantry Regiments
3rd Brigade
49th and 50th Jager Regiments

Artillery
32nd Battery Company

2nd Combined Grenadier Division
1st Brigade
1st and 2nd Combined Grenadier Battalions of the 7th Division
1st and 2nd Combined Grenadier Battalions of the 24th Division
2nd Brigade
1st and 2nd Combined Grenadier Battalion of the 2nd Grenadier Division
1st and 2nd Combined Grenadier Battalion of the 12th Division
2nd Combined Grenadier Battalion of the 26th Division
1st and 2nd Combined Grenadier Battalion of the 27th Division

Artillery
1st Don Horse Company

Artillery Attached to the 8th Corps
1st Brigade
3rd Battery Company
3rd Brigade
1st Battery Company
3rd Reserve Artillery Brigade

31st Battery Company

Cavalry of the 2nd Western Army
Commanded by Lieutenant General Dmitri Golitsyn V

2nd Cuirassier Division
1st Brigade
Ekaterinoslav and Military Order Cuirassier Regiments
2nd Brigade
Glukhov and Malorossiisk Cuirassier Regiments

4th Reserve Cavalry Corps
1st Brigade
Kharkov and Chernigov Dragoon Regiments
2nd Brigade
Kiev and Novorossiisk Dragoon Regiments
3rd Brigade
Akhtyrsk Hussar and Lithuanian Uhlan Regiments

Artillery
8th Horse Artillery Company

Irregular Troops of the 2nd Western Army
Major General Akim Karpov II
Cossack Forces
Bykhalov I, Grekov XXI, Ilovaisky X, Ilovaisky XI, Karpov II, Komissarov I, Melnikov IV and
    Sysoyev III Don Cossack Regiments

Artillery Reserve of the 2nd Western Army

12th Artillery Brigade
12th Battery Company and 22nd and 23rd Light Artillery Companies
2nd Artillery Brigade
20th and 21st Light Artillery Companies
23rd Artillery Brigade
23rd Battery Company
26th Artillery Brigade
48th Light Company
3rd Reserve Artillery Brigade
4th Pontoon Company

Engineer Troops
Zotov's Pioneer Company of the 2nd Pioneer Regiment.

3rd Observation Army

Commanded by General of Cavalry A. P. Tormassov

General of Infantry S. M. Kamenski's Corps

18th Infantry Division
1st Brigade
Vladimir and Tambov Infantry Regiments
2nd Brigade
Kostrom and Dniepov Infantry Regiments
3rd Brigade
28th and 32nd Jager Regiments
Combined Grenadier Brigade
Grenadiers companies from 9th, 15th and 18th Infantry Divisions
Pavlograd Hussar Regiment
11th Horse artillery company

Lieutenant General Markov's Corps

15th Division
1st Brigade
Kozlov and Kolivan Infantry Regiments
2nd Brigade
Kurin and Vitebsk Infantry Regiments
3rd Brigade
13th and 14th Jager Regiment
15th Field Artillery Brigade (15th Battery, 28th and 29th Light Companies)

9th Division
1st Brigade
Nashyeburg and Yakut Infantry Regiment
2nd Brigade
Apsheron and Ryazh Infantry Regiment
3rd Brigade
10 and 38 Jager Regiments
9th Field Artillery Brigade (9th Battery, 16th and 17th Light Companies)
Alexsandir Hussar Regiment
12th Horse Artillery Company

Lieutenant General F. V. Osten-Sacken's Corps

Infantry
18 Reserve battalions of the 9th, 15th and 18th Infantry Divisions

Cavalry
11th Cavalry Division
16 Reserve squadrons 4th, 5th and 2nd Cuirassier Divisions
Luben Hussar regiment
4th Reserve Artillery Brigade (33rd Battery and 13th Horse companies)

Major General K. O. Lambert's Cavalry Corps

5th Cavalry Division
Tatar Uhlan Regiment

15th Brigade
Starodubov and Tver Dragoon Regiments
16th Brigade
Zhitomir and Arzanms Dragoon Regiments

8th Cavalry Division
24th Brigade
Vladimir and Taganrog Dragoon Regiment
Reserve
4th Reserve Artillery (34th Battery, 4th Pontoonier Companies
Cossack Detachments
Barabanshikov 2nd, Platov 5th, Vlasov 2nd, Dyachkin, Chikilev Don Cossack Regiments
Feodosii and Evpatorii Horse Tatar Regiments
2nd Bashkir Regiment
1st and 2nd Kalmick Regiments

Ukranian Cossack Division
1st, 2nd, 3rd and 4th Ukranian Cossack Regiments

Army of the Danube

Commanded by Admiral P.V. Chichagov

1st Corps
Commanded by General of Infantry A. F. Langeron

22nd Division
1st Brigade
Vyatsk and Starooskol Infantry Regiments
2nd Brigade
Viborg Infantry Regiment
3rd Brigade
29th and 45th Jager Regiment
22nd Field Artillery Brigade
22nd Battery, 41st and 42nd Light Companies

Cavalry
Grekov 4th and Panteleev 2nd Don Cossack Regiments
1st Ural Cossack Regiment
14th Horse Artillery Company
18th Brigade of 6th Cavalry Division
St Petersburg and Finland Dragoon Regiments

2nd Corps
Commanded by Lieutenant General P. K. Essen
1st Brigade
Arhangelogorod and Ukraine Infantry Regiments
2nd Brigade
Shlisselburg and Staroingermanland Infantry Regiment
3rd Brigade
37th Jager Regiment (3 btns)
22nd Field Artillery Brigade
8th Battery, 14th and 15th Light Companies.

Cavalry
Seversk and Smolensk Dragoon Regiments
Grekov 8th Don Cossack Regiment
2nd Ural Cossack Regiment
15th Horse artillery company

3rd Corps
Commanded by Lieutenant General A. L. Voinov

10th Division
1st Brigade
Belostok and Crimean Infantry Regiments
2nd Brigade
Kursk Infantry Regiment
3rd Brigade
8th and 39th Jager Regiments
10th Field Artillery Brigade
10th Battery, 18th and 19th Light Companies
7th Reserve Artillery Brigade
30th Battery and 50th Light Companies

Cavalry
Kinburn Dragoon Regiment
Belorussia Hussar Regiment

Mel'nikkov 5th Don Cossack Regiment
3rd and 4th Ural Cossack Regiment

4th Corps
Commanded by Lieutenant General A. P. Zass

16th Division
1st Brigade
Ohotsk Infantry Regiment
2nd Brigade
Kamchatka and Mingrel Infantry Regiments
16th Field Artillery Brigade
16th Battery and 31st Light Artillery Companies
7th Cavalry Division
Pereyaslav, Chugyev, Derptski and Tiraspol Dragoon Regiments
Reserve
Mel'nikov 3rd and Kutyeinikov 4th Don Cossack Regiments
17th Horse and 39th Battery Companies

Reserve
Olonets and Yaroslav Infantry Regiments
7th Jager Regiment
Ol'viopol Hussar Regiment
Lukovkin Don Cossack Regiment
16th Horse Artillery Company

Riga Corps
Commanded by Lieutenant General I. N. Essen 1st

30th Infantry Division
Depot Battalions of the regiments of 4th and 14th Infantry Divisions

31st Infantry Division
Depot Battalions of the regiments of 5th and 17th Infantry Divisions

39th Infantry Division
Reserve Battalions of the regiments of 14th and 25th Infantry Divisions

40th Infantry Division
Reserve Battalions of the regiments of 5th Infantry Divisions

Finland Corps
Commanded by Lieutenant General F. F. Sheingell

6th Division
1st Brigade
Bryansk and Nizov Infantry Regiments
2nd Brigade
Azov Infantry Regiment
3rd Jager Regiment
6th Field Artillery Brigade
6th Battery and 11th Light Companies

21st Division
1st Brigade
Petrov and Podolsk Infantry Regiments

2nd Brigade
Nevsk and Litovski Infantry Regiments
3rd Brigade
2nd and 44th Jager Regiments
21st Field Artillery Brigade
21st Battery and 40th Light Companies

25th Division
1st Brigade
1st and 2nd Marine Regiment
2nd Brigade
3rd and 4th Marine Regiment
3rd Brigade
31st and 47th Jager Regiments
25th Field Artillery Battery
25th Battery company and 3rd Marine half company
Isaev 2nd, Loshilin and Kiselev 2nd Don Cossack Regiments
27th Cavalry Brigade
Finlandski and Mitavsk Dragoon Regiments

1st Reserve Corps
Commanded by Adjutant General E. I. Miller–Zakomelski

32nd Division
Depot Battalions of the regiments of 1st Grenadier, 11th and 23rd Infantry Divisions

33rd Division
Depot Battalions of the regiments of 3rd and 7th Infantry Divisions

Cavalry
Depot Squadrons of regiments from 3rd Cavalry Division

9th Cavalry Division
Depot Squadrons of the regiments of Guard cavalry, 1st Cuirassier, 1st and 2nd Cavalry Divisions.

2nd Reserve Corps
Commanded by Lieutenant General F. F. Ertel
Infantry
Depot Battalions of the regiments of 2nd Grenadier, 12th and 27th Infantry Divisions.
Cavalry
Depot Squadrons of the Ahtirsk Hussar Regiment, Lithuanian Uhlan Regiment, Bihalov 1st,
    Grekov 21st and Komissarov Don Cossack Regiments

Smolensk Reserve Corps
Commanded by Adjutant General F. F. Vintsingerod

40th Division
Reserve Battalions of the regiments of the 4th Infantry Division

41st Division
Reserve Battalions of the regiments of the 3rd and 17th Infantry Divisions

42nd Division
Reserve Battalions of the regiments of the 11th and 23rd Infantry Divisions

13th Cavalry Division

Reserve Squadrons of the regiments of the 3rd Cavalry Division and 8th Brigade of the 2nd
   Cavalry Division
2nd Depot Artillery Brigade
46th and 51st Battery, 59th, 60th, 61st and 62nd Light, 20th and 24th Horse Companies.

Kaluzsk Reserve Corps

Commanded by General of Infantry M. A. Miloradovich

42nd Division

Reserve Battalions of the regiments of the 7th Infantry Division

43rd Division

Reserve Battalions of the regiments of the 18th and 24th Infantry Divisions

44th Division

Reserve Battalions of the regiments of the 12th and 26th Infantry Divisions

45th Division

Reserve Battalions of the regiments of the 9th and 15th Infantry Divisions

14th Cavalry Division

Reserve Squadrons of the regiments of 4th Cavalry Division

15th Cavalry Division

Reserve Squadrons of the regiments of 5th Cavalry Division

APPENDIX TWO

OPOLCHENYE FORCES AT BORODINO

Moscow Opolchenye

Lieutenant General Morkov
(Each regiment 4 battalions strong)

1st Division
1st Jager Regiment, armed with muskets
4th Dismounted Cossack Regiment, armed with pikes
6th Dismounted Cossack Regiment, armed with pikes

2nd Division
7th Dismounted Cossack Regiment, armed with pikes

3rd Division
2nd Jager Regiment, armed with muskets.
3rd Jager Regiment, armed with muskets
1st Dismounted Cossack Regiment, armed with muskets
3rd Dismounted Cossack Regiment, armed with pikes

Militia
Troops of Vereya and Volokolamsk District (946 men)

Smolensk Opolchenye

Total of 12,530 men (up to 2,000 men left near Mozhaisk)
Lieutenant General Nikolay Lebedev
Belsk District (1,341 men)
Vyazma District (1,143 men)
Gzhatsk District (993 men)
Dorogobouzh District (1,084 men)
Dukhovo District (1,190 men)
Yelna District (1,282 men)
Krasnyi District (212 men)
Roslavl District (1,293 men)
Smolensk District (1,203 men)
Sychev District (1,336 men)
Yukhnov District (1,453 men)

APPENDIX THREE

FRENCH LOSSES

Date	Event	Killed	Prisoners	
			Officers	Other Ranks
9-Jul	Taken by Platov at Mir	200	9	185
10-Jul	Taken by Platov at Romanov	500	18	300
Mid July	Taken by Col. Koulev from Wittgenstein's Army & garrison of Daunberg	700	10	1,000
21-Jul	Taken by Col Sizoev from 2nd Army near Molihev	100	11	245
23-Jul	Action near Daschkorke by General Raevski's Corps	1,400	8	250
25–27 July	Different actions near Vitebsk with 2nd Corps & rear guard of 1st Army	2,100	18	850
25-Jul	In Platov's march from the 2nd to 1st Army	50	12	211
27-Jul	At the battle of Kobrin by 3rd Army	1,000	67	2,334
30 Jul–1 Aug	Series of battles near Polotsk by Wittgenstein's Army	3,300	25	3,100
c. 1 Aug	By same army at Drissa	100	16	684
7-Aug	At Shlok by the garrison of Riga	100	1	52
8-Aug	Action at Leshney near Vloudni by Platov's Corps	200	9	450
11-Aug	Action at Kochanov by Wittgenstein	600	5	250
12-Aug	Battle of Gorodetchina by 3rd Army	1,650	4	230
Early Aug	By a detachment of Wittgenstein's Army at Dwina	100	11	620
13–16 Aug	Platov's Corps near Roudni, Portjetchie & Loubavitch, also a detachment of Wintzengerode's Army near Velij	350	31	922
15-Aug	Action at Krasnoe & battles of 4–5 at Smolensk	7,000		700
17–18 Aug	Action at Polotsk by Wittgenstein	3,500	39	3,201
19-Aug	Battle at Gedeonova & Bredichino by 2nd Corps & rearguard of 1st Army	3,000	13	600
22-Aug	Action near Riga by the garrison	500	35	1,140
22-Aug	Near Bielo by Wittgenstein's vanguard	350	3	240
5–7 Sept	Battle of Borodino	18,000	11	1,550
Aug–Sept	Brought in by detachments of Wittgenstein's Army			
Mid-Sept	A detachment of Wittgenstein's Army on the Dwina	100	29	238
Mid-Sept	General Oertils Corps in the government of Minsk	800	13	574
15-30 Sept	By various detachments & outposts of the Main Army	1,100	24	5,500

Date	Event	Killed	Prisoners Officers	Prisoners Other Ranks
19-Sep	By General Ilovayski's detachment at Zamanskoe	100	7	240
20-Sep	Count Lambert's Corps of the 3rd Army at Nesevitch	200	13	187
20-21 Sept	General Dorochov's detachment on the Mozhaisk	400	21	500
24 Sep-3 Oct	Dorochov, Korf, Col Ephremov & vanguard of	1,150	34	1,573
26 Sep-2 Oct	Main Army Detachments of Wintzengerode's Army near Moscow	350	2	378
28-Sep	Taking of Mittau by the garrison of Riga			240
2–6 Oct	By Wintzengerode's detachment near Moscow	175	2	289
6-Oct	By Bedriah under Wittgenstein on the Dwina	150	3	87
6–8 Oct	By Wintzengerode's detachment near Moscow	300	6	215
8–20 Oct	Chernichov's detachment in the Duchy of Warsaw	270	6	220
9-Oct	By Tchernerzubov's detachment between Mozhaisk & Gjatsk			
11-Oct	By Dorochov's detachment at the taking of Vercia	325	15	437
4–23 Oct	Various detachments of partizans acting on different	600	15	377
	roads & reported to Kutuzov	1,300	18	1,280
Oct	In pursuit by the 3rd Army & that of the Danube Army			
13–15 Oct	Partizans corps & parties from the Main Army	1,100	15	1,552
13–20 Oct	By detachments of Wintzengerode's Corps	600	5	499
16–20 Oct	By partizans	400	9	
18-Oct	Battle of Tchernishma by the Main Army	600	13	770
18-Oct	Battle of Polotsk & taking the city by Wittgenstein	2,000	60	1,500
19-Oct	Battle of Oushatch by Count Steinhel's Corps	3,600	45	1,980
20-Oct	General Chaplitz's detachment at Slonim	1,000	38	490
20–27 Oct	Detachments of the Main Army & Battle of Maloyaslavetz	100	14	450
8–19 Oct	Pursuit of the enemy from Polotsk to Lapelle by Wittgenstein	5,000	24	1,800
22-Oct	The retaking of Moscow by Colonel Ilovayski	1,200	50	3,620
24–26 Oct	Two actions near Koublitcj & Glouboki by Steinhel's Corps		58	1,800
25–30 Oct	By Iloivayski in the vicinity of Moscow	600	18	350
28 Oct–5	By Platov Corps & other detachments on different	325	5	652
Nov	roads during the pursuit from Maloyaroslavets	1,000	8	440
31-Oct	By Platov near the monastery of Polotsk			
31-Oct	Wittgenstein near Chashniki	800	9	200
2-Nov	By Orlov-Denisov near Viasma	1,200	12	1,000
3-Nov	Battle of Viasma & pursuit of 23 Oct by Miloradovitch	200	6	130
3–21 Nov	Kutuzov commanding Wintzengerode's Corps who	1,800	24	3,500
	had taken prisoner & pursuing the enemy from	500	18	900
	Mocow to Babinovitch			
5–6 Nov	By the pursuit from Viasma to Dorogobough by Miloradovitch & Platov	900	29	1300
7 Nov	By Platov near the village of Mantorovaca.			
7-Nov	Near Douchovshchina by Ilovaysky	1,600	109	2,800
7-Nov	By Andrianov from Platov's Corps near Bazikova	450	23	502
7-Nov	Taking of Dorogobough by Miloradovitch	220	3	175
7-Nov	Taking of Vitebsk by General Harpe of Wittgenstein's Army	1,000	1	580

Date	Event	Killed	Prisoners	
			Other	Ranks
9-Nov	Pursuit & crossing of the Dnieper at Solovievo by	280	12	307
8–9 Nov	Orlov Denisov	700	7	563
9-Nov	Pursuit from Dorogobough to Solovievoi,	600	11	200
9-Nov	crossing the Dnieper by general Ourkousky of Miloradovitch's Army.			
9–11 Nov	By Partizans Seslavin, Figner & Davidov near Liachov	175	61	655
10-Nov	Crossing of the Dnieper at Solovievo by Orlow-Denisov	700	7	563
11-Nov	Various detachments of the Main Army	400	27	655
12-Nov	From action at Vop by Platov	600	5	200
12-Nov	Taking of Kraytzburg by Marquis of Pauluzzi	100	2	63
12–13 Nov	By Orlov-Denisov on roads between Elnia & Smolensk	1,300	9	1,291
Mid-Nov	By Platov at Douchovshchina	450	5	800
14-Nov	By Orlov-Denisov	300	6	620
14-Nov	By Sacken near Slonin		12	1,000
14-Nov	By the pursuit of Platov to Smolensk	400	5	380
14-Nov	By Count Ojarovski near Krasnoe	150	1	260
14-Nov	By Ostermann-Tolstoy on the Smolensk Road		5	290
15-Nov	Battle of Smolnia by Wittgenstein's Army	1,200	19	1,300
15-Nov	Potolsk by General Vlaslov of Wittgenstein	50		83
15-Nov	Orlov Denisov near Krasnoe	100	23	400
15-Nov	Ostermann-Tolstoy near Krasnoe	300	4	820
15–16 Nov	Miloradovitch at Kobizeva near Krasnoe	800	21	1,100
16-Nov	Lambert near ″ ∙ydanov of Chichagov's Army	1,200	64	3,870
16-Nov	Taking Smolensk	300	3	217
16-Nov	Battle near Krasnoe by Miloradovitch	1,000	41	1,500
16-Nov	Korf and Karpov near Krasnoe and on the Dnieper	800	13	1,199
17-Nov	General Borozdin's detachment at [blank]	125	1	92
17-Nov	Taking of Minsk by Lambert of Chichagov's Army		45	2,224
17-Nov	Battle near Krasnoe with Main Army	4,000	60	9,170
17–22 Nov	Taking of Liadi by Borozdin	100		180
18-Nov	By Platov between Smolensk & Krasnoe	180	5	380
19-Nov	Pursuit on both sides of the Dnieper as far as Orsha by Platov	1,500	72	5,000
19-Nov	Battle near Krasnoe with Miloradovitch's Army	6,000	100	12,000
20-Nov	Pursuit from Liadi to Doubrovna by Borozdin			120
21-Nov	Near Vinnielouki by part of Gen Miller Zakomelski's Corps		8	2,300
21-Nov	Count Ozharovski near Gorki	120	4	850
21-Nov	Borozdin at the taking of Dutrova	100	8	400
21-Nov	Taking of Borissov by Lambert	1,500	40	2,100
24-Nov	By Colonel Loukovkin of Chichagov's Army near Orsha	100	13	284
24-Nov	By Davidov near Kopyss	100	3	285
24-Nov	Detachment of Platov's Corps near Liubavitch	800		2,500
25-Nov	Taking of Moghilev by Ozharovski	200	1	100
26-Nov	Action near Baturi by Wittgenstein's Advance Guard and in the pursuit of 13 Nov	600	37	1,800
27-Nov	Orsha to Tolotchin by Platov	400	5	396

Date	Event	Killed	Prisoners Other	Ranks
27–28 Nov	Taking of Bielinitsch by Davidov	100	8	578
28-Nov	Village of Glinki by Advance Guard on Main Army	50	2	100
29-Nov	By Wittgenstein & Platov near Studentzi	4,500	309	12,691
30 Nov–1 Dec	By Chichagov near Stockov & Brilov on the Berezina	2,500	7	3,300
1-Dec	General Lanskoy of Chitchagov's Army near Pleshtenitza	150	31	217
1-Dec	Pursuit by Chichagov's Advanced Guard	400	7	380
1–2 Dec	By Chichagov near Chotinitch	300	7	527
2-Dec	Further pursuit by Platov	370	8	892
3-Dec	Kutuzov's pursuit from Babinovitch to the Berezina	1,200	73	5,929
3-Dec	By Colonel Tetterborn near Dolgikov	100	26	1,000
4-Dec	Elements of Platov's Corps and Chichigov's Army near Latigal	300	33	1,500
Early Dec	Detachment of Chichagov's Army near Roubetova	200	4	200
5-Dec	Count Orourk near Molodetchino	200		500
5-Dec	In pursuit of the Bavarian Corps by Kutuzov	425	126	2,024
7-Dec	Seslavin's partizans near Zabreg	50	12	211
8-Dec	Platov near Molodetchino	375	6	500
8-Dec	Count Orourk between Molodetchino & Bielitza	180	11	1,500
9-Dec	Chichagov's vanguard under Chaplitz near Smorgoni	600	42	2,500
10-Dec	Same between Smorgono & Otmianami	600	2	1,900
10-Dec	Partizan Seslavin near Vilna	200	4	170
11–17 Dec	Taking of Vilna by Chitchagov	300	7	14,656
11–28 Dec	Between Vilna and Kovno by Platov	1,000	27	1,100
13-Dec	Pursuit from Vilna & the capture of Kovno by Platov	1,220	162	4,600
13–18 Dec	Pursuit from Vilna to Kovno & Suberg and the taking of Tilsit by Kutuzov	1,000	212	3,152
15–17 Dec	Pursuit from Kovno to Vilkovitch by Platov	1,200	210	3,000
16–17 Dec	Lanskoy of Chitchagov's Army near Warsaw	500	75	2,176
20-Dec	By Chitchagov's Army near Preni, Puni & Vikovitch	300	21	997
? Dec	By small parties of the same			700
26-Dec	Capturing Grodno by Davidov		60	661
27–28 Dec	Pursuit from Mittav & capture of Memel by Pauluzzi	300	22	1,104
27 Dec–2 Jan	Capture of Istenberg & Gounmbienn by Kutuzov	100	66	2,820
2-Jan	By Wittgenstein's Corps near Vilna & Ragnita	50	3	131
4-Jan	Detachment of Sacken's Corps near the frontier	600	40	2,600
11-Jan	Between Tilsit and Liebau by Wittgenstein	300	7	700
11-Jan	In action bear Liebau in pursuit to Konigsberg & taking of city by Wittgenstein	1,000	100	9,150
12-Jan	Taking Ebbing by Platov	400	35	1,300
Jun–Dec	Pursuit to Vistula, Danzig & Marienweder by Platov	800	40	1,227
	Taking of Marienwerder by Chernishev	300	6	180
	In addition several retreats and skirmishes between Russian rearguard and the vanguard of the French Army	8,000	80	4,120
		135,635	4,654	210,530

Source: Colonel Tchuyhevitch *Reflections of the War of 1812* (Munroe & Frances, 1813)

Russian Army – December 1812

Main Army

Field Marshal M. I. Kutuzov

Advance Army

Commanded by Adjutant General Wintsingerode
33 battalions, 51 squadrons, 14 Cossack Regts and 72 guns

Advance Guard
Commanded by Major General S. N. Lanskoi

Aleksander and Belorussia Hussars, Lithuanian and Chernigov Horse Jagers, 6th and 32 Jager
  Regiments, 7th Horse Artillery
Light Detachment
Popov 13th Don Cossack Regiment and 1st Bug Cossack Regiment
Cossack Detachment
Grekov 9th, Grekov 21st, Kutyeinikov 4th, Semenchenkov and Iloviak 12th Don Cossack
  Regiments and 3rd Ural Cossack Regiment

2nd Corps
Lieutenant General Prince Eugene von Wurttemberg

3rd Division
Muromsk, Revel and Chernigov Infantry Regiments and 20th Jager Regiment

4th Division
Ryazhsk, Kremenchug, Tobol and Volinsk Infantry Regiment and 4th Jager Regiment
1st Battery, 6th and 7th Light Artillery Companies

Reserve Corps
Major General N. N. Bahmetyev
Brigade
Depot Battalions of Vitebsk, Kurinsk, Kozlov, Kolivan, Narva Infantry Regiments and 4th and 5th
  Jager Regiments

Brigade

Depot Battalions Vladimir, Tambov, Dnieper, Kostrom Infantry regiments and 13th and 14th Jager Regiments.

33rd Battery Company

Cavalry Corps

Adjutant General V. S. Trubetskoi

Depot Squadrons of Sumi and Orenburg Hussar Regiments, Siberian and Lithuanian Uhlan Regiments and 8th Horse Artillery company.

Brigade

1st and 3rd Ukraine Cossack Regiment

Brigade

Tatar Uhlans and Evpatorii Horse Taters Regiments

Brigade

Novorussia Hussar and Combined Dragoon Regiments

Flying Corps

Commanded by Lieutenant General P. P. Palen 3rd

Sumsk, Mariupol and Elisavetgrad Hussars, Kurland Dragoon and Vlasov and Isaev Don Cossack Regiments, 1st and 11th Jager Regiments

General of Cavalry A. P. Tormasov's Column

36 battalions, 39 squadrons, 184 guns

3rd Corps

Commander Lieutenant General Karl Mecklandburg

1st Grenadier Division

Lieb Grenadier, Count Arackcheev, Ekateringburg, Pavlov, St Petersburg, Tauride Grenadier Regiments.

2nd Grenadier Division

Kiev, Moscow, Astrakan, Fanagori, Siberia and Malorussia Grenadier Regiments

5th (Guard) Corps

Brigade

Preobrazhenski and Semenovski Regiments of the Imperial Guard

Brigade

Izmailovski and Lithuania Regiments of the Imperial Guard

Brigade

Jager and Finland Regiments of the Imperial Guard

Artillery

1st and 2nd Guard Batteries and 1st and 2nd Light Guard Artillery companies

Cuirassier Corps

1st Cuirassier Division

Kavalergrad Horse, Lieb Cuirassier, His and Her Cuirassier and Astrahan Cuirassier Regiments

2nd Cuirassier Division

Ekaterinoslav, Military Order, Gluhov, Malorussia and Novgorod Cuirassier Regiments

Horse Artillery company of the Imperial Guard

Reserve

Cossacks of the Guard and Combined Guard Regiments

3 Battery and 5th Light Artillery Companies, plus reserve of 100 guns

General of Infantry D. S. Dohturov Column
22 battalions and 72 guns

6th Corps

7th Division
Pskov, Moscow, Libavsk, Sofia Infantry Regiments, 36th Jager Regiment.

24th Division
Shirvan, Ufa, Butirsk Infantry Regiments and 19th Jager Regiment
7th Battery, 13th and 46th Light Artillery Companies

8th Corps
Commanded by Lieutenant General A. I. Gorchakov

17th Division
Ryazan, Brest, Belozersk Infantry Regiments and 48th Jager Regiment
32nd Battery, 32nd and 33rd Light Artillery Companies
General of Infantry M. A. Miloradovitch's Column
26 battalions, 34 squadrons, 4 Cossack Regts and 96 guns

4th Corps
Lieutenant General E. I. Markov

11 Division
Ekaterinburg, Rilsk, Yelets and Polotsk Infantry Regiments and 33rd Jager Regiments.
2nd Battery, 3rd and 44th Light Artillery Companies

7th Corps
Major General I. F. Paskevitch

12th Division
Smolensk, Narva, Aleksopol Infantry Regiments and 6th Jager Regiment
26th Battery, 47th and 48th Light Artillery Companies

26th Division
Orlov, Ladozhsk, Poltava Infantry Regiments and 5th Jager Regiment
26th Battery, 47th and 48th Light Artillery Companies
Cavalry
Commanded by Major General F. K. Korf and Adjutant General I. V. Vasilchikov
Starodubov and Pskov Cuirassier Regiments, 6th and 7th Horse Artillery companies
Slusarev, Chernozubov 3rd and Karpov 2nd Don Cossack Regiments, and the Tula Cossack
    Opolchenye Regiment.
Brigade
Lithuania and Chuguev Uhlan and Ahtirsk Hussar Regiments
Brigade
Kiev and Moscow Dragoon Regiments
Brigade
Harkov and Kargopol Dragoon Regiments

Right Wing

Commanded by Admiral Chichagov
130 battalions, 82 squadrons, 49 Cossack Regts and 310 guns

Cossack Corps

Commanded by General of Cavalry M.I. Platov
Bihalov, Grevtsov, Denisov 7th, Sisoev 3rd, Grekov, Vlasov 3rd, Sulin 9th, Komissarov, Ilovaisk 11th, Zhipov, Belogorodtsev, Mel'nikov 4th, Grekov 1st, Andriyanov 2nd, Ilovaisk 5th Grekov 5th, Ilovaisk 10th, Rebrikov, Ilovaisk 3rd, Haritonov 7th, Kutyeinikov 6th and the Ataman Don Cossack Regiments.
2nd Bashkir Regiment, Simferopol and Perekop Horse Tatar Regiments, 1st and 2nd Don Battery Artillery Companies.

Army

Commanded by General of Cavalry P. H. Wittenstein

1st Advance Guard

Commanded by Adjutant General P.V. Golenicshchev-Kutuzov
Litovsk Infantry Regiment and 24th Jager Regiment, 1st and 9th Druzhini St Petersburg Opolchenye, 28th Battery and 11th Light Artillery Companies.
Detachment of Major General A.I. Chernishev
Izum Hussars, Kazan and Finland Dragoon Regiments
Cossack Detachment
Platov 4th, Loshchilin, Ilovaisk 4th, Grekov 17th Suchilin, Yagodin and Ilovaisk 9th Cossack Regiments.

2nd Advance Guard

Major General D.D. Shepelev
Tenginsk Infantry Regiment, 23rd and 25th Jager Regiments, Grodnensk and Combined Hussars, Combined Dragoons, Stavropol Kalmucks, Rodionov 2nd and Chernozubov Don Cossack Regiments, 1st and 23rd Horse Artillery Companies.

Lieutenant General F. F. Shteingel's Corps

3rd Jager Regiment, 2nd, 7th and 8th Druzhini St Petersburg Opolchenye, 7th and 8th Druzhini Novgorod Opolchenye, 21st Battery, 26th Light and 3rd Horse Artillery Companies.

14th Division

Tula, Navagin, Estland Infantry Regiments and 26th Jager Regiment

21st Division

Nevsk, Petrov Infantry Regiments, 2nd Jager Regiment

25th Division

1st and 3rd Marine Regiment
Brigade
Mitav and Finland Dragoon Regiments

Lieutenant General G. M. Berg's Corps

Yamburg Uhlan, 2 Druzhini Novgorod Opolchenye, 5th and 14th Battery, 27th Light and 19th Horse Artillery Companies.

5th Division

Perm, Sevsk, Kaluzhsh Infantry Regiments

6th Division

Azov Infantry Regiment, 6 Combined Battalions 5th Druzhini St Petersburg Opolchenye.

Lieutenant General F. F. Leviz's Corps

Brigade
10th, 40th and 53rd Jager Regiments

Division

8 Combined Battalions
Selivanov 2nd Don Cossacks, Volunteers of Yahontov, Bodye, and Nirota Regiments, Combined Dragoon and Cuirassier Regiments, 6th Battery, 10th, 40th and 53rd Light Artillery Companies.

Reserve

Commanded by Major General A. B. Fok

4th, 6th, 17th and 18th Druzhini St Petersburg Opolchenye, 28th Battery, 11th Light, 1st and 23rd Horse Artillery Companies.
Brigade
5 battalions
Molilev, Nizov, Voronezh Infantry Regiments
Brigade
10 battalions
Reserve Battalion of 1st Grenadier Division, Combined Grenadier Battalions of 5th and 14th Infantry Divisions.

3rd Western Army

Commanded by Admiral P.V. Chichagov
46 battalions, 39 squadrons, 10 Cossack Regts and 136 guns

Flying Corps

Combined Grenadier Battalions of 9th, 15th and 18th Infantry Division, 11th and 13th Horse Artillery Companies.
Cossack Brigade
Lukovkin, Barabanshchikov and Panteleev Don Cossack Regiments
Brigade
13th and 14th Jager Regiments

Advance Guard

Commanded by Lieutenant General E. I. Chaplitz
Nasheburg Infantry Regiment, 11th and 26th Horse Artillery Companies
Cossack Detachment
Isaev, Grekov 8th, Kireev, Dyachkin, Mel'nikov Don Cossack Regiments
Brigade
Ol'viopol Hussar, Zhitomir Uhlan, Arzamask Horse Jager Regiments
Detachment
Pavlovgrad Hussars, Volinsk Uhlan, Tver and Kinburn Dragoon Regiments
Brigade
10th and 38th Jager Regiments
Brigade
7th and 27th Jager Regiments

Brigade
28th and 32nd Jager Regiments

General of Infantry A. F. Langeron's Corps
10 battalions, 36 guns

15th Division
Vitebsk. Kozlov and Kolivan Infantry Regiment
Brigade
12th and 22nd Jager Regiment
Artillery
15th Battery, 28th and 29th Light Artillery Companies

Lieutenant General A. L. Voinov's Corps
12 battalions, 36 guns

18th Division
Vladimir, Tambov, Dneprov and Kostrom Infantry Regiments
Brigade
Apsheron, and Yakut Infantry Regiments
Artillery
12th Battery, 34th and 35th Light Companies

Reserve
Lieutenant General A. P. Zass
13 Squadrons, 1 Cossack Regiment and 36 guns
Mariupol Hussars, Derptsk and Seversk Horse Jager , Starodubov Cuirassiers, Volunteers of
   Skarzhin Regiments
18th and 34th Battery, 25th Light Artillery Companies.

Lieutenant General F. V. Osten Sacken's Independent Corps
39 battalions, 28 squadrons, 7 Cossack Regts and 96 guns

Right Wing
Major General M. L. Bulatov
1st Kalmuck and 4th Ural Cossacks, Chuguev Uhlan, Smolensk Dragoons, Pereyaslav Horse Jager
   Regiments
22nd Battery and 31st Light Artillery Companies

16th Division
Ohotsk, Mingrel, Kamchatka Infantry Regiments and 45th Jager Regiment

22nd Division
Vyatsk, Starooskol, Olonetz Infantry Regiments and 29th Jager Regiment
Brigade
Talitsk and Saratov Infantry Regiments

Left wing
Major General I. A. Lieven 3rd

10th Division
Biborg, Crimean, Yaroslav, Belostok Infantry Regiments and 8th and 39th Jager Regiments
Vlasov Don Cossacks

10th Battery and 41st Light Artillery Regiment

Lieutenant General D. M. Volkonski's 1st Corps

8th Division

Arhangelogod, Shlisselburg, Ukraine Infantry Regiments and 37th Jager Regiments
Brigade
Lubensk Hussars, Vladimir and Seruhov Dragoon Regiments
Chikilev Don Cossacks, 2nd Bashkir, 2nd Kalmits, 2nd Ukraine Cossack and 4th Ural Cossack
   Regiments.
18th Battery 14th, 18th and 42nd Light Artillery Companies.

Lieutenant General P. K. Musin-Pushkin's Independent Corps

11 batalions, 4 squadrons, 1 Cossack Regt and 22 guns

16th Division

Neishlot Infantry Regiment, 43rd Jager Regiment and Depot Battalions of Ohotsk and Mingrel
   Infantry Regiments.

13th Division

(5 battalions)
Penzen, Velikoluts and Saratov Infantry Regiments
Turchaninov Don Cossack and Tiraspol Horse Jager Regiments,
18th Horse, 38th Battery, 19th and 21st Light Artillery Companies

BIBLIOGRAPHY

Primary Sources and Early Works

British Library

Add ms 30133 Plans etc of the French campaign in Russia

Add ms 30132 Sir Robert Wilson's correspondence and Mr Levy's Journal and plans of operations against the Duchy of Warsaw, 1812

Add ms 38363 Sovereigns of Russia, Alexander I

Add ms 41366 Sovereigns of Russia, Alexander I

Russian State Military Archives

(Microfilms in London School of Economics)

Fonts 3465-3470, 3481-3486, 3489-3503, 3506, 3512, 3515-3519, 3521-3533, 3535-3671, 3673, 3681-3701, 3708, 3718, 3720–3836.

Newspapers

The Times 1812

The *Edinburgh Courant* 1812

Windsor and Eton Express 1812

St James Chronicle 1812

Russkii Invalid 1813, 1912

Caledonian Mercury 1812

Polnoe Sobranie Zakonov Rossiskoi Imperii

Aglaimov, S. P. *Otechestvennia Voina 1812 goda, istoricheskie materially Lieb Gvardii Semenovskago polka* (Poltava 1912)

Alexander I. *Correspondence de l'Empereur Alexandre Ier avec sa soeur la Grande Duchesse Catherine,* (St Petersburg, 1910)

Al'tsuller, R. E. *Borodino, dokumenti, pis'ma, vospominaniya* (Moscow, 1962)

Istoriya Leib Guardii Yegerskogo Polka (St Petersburg, 1896)

Andeev, N. I 'Iz vospominanii Nikolaia Ivanovicha Andreev' in *Russkii Arkhiv* (Moscow, 1879)

Asvarishch, B. *Otechestvennia Voina 1812 goda v kartinakh Petera Khess* (Leningread, 1984)

Babkin, V. I. *Narodnoe Opolchenye v Otechestvennoi Voine 1812,* (1962)

Bagration, P. *General Bagration, sbornik, dokumentov I materialov* (Moscow, 1945)

Benkendorf, A. K. *Zapiski Benkendorfa 1812* (Russia 2001)

Bennigsen, L. *Memoires du General Bennigsen* vol. 3 (Paris, 1908)

Beskrovnuy, L. G. *Dnevnik Aleksandra Chicherina, 1812–1813* (Moscow, 1966)

Beskrovnuy, L. G. *Narodnoe Opolchenye v Otechestvennoi Voine 1812* (1962)

Bogdanovich, M. I. *Istoriya Otechestvennoi Voini 1812 goda* (St Petersburg, 1859)

Boitsov, M. *Kchesti Rossi, iz chastnoi perepiski 1812 goda* (Moscow, 1988)

Brandt, H. *In the Legions of Napoleon* (London, 1999)

Brett-James, A. *1812, eyewitness accounts of Napoleon's defeat in Russia* (New York, 1966)

Brett-James, A (ed.) *General Wilson's journal 1812–1814* (London, 1964)

Buturlin, D. P. *Historie militaire de la campagne de Russie en 1812* (Paris, 1824)

Chicherin, A.V. *Dnevnik Aleksandr Chicherina 1812–1813* (Moscow, 1966)

Choiseul-Gouffier, Countess de *Memoirs of Alexander I and the court of Russia* (Paul Kegan, 1904)

Clausewitz, Carl von *The campaign of 1812* (London, 1992)

Durova, N. *The Cavalry Maiden* (Paladin Books, 1990) translated by Mary Fleming Zirin

Dushenkich, Dmitri 'Iz moikh vospominanii' in *1812, v vospominaniyakh sovremennikov* (Moscow, 1995)

Ermolov, A. P. *Materiyali dla istorii voinoi 1812, Zapiski A P Ermolova* (London, 1863)

Fusil, Madame Louise *Souvenirs d'une Femme sur la Retraite de Russie* (1910)

Garin, F. A. *Izgananye Napoleona iz Moskvy* (Moscow, 1938)

Glinka, F. *Pisma Russkavo Ofitsera* (Moscow, 1985)

Glinka, F. *Ockerki Borodinskogo srazhenia* (Moscow, 1839)

Glinka, Sergei *Iz Zapisok o 1812 goda*

Golitsuin, N. B. *Ofitserskiya zapiski ili vospominaniya o pohodah 1812, 1813 I 1814* (Moscow, 1838)

Karpov, E. P. *Pozhar Moskbi 1812* (St Petersburg, 1903)

Kharkevich, V. I. *Voina 1812 goda, ot Nieman do Smolenska* (Vilna, 1901)

Kharkevich, V. I. Barklay-de-Tolli v *Otechestvennia Voina nosl sosdineniya armii nod Smolensk.* (St Petersburg, 1904)

Langeron, Comte de *Memories du Langeron, General d'Infantrie dans l'Armée Russe* (Paris, 1902)

Lipandi I. P. *Materali dla Otechestvennoi Voini 1812 goda* (St Petersburg, 1867)

von Loewenstern, Baron Woldemar *Memoires du general major russe baron de Lowenstern,* (1903)

Lubenkov, N. *Raskas artilerista o dele Borodinskom* (St Petersburg, 1837)

Mikhailovsky-Danielevsky, A. *Opisaniye Otechestvennoi v 1812* (St Petersburg, 1839)

Mitarevsky, N. E. *Vospominaniya o vonia 1812 goda* (Moscow, 1871)

Nesselrode, Count von *Lettres et papiers du Chancellor comte de Nesselrode* (Paris, 1904–11) 11 volumes

'Zapiski Generala Neverovskavo o sluzhbe svoiei v 1812' in *Shternia v obshchestvie istorii I Drevnostiei Rossiishikh* no. 1 (1859)

Okunev, N. A. *Considerations sur les Grandes Operations, les Batailles et la campagne de 1812 en Russie* (Brussels, 1841)

Oginski, M. *Memoirs de Michel Oginski sur la pologne et les Polonais* (Paris, 1826)

Petrov, F. A. *1812 goda vospominaniia voinov Russkoi Armii iz sobraine pismennykh* (Moscow, 1991)

Pogodin, M. *A. P. Ermolov: Materiali dlia ego biografii, sobrannie Pogodinim* (Moscow, 1864),

Porter, Sir Robert Ker *Narrative of the Campaign in Russia During the Year 1812* (Hartford, 1814)

Radozhitsky, I. *Poxodnie zapiski artilerista s 1812 po 1816* (Moscow, 1835)

Memoirs of the Count de Rochechouart (London, 1920) translation by Frances Jackson.

Samarin, Y. F. *Zapiski mn'niya I perepiska Admirala A S Shichkova* (Berlin, 1870)

Shishkov, A. S. *Krarkiya zapiski Admirala A Shishkova...* (St Petersburg, 1831)

Surrugues *Lettres sur l'incendie de Moscou* (Paris 1823)

Vasiliev, I. N. *Neskoi'ko gromkikh udarov po khvostu tigra; operat'sion Berezine osenou 1812* (Moscow, 2001)

Tartakovsii, A. G. *1812 god, voennye dnevniki* (Moscow, 1990)

Tartakovsii, A. G. *1812 god, v vospominaniiakh sovremennikov* Moscow, 1995)

Troubetzkoy, G *In the service of the Tsar against Napoleon: The Memoirs of Denis Davidov*

'Pismo Imperatora Aleksandra I k Admiralu Chichagovu' in *Sbornik Russkago Istoricheskogo Obshchestva* vol 6 (1871)

Borodinskoe Srazhenie (Moscow, 1872)

Uxhull, B. *Arms and the woman, the diary of Baron Boris Uxhull* (London, 1966) ed. Joel Carmichael

Valkovich, A. M. *Feldmarshal Kutuzov* (Moscow, 1995)

Wilson, Sir Robert *The French Invasion of Russia* (London, 1860)

Wurttemberg, Prince Eugene de *Memoires of Prince Eugene de Wurttemberg* (Paris 1907)

Yermolov, A. *The Czar's General, memoirs of a Russian General* ed. Aleaxander Mikaberidze (Ravenhall Books, 2005)

Rafail Mikhailolovich Zotov Razskazi o pohodah 1812 i 1813, praporshchika Sankt Petersburg Opolchenye (St Petersburg, 1836)

Pohod Russkoi Armii protiv Napoleona v 1813 (Nauka, 1964)

Izvestiya o voennih deistviyah Rossiisskoi Armii protiv Frantsuzov 1812 goda (St Petersburg, 1813)

Secondary Sources

Beskrovny, L. G. *The Russian Army and Fleet in the Nineteenth Century* (Academic International Press, 1996)

Bragin, M. *Field Marshal Kutuzov* (Moscow, 1944)

Britten Austin, P. *1812* 3 vols. (Greenhill Books, 1993)

Duffy, C. *Borodino, Napoleon against Russia, 1812* (Sphere Books, 1972)

Holmes, E. R. *Borodino 1812* (London, 1971)

Josselson, Michael & Diana *The Commander, a life of Barclay de Tolly* (Oxford University Press, 1980)

Makhneva, E. O. *Geroi Otechestvennoi Voini 1812* (Russia 1991)

Metternich, T. *Les Stroganov* (Neuilly, 1991)

Mikaberidze, A. *The Battle of Borodino* (Pen and Sword, 2007)

Mikaberidze, A. *Bagration, the Lion of the Army* (doctoral dissertation, Florida State University, 2003)

Mikaberidze, A. *The Russian Officer Corps* (Savas Beatie, 2005)

Nafziger, G. *Napoleon's invasion of Russia* (Presidio Press, 1998)

Parkinson, R. *The Fox of the North* (London, 1976)

Podmazo, A. A. *Bolshaya Evropeiskaya Voina 1812–1814* (Rosspen, 2003)

Smith, D. *Borodino* (Windrush Press, 1998)

Smith, D. *Charge, Great cavalry charges of the Napoleonic Wars* (Greenhill Books 2003)

Smith, D. *Napoleon against Russia* (Pen & Sword, 2004)

Spring, L. *Russian Grenadiers and Infantry, 1799–1815* (Osprey, 2002)

Spring, L. *Cossacks, 1799–1815* (Osprey, 2003)

Henri Troyat *Alexander of Russia* (New English Library, 1982)

Various, *Otechyestvennaya Boina 1812 goda Entsklopediya* (Rosspen, 2004)

Various, *Otechyestvennaya Boina I Russkoe obshchyestvo 1812–1912* (Moscow, 1912)

Various, *The Kiwer, the newsletter of the Russian Study Group*

Verestchagin, V. *1812, Napoleon I in Russia* (New York, 1899)

Zamoyski, A. *1812, Napoleon's fatal march on Russia* (Harper Collins, 2004)

Zhilin, P. A. *Otechestvennoi Voini 1812 goda* (Moscow, 1988)

INDEX